Revit® Architecture 2009
A Comprehensive Guide

H. Edward Goldberg, AIA

PEARSON

Prentice Hall

Upper Saddle River, New Jersey
Columbus, Ohio

Library of Congress Control Number: 2008921497

Editor in Chief: Vernon Anthony
Acquisitions Editor: Jill Jones-Renger
Editorial Assistant: Doug Greive
Production Coordination: Lisa S. Garboski, bookworks publishing services
Project Manager: Louise Sette
AV Project Manager: Janet Portisch
Operations Supervisor: Deidra Schwartz
Art Director: Michael Fruhbeis
Cover Designer: Iize Lemesis
Cover Image: H. Edward Goldberg
Director of Marketing: David Gesell
Senior Marketing Coordinator: Alicia Dysert
Copyeditor: Bret Workman

This book was set in TimesNewRomanPS by Aptara, Inc. and was printed and bound by Bind-Rite Graphics. The cover was printed by Coral Graphic Services.

Disclaimer:

This publication is designed to provide tutorial information about AutoCAD® and/or other Autodesk computer programs. Every effort has been made to make this publication complete and as accurate as possible. The reader is expressly cautioned to use any and all precautions necessary, and to take appropriate steps to avoid hazards, when engaging in the activities described herein.

Neither the author nor the publisher makes any representations or warranties of any kind, with respect to the materials set forth in this publication, express or implied, including without limitation any warranties of fitness for a particular purpose or merchantability. Nor shall the author or the publisher be liable for any special, consequential, or exemplary damages resulting, in whole or in part, directly or indirectly, from the reader's use of, or reliance upon, this material of subsequent revisions of this material.

Pearson Education Ltd., London
Pearson Education Singapore Pte. Ltd.
Pearson Education Canada, Inc.
Pearson Education—Japan

Pearson Education Australia Pty. Limited
Pearson Education North Asia Ltd., Hong Kong
Pearson Educación de Mexico, S.A. de C.V.
Pearson Education Malaysia Pte. Ltd.

9 8 7 6 5 4 3 2 1
ISBN-13: 978-0-13-513475-7
ISBN-10:   0-13-513475-7

I dedicate this book to the women I love:
my 95-year-old mother, Lillian,
my wife of 35 years, Judith Ellen,
and my daughter, Allison Julia.

I want to thank all the people at Autodesk for their help on this book, especially Rick Rundell,
Paul Donnelly, David Mills, and Noah Cole.

THE NEW AUTODESK DESIGN INSTITUTE PRESS SERIES

Pearson/Prentice Hall has formed an alliance with Autodesk® to develop textbooks and other course materials that address the skills, methodology, and learning pedagogy for the industries that are supported by the Autodesk® Design Institute (ADI) software products. The Autodesk Design Institute is a comprehensive software program that assists educators in teaching technological design.

Features of the Autodesk Design Institute Press Series

JOB SKILLS—Coverage of computer-aided drafting job skills, compiled through research of industry associations, job websites, college course descriptions, and the Occupational Information Network database has been integrated throughout the ADI Press books.

PROFESSIONAL and **INDUSTRY ASSOCIATIONS INVOLVEMENT**—These books are written in consultation with and reviewed by professional associations to ensure they meet the needs of industry employers.

FEATURES OF *Revit® Architecture 2009*

This text presents a modern approach to using Revit® Architecture. That is, it addresses advances in technology and software evolution and introduces commands and procedures that reflect a modern, efficient use of Revit® Architecture 2009. Features include:

A "Getting Started" section at the beginning of the book provides essential information, preparing users for the guided tutorial on Revit Architecture 2009, including Definitions and Abbreviations, and more.

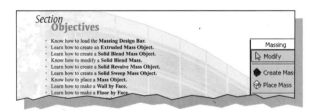

Section Objectives, a bulleted list of learning objectives for each section, provide users with a road map of important concepts and practices that will be introduced in the section.

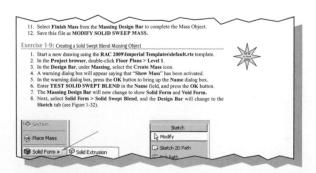

A New to 2009 icon flags features that are new to the 2009 version of the Revit Architecture software, creating a quick "study guide" for instructors who need to familiarize themselves with the newest features of the software to prepare for teaching the course. Additional details about these new features can be found in the Online Instructor's Manual.

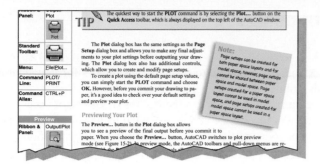

NOTE boxes highlight additional helpful information for the student.

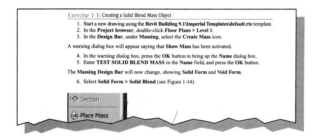

Exercises throughout the sections provide step-by-step walk-through activities for the student, allowing immediate practice and reinforcement of newly learned skills.

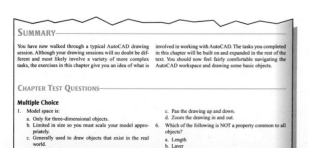

End-of-Section material, easily located by shading on page edges, provides:

* Summaries
* Section Test Questions

to help students check their own understanding of important section concepts.

INSTRUCTOR'S RESOURCES

An Online Instructor's Manual is available to qualified instructors for downloading. To access supplementary materials online, instructors need to request an instructor access code. Go to **www.pearsonhighered.com/irc**, where you can register for an instructor access code. Within 48 hours after registering, you will receive a confirming e-mail including an instructor access code. Once you have received your code, go to the site and log on for full instructions on downloading the materials you wish to use.

A Note from the Author

A personal philosophy lies behind the tutorial method used in this book. These tutorials are designed to give the student an experience of the operational methodology that I believe is most effective in learning Revit Architecture. I like to compare the operation of any architectural design and documentation software to driving an automobile and to playing a game of chess.

I often remind students how much difficulty they had when they first drove an automobile, especially one with a manual transmission. Then I ask them whether they can remember the specific tasks they performed while driving to class. For example, if they had a manual transmission, did they remember changing gears? The analogy here is that, like mastering driving, repeated practice with Revit Architecture tools on simple tasks eventually makes performing them routine. Then, adding more tasks builds a repertoire of solutions. Operating the program effectively depends on picking the correct tool for a particular task.

Chess is a game of strategy, and the effective operation of Revit Architecture is similar to playing chess. The object, in both cases, is to get the most results with the least effort (moves). Succeeding at the game (or the project) requires thinking several moves ahead with a clear goal in mind. As with an opponent in chess, the building project will always oppose you (as all projects do). Don't be afraid of trying a new strategy (unless you are on a deadline), and practice, practice, practice.

Finally—experiment! Be open to operating Revit Architecture in different ways. After completing a series of tutorials, go back and experiment with the settings to see what changes occur. Also, be aware that no book can possibly cover every feature of the Revit Architecture program. Although Revit Architecture is relatively easy to understand, it is a very deep and complex program, and different users often use different features and operate the software in different ways.

Acknowledgments

I would like to thank the reviewers of this text: Terry Kirkham, Consumnes River College; Patrick E. Connolly, Purdue University; Brian Myers, Seiler Instrument; Fred Brasfield, Tarrant County College; Ronald D. Spangler, Berea College; Tom Bledsaw, ITT; Hadi Hamid, Technical College of the Lowcountry; Harry R. Glesner, III, Community College or Denver; and Mohd Fairuz Shiratuddin, The University of Southern Mississippi.

STYLE CONVENTIONS IN *Revit*® *Architecture 2009*

Text Element	Example
Revit commands—Bold and uppercase.	Start the **LINE** command.
Toolbar names, menu items and dialog box names—Bold and follow capitalization convention in Revit toolbar or pull-down menu (generally first letter capitalized).	The **Layer Manager** dialog box The **File** pull-down menu
Toolbar buttons and dialog box controls/buttons/input items—Bold and follow capitalization convention of the name of the item or the name shown in the Inventor tooltip.	Choose the **Line** tool from the **Draw** toolbar. Choose the **Symbols and Arrows** tab in the **Modify Dimension Style** dialog box. Choose the **New Layer** button in the **Layer Properties Manager** dialog box. In the **Line and Arrows** tab, set the **Arrow size:** to **.125**.

Contents

PART III   *Putting It All Together*

The BIM

THE BUILDING INFORMATION MODEL AND BIM SOFTWARE

Twenty-five years ago, Autodesk created AutoCAD, and revolutionized architectural drafting for the masses. When AutoCAD was introduced, production time decreased significantly. Regardless, AutoCAD was only electronic drawing—quicker perhaps, but still following the concept of 2D plan, elevation, section, and detail that had been in use for hundreds of years. Today, with Revit Architecture, which is BIM (Building Information Model) authoring software, buildings are designed in a new way. Instead of depending on 2D views, architects are designing buildings virtually. This has several benefits. The first benefit of the virtual building is its ability to allow easy examination of the building from any direction. This allows the designer to better visualize his/her design. The second benefit is the ability to test, analyze, and quantify the building. Because the virtual building acts like its real-world counterpart, it is possible to analyze things such as energy usage, shading, and component clashes. Another benefit of the BIM is that it allows the contractors to simulate the construction of the building while checking different construction scenarios. This last capability, often called "4D," has been used by many large construction companies to schedule material deliveries. Programs such as NavisWorks combine a Microsoft Project or Primavera schedule with a BIM model, allowing one to construct a simulation based on these scheduling programs. Finally, because the components of the BIM model are 3D digital models, they are often prime candidates for automated manufacturing. It is becoming quite common for steel beams and stairs designed in BIM models to be sent directly to computerized steel cutting and assembly machines.

All this BIM capability, however, has its drawbacks. BIM operators can no longer be just draftspersons; they will have to has a much better understanding of how buildings go together. The BIM is opening up new opportunities for those that understand how to build and analyze models. As the BIM and Revit Architecture become an industry standard, one might expect to see new operator definitions such as Virtual Contractor or Virtual Architect. Although designing a building in Revit Architecture is a new paradigm, the programmers have taken great pains to make this software as easy as possible to understand and be productive.

BIG BIM, LITTLE bim

The BIM, or "Building Information Model," is a new paradigm in architectural design management that has been popularized by Autodesk since 2002. Although the BIM utilizes a three-dimensional digital model, it is more than just drawing and visualization. Much has been written about the BIM, but few people really understand its meaning and its impact. A new book by Finith E. Jernigan, AIA, *Big BIM, little bim,* does a great job in explaining the difference between the concept of the BIM (the Big BIM) and the software utilized to create it (the little bim), and is highly recommended reading. Basically, the Big BIM is defined by Jernigan "as all the information about a project within its property lines to the center of the earth and infinitely to the sky from; its inception thru construction and use until its final decommission and elimination. This includes the structures and associated information, weather history, taxes, ground compaction, utilities, manufactures, equipment, and more." Eventually the BIM will include all the available digital databases of information available through the Internet. The BIM is also about collaboration, often real-time, with other resources such as owners, engineers, contractors, manufacturers, and so on. This collaboration should increase productivity because more information will be available at the earlier stages of a project, rather than later as is presently done. When informed decisions are made early in a project design, mistakes are reduced and costs are lowered.

The **little bim**, as Jernigan states, is the software used to create the **big BIM**. To be truly viable, a BIM software solution must contain a modeler capable of quickly and easily modeling a 3D model. If it takes longer to create a 3D model than it would take to draw the model in three views, much of the design benefit of the BIM is lost. To this end, the major BIM software player, Revit Architecture, includes routines that allow for ease of modeling. Because the Building Information Model mimics a real project, some of the real benefits on the design side can be fully realized only when the architect or designer is the computer operator. This issue should be noted by the large architectural firms that use CAD as an electronic drafting tool, and have structured their practice as a hierarchy in which a project architect sketches a concept, and the CAD operator merely acts as a scribe. One advantage of using Revit Architecture at the design stage is that the designer can understand the relationships of the building and its systems virtually instantaneously. This understanding may be in regards to aesthetic, special, performance, or program issues. Until recently, the modeling of virtual buildings has focused primarily on improving drawing productivity in creating construction documents, and one great productivity feature of Revit Architecture software is its ability to generate elevations and sections automatically from the model and to coordinate and update them whenever the model is changed. Another advantage of Revit Architecture is its ability to create and maintain schedules for doors, windows, walls, and other objects. The following figures show examples of buildings built using BIM software. As of today, though, very few buildings that are designed using BIM software are being designed for the Big BIM concept.

AUTODESK DEFINES THE BIM

Autodesk says: "(BIM) refers to the creation and use of coordinated, consistent, computable information about a building project in design—information used for design decision making, production of high-quality construction documents, predicting performance, cost-estimating and construction planning, and, eventually, for managing and operating the facility."

LITTLE

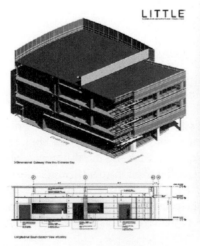

While Revit has features that speed construction documentation, new applications have been found for the information contained in the BIM model. With Revit Architecture as the base modeling product, one can analyze, estimate, construct, and finally manage the operation of a project. The following are some of the additional software and services that extend the viability of Revit Architecture.

e-SPECS® AUTOMATED SPECIFICATIONS

http://www.e-specs.com/

e-SPECS automates the preparation of construction specifications by extracting the product and material requirements directly from the project's model.

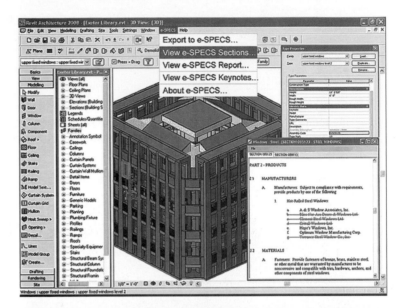

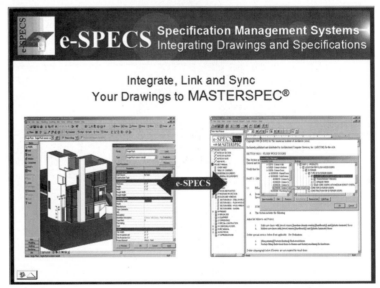

GREEN BUILDING STUDIO

http://www.greenbuildingstudio.com

This Web service, now owned by Autodesk, assists in the energy analysis of buildings in the design stages as well as with the selection of energy-efficient green building products and materials. The Green Building Studio Web service was developed by Green Building Studio, Inc., and funded through grants from the California Energy Commission Public Interest Energy Research (PIER) Program, Pacific Gas & Electric Company, United States Environmental Protection Agency, Northwest Energy Efficiency Alliance, and other organizations. The following are some of the data that can be generated from the BIM model by Green Building Studio V3.0:

> **Carbon Neutral Building Check** – Automatically estimates the feasibility for each building to achieve carbon neutral status using local grid emission data.

U.S. EPA ENERGY STAR Score – Computes each building's U.S. EPA ENERGY STAR score or Architecture 2030's targets.

Water Use Analysis – Estimates water needs, savings associated with efficiency measures, rain capture potential, and LEED credits for the building.

Daylighting with Energy Savings – Automatically determines the LEED Glaze factor for each room with lighting control energy savings.

Natural Ventilation Potential – Automatically determines if the building location and loads are well suited for naturally ventilating the building.

Local Weather Data – Provides access to over 60,000 weather locations, ensuring that the design team uses local hourly weather data obtained from within 14 km of your building rather than from the typical 230 airport locations.

Corporate Accounts – Provides firmwide management of users, building designs, building templates, and review of corporate-wide CO2 emission, energy, and water use analyses. Leverages key staff on every project no matter which office they are in.

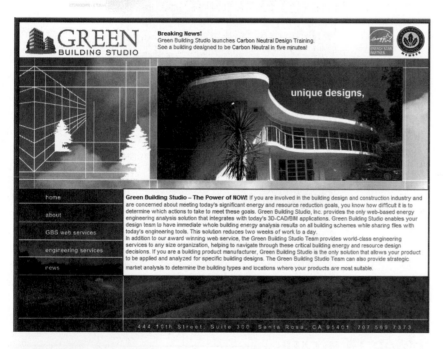

General Information: The General Building information section at the top of the page describes the project scenario, building type, geographic location, and gross floor area.

Estimated Energy & Cost Summary: Most building energy cost comparisons and early compliance decisions can be made using annualized energy cost and consumption information. Costs are estimated using local utilities rates. The following information is provided:
- Annual Energy Cost
- Lifecycle Energy Costs (30 year)
- Annual Energy Consumption (electric and gas)
- Peak Electric Energy Demand (kW)
- Lifecycle Energy Consumption (electric and gas)

Energy End-Use Charts: Further breakdowns of energy use for major electric and gas end uses like lighting, HVAC, and space heating are provided in graphical format. Numbers associated with each category can be seen by clicking on the pie charts with your mouse.

IES <Virtual Environment>

http://www.iesve.com

This is a unique, integrated system for building performance assessment. IES VE consists of analysis modules that evaluate most building performance properties.

The <VE> Sustainability Toolkit makes it extremely easy for Revit users to undertake a range of building simulation analyses. Within Revit MEP an interface is launched that enables the user to assign information to the building and individual rooms. This information is then passed through the IES <VE>, and the <VE> Toolkit is displayed. Select any button and the toolkit will run the chosen analysis by using the model transferred from Revit. Interrogate the results of the analysis via an html report, or conduct a more detailed analysis within the <VE> using one or more of the integrated performance assessment modules.

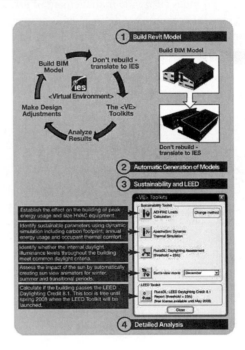

Solibri Model Checker

http://www.solibri.fi

"Think of Solibri Model Checker as a spell checker for virtual models." This program analyzes building models for integrity, quality, and physical security. It checks for potential flaws and weaknesses in the design, highlights clashing components, and determines whether the model complies with building codes and the organization's own best practices. You can set up rules to check just about anything in your BIM model. In the following figure, Solibri is checking escape routes.

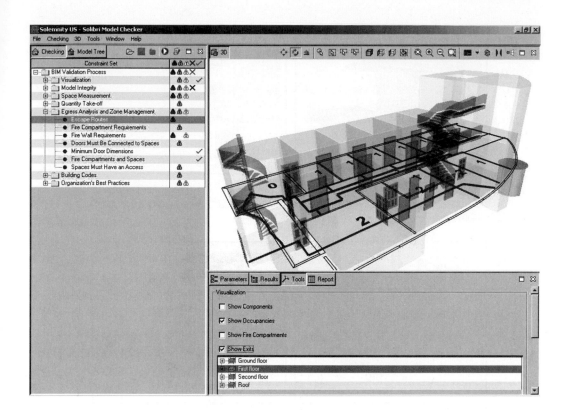

Automatic code checking will be a boon to the architectural design industry. The ICC (International Code Council) is developing a code checking capability that will automatically check 80% of all the building codes in the United States. You can try the **Smart Codes Instant Code Compliance Checking** demonstration using Solibri Model Viewer at http://www2.iccsafe.org/io/smartcodes/.

ADS—ARCHITECTURAL DATA SYSTEMS, ADSYMPHONY

http://architecturaldatasystems.com/

This Web-based solution automatically integrates 3D content from manufacturers into your Revit Architecture projects. It is free for one named user, with a minimal cost for additional users. (Several users in the same office can access the system for free, but not at the same time.) To use **ADSymphony**, you log on to the ADS website. You then use Revit Architecture as you normally would, placing generic content such as doors, windows, and so on, into your project. You then go to the ADS website from within your program, select the manufacturer's catalog and content, and your generic content is changed to the manufacturer's content. In Revit Architecture, everything is automatic; this includes changes to the actual manufacturer's content as well as creation of the schedule and specifications. There is a growing library of over 900 product catalogs, complete with 3D content, and more are being created all the time.

ECOTECT

http://squ1.com/project/ecotect

ECOTECT is a full-featured building performance analysis and design solution. It combines an interactive building design interface and 3D modeller with a wide range of environmental analysis tools for a detailed assessment of **solar**, **thermal**, **lighting**, **shadows and shading design**, **energy and building regulations**, **acoustics**, **air flow**, and **cost and resource** performance of buildings at any scale. Even more importantly, it has been written and developed by designers, for designers, to be as useful at concept stage as it is during final design development.

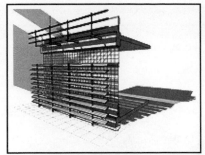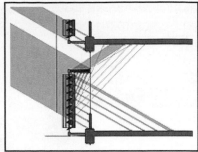

Alternatively, by tracking solar rays you can quickly see how your own more complex shading and light redirection systems are likely to work under different conditions throughout the year.

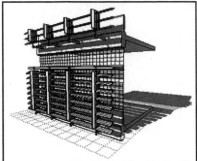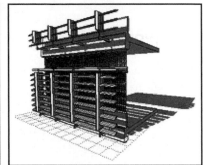

Once a complex shading system has been remodeled, you can quickly calculate how much solar radiation actually hits any part of the window, either instantaneously or over any date and time range.

NavisWorks JetStream V5

http://www.navisworks.com/en/jetstream

This company was recently purchased by Autodesk. The software can import file formats and models from most of the different BIM software vendors. Using NavisWorks, one can bring together models from different disciplines and analyze the entire model.

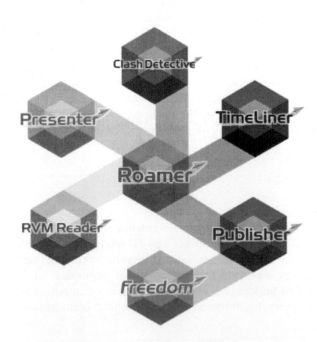

Roamer – Smooth real-time walkthrough of all major native 3D design and laser scan file formats to combine models produced in different applications for review.

Publisher – Share 3D models faithful to the original design data with anyone using the free JetStream Freedom viewing software.

Freedom – Free NavisWorks viewing software.

Presenter – Easily create compelling images and animations to accurately and effectively convey design ideas and intent.

Clash Detective – Effective identification, inspection, and reporting of interferences in a 3D project model.

TimeLiner – Visual simulation of work processes by linking 3D model data to project schedules.

INNOVAYA VISUAL ESTIMATING

http://www.innovaya.com/

Innovaya Visual Estimating 9.4 is a true BIM-based estimating solution that integrates Revit® applications with Sage Timberline Estimating. This program is used by many large construction companies for estimating and scheduling.

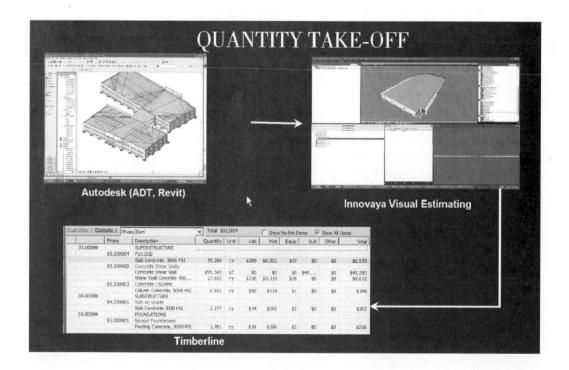

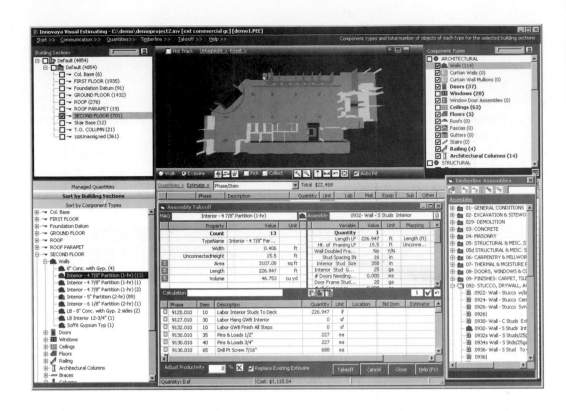

Presently, most of the major architecture firms (e.g., SOM, HOK, HNTB, RTKL, etc.) use Revit Architecture, and the user base is growing exponentially. In the near future, the BIM and Revit Architecture (bim software) will very likely become the standard for the design, analysis, construction, and operation of buildings.

SUMMARY

This section discussed the concepts behind the BIM (Building Information Model), BIM software (BIM authoring tools), and the benefits of the BIM.

SECTION TEST QUESTIONS

True/false

1. True or False: The BIM is an evolution of CAD.

2. True or False: BIM software can be used as traditional 2D CAD software.

3. True or False: One advantage of the BIM is that it enables the designer to understand the relationships of a building and its systems.

4. True or False: The BIM model can be used for manufacturing.

5. True or False: Eventually the BIM will include all the digital databases of information available through the Internet.

Questions

1. What is the difference between the BIM and BIM authoring software?

2. How does BIM software differ from traditional 2D CAD software?

3. What does 4D mean in relationship to BIM software?

4. How can the BIM be used for analysis?

5. What is your interpretation of the Virtual Contractor or Virtual Architect?

Part One

Getting Started

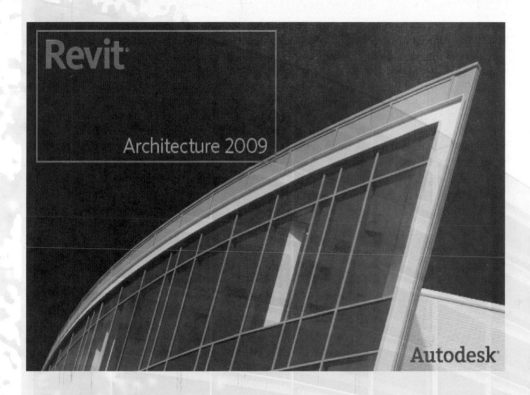

Whenever you start Revit Architecture 2009, or minimize your projects, the Recent Files screen appears. Here you can start new projects, browse existing ones, and also select the Revit 2008 Content Distribution Center on the Web. (See next page.)

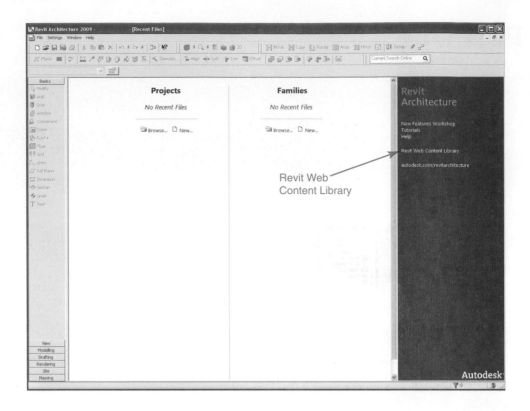

Revit Web
Content Library

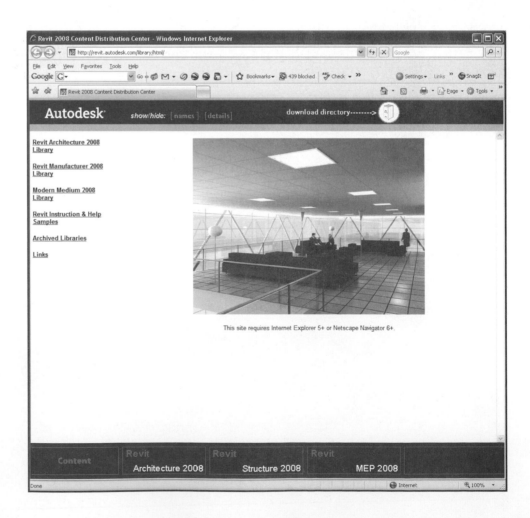

To best learn Revit Architecture, some basic concepts must be mastered. All of these concepts will be demonstrated in the Exercises in Part II, but it is best that you read this section first.

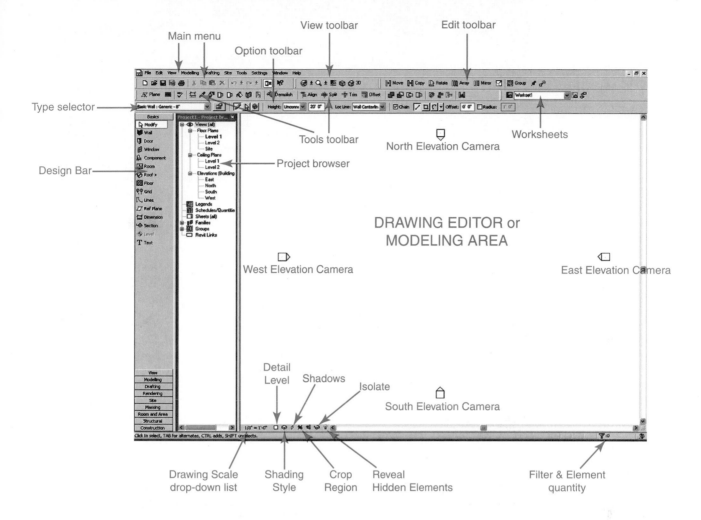

Abbreviations

Revit	Refers to Revit Architecture 2009.
Browse	Refers to searching through the file folders and files.
Contextual menu	Refers to any menu that appears when an object or entity is selected with the **Right Mouse Button** (**RMB**).
Dialog box	Refers to any menu containing parameters or input fields.
Display tree	Refers to the Microsoft Windows folder listing consisting of + and − signs. If a + sign appears, the listing is compressed with more folders available.
Drawing Editor	Refers to the drawing area where drawings are created.
Drop-down list	Refers to the typical Windows operating system list. When selected, a series of options appear in a vertical list.
DWG	Refers to an AutoCAD Drawing.
Elevation View	Refers to **Front**, **Back**, **Right**, or **Left Views**, perpendicular to the ground plane.
Floor Plan View	Refers to looking at a plan from the **Top View**.
Model, Virtual model	Refers to a 3D representation of a real building or component.
Press the Enter button	Refers to any **Enter** button in any dialog box on the screen.
Press the \<Enter\> key	Refers to the keyboard **\<Enter\>** key.
Press the OK button	Refers to any **OK** button in any dialog box on the screen.
Project browser	Refers to the list of Views in the Drawing Editor.
RMB	Refers to clicking using the **Right Mouse Button**. This is most often used to bring up contextual menus.
Section View	Refers to a longitudinal or transverse cut through the model.
Tooltips	Refers to the information that appears when the cursor is held momentarily over an icon.

Definitions

PARAMETRIC BUILDING MODELING TECHNOLOGY

Parametric Building Modeling (PBM) is analogous to the decision instruments used in the financial community, which combine a data model (geometry and data) with a behavioral model (change management) that gives meaning to the data through relationships. Just as a spreadsheet is a tool for analyzing numbers, software built on parametric building modeling technology is a tool for analyzing buildings. A change made anywhere in a spreadsheet updates everywhere with no further intervention from the user; a change made anywhere in a parametric building modeler is immediately reflected everywhere. In PBM, all building information and a complete set of design documents are stored in an integrated parametric database and therefore are completely interconnected. This interconnectivity allows changes to the relationships, enabling real-time self-coordination of information in every view.

FAMILIES

All objects in Revit Architecture are "Family based." The term *Family* describes a concept used throughout Revit Architecture to help you to manage your data and to make changes easily. Each Family element can have multiple types defined within it, each with a different size, shape, material set, or other parameter variables as designed by the Family creator. Changes to a Family type definition propagate through a project and are automatically reflected in every instance of that Family type within the project. This keeps objects coordinated and saves you the time and effort of manually keeping components, and schedules, up to date (see Figure 1).

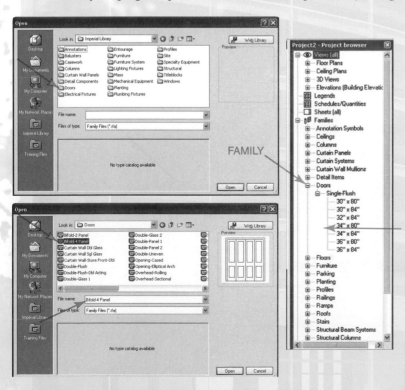

Figure 1

LEVELS

Levels are horizontal planes that act as a reference for elements, such as roofs, floors, ceilings, and so on. These levels, which are seen only in the elevations, correspond to levels in the Project browser. Adding new levels in any elevation will add corresponding levels in the Project browser (see Figure 2).

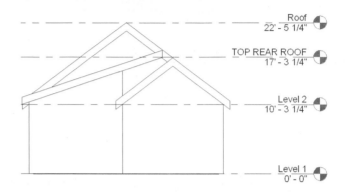

Figure 2

ELEMENTS

All objects in Revit Architecture are referred to as *elements*. These include, but are not limited to Lines, Circles, Components, Walls, Windows, Doors, Roofs, and Stairs.

CHECK BOXES

Check boxes indicate the on or off state of available options. If they are in a group, several check boxes can be selected at the same time (see Figure 3).

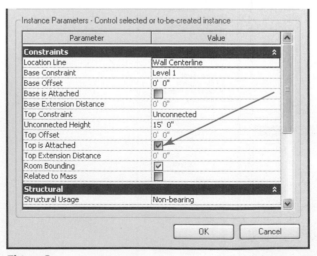

Figure 3

RADIO BUTTONS

Radio buttons (the name comes from the button selectors on car radios) indicate the on or off state of available options. Only one button in a group of buttons can be chosen (see Figure 4).

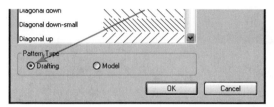

Figure 4

CONTEXTUAL MENUS

Contextual (context-sensitive) menus became popular when Microsoft introduced Windows 95. Revit Building uses these menus to control options and subcommands of various components. Contextual menus typically are summoned by clicking the right mouse button on a specific object, entity, or spot in the interface. Through programming, the appropriate menu or "context" will appear for that object at that point in its command structure. As an example, clicking the right mouse button on a door within a wall will provide all the commands available for the door and its relationship to the wall (see Figure 5).

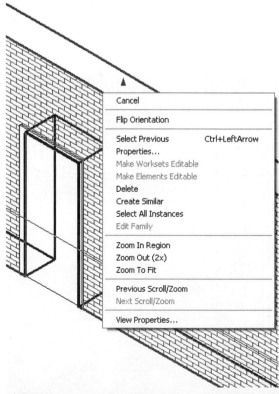

Figure 5

CONSTRAINTS

You create constraints either by placing dimensions and locking them or by creating equality constraints. Constraints are very helpful when you wish to hold a wall in place while changing the dimension of an adjacent wall (see Figure 6).

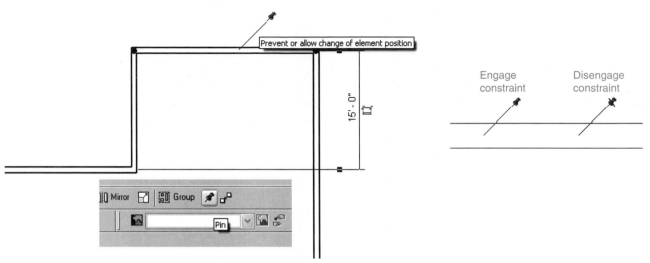

Figure 6

DIALOG BOXES

Dialog boxes contain fields, drop-down lists, and other features that you fill in to change settings.

In Revit Architecture, right mouse clicking on an object brings up a context-sensitive menu that contains commands that can be used on that particular object in that particular situation. Right mouse clicking in the Drawing Editor (drawing area) also brings up a contextual menu with controls for that editor (see Figure 7).

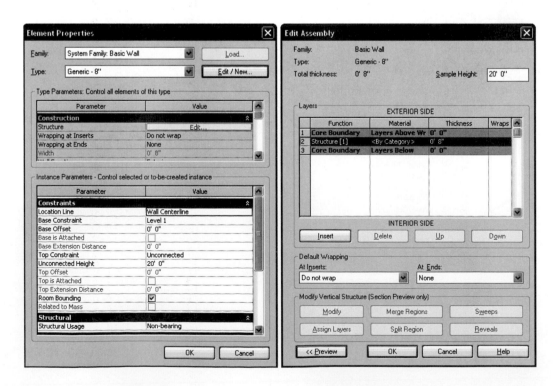

Figure 7

OBJECT SNAPS

Object snaps allow you to grab onto objects and lines at predetermined locations, automatically, when doing operations such as move, copy, rotate, and so on. This concept comes to Revit Architecture from 2D CAD programs. The **Snaps** dialog box can be reached by selecting **Settings** > **Snaps** from the **Main** menu. Revit Architecture displays snap points and snap lines to assist in lining up elements, components, or lines with existing geometry. Snap points depend on the type of snap, and are represented in the drawing area as shapes (triangles, squares, diamonds, etc.). Snap lines are represented as dashed green lines in the drawing area.

In the **Snaps** dialog box, you can check which snaps you wish to automatically appear when you perform an operation. You can enable or disable object snaps, and specify dimension snap increments. You can also override snap settings using keyboard shortcuts (see "Keyboard Shortcuts"). Settings are held for the duration of the Revit Architecture session. Snap settings apply to all files open in the session, but are not saved with a project (see Figures 8 and 9).

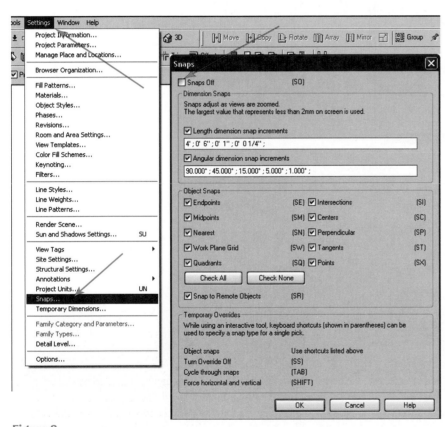

Figure 8

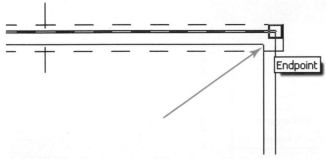

Figure 9

MAIN MENU

The **Main** menu appears at the very top of the Revit Architecture interface. It contains drop-down menus with names. When a horizontal triangle appears after a name, clicking on that name will bring up more menu names. Picking one of these names will take you to a dialog box. These are often called "nested menus." Menu names with three dots after them will take you directly to dialog boxes (see Figure 10).

Figure 10

TOOLBARS

Toolbars are located at the top of the Revit Architecture interface. They can be activated by right mouse clicking on an empty spot in the toolbar area, and checking the toolbars that you wish to display. If you check **Text Labels,** the names of the tools will appear next to their respective tools (see Figure 11).

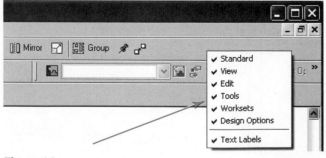

Figure 11

Standard toolbar

The **Standard** toolbar contains many basic commands such as **New Project, Save, Cut, Paste,** and so on (see Figure 12).

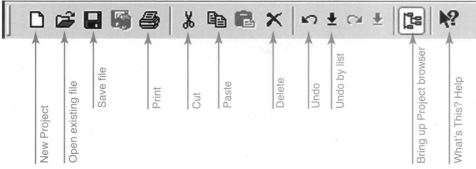

Figure 12

New Project	Creates a new project.
Open Existing File	Brings up browser to locate existing files.
Save File	Brings up Save As dialog box to save files.
Print	Brings up Print dialog box.
Cut	Removes objects from Drawing Editor, and saves them in the Clipboard.
Paste	Pastes objects from the Clipboard into the Drawing Editor.
Delete	Removes selected objects from the Drawing Editor.
Undo & Redo	Sequences backwards and forwards through past commands.
Undo by List	Sequences backwards through a list of past commands.
Bring up Project Browser	Makes Project browser visible or not visible.
What's This?	Point at any toolbar icon to bring up help files for that icon.

View toolbar

The **View** toolbar contains the commands to control the views (see Figures 13).

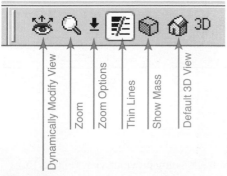

Figure 13

Dynamically Modify View	Brings up Dynamic View dialog box with buttons for Scroll, Zoom, and Spin (depending on View type).
Zoom	Zooms dynamically with magnifying glass icon.
Zoom Options	Different Zoom methods.
Thin Lines	Changes all lines to thin lines.
Show Mass	Shows the Mass Object.
Default 3D View	Creates a 3D view in the Project browser, and displays that view in the Drawing Editor.

Steering Wheels

New for Revit 2009, Steering Wheels appear when you click on the **Steering Wheels** icon (Figure 14) in the **View** toolbar. Different Steering Wheels with different capabilities appear in Plan views and 3D views (Figure 15).

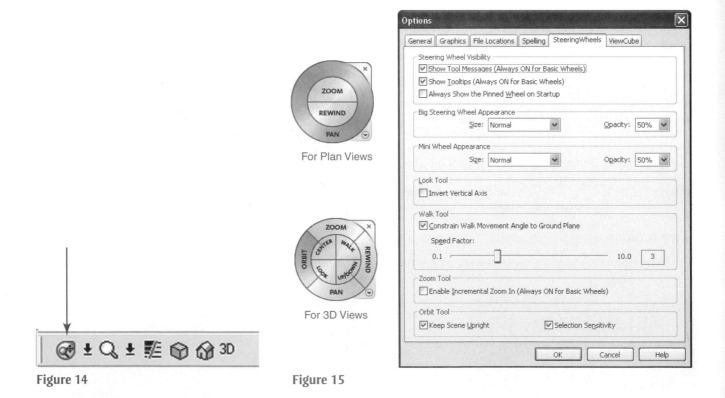

For Plan Views

For 3D Views

Figure 14   **Figure 15**

The **Rewind** option in the Steering Wheel allows you to re-track to any previous view (Figure 16.) Click as shown in Figure 17 to show Steering Wheel options.

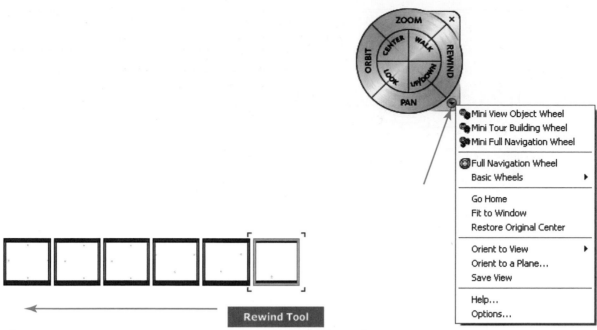

Figure 16   Figure 17

ViewCube

New for Revit 2009, the ViewCube appears when you are in a 3D or camera view. Clicking on the cube places you in a **Top**, **Front**, **Right**, **Left**, **Back**, or **Bottom** view. Clicking on the "**house**" icon adjacent to the cube returns you to the 3D view. Moving the compass "orbits the view" in real-time. You can turn the ViewCube on or off in the **Options** dialog box, which is found in the **Settings** drop-down menu (Figure 18).

Figure 18

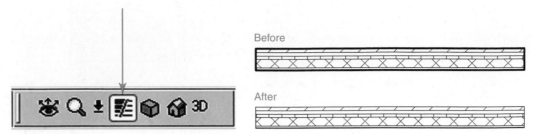

Figure 19

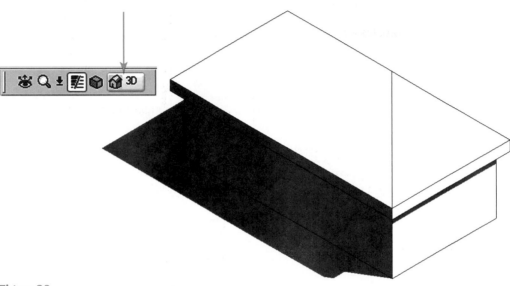

Figure 20

Edit

The **Edit** toolbar contains routines for moving, copying, arraying, and performing other operations on objects and lines (see Figure 21)

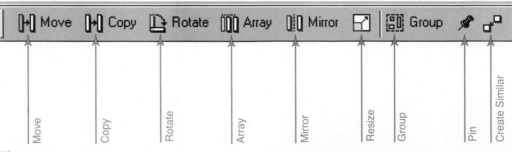

Figure 21

Move	Moves objects.
Copy	Copies objects.
Rotate	Rotates objects.
Array	Arrays objects.
Mirror	Mirrors objects.
Resizes	Resizes elements and walls with the same base level. Resizes symbols.
Group	Groups objects.
Pin	Constrains objects.
Create Similar	Creates a new object similar to a selected object.

Tools toolbar

The **Tools** toolbar contains the commands for working with objects (see Figure 22).

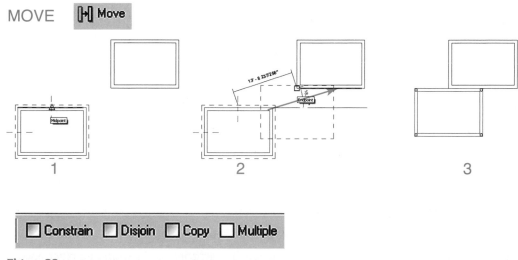

Figure 22

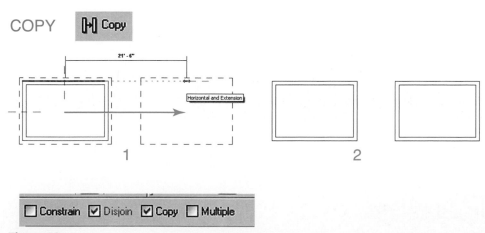

Figure 23

ROTATE

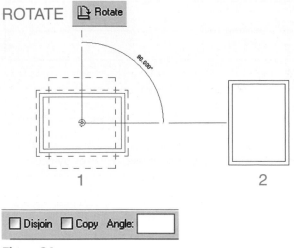

Figure 24

ARRAY

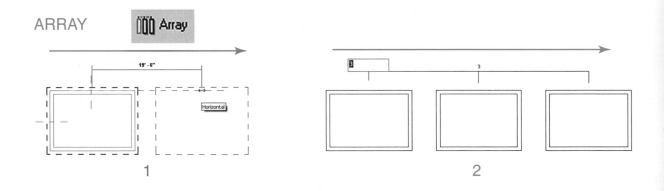

Figure 25

MIRROR

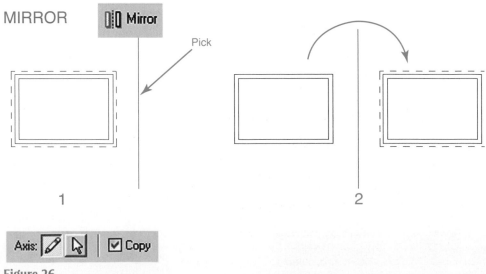

Figure 26

RESIZE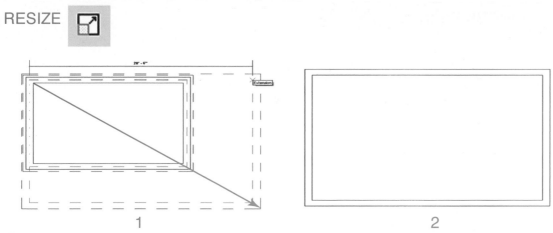

Figure 27

Tools (1)

The **Tools** toolbar contains the commands for working with objects (see Figure 28).

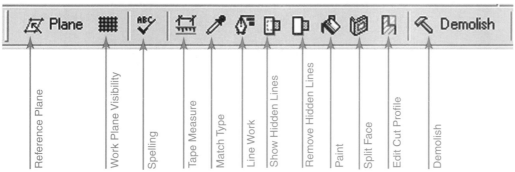

Figure 28

Reference Plane	Creates a plane to draw on.
Work Plane Visibility	Turns Work Plane grid on and off.
Spelling	Spell checker.
Tape Measure	Measuring tool.
Match Type	Changes the type of other objects to match the first selected.
Line Work	Changes line styles.
Show Hidden lines	Shows lines that are hidden.
Remove Hidden lines	Removes hidden lines.
Paint	Assigns textures to surfaces.
Split Face	Splits the faces of objects.
Edit Cut Plane	Cuts objects in sections.
Demolish	Changes object to demolish display.

WORK PLANE

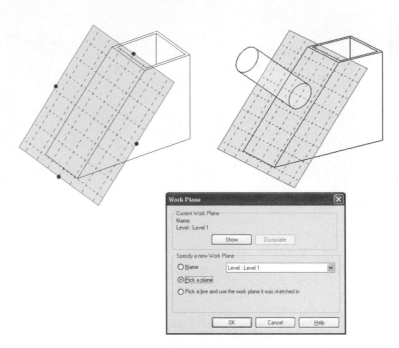

Figure 29

LINE WORK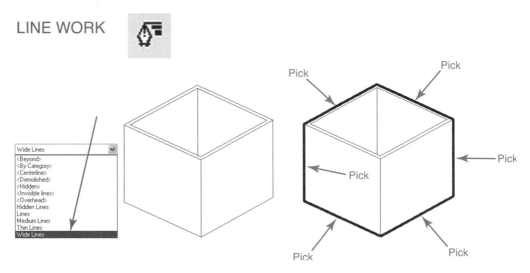

Figure 30

PAINT

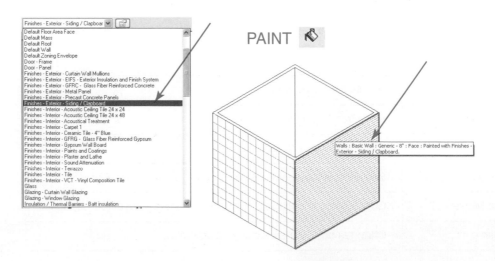

Figure 31

SPLIT FACE 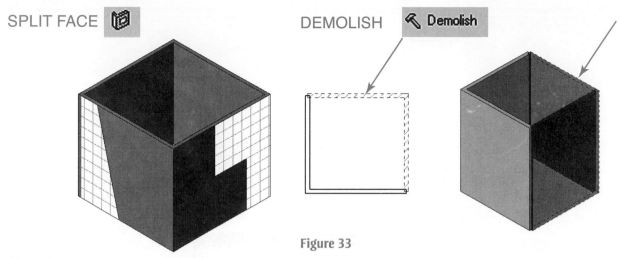   DEMOLISH

Figure 33

Figure 32

Tools (2)

See Figure 34.

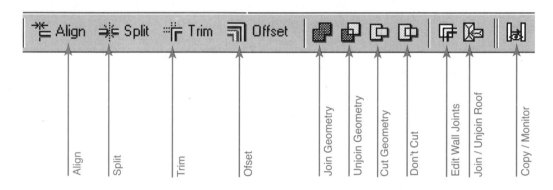

Figure 34

Align	Aligns one object or element to another. Select first the element to be aligned to, and then select the element to align to it.
Split	Splits walls horizontally and vertically; splits lines.
Trim	Trims walls and lines.
Offset	Offsets objects.
Join Geometry	Cleans joints between two or more host elements that share a common face.
Unjoin Geometry	Removes a join between two or more elements that were joined using the Join Geometry command.
Cut Geometry	
Don't Cut	
Edit Wall Joins	Edit conditions at wall ends and joints (see Section 2 on Walls).
Join / Unjoin roof	Used to join or unjoin roofs to other roofs or walls (see Section 5 on Roofs).
Copy / Monitor	Use for monitoring Multi-discipline Coordination.

ALIGN

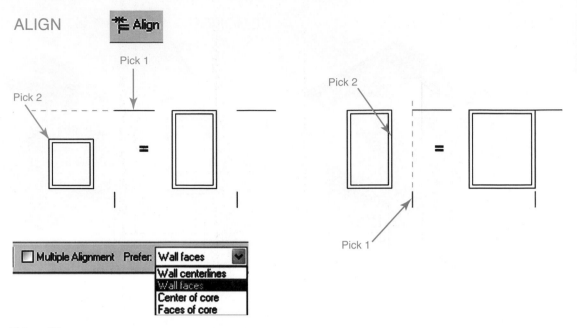

Figure 35

SPLIT

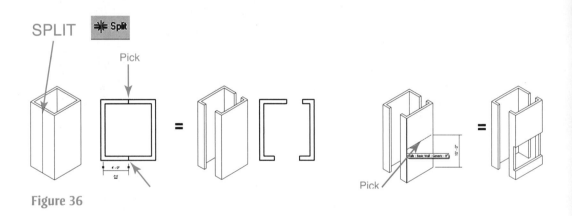

Figure 36

TRIM

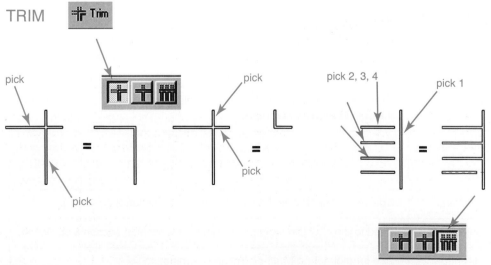

Figure 37

JOIN GEOMETRY

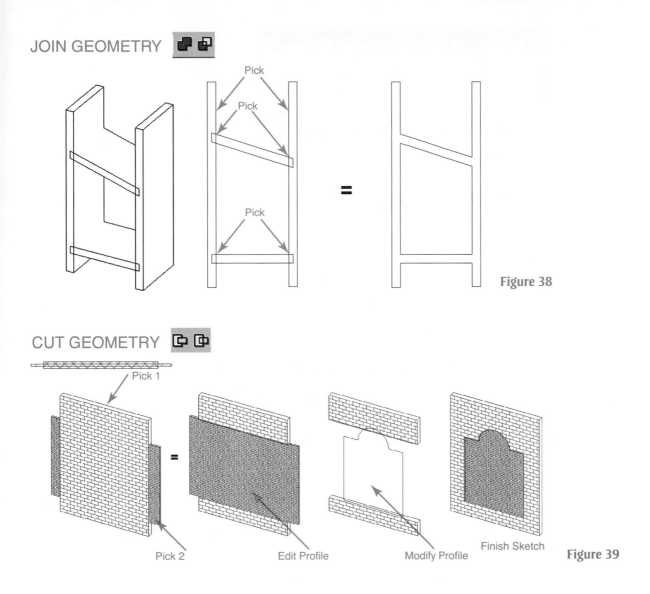

Figure 38

CUT GEOMETRY

Figure 39

Worksets

Figure 40 shows the Worksets toolbar. See Section 17 on Worksharing for more information.

Figure 40

View Properties

Every view has View Properties that control it. To activate the dialog box, type **VP** on your keyboard, or **RMB** (right mouse click) in an empty space in the **Drawing Editor** (drawing space) to bring up the **Element Properties** dialog box (see Figure 41) for that view. View Properties control such things as scale, hidden line display, shadows, and,other features. Some of these controls are redundant because they are also controlled through icons at the bottom of the screen. Every view is independent—this means that turning shadows on in a floor plan does not turn them on in the elevation or other features.

Please explore all the fields, and pay particular attention to the **Underlay** drop-down list. When you are working on floor plans, Underlay will allow you to see another view under the view on which you are working. This is especially helpful in checking to see if walls line up.

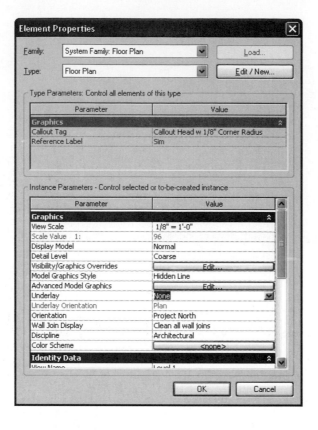

Figure 41

Visibility Graphics

The **Visibility Graphics** dialog box (see Figure 42) allows you to control the visibility of parts of the model, the annotations, and any imported information such as bitmap pictures and CAD files.

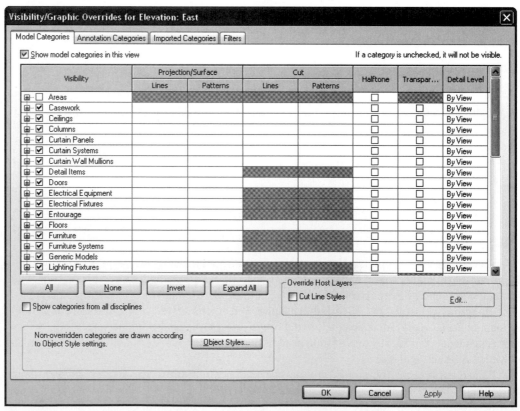

Figure 42

You can bring up the **Visibility Graphics** dialog box by typing **VG** on your keyboard or selecting it from the **Visibility Graphics/Overrides** field in the **View Properties** dialog box (see Figure 41).

Keyboard Shortcuts

Although you can operate Revit by picking commands from menus and icons with the mouse, many people prefer keyboard shortcut commands. To execute these keyboard commands all you need to do is press the two letter commands in order, or hold down the **<Ctrl>** key and then press the letter key together for the "**<Ctrl>** +" commands.

As with most architectural and CAD programs, there are multiple methods for evoking commands. The following menus (see Figures 43 through 50) show the keyboard shortcut commands, but you can also pick these commands directly from the menus or from the duplicate icon commands on the toolbars.

File Menu

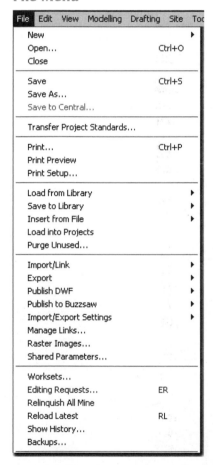

Figure 43

1	Ctrl + O	Open
2	Ctrl + S	Save
3	Ctrl + P	Print
4	ER	Editing Requests
5	RL	Reload Latest

Edit Menu

1	Ctrl + Z	Undo	16	UG	Ungroup
2	Ctrl + Y	Redo	17	LG	Link Group
3	Ctrl + X	Cut	18	EX	Exclude Member
4	Ctrl + C	Copy to Clipboard	19	RB	Restore Excluded Member
5	Ctrl + V	Paste from Clipboard	20	RA	Restore All
6	MD	Modify	21	AP	Add to Group
7	SA	Select all Instances	22	RG	Remove from Group
8	MV	Move	23	AD	Attach Detail
9	CO	Copy	24	PG	Group Properties
10	RO	Rotate	25	FG	Finish Group
11	AR	Array	26	CG	Cancel Group
12	MM	Mirror	27	pp	Pin Position
13	RE	Resize	28	UP	Unpin Position
14	GP	Create Group	29	CS	Create Similar
15	EG	Edit Group	30	PR	Properties

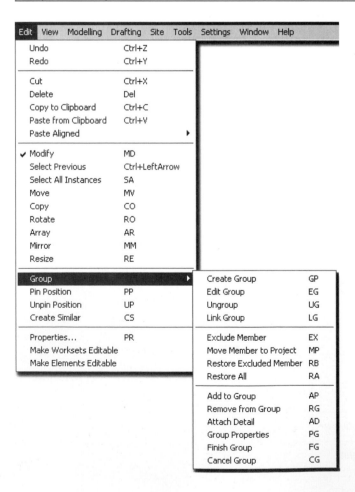

Figure 44

View Menu

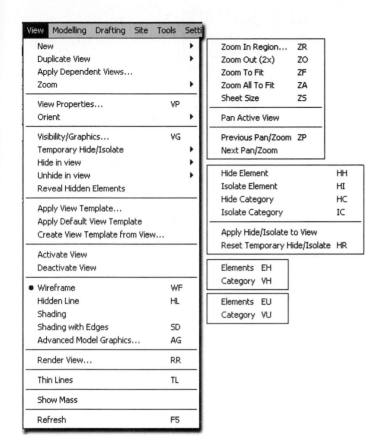

Figure 45

1	VP	View properties	13	HR	Reset Temporary Hide
2	ZR	Zoom In Region	14	EH	Hide in View/Elements
3	VG	Visibility/Graphics	15	VH	Hide in View/Category
4	ZO	Zoom Out	16	EU	Unhide in View/Elements
5	ZF	Zoom to Fit	17	VU	Unhide in View/Category
6	ZA	Zoom All to Fit	18	WF	Wireframe
7	ZS	Sheet Size	19	HL	Hidden Line
8	ZP		20	SD	Shading with Edges
9	HH	Hide Element	21	AG	Advanced Model Graphics
10	HI	Isolate Element	22	TL	Thin Lines
11	HC	Hide Category	23	F5	Refresh
12	IC	Isolate Category			

Modeling Menu

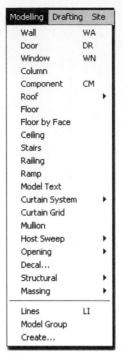

1	WA	Wall
2	DR	Door
3	WN	Window
4	CM	Component
5	LI	Lines

Figure 46

Drafting Menu

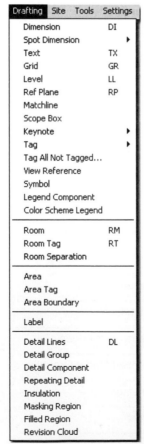

1	DI	Dimension
2	TX	Text
3	GR	Grid
4	LL	Level
5	RP	Reference Plane
6	RM	Room
7	RT	Room Tag
8	DL	Detail Lines

Figure 47

Tools Menu

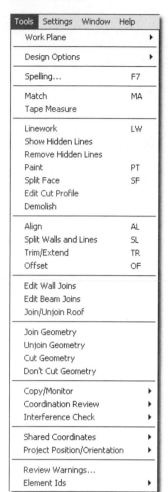

Figure 48

Settings Menu

Figure 49

1	SU	Sun and Shadow Settings
2	UN	Project Units

1	F7	Spelling
2	MA	Match
3	LW	Linework
4	PT	Paint
5	SF	Split Face
6	AL	Align
7	SL	Split Walls and Lines
8	TR	Trim/Extend
9	OF	Offset

Snaps Menu

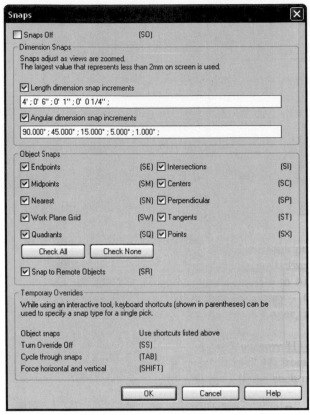

1	SO	Snaps Off
2	SE	Object snap - Endpoints
3	SM	Object snap - Midpoints
4	SN	Object snap - Nearest
5	SW	Object snap - Work Plane Grid
6	SQ	Object snap - Quadrants
7	SI	Object snap - Intersections
8	SC	Object snap - Centers
9	SP	Object snap - Perpendicular
10	ST	Object snap - Tangents
11	SX	Object snap - Points
12	SR	Snap to Remote Objects
13	SS	Turn Override Off

Figure 50

CUSTOMIZING KEYBOARD SHORTCUTS

1. Open the **KeyboardShortcuts.txt** file in a text editor. This file is typically located in the following directory: **C:\Program Files\Revit Architecture 2008\Program**. The path may vary depending on your operating system or where you installed Revit Architecture.

   At the top of the file you will see several paragraphs with each line preceded by a semicolon. A list of commands begins after the text. Command lines are not preceded by semicolons. Command syntax is as follows:

   "key(s)" menu: "menu-string"

   Function key menu: "menu-string"

   For example, in the following command line, **M** launches the menu command **Edit > Move.**

   M menu: **Edit > Move**

   Function key **(F2–F12)** command syntax does not require the shortcut key in quotes. For example, in the following command line, the shortcut key **<F5>** has no quotes. **<F5>** launches the menu command **View > Refresh.**

   <F5> menu: **View > Refresh**

2. Insert a new line between any two existing commands.
3. Type the new command using the examples above, or modify existing lines.
4. Save and close the file.
5. Restart Revit Architecture.

   The **KeyboardShortcuts.log** file (located in the same directory as **KeyboardShortcuts.txt**) contains any errors encountered while reading the KeyboardShortcuts.txt file.

Part Two: Sections and Tutorials

Massing

Section
Objectives

- Know how to load the **Massing Design Bar.**
- Learn how to create an **Extruded Mass Object.**
- Learn how to create a **Solid Blend Mass Object.**
- Know how to modify a **Solid Blend Mass.**
- Learn how to create a **Solid Revolve Mass Object.**
- Learn how to create a **Solid Sweep Mass Object.**
- Know how to place a **Mass Object.**
- Learn how to make a **Wall by Face.**
- Learn how to make a **Floor by Face.**
- Learn how to make a **Curtain System by Face.**
- Learn how to make a **Roof by Face.**
- Know how to create multiple **Mass Objects.**

MASSING AND MASS MODELING

Computerized mass modeling replicates the design system frequently used by architects to design large buildings. The initial design studies for these buildings are often modeled in clay or wood first. These small models generally show the relationship between parts of the building while indicating scale as well as how light and shadow react with the facades. Mass modeling is meant to be a quick process, akin to the building blocks we all played with as children.

The Mass Family comes with 15 preconfigured primitives (3D shapes). These primitives can be placed into your drawing from the **Mass Design Bar**. Building models can be made from Massing primitives. These primitives can then be individually changed to quickly change the building model. After the building model has been created, Walls, Floors, Roofs, and Curtain Wall Systems can be placed on the Mass model faces.

The following exercises are designed to give you a hands-on feel for using the **Mass** feature of the program. After doing these exercises, I recommend that you explore all the primitives, and try to create some new ones.

Exercise 1-1: Loading the Massing Menu

1. **RMB** (click the right Mouse Button) in the **Design Bar** to bring up the contextual menu.
2. In the contextual menu, select **Massing**. (If it is checked, the Massing menu has already been loaded.) (See Figure 1-1.)

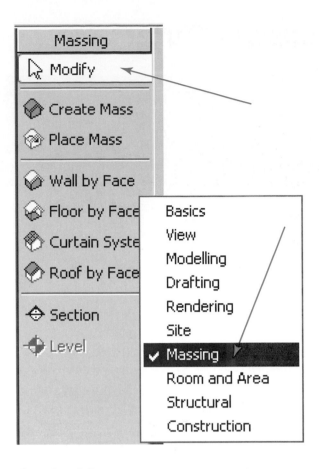

Figure 1-1

Exercise 1-2: Creating an Extruded Mass Object

1. Start a new drawing using the **RAC 2009\Imperial Templates\default.rte** template.
2. In the **Project browser**, double-click **Floor Plans > Level 1**.
3. In the **Design Bar**, under **Massing**, select the **Create Mass** icon.

A warning dialog box will appear saying that the "**Show Mass**" mode has been activated.

4. In the warning dialog box, press the **OK** button to bring up the **Name** dialog box.
5. Enter **TEST EXTRUDED MASS** in the **Name** field, and press the **OK** button (see Figure 1-2).

Figure 1-2

6. The **Massing Design Bar** will now change, showing **Solid Form** and **Void Form.**
7. Select **Solid Form > Solid Extrusion** (see Figure 1-3).

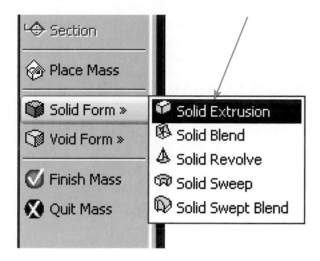

Figure 1-3

8. Move your cursor to the **Options** toolbar; change the **Depth** to **20′-0″**, pick the pencil icon, check the **Chain** check box, and pick the **Line** icon (see Figure 1-4).

Figure 1-4

9. In the drawing area, draw a **30′-0″ × 35′-0″** rectangle, and then press **Finish Sketch** in the **Massing Design Bar**.
10. Select the **3D** icon in the **View** toolbar to change to the 3D view (see Figure 1-5).

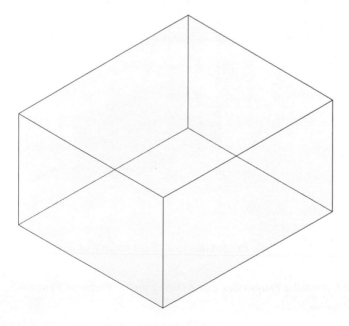

Figure 1-5

11. In the **Project browser**, double-click **Floor Plans > Level 1** to return to the plan view.
12. Select **Void Form > Void Extrusion** from the **Massing Design Bar**.
13. Move your cursor to the **Options** toolbar; change the **Depth** to 10′-0″, pick the pencil icon, check the **Chain** check box, and pick the **Line** icon.
14. Draw a **17′-0″ × 30′-0″** rectangle overlapping the Mass Object you previously created and then press **Finish Sketch** in the **Massing Design Bar** (see Figure 1-6).
15. Again, select the **3D** icon in the **Main** menu to change to the 3D view.
16. In the 3D view, hold down the **<Shift>** key on your computer while holding down the roller button on the mouse to rotate the **TEST EXTRUDED MASS** (see Figure 1-7).

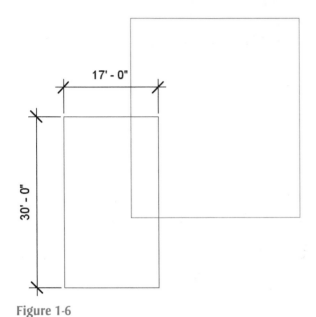

Figure 1-6

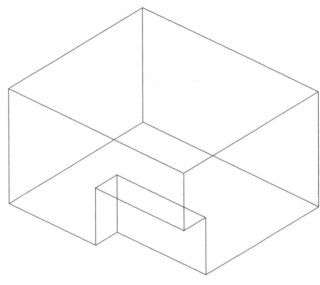

Figure 1-7

17. Select the corner shown in Figure 1-8 to expose the **Void Form** with arrow handles that you can use to stretch the Void Form in all directions (see Figure 1-8).

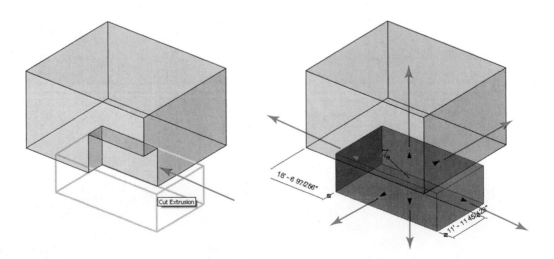

Figure 1-8

With the **Void Form** selected, you can now select the **Properties** icon, **Edit** button, or change the **Depth** in the **Options** toolbar (see Figure 1-9).

18. With the **Void Form** selected, press the **Properties** icon to bring up the **Element Properties** dialog box.

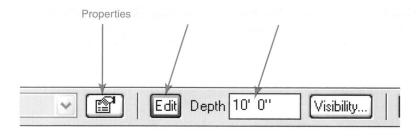

Properties

Figure 1-9

Here you can change the **Void Form Extrusion Start** and **Extrusion End** heights (see Figure 1-10).

19. Select the **Edit** button to put the Void Form into **Edit** mode.
20. While in **Edit** mode, use **Lines** to modify the Void Form, and then press **Finish Sketch** to finish the Void Form (see Figures 1-11 and 1-12).

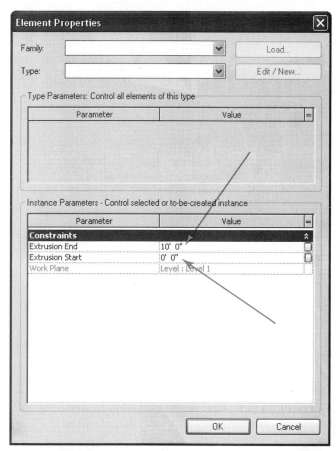

Figure 1-10

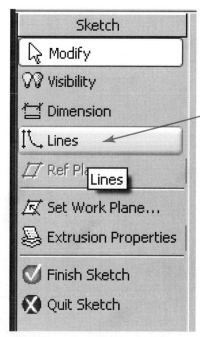

Figure 1-11

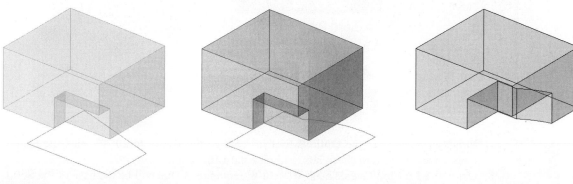

Figure 1-12

21. Select the **Void Form** again, and change the **Depth** on the **Options** toolbar to **20′-0″**.
22. Deselect the **Void Form**, and then press **Finish Mass** to complete the **TEST EXTRU-SION MASS** (see Figure 1-13).

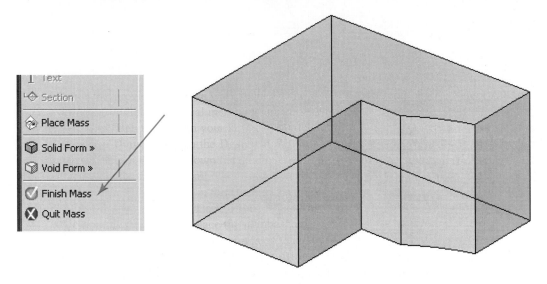

Figure 1-13

23. Save this file as **TEST EXTRUDED MASS**.
24. Select **File > Close** from the **Main** menu to close the project.

Exercise 1-3: Creating a Solid Blend Mass Object

1. Start a new drawing using the **Revit Building 9.1\Imperial Templates\default.rte** template.
2. In the **Project browser**, double-click **Floor Plans > Level 1**.
3. In the **Design Bar**, under **Massing**, select the **Create Mass** icon.

A warning dialog box will appear saying that **Show Mass** has been activated.

4. In the warning dialog box, press the **OK** button to bring up the **Name** dialog box.
5. Enter **TEST SOLID BLEND MASS** in the **Name** field, and press the **OK** button.

The **Massing Design Bar** will now change, showing **Solid Form** and **Void Form**.

6. Select **Solid Form > Solid Blend** (see Figure 1-14).

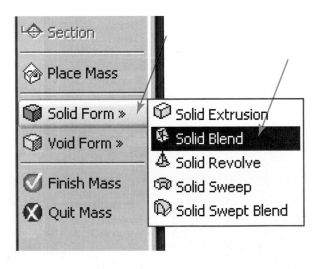

Figure 1-14

7. Move your cursor to the **Options** toolbar; change the **Depth** to **20′-0″**, pick the pencil icon, check the **Chain** check box, and pick the **Line** icon.
8. Using the **Line** tool, create a **30′-0″ × 30′0″** rectangle. (This will be the base of the Solid Blend.)

Figure 1-15   Figure 1-16

9. Select the **Edit Top** icon in the **Mass Design Bar** (see Figure 1-15).
10. In the **Options** toolbar, set the **Offset** to **-5′-0″**. (Note the minus sign.)
11. With the **Line** tool, trace the first rectangle to create a smaller rectangle inside the first (see Figure 1-16).
12. Press the **Finish Sketch** button in the **Massing Design Bar**.
13. Select the **3D** icon from the **View** toolbar to change to the **3D** view (see Figure 1-17).
14. Save this file as **SOLID BLEND MASSING OBJECT**.

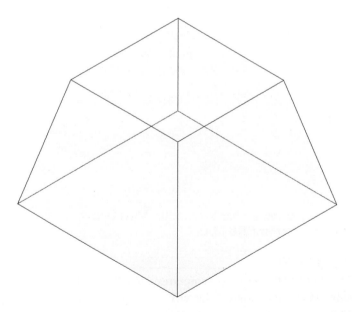

Figure 1-17

Exercise 1-4: Modifying the Solid Blend Mass

1. Select the **TEST SOLID BLEND MASSING OBJECT**, and press the **Edit Base** button in the **Options** toolbar to enter the **Edit** mode for the base (see Figure 1-18).
2. Click and drag the base to be 50′-0″ long, and then press the **Finish Sketch** button (see Figure 1-19).
3. Select the **TEST SOLID BLEND MASS**, and then select **Void Form > Void Extrusion** from the **Massing Design Bar**.

Figure 1-18

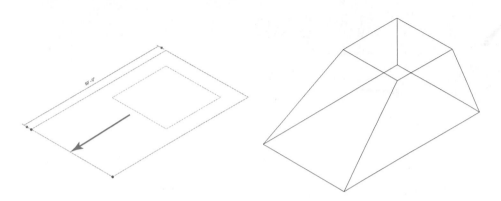

Figure 1-19

4. In the **Options** toolbar, change the **Depth** to **10′-0″**, select the **Pencil** icon, and select the **Rectangle** icon.
5. Draw a rectangle, and press **Finish Sketch** in the **Massing Design Bar** to create the mass, as shown in Figure 1-20.

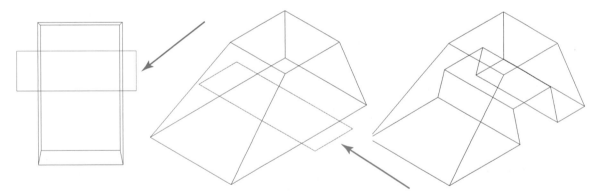

Figure 1-20

6. Select **Finish Mass** from the **Massing Design Bar** to create the Mass Object.
7. Save this file as **MODIFYING SOLID BLEND MASS.**

Exercise 1-5: Creating a Solid Revolve Mass Object

1. Start a new drawing using the **RAC 2009\Imperial Templates\default.rte** template.
2. In the **Project browser**, double-click **Floor Plans > Level 1**.
3. In the **Design Bar**, under **Massing**, select the **Create Mass** icon.

A warning dialog box will appear saying that **"Show Mass"** has been activated.

4. In the warning dialog box, press the **OK** button to bring up the **Name** dialog box.
5. Enter **TEST SOLID REVOLVE MASS** in the **Name** field, and press the **OK** button.

The **Massing Design Bar** will now change, showing **Solid Form** and **Void Form.**

6. Select **Solid Form > Solid Revolve** (see Figure 1-21).
7. Select **Revolution Properties** from the **Massing Design Bar** to bring up the **Element Properties** dialog box.

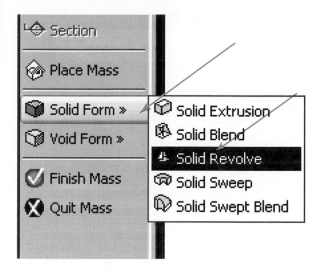

Figure 1-21

8. In the **Element Properties** dialog box, change the **End Angle** to **-180.000** and press the **OK** button to return to the drawing area (see Figure 1-22).

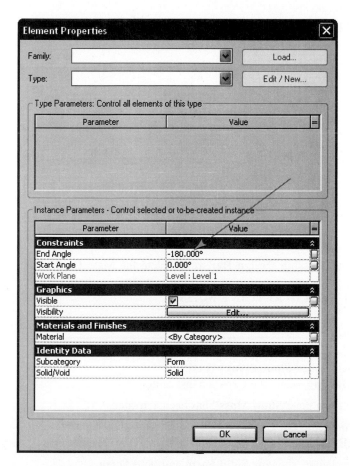

Figure 1-22

9. Move your cursor to the **Options** toolbar, pick the **Pencil** icon, check the **Chain** check box, and pick the **Rectangle** icon.
10. Create a **30'-0" × 15'0"** rectangle.
11. Select **Axis** from the **Design Bar**, and draw an **Axis** line parallel to the 30' side of the rectangle, and **7'-0"** away from it.
12. Select **Finish Sketch** from the **Massing Design Bar** to create the Mass Object (see Figure 1-23).
13. Save this file as **SOLID REVOLVE MASS OBJECT.**

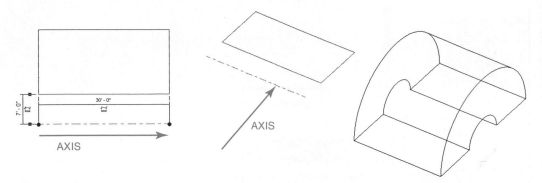

Figure 1-23

Exercise 1-6: Modifying the Solid Revolve Mass

1. Select the **TEST SOLID REVOLVE MASS**, and press the **Edit** button in the **Options** toolbar to enter the **Edit** mode.
2. Erase the **Axis** you previously placed.
3. Select **Axis** from the **Design Bar**, and draw a new **Axis** line parallel to the 15′ side of the rectangle, and 5′-0″ away from it.
4. Select **Finish Sketch** from the **Massing Design Bar** to create the Mass Object (see Figure 1-24).

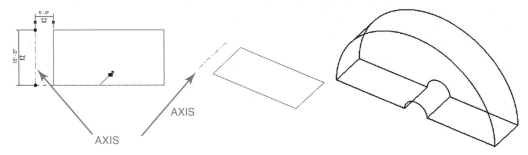

Figure 1-24

5. Select **Finish Mass** from the **Massing Design Bar** to complete the Mass Object (see Figure 1-24).
6. Save this project as **MODIFY SOLID REVOLVE MASS**.

Exercise 1-7: Creating a Solid Sweep Mass Object

1. Start a new drawing using the **RAC 2009\Imperial Templates\default.rte** template.
2. In the **Project browser**, double-click **Floor Plans > Level 1**.
3. In the **Design Bar**, under **Massing**, select the **Create Mass** icon.

A warning dialog box will appear saying that **"Show Mass"** has been activated.

4. In the warning dialog box, press the **OK** button to bring up the **Name** dialog box.
5. Enter **TEST SOLID SWEEP MASS** in the **Name** field, and press the **OK** button.

The **Massing Design Bar** will now change, showing **Solid Form** and **Void Form**.

6. Select **Solid Form > Solid Sweep** (see Figure 1-25).
7. Select **Sketch 2D Path** from the **Massing Design Bar**.
8. In the **Massing Design Bar**, select **Lines**.
9. In the **Options** toolbar, select the **Pencil** icon, check the **Chain** check box, and select the **Arc passing through three points** icon.
10. Draw a **50′-0″** long arc with an **80 degree** angle as shown in Figure 1-26.
11. Press **Finish Path** in the **Massing Design Bar** to complete the path.
12. Select **Sketch Profile** in the **Massing Design Bar**.

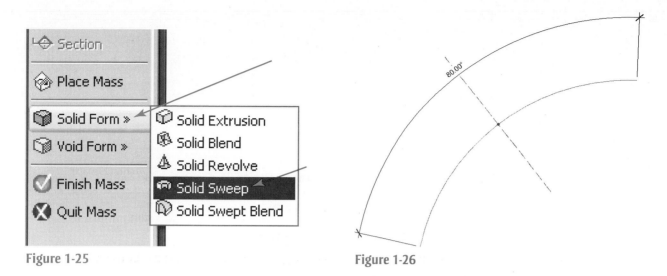

Figure 1-25

Figure 1-26

The **Go To View** dialog box will now appear with the views available for sketching the profile.

13. Select **Elevation: East** and press the **Open View** button to go to the **East View** (see Figure 1-27).

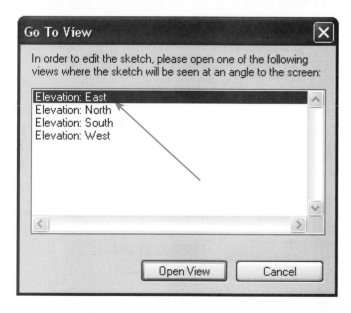

Figure 1-27

In the **East View**, you will see reference planes and a red dot signifying the location of the **Path.**

14. In the **East View**, using **Lines**, place a **6′** wide × **10′** high rectangle centered on the dot (see Figure 1-28).

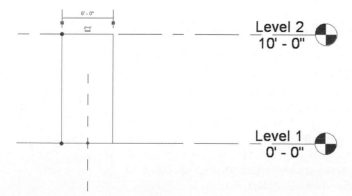

Figure 1-28

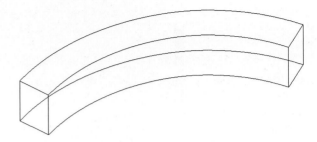

Figure 1-29

15. Press **Finish Sweep** in the **Massing Design Bar**, and then select the **3D** icon from the **View** toolbar to change to the **3D** view (see Figure 1-29).
16. Save this file as **Solid Sweep Mass Object.**

Exercise 1-8: Modifying the Solid Sweep Mass

1. Select the **TEST SOLID SWEEP MASS**, and press the **Edit Sweep** button in the **Options** toolbar to enter the **Edit** mode.
2. Change to **Level 1** from the **Project browser**.
3. Select **Sketch 2D Path** from the **Massing Design Bar**.
4. Using **Lines** from the **Massing Design Bar**, change the path, and then select **Finish Path**.
5. Select **Finish Sweep** from the **Massing Design Bar**, and then select the **3D** icon from the **View** toolbar to change to the **3D** view (see Figure 1-30).

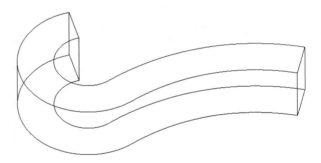

Figure 1-30

6. Select the **TEST SOLID SWEEP MASS** again, and press the **Edit Sweep** button in the **Options** toolbar to enter the **Edit** mode.
7. Change to the **East Elevation** from the **Project browser**.
8. Select **Sketch Profile** from the **Massing Design Bar**.
9. Using **Lines** from the **Massing Design Bar**, change the profile as shown in Figure 1-31, and then select **Finish Profile**.
10. Select **Finish Sweep** from the **Massing Design Bar**, and then select the **3D** icon from the **View** toolbar to change to the **3D** view (see Figure 1-31).

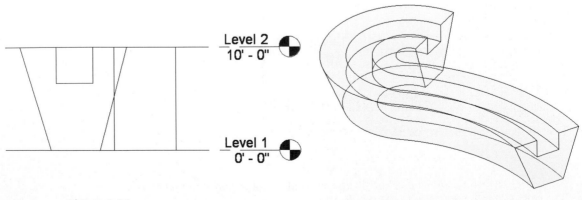

Figure 1-31

11. Select **Finish Mass** from the **Massing Design Bar** to complete the Mass Object.
12. Save this file as **MODIFY SOLID SWEEP MASS.**

Exercise 1-9: Creating a Solid Swept Blend Massing Object

1. Start a new drawing using the **RAC 2009\Imperial Templates\default.rte** template.
2. In the **Project browser**, double-click **Floor Plans > Level 1**.
3. In the **Design Bar**, under **Massing**, select the **Create Mass** icon.
4. A warning dialog box will appear saying that "**Show Mass**" has been activated.
5. In the warning dialog box, press the **OK** button to bring up the **Name** dialog box.
6. Enter **TEST SOLID SWEPT BLEND** in the **Name** field, and press the **OK** button.
7. The **Massing Design Bar** will now change to show **Solid Form** and **Void Form.**
8. Next, select **Solid Form > Solid Swept Blend**, and the **Design Bar** will change to the **Sketch** tab (see Figure 1-32).

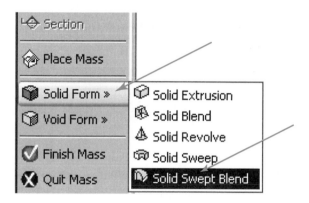

Figure 1-32

9. In the **Sketch** tab, select the **Sketch 2D Path** tool, and the tab will change to the **Sketch** mode.
10. Select the **Lines** tool in the **Sketch** tab; select the **Pencil** (Draw) tool in the **Options** toolbar.
11. In the **Options** toolbar, pick the **Spline** tool (see Figure 1-33).

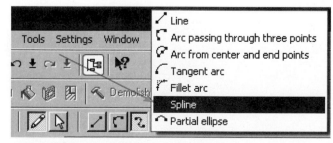

Figure 1-33

12. In the **Drawing Editor**, draw a **70′ Spline** similar to that shown in Figure 1-34.
13. In the **Sketch** tab, select the **Finish Path** icon.

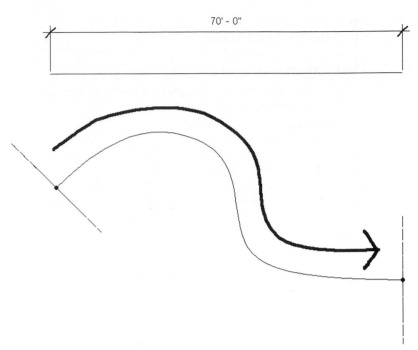

Figure 1-34

The **Sketch** mode tab will change to the **Sketch Profile** mode.

14. In the **Sketch** tab, select the **Sketch Profile 1** icon (see Figure 1-35).

Figure 1-35

15. In the **Go To View** dialog box, select the **3D View {3D}** view (see Figure 1-36).

Note:
The **Go To View** dialog box will appear with optional views for you to pick. This is because the **Sketch Profiles** will have to be created perpendicular to the path.

Note:
After you understand the method, you should use the other elevations to be able to create more accurate profile sketches.

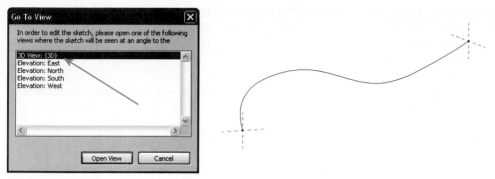

Figure 1-36

16. In the **Sketch** tab, select the **Lines** icon.
17. In the **Options** toolbar, select the **Pencil** (Draw) icon.
18. In the **Options** toolbar, select the **Rectangle**.
19. The **Sketch Profile 1** center location will appear as a red dot with dashed green "cross hairs."
20. Place a rectangle similar to that shown in Figure 1-37.

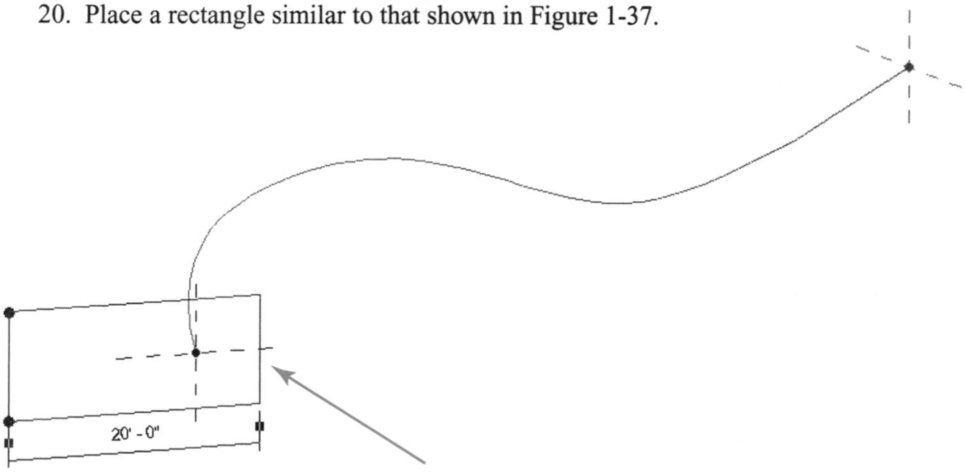

20' - 0"

Figure 1-37

21. In the **Sketch** tab, press the **Finish Profile** icon.
22. In the **Sketch** tab, select the **Sketch Profile 2** icon.
23. In the **Options** toolbar, select the **Pencil** (Draw) icon.
24. In the **Options** toolbar, select the **Rectangle**.
25. The **Sketch Profile 2** center location will appear as a red dot with dashed green "cross hairs."
26. Place a rectangle similar to that shown in Figure 1-38.

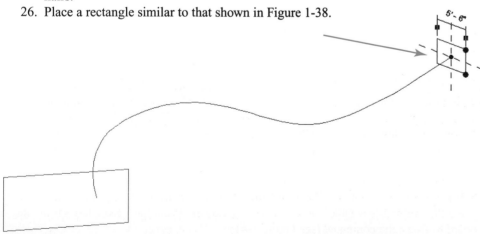

6'- 6"

Figure 1-38

27. In the **Sketch** tab, press the **Finish Profile** icon again.
28. In the **Sketch** tab, press the **Finish Swept Blend** icon to return to the **Mass** tab.
29. In the **Mass** tab, select the **Finish Mass** button to create the Mass Object, and return to the **Massing** tab in the **Design Bar**.
30. In the **Design Bar,** select the **Wall by Face** icon.
31. In the **Options** toolbar, select the **Basic Wall : Generic – 4″ Brick**, and select the side faces of the Massing Object you just created.

You have now created a Solid Swept Blend Massing Object, and added brick walls to it (see Figure 1-39).

32. Save this file as **SOLID SWEPT BLEND MASS**.

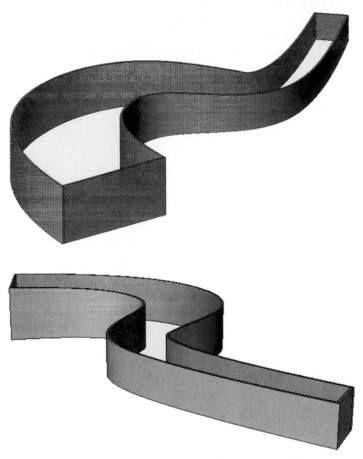

Figure 1-39

Exercise 1-10: Placing a Mass

Placing a mass allows you to place a mass that has been previously created. If no mass has been loaded in the program, you will get a warning dialog box asking if you wish to load one. Pressing the **Yes** button in this dialog box will automatically take you to the **Open** dialog box of the **Library**. If you scroll down to the **Mass** folder, you will find 15 premade Mass Objects (see Figure 1-40).

1. From the **Mass** folder, select the **Gable** mass.
2. Select **Gable**, and then the **Place on Work Plane** icon from the **Options** toolbar, and place the **Gable** Mass Object in the **Drawing Editor**. Press the **<Esc>** key on the keyboard to finish the command (see Figure 1-41).
3. Save this file as **PLACING A MASS**.

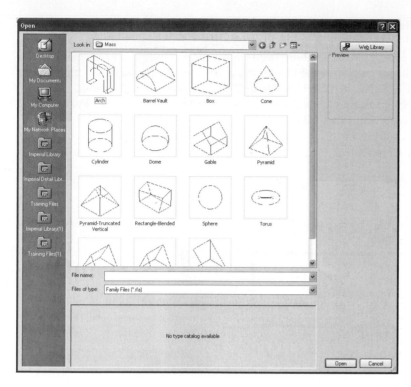

Figure 1-40

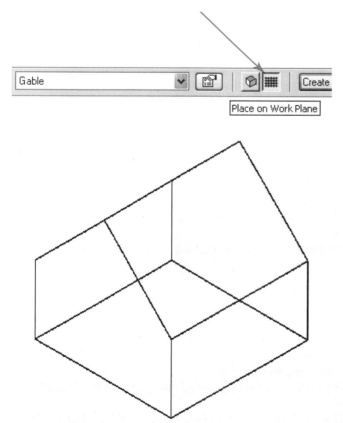

Figure 1-41

Exercise 1-11: Creating a Wall by Face, a Floor by Face, a Curtain System by Face, and a Roof by Face

A great feature of Revit is its ability to automatically convert Mass Objects into Walls, Floors, and Roofs.

1. Start a new drawing using the **Revit Building 9.1\Imperial Templates\default.rte** template.
2. In the **Project browser**, double-click **Floor Plans > Level 1**.

3. In the **Design Bar**, under **Massing** select the **Create Mass** icon.

A warning dialog box will appear saying that **"Show Mass"** has been activated.

4. In the warning dialog box, press the **OK** button to bring up the **Name** dialog box.
5. Enter **TEST BUILDING MASS** in the **Name** field, and press the **OK** button.
6. The **Massing Design Bar** will now change, showing **Solid Form** and **Void Form.**
7. Select **Solid Form > Solid Extrusion.**
8. Move your cursor to the **Options** toolbar; change the **Depth** to **80′-0″**, pick the **Pencil** icon, check the **Chain** check box, and pick the **Line** icon. Create the figure shown in Figure 1-42.

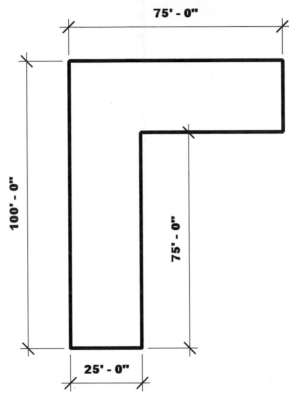

Figure 1-42

9. Press **Finish Sketch**, and then **Finish Mass** in the **Massing Design Bar** to create the first mass.
10. Change to the **East Elevation**.

Creating the Floors by Face

11. Select the **Level** icon from the **Mass Design Bar**, and add levels at **10′-0″** increments. Rename the last **Level** as **ROOF** (see Figure 1-43).
12. Change to the 3D view, and select the **Building** mass.
13. Select the **Floor Area Faces** button in the **Options** toolbar to open the **Floor Area Faces** dialog box.
14. In the **Floor Area Faces** dialog box, check all the check boxes *except* the **ROOF** check box (see Figure 1-44).
15. Press the **OK** button in the **Floor Area Faces** dialog box to return to the **Drawing Editor** (see Figure 1-45).
16. In the **Options** toolbar, select the floor type, check the **Select Multiple** check box, and select all the floors with a "window" selection.
17. In the **Options** toolbar, select the **Create Floors** button to create all the floors (see Figure 1-46).

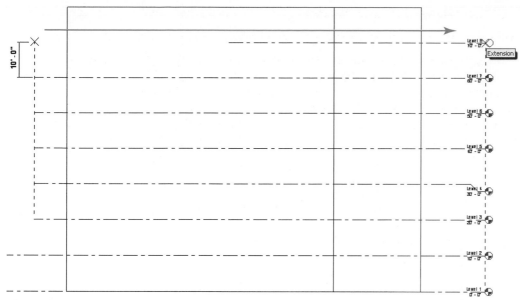

Figure 1-43

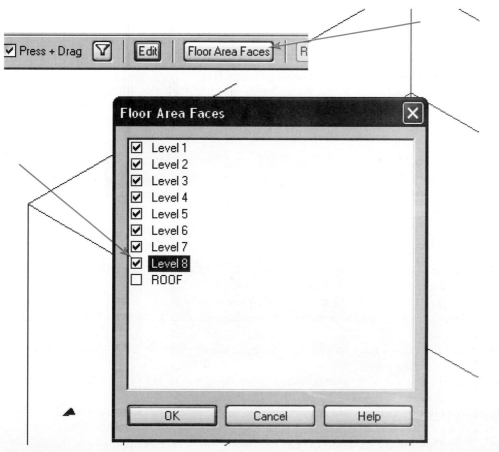

Figure 1-44

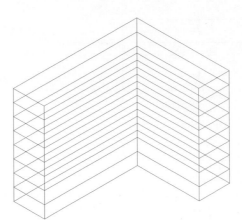

Figure 1-45

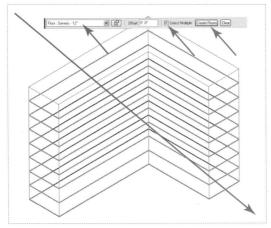
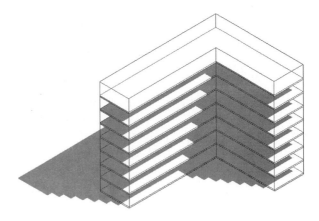

Figure 1-46

Creating the Walls by Face

18. Select **Wall by Face** from the **Massing Design Bar**.
19. In the **Options** toolbar, select the wall type, pick the **Pick Faces** icon, and select **Finish Face Interior** from the **Loc Line**.
20. Pick all the faces of the Mass Object shown in Figure 1-47.

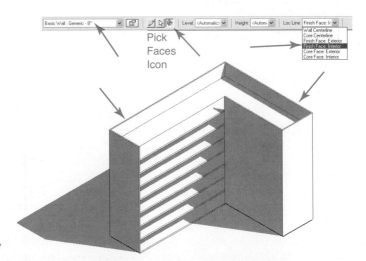

Figure 1-47

Creating Curtain System by Face

21. Select **Curtain System by Face** from the **Massing Design Bar**.
22. Pick the remaining face of the **Building** mass.

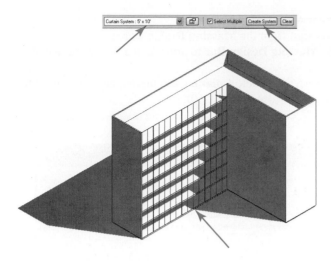

Figure 1-48

23. Select the curtain system type, and then press the **Create System** button in the **Options** toolbar (see Figure 1-48).

Creating the Roof by Face

24. Select **Roof by Face** from the **Massing Design Bar**.
25. In the **Options** toolbar, pick the top of the **Building** mass, select the **Roof** type, and then press the **Create Roof** button (see Figure 1-49).
26. Save this file as **WALLS_FLOORS_CEILINGS BY FACE**.

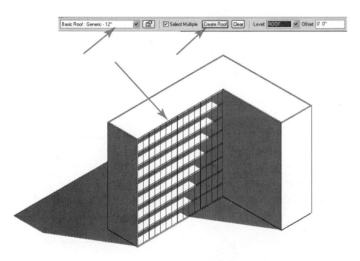

Figure 1-49

Exercise 1-12: Creating a Building from Multiple Mass Objects

1. Start a new drawing using the **Revit Building 9.1\Imperial Templates\default.rte** template.
2. In the **Project browser**, double-click **East Elevation** to bring up the East Elevation in the **Drawing Editor**.
3. In the **East Elevation**, create **6** levels **10'-0"** apart.
4. In the **Project browser**, double-click **Level 1** to bring up Level 1 in the **Drawing Editor**.
5. In the **Design Bar**, under **Massing**, select the **Create Mass** icon.
6. Enter **MULTIPLE BUILDING MASS** in the **Name** field, and press the **OK** button.
7. The **Massing Design Bar** will now change showing **Solid Form** and **Void Form.**
8. Select **Solid Form > Solid Extrusion** from the **Massing Design Bar**.
9. Move your cursor to the **Options** toolbar; set the **Depth** to **50'-0"**, pick the **Pencil** icon, check the **Chain** check box, and pick the **Line** icon. Create a **70'** long × **25'** wide mass, press **Finish Sketch** in the **Massing Design Bar**, and then press **Finish Mass**.

10. Create a second mass, and name it **ATRIUM**.
11. Select **Solid Form > Solid Extrusion** from the **Massing Design Bar**.
12. Select **Set Work Plane** from the **Massing Design Bar** to bring up the **Work Plane** dialog box.
13. In the **Work Plane** dialog box, select the **Pick a plane** radio button, and press the **OK** button to return to the **Drawing Editor** (see Figure 1-50).

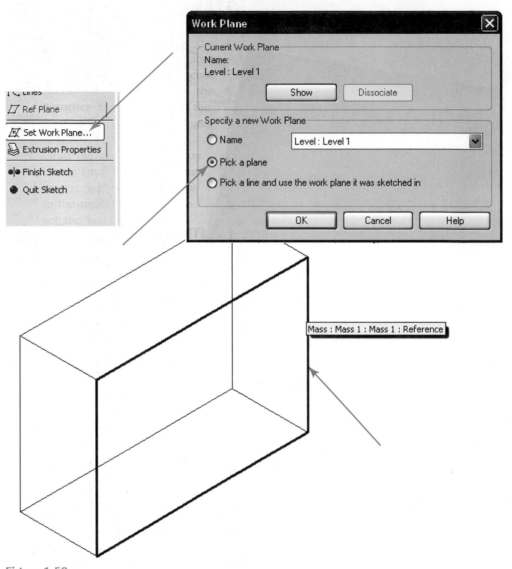

Figure 1-50

14. Double-click the **East Elevation** in the **Project browser** to bring up the **East** view in the **Drawing Editor**.
15. Using the **Lines** tool from the **Massing Design Bar**, in the **East** view draw the form shown in Figure 1-51.
16. Select **Extrusion Properties** from the **Massing Design Bar** to bring up the **Element Properties** dialog box.
17. In the **Element Properties** dialog box, enter **50′-0″** in the **Extrusion End** field and press the **OK** button.
18. Press **Finish Sketch** in the **Massing Design Bar**, and press the **3D** icon in the **View** toolbar (see Figure 1-52).
19. Again select **Solid Form > Solid Extrusion** from the **Massing Design Bar**.

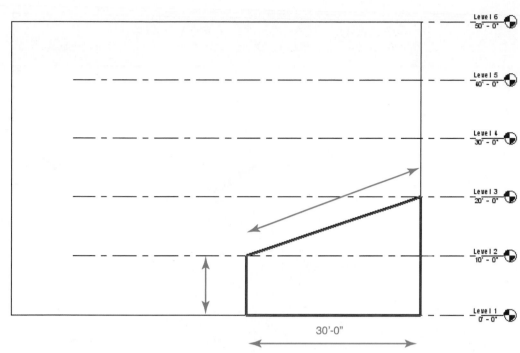

Figure 1-51

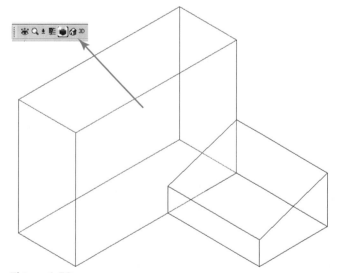

Figure 1-52

20. Again select **Set Work Plane** from the **Massing Design Bar** to bring up the **Work Plane** dialog box.
21. In the **Work Plane** dialog box, select the **Pick a plane** radio button, and press the **OK** button to return to the **Drawing Editor**.
22. Pick the sloped top plane of the **ATRIUM** to select it.
23. Move your cursor to the **Options** toolbar; set the **Depth** to **15'-0"**, pick the **Pencil** icon, check the **Chain** check box, and pick the **Circle** icon. Create a 7'-0" radius circle, press **Finish Sketch** in the **Massing Design Bar**, and then press **Finish Mass**.
24. Using the **Wall by Face, Floor by Face, Curtain System by Face**, and **Roof by Face** tools, complete the multiple Mass Objects (Figure 1-53). Try experimenting with all the different Mass tools to create different masses.
25. Save this file as **MULTIPLE MASS**.

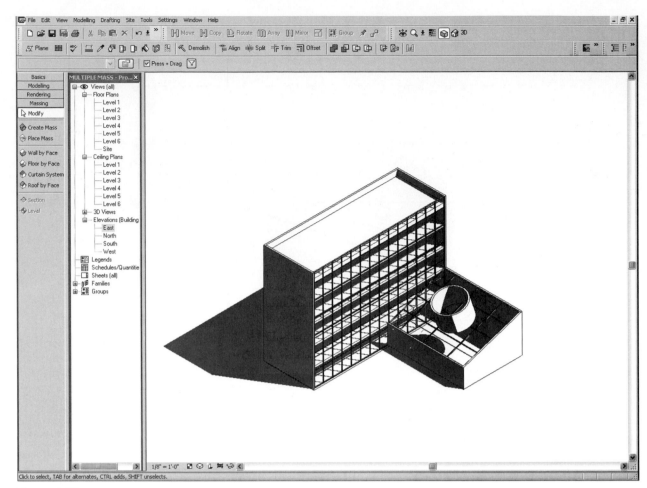

Figure 1-53

Summary

This section discussed the methods for creating Massing models. It also showed how to use Massing models as beginning building blocks for buildings in Revit Architecture 2009.

Section Test Questions

True or false

1. True or False: A Mass Object is similar to a solid wood model.

2. True or False: You cannot use a Mass Object in the Construction Documents.

3. True or False: A Solid Swept Blend profile can be created in a 3D view.

4. True or False: The **Pencil** and the **Draw** tools are the same tool.

5. True or False: The **Solid Form Extrusion Depth** is not located on the **Options** toolbar.

Questions

1. How do you add walls to a Mass Object?

2. How many types of **Mass** models are there?

3. What is the purpose of the **Void Form**?

4. What is the purpose of **Place Mass**?

5. How could you use a **Solid Revolve**?

Walls

2

Objectives

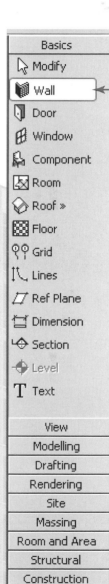

- Know how to place a wall with the **Pencil** tool.
- Learn how to use **Pick Lines** on an imported 2D CAD file.
- Learn how to create **Wall Sweeps** and **Reveals**.
- Use **Join Geometry, Cut Geometry**, and **Wall Joins**.
- Learn how to modify **Vertically-Compound Walls**.
- Know how to create a **Profile** for a **Wall Sweep**.
- Know how to create a compound wall with **Sweep**.
- Know how to modify **End Caps** and **Insert** conditions.
- Use **Embed Walls**.
- Create a new wall table.

WALLS

Wall objects are the basis of all buildings; they enclose space and give the building its character. Because buildings require a vast variety of wall types and configurations, these objects have become very sophisticated in Revit Building. Walls can function as interior, exterior, foundation, and retaining. All walls have a structure that can be defined through the type properties of the wall. In addition, various instance and type properties can be specified to define the appearance of the wall.

You create a wall by sketching the location line of the wall in a plan view or a 3D view. Revit Architecture applies the thickness, height, and other properties of the wall around the location line of the wall. The location line is a plane in the wall that does not change, even if the wall type changes. For example, if you draw a wall and specify its location line as Core Centerline, the location line remains there, even if you select that wall and change it to another type or change its structure.

Exercise 2-1: Placing a Wall with the Pencil Tool

1. Start a new drawing using the **RAC 2009\ImperialTemplates\default.rte** template.
2. In the **Project browser**, double-click **Floor Plans > Level 1**.
3. In the **Design Bar**, under **Basics**, select the **Wall** icon.
4. Set the **Detail** to **Medium** (see Figure 2-1) so that you can see the wall components in plan view.

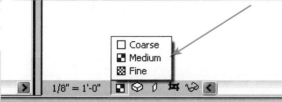

Figure 2-1

Wall Type

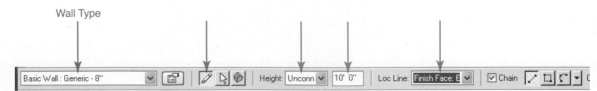

Figure 2-2

5. Move your cursor to the **Options** toolbar; select **Basic wall: Exterior – Brick on CMU** from the drop-down list, pick the **Pencil** icon, and set the **Height** to **Unconnected**. Then set the height to **10′-0″**, set the **Loc line** to **Finish Face: Exterior**, check the **Chain** check box, and pick the **Line** icon (see Figure 2-2).
6. Place the wall horizontally by clicking a spot in the **Drawing Editor**, releasing the mouse button, moving the mouse to the right, and clicking again when the number above the wall reads **28′-0″**.

> **Note:**
> When you set the **Height** to **Unconnected**, the wall top is not connected to a **Level**; thus, you must set its height.

Notice that the wall is being drawn in relation to the face of the wall; this is the **Loc Line**.

7. Again, select the **Wall** icon from the **Design Bar**.
8. Change the **Loc Line** to **Core Face: Exterior**, and place another wall **28′-0″** long.

Notice that the wall is now being drawn in relation to the face of the CMU core. Repeat steps 5 and 6 with all the different Loc Lines (see Figure 2-3).

Loc Line
at Exterior
Face

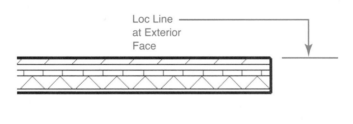

Loc Line
at Core
Face

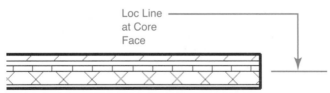

Figure 2-3

9. Select the walls you placed, and press the **<Delete>** key on your keyboard to delete the walls.
10. Click a spot, move your cursor vertically, enter **11** (11′-0″) on your keyboard, and press the **<Enter>** key to create an 11′-0″ long wall.
11. Repeat this process, moving your cursor horizontally, entering **28 6** (28′-6″).
12. Move your cursor vertically downward until a dashed line appears that shows you are aligned with the bottom of the first wall you placed.
13. Click at this spot, and then press the **<Esc>** key on your keyboard twice, or select the **Modify** tool in the **Design Bar** to finish the command (see Figure 2-4).
14. Select the left vertical wall to expose the temporary dimension lines. If the temporary dimensions are not from face to face, double-click the witness line node as shown in Figure 2-5 until the witness line is in the correct position. Repeat for both sides.

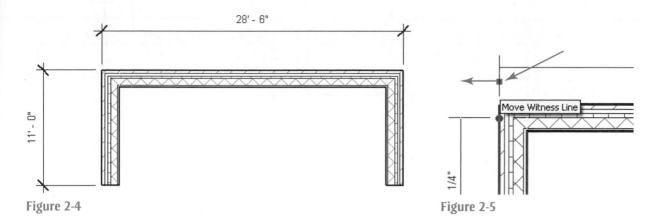

Figure 2-4   **Figure 2-5**

15. Select the dimension for the horizontal wall, change it to **35** (35'-0"), and press the **<Enter>** key on your computer.

The horizontal wall becomes 35'-0" long, and the left vertical wall moves left.

16. Press **<Ctrl> +Z** on the keyboard, or the **Undo** icon on the **Standard** toolbar (see Figure 2-6).

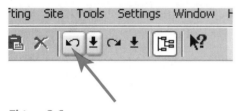

Figure 2-6

17. Select the right vertical wall to expose the temporary dimension lines.
18. After adjusting the witness lines, select the dimension for the horizontal wall, change it to **35** (35'-0"), and press the **<Enter>** key on your computer.

This time the horizontal wall becomes 35'-0" long, and the right vertical wall moves right.

19. Select a wall, **RMB**, and select **Create Similar** from the contextual menu that appears.
20. Add and adjust walls to create the enclosure shown in Figure 2-7.

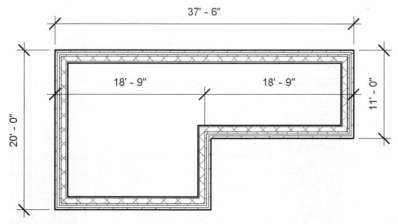

Figure 2-7

21. Select the wall shown in Figure 2-8.

By entering numbers in the temporary dimension area, you can move the selected wall.

22. Save this file as **WALLS BY PENCIL**.

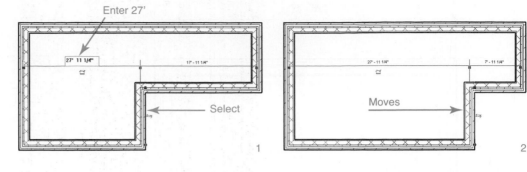

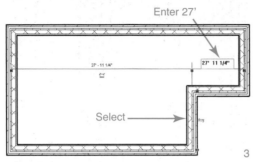

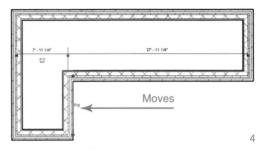

Figure 2-8

USING PICK LINES ON AN IMPORTED 2D CAD FILE

Using the **Pick Lines** option for creating Walls allows you to pick any 2D CAD or line drawing. This is especially useful when you import a DWG, DXF, or MicroStation DGN file.

Exercise 2-2: Using the Pick Lines Tool

1. Download the CARRIAGE HOUSE WALLS CAD file from the Internet at http://www. hegra.org/REVIT_BOOK_PRACTICE_FILES.html, and place it in a new directory on your computer called WALLS.
2. Start a new drawing using the **RAC 2009\Imperial Templates\default.rte** template.
3. In the **Project browser**, double-click **Floor Plans > Level 1**.
4. Select **File > Import/Link > CAD Formats** from the **Main** menu to bring up the **Import/Link** dialog box.
5. In the **Import/Link** dialog box, uncheck the **Link** check box, and select the radio buttons as shown in Figure 2-9, and then open the **CARRIAGE HOUSE WALLS** file from the **WALLS** directory (see Figure 2-9).

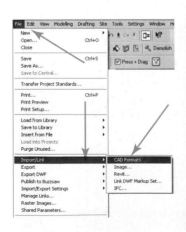

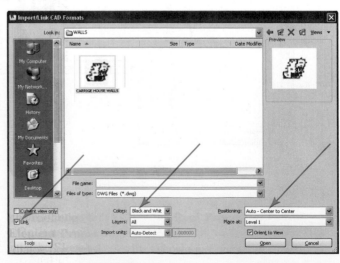

Figure 2-9

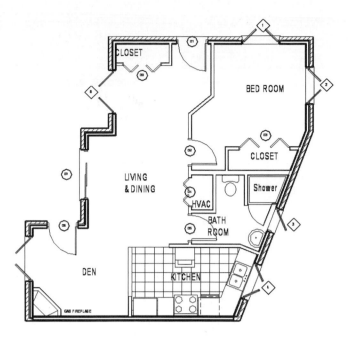

Figure 2-10

The 2D CAD drawing will now appear in the **Drawing Editor** (see Figure 2-10).

6. Select **View > Visibility/Graphics**, or type **VG** on the keyboard to bring up the **Visibility Graphics Overrides** dialog box.
7. In the **Visibility Graphics Overrides** dialog box, change to the **Imported Categories** tab.
8. In the **Imported Categories** tab, check the **Halftone** check box for the **CARRIAGE HOUSE WALLS** drawing.
9. Expand the **CARRIAGE HOUSE WALLS** drawing, and uncheck all the layers except **A-Wall** and **B-Wall**.

This will turn off all the walls except those on layers A-Wall and B-Wall, and give them a halftone appearance (see Figure 2-11).

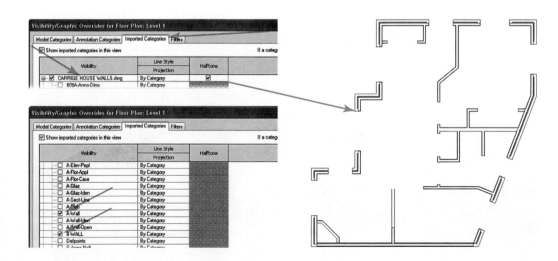

Figure 2-11

10. Select the **Wall** tool from the **Design Bar**.
11. Select the **Pick Lines** tool and **Finish Face Exterior** from the **Options** toolbar (see Figure 2-12).
12. Pick lines as shown in Figure 2-13.
13. Pick the **Trim** tool from the **Tools** toolbar, and then **Trim/Extend to Corner** from the **Options** toolbar.
14. Trim all the corners to complete the exterior walls (see Figure 2-14).

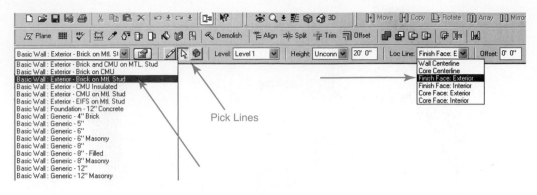

Figure 2-12

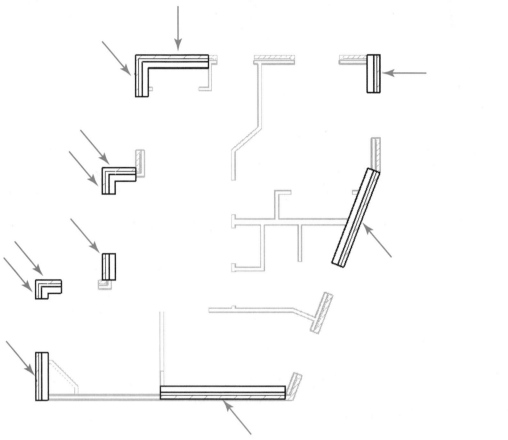

Figure 2-13

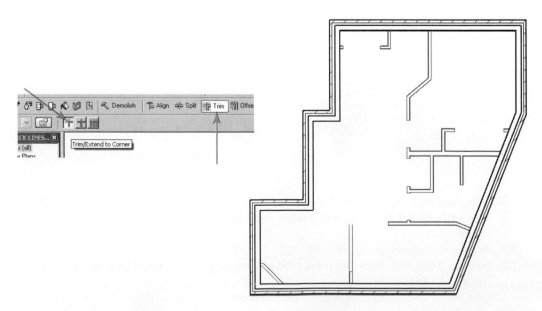

Figure 2-14

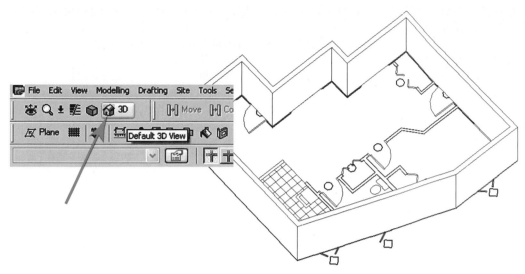

Figure 2-15

15. Select the **Default 3D View** tool from the **View** toolbar, and place the model into **3D** (see Figure 2-15).
16. Repeat steps 5–10 using the **Basic Wall: Interior 5-1/2″ Partition (1-hr)** wall, and the other **Trim** options to create the interior walls.
17. Again, select the **Default 3D View** tool from the **View** toolbar, and place the model into **3D**.
18. Finally, press the **Shadows** icon at the bottom of the **Drawing Editor** (see Figure 2-16).

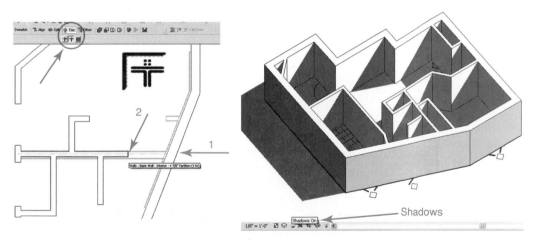

Figure 2-16

You have now traced your 2D CAD drawing, and converted it into a 3D Revit model.

19. Save this file as **WALLS by PICK LINES**.

USING THE PICK FACES OPTION

The **Pick Faces** option is used to place Walls on a Mass Object. This is covered in detail in Section 1 on Massing.

Exercise 2-3: Creating and Modifying Wall Sweeps and Wall Reveals

Wall sweeps and reveals are used to add details such as moldings, handrails, indentations, and so on, to walls without adding extra objects. Although you could create separate moldings as well as other details, it is quicker to have them as part of the walls so that they are created at the same time as the walls.

1. Start a new drawing using the **RAC 2009\Imperial Templates\default.rte** template.
2. In the **Project browser**, double-click **Floor Plans > Level 1**.
3. In the **Design Bar**, under **Basics**, select the **Wall** icon.
4. Set the **Detail** to **Medium** so that you can see the wall components in plan view.
5. Move your cursor to the **Options** toolbar; select **Basic wall: Generic – 12** from the drop-down list, pick the **Pencil** icon, set the **Height** to **Unconnected**, set the height to **8′-0″**, and set the **Loc line** to **Finish Face: Exterior**.
6. Place a **16′-0″** long wall, and then press the **3D** tool in the **View** toolbar to place the wall in 3D.

Loading the Profile

Profiles are 2D lines that create the cross sections (Profiles) of Revit's Sweeps and Reveals.

7. Select **File > Load from library > Load Family** to bring up the **Imperial Library** folder in the **Load Family** dialog box.
8. In the **Imperial Library** folder, open the **Profiles** folder.
9. In the **Profiles** folder, select the **Base-Built-Up** family, and then press the **Open** button to load the family (see Figure 2-17).

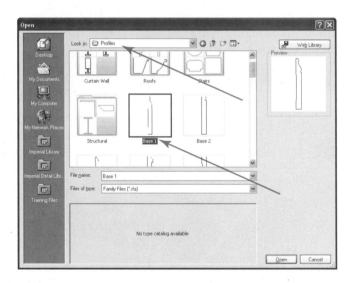

Figure 2-17

Using the Profile

10. Select the wall you placed, **RMB**, and select **Element Properties** from the contextual menu to bring up the **Element Properties** dialog box.
11. In the **Element Properties** dialog box, press the **Edit/New** button at the top right of the dialog box to bring up the **Type Properties** dialog box.
12. In the **Type Properties** dialog box, press the **Duplicate** button at the top right to bring up the **Name** dialog box.
13. In the **Name** dialog box, enter **TEST WALL SWEEP** and press the **OK** button to return to the **Type Properties** dialog box (see Figure 2-18).
14. In the **Type Properties** dialog box, set the **Sample Height** to **8′-0″**.
15. Press the **Preview** button at the bottom left of the **Type Properties** dialog box.

Notice that the **Sweeps** button as well as the **Reveals, Merge Regions, Split Regions**, and so on, are not lit. This is because you can modify these only in section, not in plan.

16. Select **Section: Modify type attributes** from the **View** drop-down list as shown in Figure 2-19.
17. In the **Type Properties** dialog box, press the **Sweeps** button to bring up the **Wall Sweeps** dialog box.

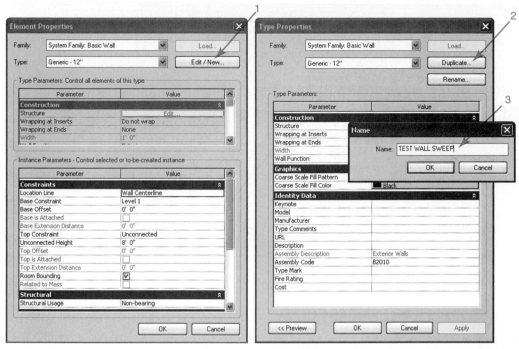

Figure 2-18

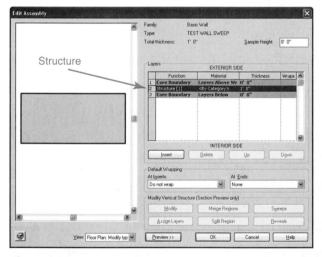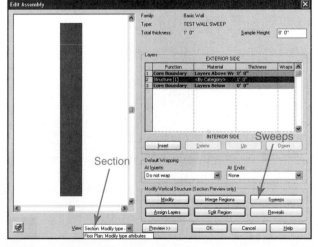

Figure 2-19

18. In the **Wall Sweeps** dialog box, press the **Add** button to add a **Default** profile.
19. Press the **Default** profile drop-down list, select **Base 1: 7 1/4″ × 5/8″,** and press the **OK** button.
20. The Wall will now have a wall sweep profile assigned to it (see Figure 2-21).
21. Press the **Sweeps** button again to bring up the **Wall Sweeps** dialog box.
22. In the **Wall Sweeps** dialog box, press the **Add** button to add a another **Default** profile.
23. Press the **Default** profile drop-down list, and this time, select **Base 1: 3 1/2″ × 5/8″,** and set its distance (Figures 2-22 and 2-23).
24. Save this file as **WALL SWEEPS**.

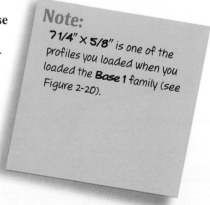

Note:
7 1/4″ × 5/8″ is one of the profiles you loaded when you loaded the **Base 1** family (see Figure 2-20).

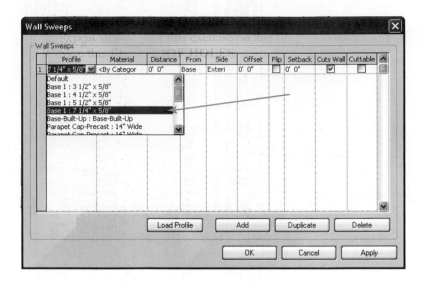

Figure 2-20

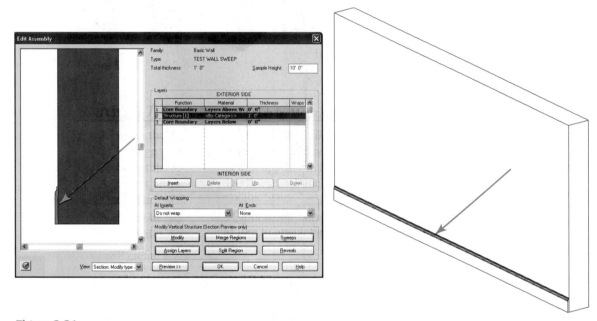

Figure 2-21

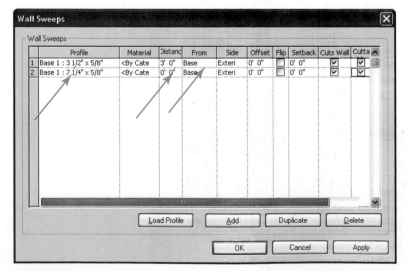

Figure 2-22

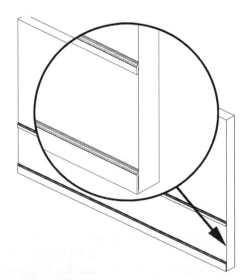

Figure 2-23

Exercise 2-4: Using the Join Geometry Tool, Cut Geometry, and Wall Joins

Join Geometry

1. Place a **Basic Wall: Generic -12″** in the **Drawing Editor**. Make it **12′-0″** long and **8′-0″** high.
2. Place a **Basic Wall: Generic -8″** in the **Drawing Editor**. Make it **8′-0″** long and **8′-0″** high.
3. Place the **8″** wall intersecting the **12″** wall.
4. Select the **Join Geometry** icon in the **Tools** toolbar.
5. Select the **12″** wall, and then select the **8″** wall to join them (see Figure 2-24).

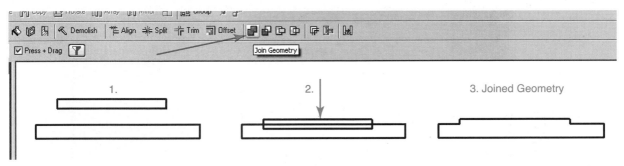

Figure 2-24

6. Select the joined walls, and make a copy by pressing the **<Ctrl>** key on your keyboard and moving the wall.
7. Select the copied set of joined walls, and select **Basic Wall: Generic -12″ Masonry** from the **Options** toolbar (see Figure 2-25).

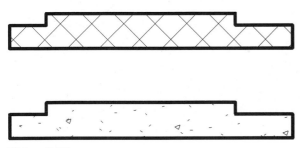

Figure 2-25

Cut Geometry

8. Place a **Basic Wall: Generic -12″** in the **Drawing Editor**. Make it **12′-0″** long and **8′-0″** high.
9. Place a **Basic Wall: Generic -8″** in the **Drawing Editor**. Make it **8′-0″** long and **8′-0″** high.
10. Place the **8″** wall inside the **12″** wall.
11. Select the **Cut Geometry** icon in the **Tools** toolbar to cut the wall.
12. Select the **Join Geometry** icon to join the two walls again.
13. Select **Basic Wall: Generic -12″ Masonry** for the **12″** section, and **Basic Wall: Generic -8″ Masonry for the 8″** section (see Figures 2-26 and 2-27).

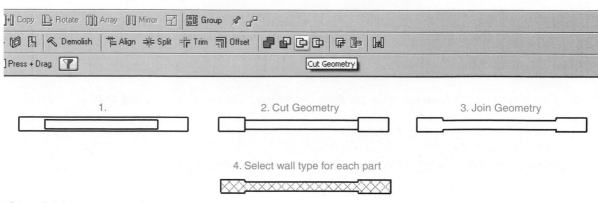

Figure 2-26

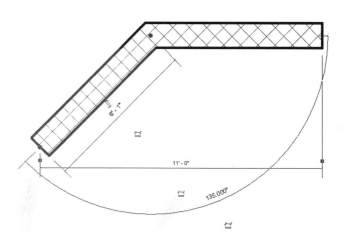

Figure 2-27

Wall Joins

14. Place a **Basic Wall: Generic -12″ Masonry** in the **Drawing Editor** as shown in Figure 2-28.

Figure 2-28

15. Select the **Edit Wall Joins** tool from the **Tools** toolbar.
16. Select a junction point of two walls and click—a rectangle will appear at the junction (see Figure 2-29).
17. Select **Don't Clean Join** from the **Display** drop-down list.
18. Select the **Butt, Miter,** and **Square off** radio buttons, and watch the changes.
19. Select the **Butt** radio button, and then press the **Next** button, and watch the changes.
20. Select the **Square off** radio button, and then press the **Next** button, and watch the changes (see Figure 2-30).
21. Save this file as **JOIN GEOMETRY_ CUT GEOMETRY _ WALL JOINS**.

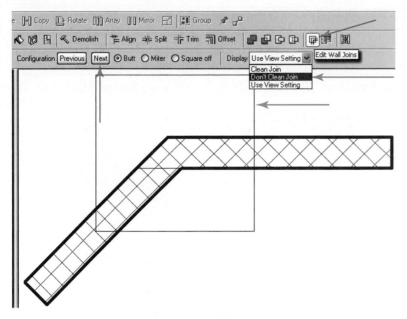

Figure 2-29

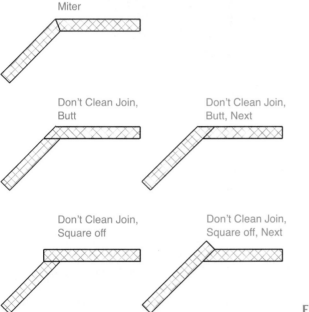

Figure 2-30

MODIFYING VERTICALLY-COMPOUND WALLS

You define the structure of vertically-compound walls using either layers or regions.

- A layer is a rectangle assigned to one row. It has a constant thickness and extends the height of the wall. You can change its thickness in the row assigned to it.

- A region is any other shape appearing in the wall that does not meet the criteria of a layer. Regions can have either constant or variable thickness. In a row assigned to a region, if the region has a constant thickness, a numerical value appears for it. If the region has a variable thickness, the value is variable.

- You cannot change a region's thickness in the row that is assigned to it. Note that the thickness value appears shaded, indicating that it is unavailable for modification. You can only change its thickness and height graphically in the preview pane.

- Because core thickness can vary in vertically-compound walls, the core centerline and core face location lines are determined by the core thickness at the bottom of the wall. For example, if the wall core is thicker at the top than at the bottom, and you specify the location line as **Core Centerline**, the centerline of the core is measured between the core boundaries at the bottom.

Exercise 2-5: Creating a Vertically-Compound Wall

1. Place a **Basic Wall: Exterior – Brick on CMU** in the **Drawing Editor**. Make it **12′-0″** long and **8′-0″** high.
2. Set the **Model Graphics Style** to **Shading with Edges** (see Figure 2-31).

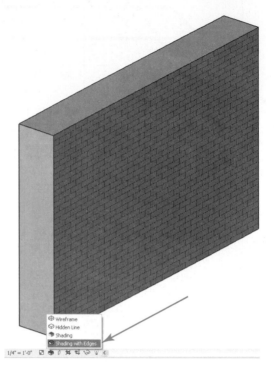

Figure 2-31

3. Select the wall, **RMB**, and select **Element Properties** from the contextual menu that appears to bring up the **Element Properties** dialog box.
4. In the **Element Properties** dialog box, press the **Edit/New** button at the top right to bring up the **Type Properties** dialog box.
5. In the **Type Properties** dialog box, press the **Duplicate** button at the top right to bring up the **Name** dialog box.
6. In the **Name** dialog box, enter **TEST COMPOUND WALL** and press the **OK** button to return to the **Type Properties** dialog box.
7. In the **Type Properties** dialog box, press the **Edit** button in the **Structure** field to bring up the **Edit Assembly** dialog box.
8. In the **Edit Assembly** dialog box, press the **Preview** button at the bottom left of the dialog box.
9. In the **Edit Assembly** dialog box, select **Section: Modify type attributes** from the **View** drop-down list.
10. Zoom with your center mouse roller so that you can see the lower portion of the wall section more clearly.

Split Regions

11. Select the **Split Region** button at the bottom of the **Edit Assembly** dialog box, and click on the exterior brick twice as shown in Figure 2-32.
12. Next, select the **Insert** button to add a new layer. (By default it will be **Structure [1]**.)
13. Change the **Function** to **Finish 1 [4]**.
14. Select the **Material** (which by default is **<By Category>**) to go to the **Materials** dialog box.
15. In the **Materials** dialog box, select **Masonry – Glass Block** and press the **OK** button at the bottom of the dialog box (see Figure 2-33).

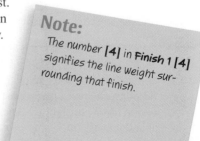

Note:
The number **[4]** in **Finish 1 [4]** signifies the line weight surrounding that finish.

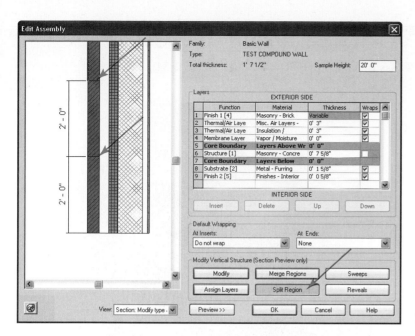

Figure 2-32

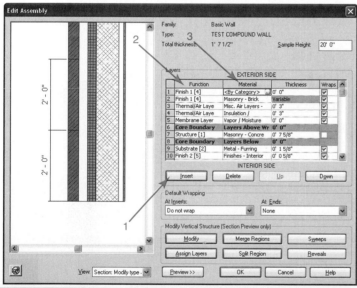

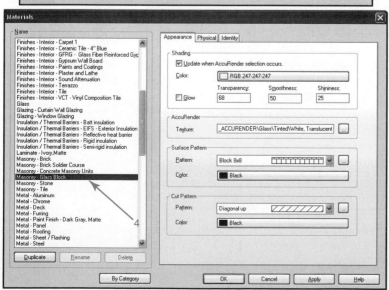

Figure 2-33

16. Select the **Assign Layers** button, and then select the **1'-4"** region you created—then press the **OK** buttons to return to the **Drawing Editor**.

You have now added a **Glass Block** to the **Brick Wall** (see Figure 2-34).

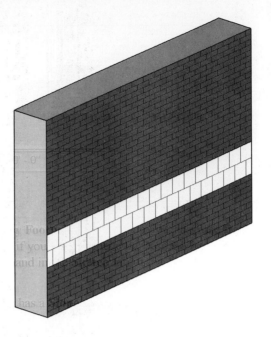

Figure 2-34

Save this file as **COMPOUND WALL**.

Exercise 2-6: Creating a Profile for a Wall Sweep

1. Open the **COMPOUND WALL** file.
2. In the **Project browser**, double-click **Floor Plans > Level 1**.
3. Select **File > New > Family** from the **Main** menu, and open the **Imperial Templates** folder.
4. In the **Imperial Templates**, select the **Profile.rft** template.
5. Using the **Lines** tool, create the 2D figure *exactly* as shown in Figure 2-35.
6. Save the profile you just created back into the **Profiles** folder as **TEST PROFILE.rfa**, and then close the file.

Note:
The **Profile** template has preset dashed lines to indicate the face of walls.

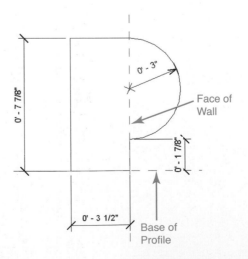

Figure 2-35

7. Select the compound wall you created in the last exercise, **RMB**, and select **Element Properties** from the contextual menu that appears to bring up the **Element Properties** dialog box.

8. In the **Element Properties** dialog box, press the **Edit/New** button to bring up the **Type Properties** dialog box.

9. In the **Type Properties** dialog box, press the **Sweeps** button to bring up the **Wall Sweeps** dialog box.

10. In the **Wall Sweeps** dialog box, press the **Load Profile** button, and locate and **Open** the **TEST PROFILE** you just created.

11. In the **Wall Sweeps** dialog box, press the **Add** button to add a **Default** profile on the **Exterior**.

12. Press the **Default** profile drop-down list, select the **TEST PROFILE,** and press the **OK** button.

13. In the **Wall Sweeps** dialog box, set the settings shown in Figure 2-36.

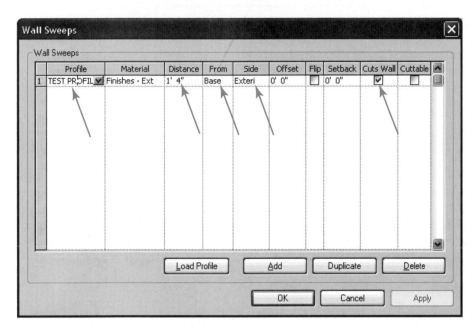

Figure 2-36

14. Finally, press the **OK** buttons to return to the **Drawing Editor** (see Figure 2-37).

15. Save this file as **COMPOUND WALL WITH SWEEP.**

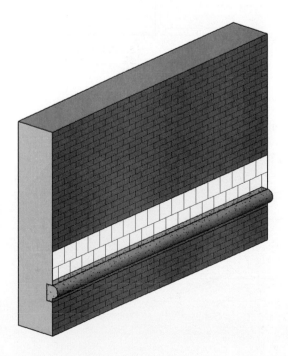

Figure 2-37

Exercise 2-7: Modifying End Caps and Insert Conditions

1. Start a new drawing using the **Revit Architecture 2009\Imperial Templates\default.rte** template.
2. In the **Project browser**, double-click **Floor Plans > Level 1**.
3. Set the **Scale** to **1″ = 1′-0″**.
4. Set the **Detail Level** to **Medium** so you can see all the detail.
5. Place an **8′-0″** long **Basic Wall: Exterior – Brick on CMU** in the **Drawing Editor**.
6. Place a **36″ × 48″** window centered on the wall (see Figure 2-38).

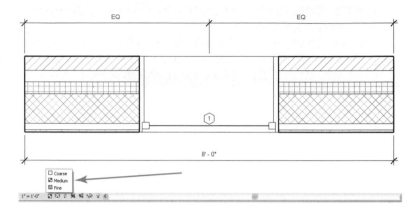

Figure 2-38

7. Select the wall, **RMB**, and select **Element Properties** from the contextual menu that appears to bring up the **Element Properties** dialog box.
8. In the **Element Properties** dialog box, press the **Edit / New** button to bring up the **Type Properties** dialog box.
9. In the **Type Properties** dialog box, press the **Wrapping at Inserts** field drop-down list and select **Exterior**. Press the **OK** buttons to return to the **Drawing Editor** (see Figure 2-39).

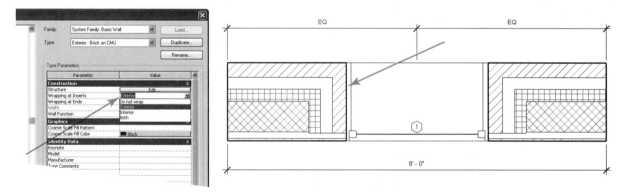

Figure 2-39

10. Repeat this process, selecting **Interior** and then **Both** (see Figure 2-40).
11. Repeat this process for the **Wrapping at Ends** (see Figure 2-41).
12. Save this file as **END CAPS _ INSERTS**.

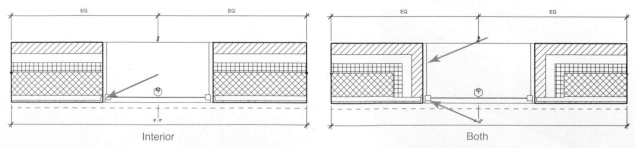

Interior   Both

Figure 2-40

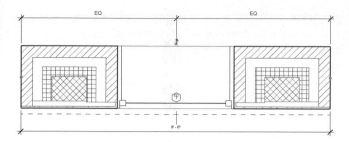

Figure 2-41

Exercise 2-8: Embedded Walls

1. Start a new drawing using the **RAC 2009\ImperialTemplates\default.rte** template.
2. In the **Project browser**, double-click **Floor Plans > Level 1**.
3. Select the **Wall** tool from the **Design Bar**.
4. Place a **Basic Wall: Exterior – Brick on CMU** horizontally in the **Drawing Editor**; make it **22'-0"** long and **10'-0"** high.
5. Place a second wall **8'-0"** high (use **Interior 4-7/8" partition**) within the first wall.
6. You will immediately get a warning telling you that the walls overlap, and you need to use the **Cut Geometry** tool to embed one wall within the other (see Figure 2-42).

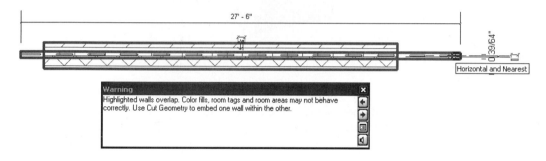

Figure 2-42

7. Change to the **Default 3D View**.
8. Select the **Cut Geometry** tool from the **Tools** toolbar (see Figure 2-43).

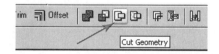

Figure 2-43

9. Select the **Brick on CMU** wall, and then select the **Interior 4-7/8" partition** wall.

The **Interior 4-7/8" partition** wall now cuts through the **Brick on CMU** wall (see Figure 2-44).

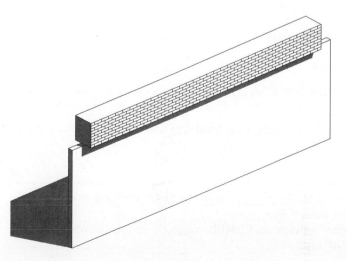

Figure 2-44

10. Select the **Interior 4-7/8″ partition** wall and press the **Edit Profile** button on the **Options** toolbar to enter **Sketch** mode for the **Interior 4-7/8″ partition** wall.
11. Using the **Lines** tool in the **Sketch** tab of the **Design Bar**, and the **Trim** tool on the **Edit** toolbar, change the shape of the partition.
12. Press the **Finish Sketch** icon in the **Sketch** tab to complete the command (see Figure 2-45).

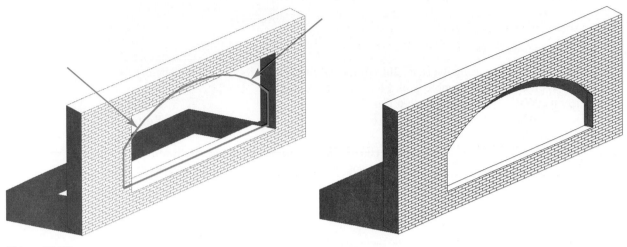

Figure 22-45

13. Select the **Interior 4-7/8″ partition** wall, and then select **Generic - 8″ Masonry** from the drop-down list on the **Options** toolbar (see Figure 2-46).
14. Save this file as **EMBEDDED WALLS**.

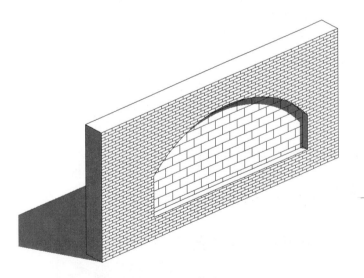

Figure 2-46

EMBEDDED CURTAIN WALLS AND STOREFRONT

Because **Storefront** is often embedded into walls, **Storefront** and **Curtain Walls** have a dedicated embedding capability.

Exercise 2-9: Embedding and Modifying Storefont Walls

1. Start a new drawing using the **RAC 2009\ImperialTemplates\default.rte** template.
2. Select the **Wall** tool from the **Design Bar**.
3. Place a **Basic Wall: Exterior – Brick on CMU** horizontally in the **Drawing Editor**; make it **22′-0″** long and **10′-0″** high.

4. Select the **Wall** tool again.
5. This time place a **Curtain Wall: Storefront** wall in the **Brick on CMU** wall; make it **18'-0"** long and **8'-0"** high.
6. Select the **Curtain Wall: Storefront** wall you just placed, and then press the **Element Properties** button on the **Options** toolbar to bring up the **Element Properties** dialog box for the storefront.
7. In the **Element Properties** dialog box, press the **Edit/New** button to bring up the **Type Properties** dialog box.
8. In the **Type Properties** dialog box, notice the **Automatically Embed** check box (see Figure 2-48).

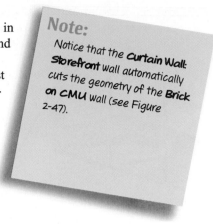

Note:
Notice that the **Curtain Wall: Storefront** wall automatically cuts the geometry of the **Brick on CMU** wall (see Figure 2-47).

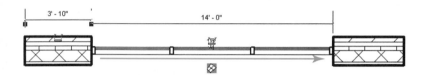

Figure 2-47

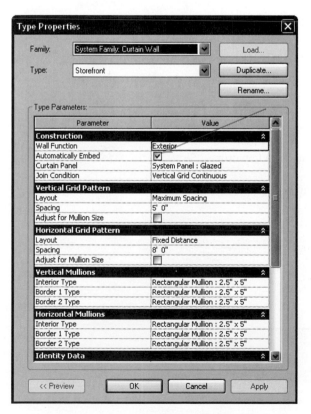

Figure 2-48

9. Once you have placed the **Storefront** wall, you can modify its profile as you did in the previous exercise (see Figure 2-49).
10. Save this file as **EMBEDDED STOREFRONT**.

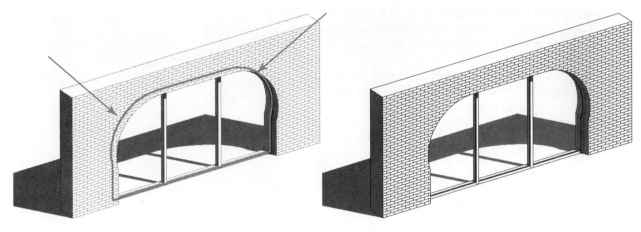

Figure 2-49

Exercise 2-10: Creating a New Wall Type

1. Start a new drawing using the **RAC 2009\ImperialTemplates\default.rte** template.
2. In the **Design Bar**, in the **Basics tab**, select the **Wall** icon.
3. In the **Options** toolbar, select **Basic Wall: Generic -8″** from the drop-down list.
4. In the **Options** toolbar, select the **Element Properties** icon to bring up the **Element Properties** dialog box.
5. In the **Element Properties** dialog box, select the **Edit/New** button at the top right of the dialog box to bring up the **Type Properties** dialog box.
6. In the **Type Properties** dialog box, select the **Duplicate** button at the top right of the dialog box to bring up the **Name** dialog box.
7. In the **Name** dialog box, enter **NEW BRICK and CMU WALL**, and press the **OK** button to return to the **Type Properties** dialog box.
8. In the **Type Properties** dialog box, press the **Preview >>** button to open the preview pane.
9. In the **Type Properties** dialog box, select **Floor Plan: Modify type attributes** from the **View** drop-down list.
10. Press the **Edit** button in the **Structure** field to bring up the **Edit Assembly** dialog box (see Figures 2-50 and 2-51).

Note: Floor Plan: Modify type attributes allows you to see and check the wall in plan view.

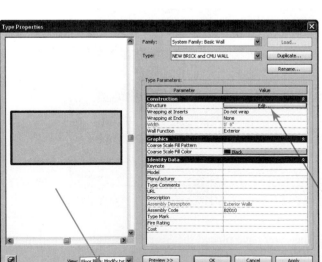

Figure 2-50

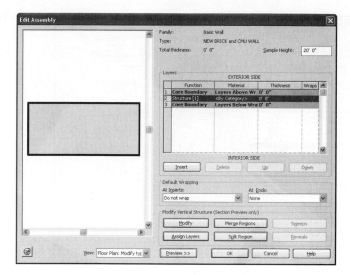

Figure 2-51

11. In the **Edit Assembly** dialog box, change the **Sample Height** to **10′-0″**.

12. Press the **Insert** button, and insert five structures between the **Core Boundary** (see Figure 2-52).

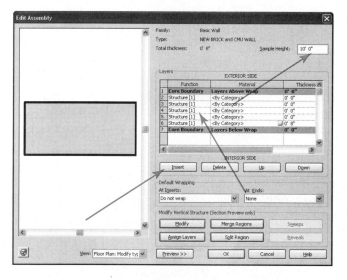

Figure 2-52

13. Select the number **2 <By Category>** field to activate it, and click the three dots that appear to its right to bring up the **Material Browser** dialog box (see Figure 2-53).

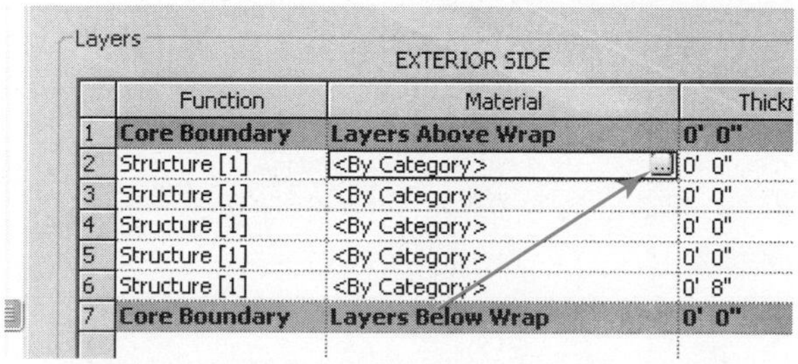

	Function	Material	Thick
1	**Core Boundary**	**Layers Above Wrap**	**0' 0"**
2	Structure [1]	<By Category>	0' 0"
3	Structure [1]	<By Category>	0' 0"
4	Structure [1]	<By Category>	0' 0"
5	Structure [1]	<By Category>	0' 0"
6	Structure [1]	<By Category>	0' 8"
7	**Core Boundary**	**Layers Below Wrap**	**0' 0"**

EXTERIOR SIDE

Layers

Figure 2-53

14. In the **Material Browser** dialog box, select **Masonry – Brick**, and press the **OK** button to return to the **Edit Assembly** dialog box (see Figure 2-54).

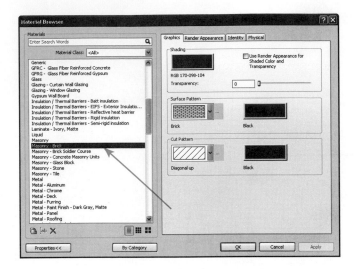

Figure 2-54

15. Repeat the previous process, assigning materials to each of the layers between the **Core Boundary**.
16. Assign layers **3–6** to **Air Barrier - Air Infiltration Barrier, Masonry - Concrete Masonry Units, Metal - Stud Layer**, and **Gypsum Wall Board**, respectively.
17. Click on **Structure [1]** on the number **2** layer, and select **Finish 1 [4]** from the drop-down list.
18. Set the width of each material in the **Thickness** column.
19. Press the **Up** and **Down** buttons to move the **Brick** and **Air Infiltration Barrier** to the **Exterior Side** of the **Core Boundary**, and move the **Metal Stud Layer** and **Gypsum Wall Board** to the **Interior Side** of the **Core Boundary.**
20. In the **Edit Assembly** dialog box, select **Section: Modify type attributes** from the **View** drop-down list.
21. Press the **OK** buttons in the dialog boxes to return to the **Drawing Editor**.

To test the wall, change to the **Floor Plan** view, select the **Wall** tool from the **Basics** tab, choose **NEW BRICK** and **CMU WALL** from the **Options** toolbar, and place the wall.

22. Save this file as **CREATING NEW WALL TYPES**.

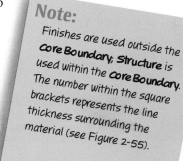

Note:
Finishes are used outside the **Core Boundary**; **Structure** is used within the **Core Boundary**. The number within the square brackets represents the line thickness surrounding the material (see Figure 2-55).

Note:
The **Masonry - Concrete Masonry Units** are the core of the wall and are thus inside the **Core Boundary** (see Figure 2-56).

Note:
Section: Modify type attributes allows you to see and check the wall in section view (see Figure 2-57).

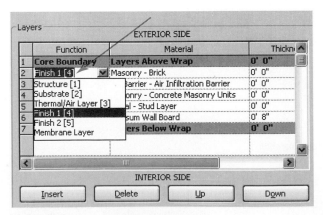

Figure 2-55

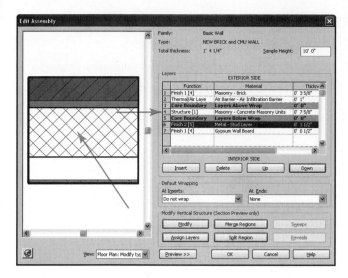

Figure 2-56

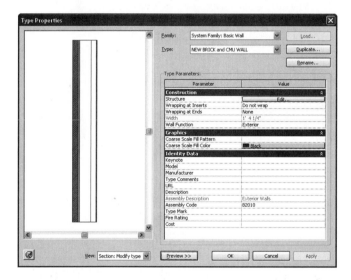

Figure 2-57

SUMMARY

This section gives the basics needed to create, modify, and place most wall types in Revit Architecture. It is a good idea to create a library of custom wall types and profiles that you can easily load into your project.

SECTION TEST QUESTIONS

True/false

1. True or False: Revit Walls can be directly imported from AutoCAD Architecture or AutoCAD.

2. True or False: Revit Walls cannot be placed on an angle.

3. True or False: **Vertically-Compound Walls** are used to join two walls together.

4. True or False: **Wall Sweeps** are used to create curved walls.

Questions

1. What is the purpose of the Pin?

2. How does the **Detail** icon at the bottom of the screen affect the wall display?

3. What is the difference between the **Draw** and **Pick Lines** tools in relation to walls?

4. What is the purpose of a Profile?

5. How many **End Cap** and **Insert** conditions are there?

6. What is the purpose of the embedded wall?

Doors

3

Section Objectives

- Learn how to place and control doors.
- Learn how to tag doors.
- Use **Wall Closure** at doors.
- Know how to modify doors.
- Know how to change door sizes.
- Know how to change door materials.
- Understand how to edit **Doors** in place.
- Understand how to set **Head** and **Sill** location.

In Revit Architecture 2009, door objects are totally customizable. All is possible in this program—from customizing the size and shape of the door or the size and shape of the jamb to including side lights, mullions, or a sill. As with other features of this program, a premade library of door styles greatly enhances productivity. Websites such as Architectural Data Systems (http://www.architecturaldatasystems.com) and BIM WORLD (http://www.bimworld.com) are currently offering content from many manufacturers. You can also go directly to the Revit Web Library from inside Revit and quickly **idrop** premade doors and door accessories.

Exercise 3-1: Placing and Controlling Doors

1. Start a new drawing using the **RAC 2009\ImperialTemplates\default.rte** template.
2. In the **Project browser**, double-click **Floor Plans > Level 1**.
3. In the **Design Bar**, under **Basics**, select the **Wall** icon.
4. Move your cursor to the **Options** toolbar; select **Basic wall: Exterior - Brick on CMU** from the drop-down list, pick the **Pencil** icon, set the height to **10′-0″**, and place a **20′-0″** long wall in the **Drawing Editor**.
5. Select the **Door** tool from the **Design Bar**.
6. In the **Options** toolbar, select **Single-Flush: 36″ × 84″** from the drop-down list, and click to the wall you previously made to place the wall (see Figure 3-1).

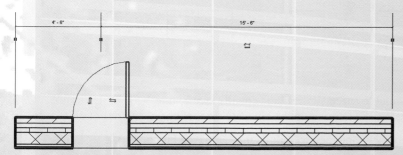

Figure 3-1

7. Click the grip shown in Figure 3-2 to move the witness line to the center or edges of the door. Drag the grip to place the witness line at the front of the door panel.

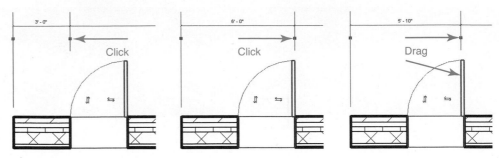

Figure 3-2

8. Select the door, and click the double arrows to flip the door swings (see Figure 3-3).

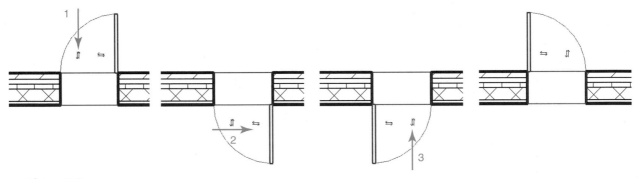

Figure 3-3

9. Select the door, **RMB**, and select **Create Similar** from the contextual menu that appears.
10. Place two more doors.
11. Select the **Dimension** tool from the **Design Bar**, and place continuous dimensions as shown in Figure 3-4.

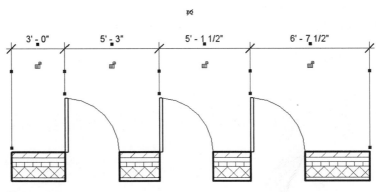

Figure 3-4

12. Click the **EQ** symbol to space all the doors equally (see Figure 3-5).
13. Select the dimension line to bring up the blue **EQ** symbol again, and turn it off.

The dimensions will then show, and they will all be the same (see Figure 3-6).

14. Save the file as **PLACING DOORS**.

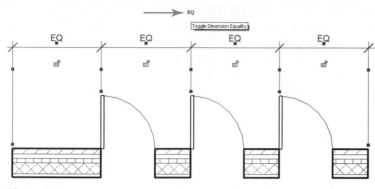

Figure 3-5

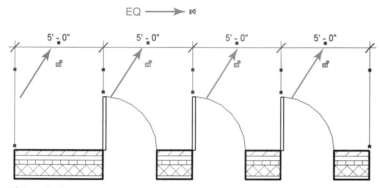

Figure 3-6

Exercise 3-2: Tagging Doors

Doors can be inserted with number tags as you place the doors, or after you place them.

Tagging on Insertion

1. Using the previous exercise, select one of the doors, **RMB**, and choose **Select All Instances** from the contextual menu that appears. All the doors will be selected.
2. Press the **<Delete>** key on your keyboard to delete the doors and their dimensions.
3. Select the **Door** tool from the **Design Bar**.
4. In the **Options** type Selector drop down list of the toolbar, select **Single-Flush: 36″ × 84″** from the drop-down list, check the **Tag on Placement** check box, and select **Horizontal** from the drop-down list shown in Figure 3-7.

Figure 3-7

5. Place a door in the wall you previously created.
6. If the number that appears in the door tag is not **1,** select the number and change it to **1.**

If you have been experimenting with the doors and tags, the door tag number will be the next available number. By changing the first tag to **1,** the succeeding tags will increment from that number.

7. Place two more doors to see the incremental numbers (see Figure 3-8).

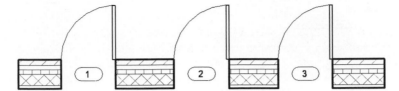

Figure 3-8

Tagging after Insertion

1. Using the previous exercise, select one of the doors, **RMB**, and choose **Select All Instances** from the contextual menu that appears. All the doors will be selected.
2. Press the **<Delete>** key on your keyboard to delete the doors and their dimensions.
3. Select the **Door** tool from the **Design Bar**. In the **Options** toolbar, select **Single-Flush: 36″ × 84″** from the drop-down list, and uncheck the **Tag on Placement** check box.
4. Place three doors in the wall.
5. Click on the **Drafting** tab in the **Design Bar** to open it.
6. In the **Drafting** tab in the **Design Bar**, select **Tag > By Category** (see Figure 3-9).
7. Click on the first door to place the number tag.
8. Once again the number will be wrong, so change it to the number **1**.
9. Select **Tag All Not Tagged** from the **Drafting** tab to bring up the **Tag All Not Tagged** dialog box.
10. In the **Tag All Not Tagged** dialog box, select **Horizontal** from the **Orientation** drop-down list, and press the **Apply** button to add number tags to the other doors (see Figure 3-10).
11. Save the file as **TAGGING DOORS**.

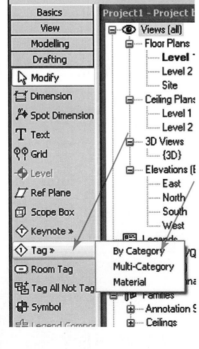

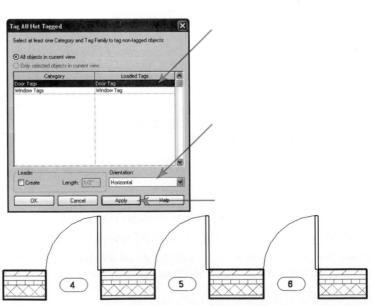

Figure 3-9   Figure 3-10

Exercise 3-3: Wall Closure

In Section 2 we discussed **Wall Wrapping at Inserts**. They were labeled **"Do not wrap"**, **"Exterior"**, **"Interior",** and **"Both".** This controls how the wall finishes wrap at these conditions. Sometimes you may want a wall to wrap differently at individual doors. To take care of these occurrences, doors are equipped with **Wall Closure** options.

1. Using the previous exercise, select one of the doors, **RMB**, and select **Element Properties** from the contextual menu that appears to bring up the **Element Properties** dialog box.
2. At the top right of the **Element Properties** dialog box, select the **Edit/New** button to bring up the **Type Properties** dialog box.
3. At the top of the **Type Properties** dialog box, press the **Duplicate** button to bring up the **Name** dialog box.
4. In the **Name** dialog box, enter **Interior**, and press the **OK** button to return to the **Type Properties** dialog box.
5. In the **Type Properties** dialog box, select **Interior** from the **Wall Closure** drop-down list (see Figure 3-11).

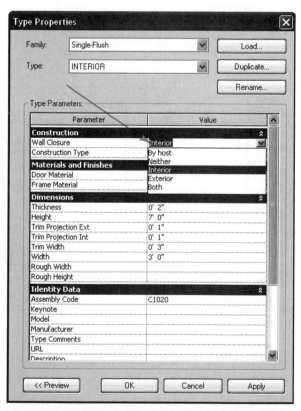

Figure 3-11

6. Press the **OK** buttons to return to the **Drawing Editor**.

Notice that the **Wrapping at Insert** or **Wall Closure** at the door has changed, but the other **Wall Closures** have not because they are either **By host** or **Neither** (see Figure 3-12).

Repeat steps 1–6 creating **Exterior** and **Both** doors and see their **Wall Closure** effects (see Figure 3-13).

7. Save the file as **WALL CLOSURE**.

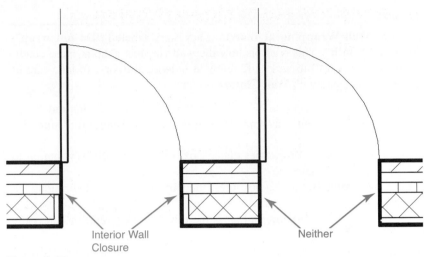

Interior Wall
Closure

Neither

Figure 3-12

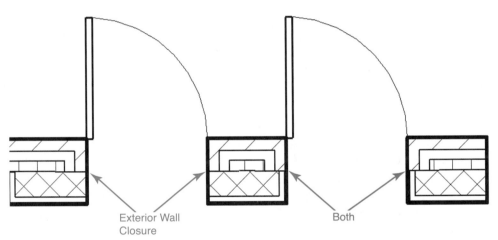

Exterior Wall
Closure

Both

Figure 3-13

Exercise 3-4: Modifying Doors

Changing Door Sizes

1. Using the previous exercise, select one of the doors, **RMB**, and select **Element Properties** from the contextual menu that appears to bring up the **Element Properties** dialog box.
2. At the top right of the **Element Properties** dialog box, select the **Edit/New** button to bring up the **Type Properties** dialog box.
3. At the top of the **Type Properties** dialog box, press the **Duplicate** button to bring up the **Name** dialog box.
4. In the **Name** dialog box, enter **TEST 24″ × 80″ DOOR**, and press the **OK** button to return to the **Type Properties** dialog box (see Figure 3-14).
5. In the **Type Properties** dialog box, enter the sizes shown in Figure 3-15, and press the **OK** buttons to return to the **Drawing Editor**.
6. In the **Project browser**, double-click on the **South Elevation** to bring it up in the **Drawing Editor** (see Figure 3-16).
7. Save this file as **CHANGING DOOR SIZES**.

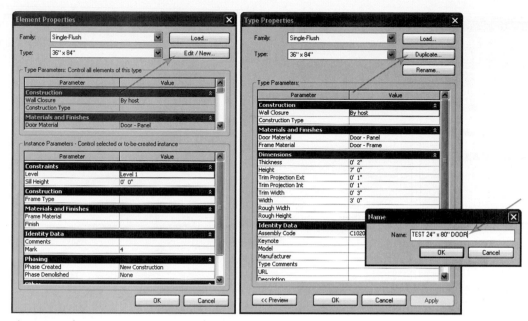

Figure 3-14

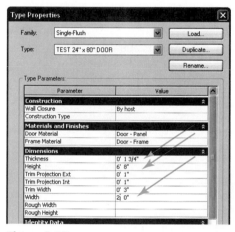

Figure 3-15

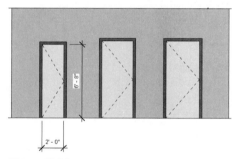

Figure 3-16

Exercise 3-5: Changing Door Materials

1. Using the previous exercise, select the **TEST 24″ × 80″ DOOR**, **RMB**, and again select **Element Properties** from the contextual menu that appears to bring up the **Element Properties** dialog box.
2. At the top right of the **Element Properties** dialog box, select the **Edit/New** button to bring up the **Type Properties** dialog box.
3. In the **Type Properties** dialog box, select the **Door-Panel** in the **Door Material** field to open the **Materials** dialog box.
4. **RMB** on a material in the **Name** area, and select **Duplicate** from the contextual menu that appears to bring up the **Duplicate Revit Material** dialog box.
5. In the **Duplicate Revit Material** dialog box, enter **TEST DOOR PANEL** and press the **OK** button to return to the **Materials** dialog box (see Figure 3-17).
6. In the **Materials** dialog box, select the **TEST DOOR PANEL** and select the **Appearance** tab.

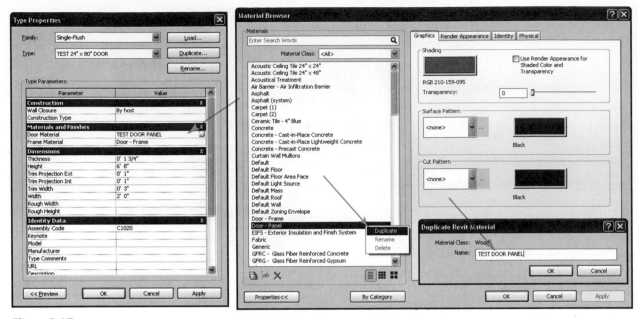

Figure 3-17

7. In the **Graphics** tab, click on the **Shading** button and set the color to **RGB 210-159-95,** the **Surface Pattern** to **Wood 3**, and the **Cut Pattern** to **None** (see Figure 3-18).

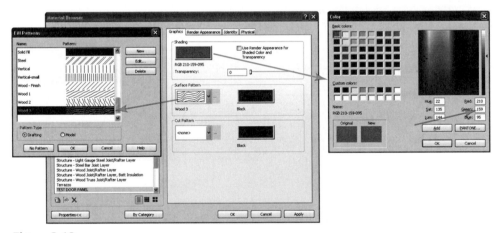

Figure 3-18

8. Press the **OK** buttons to return to the **Drawing Editor**, and again select the **South Elevation** from the **Project browser** (see Figure 3-19).
9. Save this file as **CHANGING DOOR MATERIALS**.

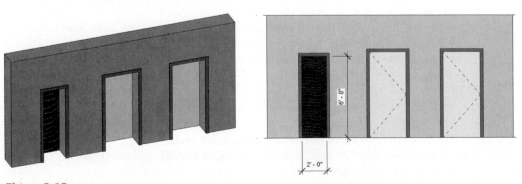

Figure 3-19

Exercise 3-6: Editing Doors in Place

Opening a Door

1. Using the previous exercise, select the **TEST 24″×80″ DOOR**, and then the **Edit Family** button that appears in the **Options** toolbar.
2. The **Revit** dialog box will appear asking if you wish to open the door for editing; select the **Yes** button to bring up the door in the **Family Editor**.
3. In the **Project browser**, expand the **Views [all]** and then expand the **Floor Plans > Ground Floor**.
4. In the **Ground Floor** plan, locate the door panel as shown in Figure 3-20.

Note:
You will recognize that you are in the **Family Editor** because the **Design Bar** has only one tab labeled **Family**.

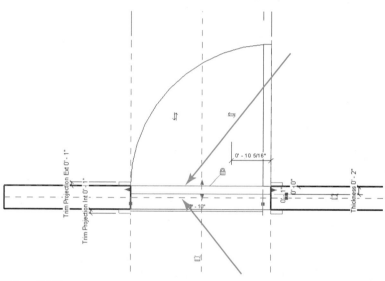

Figure 3-20

5. Select the door panel, and then press the **Rotate** button located in the top right of the screen.
6. Hold your left mouse button down and drag the **Rotate** icon to the upper right corner of the door panel to set the rotation axis, and release the mouse button.
7. Drag your mouse horizontally to the far left, and click the left mouse button.
8. Finally, drag your mouse vertically and then left mouse click to complete the rotation.
9. You will get a **Revit** error dialog box; press the **Remove Constraints** button to remove the **Constraint** and **Dimension** (see Figure 3-21).

Note:
The rotation technique may take some practice to get it right. This system is used for all rotations, and dragging the **Rotate** icon sets the center of rotation.

The reason that you have to remove the **Constraints** is because they are linked to parameters, and no longer apply to the rotated door.

10. Save the new family on your computer as **Single Flush Open**.
11. Finally, return to your 3D view of the doors, select the **TEST 24″ × 80″ DOOR**, RMB, and select **Element Properties** from the contextual menu that appears to bring up the **Element Properties** dialog box.

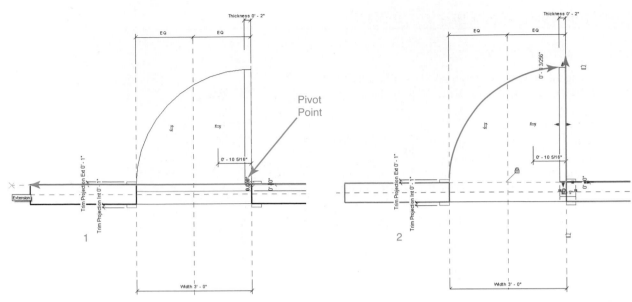

Figure 3-21

12. At the top right of the **Element Properties** dialog box, select the **Load** button, locate the **Single Flush Open** door you just created, and then press the **OK** button to return to the **Drawing Editor**.

The door will now be open (see Figure 3-22).

13. Save this file as **EDITING DOORS INPLACE**.

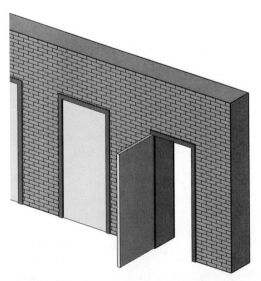

Figure 3-22

Exercise 3-7: Head and Sill Location

1. Using the previous exercise, select the **Single Flush Open** door you just created, **RMB**, and again select **Element Properties** from the contextual menu that appears to bring up the **Element Properties** dialog box.
2. Select the **Value** in the **Sill Height** field, and change it to **8″**.

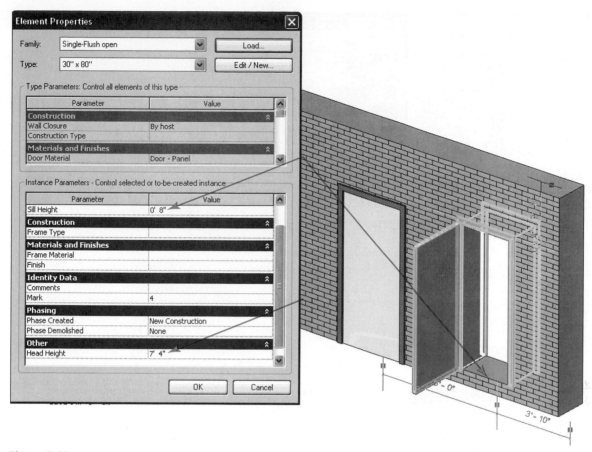

Figure 3-23

Notice that the head height changes to **7'-4"**—this is because the door height has been set to **6'-8"**. You can set either the **Sill Height** or the **Head Height**—they are related to the door panel height (see Figure 3-23).

   3. Save this file as **HEAD AND SILLS**.

Exercise 3-8: Placing Different Door Styles

Revit Architecture 2009 has a library of different door families, and you can download more families from the Internet. All Revit doors are parametric and modifiable.

   1. Start a new drawing using the **RAC 2009\ImperialTemplates\default.rte** template.
   2. In the **Project browser**, double-click **Floor Plans > Level 1**.
   3. In the **Design Bar - Basics** tab, select the **Wall** tool.
   4. In the **Options** toolbar, select the **Basic Wall: Generic - 8"**.
   5. Place a **10'** long, **10'** high wall in the **Drawing Editor**.
   6. Select **File > Load from Library > Load Family** from the **Main** menu to bring up the **Load Family** dialog box (see Figure 3-24).
   7. In the **Load Family** dialog box, select the **Double-Glass 2** door and press the **Open** button to return to the **Drawing Editor** (see Figure 3-25).
   8. In the **Project browser**, expand the **Doors** and then the **Double-Glass 2.**
   9. Under **Double-Glass 2,** drag the **68" × 80"** door into the wall you placed in the **Drawing Editor** (see Figure 3-26).
  10. Change to the **Default 3D View** (see Figure 3-27).

As mentioned previously, there are lots of places on the Internet to locate practically any door you need. If this is not enough, you can always modify an existing door Family to suit your needs—see Section 12 on Components and Families.

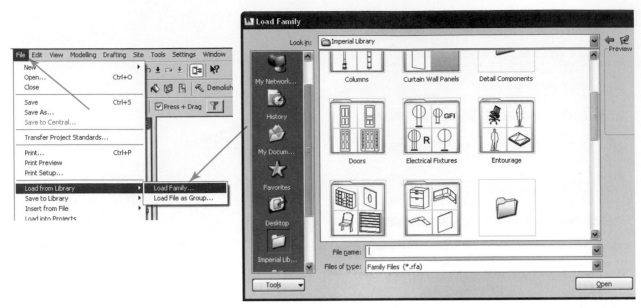

Figure 3-24

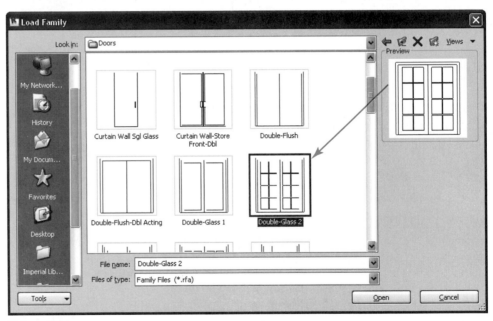

Figure 3-25

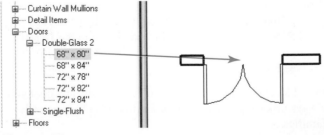

Figure 3-26

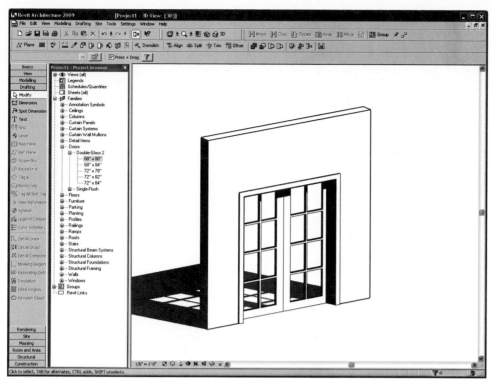

Figure 3-27

Summary

This section discussed the methods for placing, numbering, creating, and modifying all types of doors in Revit Architecture 2009.

Section Test Questions

True/false

1. True or False: Door **Families** cannot be modified.

2. True or False: Doors can be opened and closed automatically in 3D.

3. True or False: **Door Frame** materials cannot be changed.

Questions

1. What is the difference between a door **Family** and a door **Type**?

2. How do you place several doors separated by an equal distance in a wall?

3. What are door grips used for?

4. Name two places where you can get door **Families.**

5. Where do you control door tag placement?

6. How do you tag all doors that are not tagged?

7. What is **Wrapping at Insert** used for?

Windows

4

Section Objectives

- Understand the difference between Revit's **Windows** and Revit's **Doors**.
- Know how to place a **Window** object.
- Know how to place and use **Window** tags.
- Learn how to use the **View Range** option.
- Learn how to **Array** and **Group** windows.

WINDOWS

In Revit Architecture 2009, Window objects are totally customizable. All is possible in this program—from customizing the size and shape of the window or the size and shape of the jamb, to including mullions or a sill. As with other features of this program, a premade library of window styles greatly enhances productivity. Web sites such as Architectural Data Systems (http://www.architecturaldatasystems.com) and BIM WORLD (http://www.bimworld.com) are currently offering content from many manufacturers.

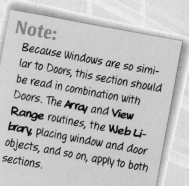

Note:
Because Windows are so similar to Doors, this section should be read in combination with Doors. The **Array** and **View Range** routines, the **Web Library**, placing window and door objects, and so on, apply to both sections.

Exercise 4-1: Loading, Placing, and Controlling Windows

1. Start a new drawing using the **Revit Architecture 2009\Imperial Templates\default.rte** template.
2. In the **Project browser**, double-click **Floor Plans > Level 1**.
3. Select **File > Load from Library > Load Family** from the **Main** menu to bring up the **Load Family** dialog box (see Figure 4-1).

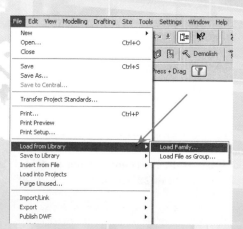

Figure 4-1

4. In the **Load Family** dialog box, press the **Imperial Library** icon on the left, and then locate the **Windows** folder (see Figure 4-2).

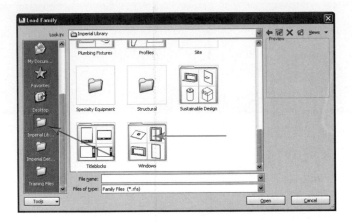

Figure 4-2

5. Double-click on the **Windows** folder, select all the windows, and then press the **Open** button at the lower right of the **Open** dialog box.

You have now loaded all the window families that are included with Revit Architecture 2009. To see what windows have been loaded and are now available, do the following.

6. Go to the **Project browser**, and locate **Families**.
7. Expand **Families**, and locate **Windows**.
8. Expand **Windows** to see all the **Window** families.
9. Expand **Double Hung** to see the sizes available (see Figure 4-3).

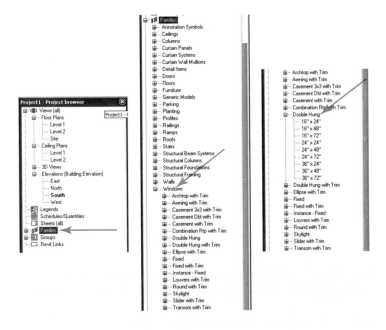

Figure 4-3

Exercise 4-2: The View Range

1. In the **Design Bar**, under **Basics**, select the **Wall** icon.
2. Move your cursor to the **Options** toolbar; select **Basic wall: Exterior – Brick on CMU** from the drop-down list, pick the **Pencil** icon, set the height to **20′-0″**, and place a **20′-0″** long wall.
3. Select the **Window** tool in the **Design Bar**.

4. In the **Options** toolbar, select **Double Hung 36″ × 48″** from the drop-down list, uncheck the **Tag on Placement** check box, and place a window at **4′-8″** from the left side of the wall you created.

5. Double-click the **South Elevation** in the **Project browser** to bring it up in the **Drawing Editor**.

6. Select **Window > Tile** from the **Main** menu to tile the **Floor Plan: Level 1** and **Elevation: South** modeling areas.

7. Set the scale of **Floor Plan: Level 1** to **1/2″ = 1′-0″**, and **Elevation: South** to **1/4″ = 1′-0″**.

8. Adjust the tiled modeling areas as shown in Figure 4-4.

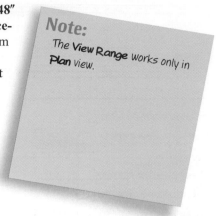

Note: The **View Range** works only in **Plan** view.

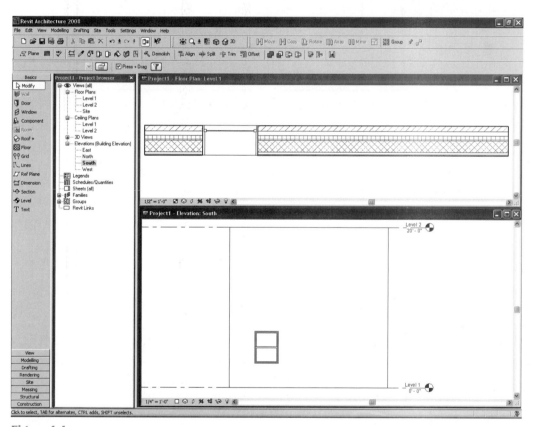

Figure 4-4

9. Select the window in the **South Elevation, RMB,** and select **Element Properties** from the contextual menu that appears to bring up the **Element Properties** dialog box.

10. In the **Element Properties** dialog box, change the **Sill Height** to **5′-0″**.

Notice that the window no longer appears in the **Level 1** view. That is because the **Cut Plane** of the **View Range** is set lower than the window (see Figure 4-5).

11. Click in the **Level 1** view, **RMB**, and select **View Properties** from the contextual menu to bring up the **Element Properties** dialog box.

12. In the **Element Properties** dialog box, select the **Edit** button in the **View Range** field to bring up the **View Range** dialog box.

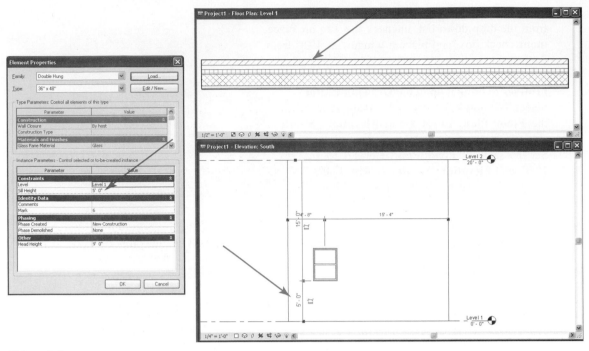

Figure 4-5

13. In the **View Range** dialog box, the **Cut plane: Offset** sets the height from the level for the cut plane (see Figure 4-6).

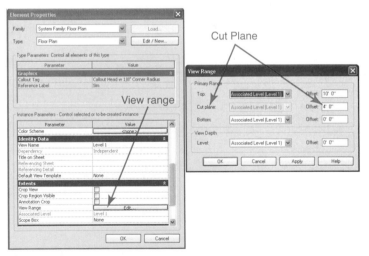

Figure 4-6

14. Change the **Cut plane** to **6′-0″**, and press the **Apply** button.

Notice that the window again appears in the plan view. That is because the cut plane is higher than the sill height of the window.

15. In the **South Elevation**, move the window up and down the wall and watch as it crosses the cut plane, and appears and disappears from the plan view.

VIEW RANGE OPTIONS

Name	Description
Top	Sets the upper boundary of the primary range. The upper boundary is defined as a level and an offset from that level. Elements display as defined by their object styles. Elements above the offset value do not display.
Cut plane	Sets a height at which elements in a plan view are cut, such that building components below the cut plane display in projection, and others that intersect it display as cut. Building components that display as cut include walls, roofs, ceilings, floors, and stairs. A cut plane does not cut components, such as desks, tables, and beds.
Bottom	Sets the level of the Primary Range's lower boundary. If you access **View Range** while viewing the lowest level of your project and set this property to a level below, you must specify a value for **Offset**, and you must set **View Depth** to a level below it.
View Depth	Sets a vertical range for the visibility of elements between specified levels. In a floor plan, it should be below the cut plane. In a reflected ceiling plan (RCP), it should be above. For example, if you are designing a multistory building, you might have a floor plan for the 10th floor that had a depth to the first level. Specifying view depth lets you display visible objects below the current level; such objects include stairs, balconies, and objects visible through holes in a floor.

Exercise 4-3: Arraying and Grouping Windows

1. Using the previous exercise, return the **Cut plane** to **4′-0″**.
2. Delete the window you previously placed.
3. Close the **Level 1** view, and expand the **South Elevation**.
4. Set the scale to **1/4″ = 1′-0″**.
5. Select the **Window** tool from the **Design Bar**.
6. In the **Options** toolbar, select the **Double Hung: 36″ × 48″** window from the drop-down list, and check the **Tag on Placement** check box.
7. Place a window as shown in Figure 4-7.

Note:
Windows can be automatically labeled in plan or elevation. Be sure to change the label annotation—windows are usually labeled by letters, and all windows of the same type will automatically have the same letter.

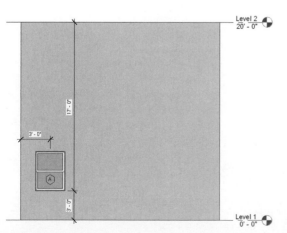

Figure 4-7

8. Select the window, and then select the **Array** icon at the top right of the interface (see Figure 4-8).

Figure 4-8

9. Select the **Linear** array icon, check the **Group and Associate** check box, enter **3** in the **Number** field, and select the **Last** radio button (see Figure 4-9).

10. Grab the window at its top center (make sure midpoint snap is on), drag the window to the right **13′-2″**, click to set the last window location, and then click again to create three windows (see Figure 4-10).

11. Select one of the windows (they are now all part of a group), change the number to **4,** and press the **<Enter>** key on your keyboard.

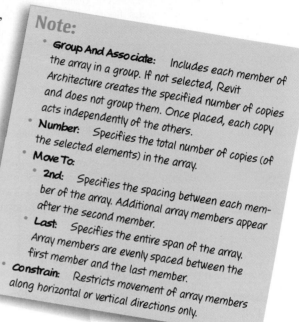

Note:

• **Group And Associate:** Includes each member of the array in a group. If not selected, Revit Architecture creates the specified number of copies and does not group them. Once placed, each copy acts independently of the others.

• **Number:** Specifies the total number of copies (of the selected elements) in the array.

• **Move To:**

• **2nd:** Specifies the spacing between each member of the array. Additional array members appear after the second member.

• **Last:** Specifies the entire span of the array. Array members are evenly spaced between the first member and the last member.

• **Constrain:** Restricts movement of array members along horizontal or vertical directions only.

Figure 4-9

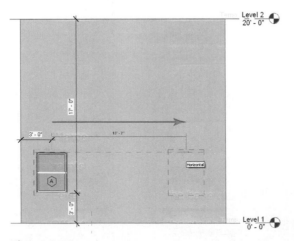

Figure 4-10

Notice that four windows now fill in the space between the first window and the last window— this is because the original **Array** had the **Last** radio button selected when it was first applied. Try changing the number to **2,** and watch what happens (see Figures 4-11 and 4-12).

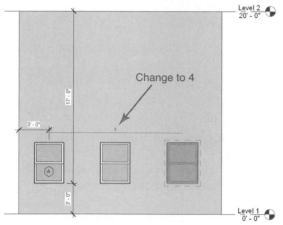

Figure 4-11

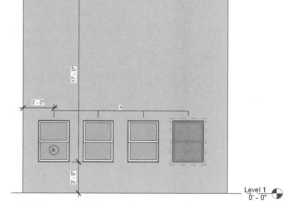

Figure 4-12

12. Select all the windows, and repeat this process vertically with the number **3** and the **Constrain** check box checked (see Figures 4-13, 4-14, and 4-15).

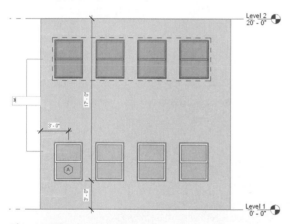

Figure 4-13

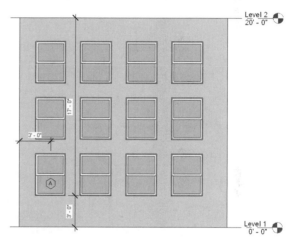

Figure 4-14

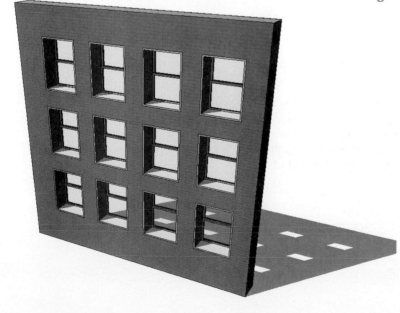

Figure 4-15

13. Change to the **South Elevation**.
14. Move the lower left window vertically up and down. Watch how the windows automatically space themselves.
15. Select the lower left window again, and select the **Ungroup** button that appears on the **Options** toolbar.
16. Move the lower left window vertically up and down again, and watch the adjacent windows automatically adjust.
17. Select the lower left window again, and again select the **Ungroup** button that appears on the **Options** toolbar to totally separate it from all window groups.

Tagging the Windows

1. Finally, change to the **Drafting** tab in the **Design Bar**.
2. In the **Drafting** tab, select the **Tag All Not Tagged** icon to bring up the **Tag All Not Tagged** dialog box.
3. In the **Tag All Not Tagged** dialog box, select the **All objects in current view** radio button, select the **Window Tag** field, and uncheck the **Leader > Create** check box (you don't want a leader on the tag).
4. Press the **Apply** button to apply all the tags, and then press the **OK** button to close the **Tag All Not Tagged** dialog box and return to the **Drawing Editor** (see Figure 4-16).

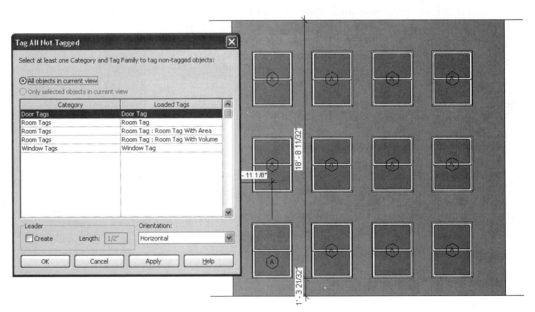

Figure 4-16

5. Open the **level 1** floor plan.
6. Change the **Scale** to **1/4″= 1′-0**.
7. Select the **Tag > by Category** icon from the **Drafting** tab.
8. Click on the left window to place the tag.
9. Select the **Tag All Not Tagged** icon from the **Drafting** tab.
10. Repeat step 3 of this exercise to place all the window tags in the plan view (see Figure 4-17).
11. Save this file as **WINDOW TUTORIAL.**

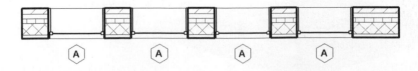

Figure 4-17

As mentioned previously, there are lots of places on the Internet to locate practically any window you need. If this is not enough, you can always modify an existing window Family to suit your needs—see Section 12 on Components and Families.

SUMMARY

This section discussed the methods for placing, numbering, creating, and modifying all types of doors in Revit Architecture 2009.

SECTION TEST QUESTIONS

Exercise

1. Go to http://www.bimworld.com on the Internet.

2. In the BIM WORLD website, select the Downloads button (see Figure 4-18).

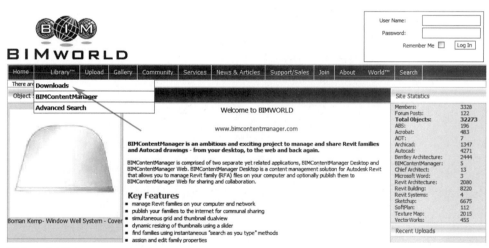

Figure 4-18

3. In the next screen, click on the Marvin icon to move to the next screen (see Figure 4-19).

Figure 4-19

4. In the Downloads screen, open the Windows > Casement & Awning folder.

5. In the Downloads screen, open the Casemaster Windows folder. Click on *Marvin -CLAD FRENCH CASEMASTER-CFCM4072* to go to the next screen (see Figure 4-20).

6. At the next screen, press "Add to Cart" for the 3D Revit Family (see Figure 4-21).

7. Press the Download button, and save the file in the Revit **Windows** folder on your computer (see Figure 4-22).

8. Place the window in a wall as shown in the exercise on placing windows.

Figure 4-20

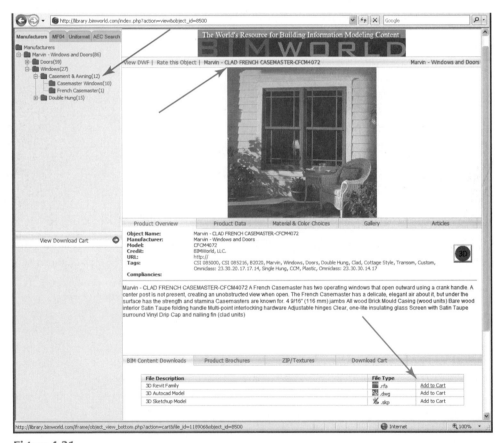

Figure 4-21

Figure 4-22

Roofs

5

Section Objectives

- Learn how to place a **Roof by Footprint**.
- Learn how to make a wall meet a roof.
- Learn how to change the **Rafter Cut**.
- Know how to modify a **Roof** slope with the **Slope Arrow**.
- Know how to create a hole in a roof.
- Know how to cut a hole in a roof slab.
- Learn how to modify a **Roof** by moving vertices.
- Learn how to create a roof by **Extrusion**.
- Know how to use the **Join/Unjoin Roof** tool.
- Learn how to create dormers.
- Learn how to create gutters.
- Learn how to create a **Roof Family**.
- Know how to use **Shape Editing** and the new roof slab editing options.

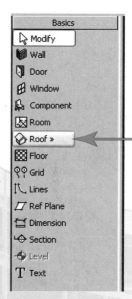

Roofs can be placed by three methods: **Roof by Footprint, Roof by Extrusion,** and **Roof by Face.**

ROOF BY FACE

Roof by Face is used to place a roof on any surface of a Mass model. The use of this feature is covered in Section 1 on Massing.

Exercise 5-1: Roof by Footprint

1. Start a new drawing using the **RAC 2009\Imperial Templates\default.rte** template.
2. In the **Project browser**, double-click **Floor Plans > Level 1** to bring it up in the **Drawing Editor**.
3. Using the **Wall** tool in the **Basics** tab of the **Design Bar**, place a **15′-0″ × 30′-0″** rectangular enclosure **10′-0″** high.
4. Change to the **South Elevation**.
5. In the **South Elevation**, double-click on the **Level 2** name and change it to **ROOF BASE**.
6. Press the **Yes** button at the **Revit** dialog box asking if you would like to rename corresponding views.
7. Make sure the **ROOF BASE** height is **10′-0″**.
8. In the **Project browser**, double-click on **ROOF BASE** to bring it up in the **Drawing Editor**. You should see Level 1 in halftone.
   a. If you do not see an underlay of **Level 1**, RMB in an empty area in the **Drawing Editor**, and select **View Properties** from the contextual menu that appears to bring up the **Element Properties** dialog box for the **ROOF BASE** view.
   b. In the **Element Properties** dialog box, select **Level 1** from the **Underlay** drop-down list (see Figure 5-1).

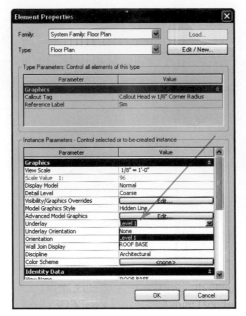

Figure 5-1

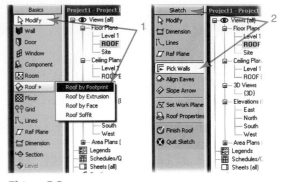

Figure 5-2

9. Select **Roof >> Roof by Footprint** from the **Basics** tab in the **Design Bar**.
10. Select **Pick Walls** from the **Sketch** tab (see Figure 5-2).
11. In the **Options** toolbar, select the **Defines Slope** check box, and enter **1'-0"** in the **Overhang** field.
12. Move your cursor above and below the northmost wall, and notice the dashed line that appears—this is the overhang location.
13. Again move your cursor above the northmost wall, and click the left mouse button.

A blue line and open angle with a number will appear above the wall. The line is the edge of the overhang, and the angle number represents the roof rise per foot of roof run.

14. Repeat steps 12–13 for the rest of the walls (see Figure 5-3).

> **Note:**
> The **Design Bar** will change to the **Sketch** tab to enable the roof sketching tools.

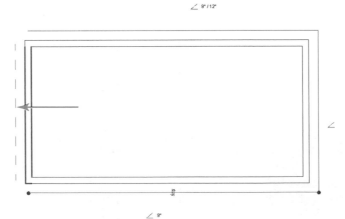

Figure 5-3

15. When you have created all the roof edge lines, select the **Roof Properties** tool from the **Sketch** tab to bring up the **Element Properties** dialog box.
16. In the **Element Properties** dialog box, set the settings shown in Figure 5-4.

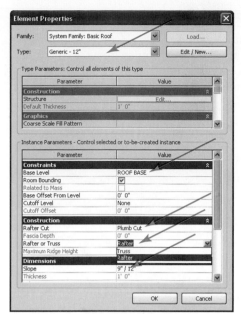

Figure 5-4

17. Press the **Finish Roof** tool in the **Sketch** tab, and select **NO** when the **Revit** dialog box asks you if you would like to attach the highlighted walls to the roof.
18. Press the **Default 3D View** icon on the **Top** toolbar to change to the default 3D view.
19. Select the **Shadows** icon at the bottom of the **Drawing Editor**, and select **Shadows On** (see Figure 5-5).
20. Save this file as **ROOF by FOOTPRINT**.

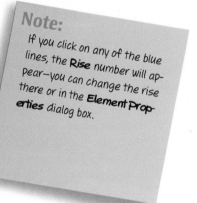

Note:
If you click on any of the blue lines, the **Rise** number will appear—you can change the rise there or in the **Element Properties** dialog box.

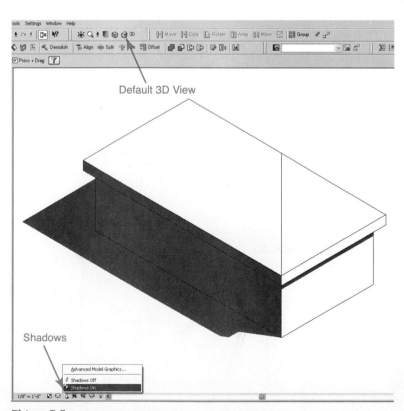

Figure 5-5

Exercise 5-2: Modifying a Roof by Footprint

1. Using the previous exercise, change to the **East Elevation**.
2. Select the **ROOF BASE** level line, **RMB**, and select **Create Similar** from the contextual menu that appears.
3. Drag a new level at the top of the roof, and name it **TOP of ROOF** (see Figure 5-6).

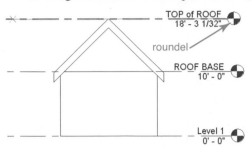

Figure 5-6

4. Double-click on the **TOP of ROOF** benchmark, or **TOP of ROOF** in the **Project browser** to bring it up in the **Drawing Editor**.
5. In the **Drawing Editor**, select the roof, and then select the **Edit** button on the **Options** toolbar.

The Roof will now be in its "Edit" state, and will return to an outline. The **Design Bar** will also return to the **Sketch** tab.

6. Select the **Right** roof line, and then uncheck the **Defines Slope** check box in the **Options** toolbar.
7. Press the **Finish Roof** tool in the **Sketch** tab, and select **NO** when the **Revit** dialog box asks you if you would like to attach the highlighted walls to the roof.
8. Press the **Default 3D View** icon on the **Top** toolbar to again change to the default 3D view (see Figure 5-7).
9. Save the file as **ROOF BY FOOTPRINT**.

Note:
The **Defines Slope** check box determines if you have a roof slope or not. If the check box is checked, you will see an angle and slope rise number. If the check box is unchecked, you will not see an angle and slope number next to a roof line.

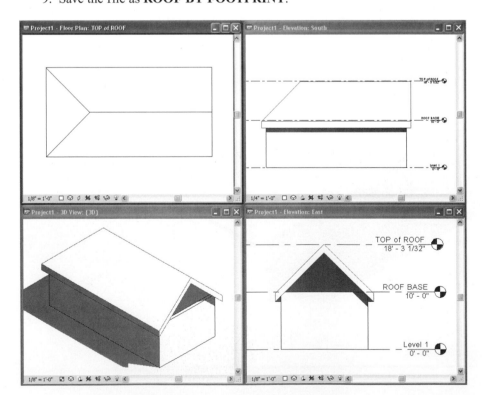

Figure 5-7

Exercise 5-3: Making a Wall Meet a Roof

1. Using the previous exercise, stay in the **Default 3D View**.
2. Select the wall below the roof, and press the **Attach** button from the **Options** toolbar.
3. Select the roof.

The wall attaches to the roof (see Figure 5-8).

4. Save the file as **WALL MEETS ROOF**.

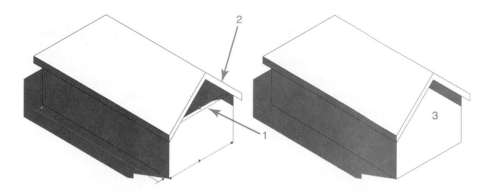

Figure 5-8

Exercise 5-4: Changing the Rafter Cut

1. Using the previous exercise, change to the **TOP of ROOF** plan view.
2. In the **Drawing Editor**, select the roof, and then select the **Edit** button on the **Options** toolbar.

The Roof will now be in its "Edit" state, and will return to an outline. The **Design Bar** will also return to the **Sketch** tab.

3. Select the **Left** roof line, and then **uncheck** the **Defines Slope** check box in the **Options** toolbar.
4. Press the **Finish Roof** tool in the **Sketch** tab, and select **Yes** when the **Revit** dialog box asks you if you would like to attach the highlighted walls to the roof.

The wall attaches to the roof.

5. Change to the **East Elevation**.
6. Select the roof, **RMB**, and select **Element Properties** from the contextual menu that appears to bring up the **Element Properties** dialog box for the roof.
7. In the **Element Properties** dialog box, select **Two Cut-Plumb** from the **Rafter Cut** field, and set the **Fascia Depth** to **6″** (see Figures 5-9 and 5-10).

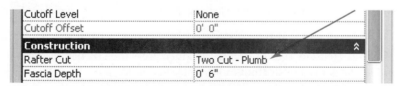

Figure 5-9

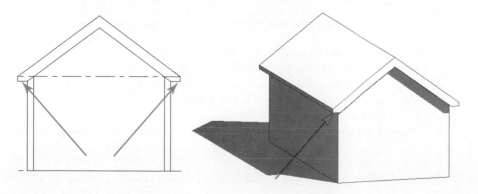

Figure 5-10

8. Experiment with the other **Rafter Cut** options, and different **Fascia Depths**.
9. Save the file as **RAFTER CUT OPTIONS**.

Exercise 5-5: Modifying a Roof Slope with the Slope Arrow

1. Using the previous exercise, change to the **ROOF BASE** plan view.
2. Delete the Roof.
3. Select **Roof >> Roof by Footprint** from the **Basics** tab in the **Design Bar**.
4. Select **Pick Walls** from the **Sketch** tab.
5. In the **Options** toolbar, uncheck the **Defines Slope** check box, and enter **1′-0″** in the **Overhang** field.
6. Select all the walls as you have in a previous exercise.
7. Adjust the lower south edge of the sketch as shown in Figure 5-29 to have no overhang.
8. Select **Slope Arrow** from the **Sketch** tab in the **Design Bar**.
9. With the **Pencil** tool selected in the **Options** toolbar, place a **Slope Arrow** as shown in Figure 5-11.

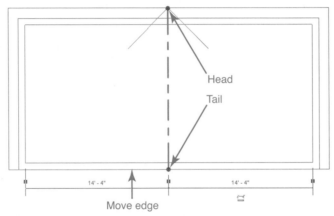

Figure 5-11

10. Change to the **Default 3D View**.
11. Select the arrow, **RMB**, and select **Element Properties** from the contextual menu that appears to bring up the **Element Properties** dialog box for the arrow.

In the **Element Properties** dialog box you can set the height of the arrow at its head and tail. Because the **Slope Arrow** controls the roof slope, you can parametrically control the roof slope.

12. In the **Element Properties** dialog box, set the **Level at Tail** to **ROOF BASE**, and **Level at Head** to **TOP of ROOF**, and then press the **OK** button.
13. Press the **Finish Roof** tool in the **Sketch** tab, and select **Yes** when the **Revit** dialog box asks you if you would like to attach the highlighted walls to the roof.

You have now set the slope of the roof by adjusting the **Slope Arrow** (see Figure 5-12).

14. Select the roof, and then select the **Edit** button that appears in the **Options** toolbar.
15. Select the **Slope Arrow** again, **RMB**, and select **Element Properties** to bring up the **Element Properties** dialog box.
16. Experiment with all the settings in the **Element Properties** dialog box, and notice the changes that happen to the roof.
17. Experiment moving the arrow head and tail, and notice the changes that happen to the roof.
18. Save the file as **SLOPE ARROW**.

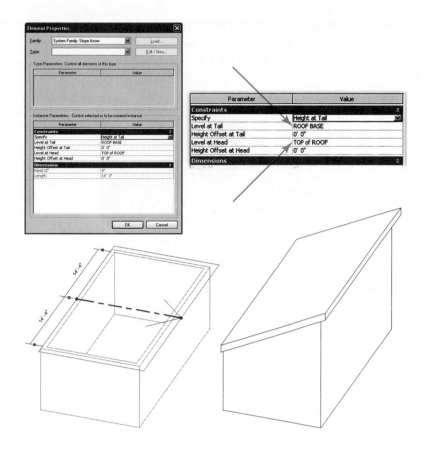

Figure 5-12

Exercise 5-6: Creating a Hole in a Roof

1. Using the previous exercise, change to the **ROOF BASE** plan view.
2. Select the Roof.
3. Select the **Edit** button that appears in the **Options** toolbar.
4. Select **Lines** from the **Sketch** tab in the **Design Bar**.
5. Place a circle, a rectangle, and an ellipse in the **ROOF BASE** view.
6. Press the **Finish Roof** tool in the **Sketch** tab, and select **Yes** when the **Revit** dialog box asks you if you would like to attach the highlighted walls to the roof.

Note:
Be sure that all the lines in the circle and rectangles do not have slope angles. If they do, select the lines and uncheck the **Defines Slope** check box.

You have now placed holes in the roof. If you select the holes, you can adjust the holes with arrow grips that appear, or repeat steps 2–3 of this exercise and change the shape of the holes there (see Figure 5-13).

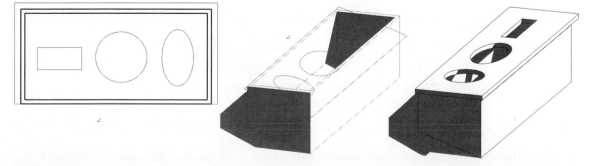

Figure 5-13

7. Open the **ROOF by FOOTPRINT** file.
8. Repeat steps 2–6 of this exercise on this file (see Figure 5-14).
9. Save this file as **ROOF HOLES**.

Figure 5-14

Exercise 5-7: Modifying a Roof Slab by Moving Vertices

1. Open the **ROOF by FOOTPRINT** file.
2. Change to the **ROOF BASE** plan view.
3. Select the **Edit** button that appears in the **Options** toolbar.
4. Select all the roof edge lines, and uncheck the **Defines Slope** check box in the **Options** toolbar.
5. Press the **Finish Roof** tool in the **Sketch** tab, and select **Yes** when the **Revit** dialog box asks you if you would like to attach the highlighted walls to the roof.

This will create a flat roof.

6. Change to the **Default 3D View.**
7. Select the flat roof, and notice that four new buttons appear in the **Options** toolbar.

These buttons are used to modify flat roofs (not extruded flat roofs) by vertices (see Figure 5-15).

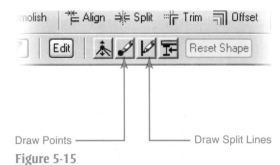

Draw Points ————————┘   └———— Draw Split Lines
Figure 5-15

8. Select the **Modify Subobjects** button, and notice that green grips appear at all four corners and on the top surface of the roof.
9. Select one of the corners, enter **6′-0″** in the number field, and then press the **<Enter>** key on your keyboard.

The corner of the roof moves upward (Z direction) 6′-0″. Because the walls are attached to the roof, they automatically move upward as well (see Figure 5-16).

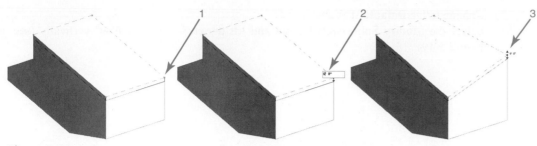

Figure 5-16

10. Experiment by moving the other vertices.
11. Select the roof again, and press the **Reset Shape** button to revert back to the roof's original flat shape.
12. Change to the **ROOF BASE** plan view.
13. Select the **Draw Points** button, and place three points.
14. Change to the **Default 3D View.**
15. Select the **Modify Subobjects** button, and lift the three points **6′-0″** vertically as shown in Figure 5-17.

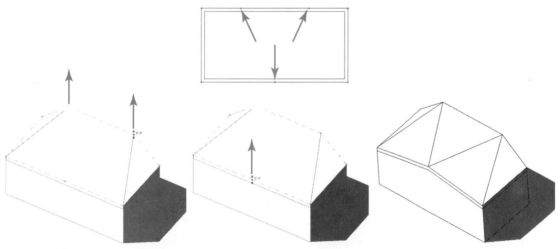

Figure 5-17

16. Change to the **ROOF BASE** plan view.
17. Select the roof again, and press the **Reset Shape** button to revert back to the roof's original flat shape.
18. Select the **Draw Split Lines** button.
19. Draw **Split Lines** across the diagonals of the flat roof (see Figure 5-18).

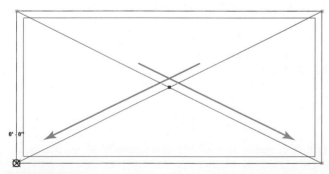

Figure 5-18

20. Change to the **Default 3D View.**
21. Select the **Modify Subobjects** button, and lift the crossing point **6′-0″** vertically (see Figure 5-19).

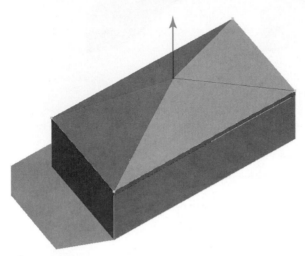

Figure 5-19

22. Change to the **ROOF BASE** plan view again.
23. Select the **Modify Subobjects** button, and move the crossing point horizontally (see Figure 5-20).

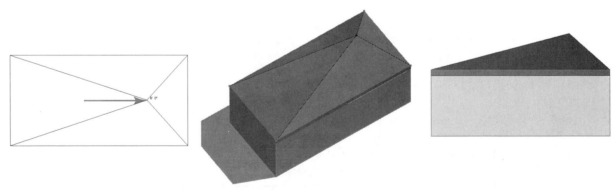

Figure 5-20

24. Select the roof again, and press the **Reset Shape** button to revert back to the roof's original flat shape.
25. Change to the **ROOF BASE** plan view.
26. Change to the **Structural** tab in the **Design Bar**.
27. In the **Structural** tab, select the **I Beam** tool.
28. With the **I Beam** tool selected, select **W-Wide Flange:W12 × 26** from the drop-down list in the **Options** toolbar, and place the beam as shown in Figure 5-21.
29. Select the **Pick Supports** button, and select the **W-Wide Flange:W12 × 26** you just placed.
30. Select the **Modify Subobjects** button again, and lift the end points **6′-0″** vertically as shown in Figure 5-22.
31. Save this file as **MOVING VERTICES**.

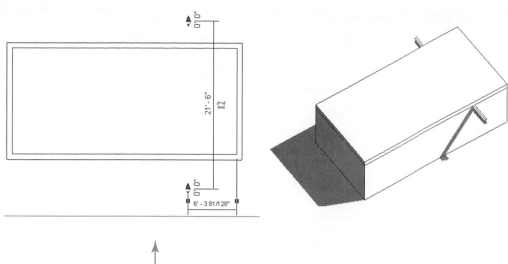

Figure 5-21

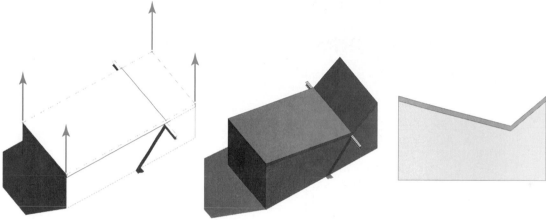

Figure 5-22

Exercise 5-8: Roof by Extrusion

1. Using the previous exercise, **Detach** the wall from the roof by selecting the wall, pressing the **Detach** button from the **Options** toolbar, and then selecting the roof.
2. Delete the roof.
3. Double-click on the **ROOF BASE** plan in the **Project browser** to bring it up in the **Drawing Editor**.
4. Select the **Ref Plane** tool from the **Basics** tab of the **Design Bar**.
5. Select the **Pick Lines** tool from the **Options** toolbar.
6. Pick the left wall of the enclosure to place a **Reference Plane**.
7. Select the **Modify** tool from the **Basics** tab of the **Design Bar**.
8. Select the **Reference Plane** you just placed, **RMB**, and select **Element Properties** from the contextual menu that appears to bring up the **Element Properties** dialog box.
9. In the **Element Properties** dialog box, enter **EXTRUDED ROOF EDGE** in the **Name** field, and press the **OK** button to return to the **Drawing Editor** (see Figure 5-23).

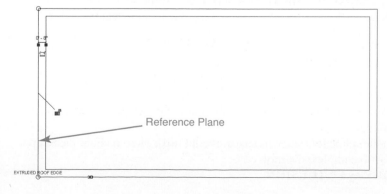

Reference Plane

Figure 5-23

Reference Planes are drawn "on edge."

10. Select **Roof >> Roof by Extrusion** from the **Basics** tab in the **Design Bar** to bring up the **Work Plane** dialog box.

11. In the **Work Plane** dialog box, select the **Pick a plane** radio button, and select **Reference Plane: EXTRUDED ROOF EDGE** from the **Specify a new Work Plane** drop-down list. Finally press the **OK** button.

12. Because you are in a plan view, the **Go to View** dialog box will now appear.

13. In the **Go to View** dialog box, select **Elevation: East** and press the **Open View** button.

14. The view will now change to the **East Elevation**, and the **Roof Reference Level and Offset** dialog box will appear.

15. In the **Roof Reference Level and Offset** dialog box, change to **ROOF BASE** from the **Level** drop-down list, and press the **OK** button (see Figure 5-24).

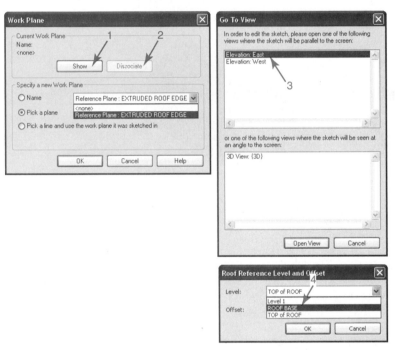

Figure 5-24

16. Select **Lines** under the **Sketch** tab in the **Design Bar**.

17. Select **Arc passing through three points** in the **Options** toolbar.

18. With the **Snaps** (on), place an arc between the left and right walls.

19. Press **Finish Sketch** under the **Sketch** tab in the **Design Bar** to complete the roof.

Notice that the line you placed becomes the top of the roof (see Figure 5-25).

20. Return to the **East** view, and delete the roof you just created.

Repeat steps 17–20 using the **Spline** tool from the **Options** toolbar (see Figure 5-26).

21. Select the roof you placed, and then select the **Edit** button in the **Options** toolbar to return to the **Sketch** mode.

22. Move the vertices in the spline to change its shape. Press **Finish Sketch** under the **Sketch** tab in the **Design Bar** to complete the roof.

23. Save this file as **ROOF by EXTRUSION**.

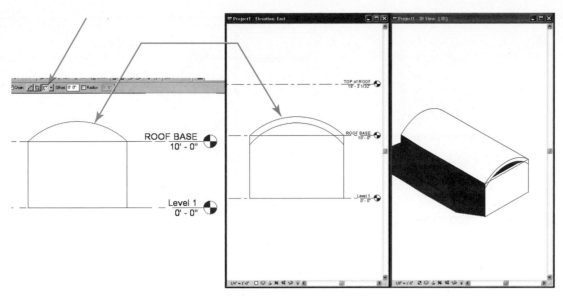

Figure 5-25

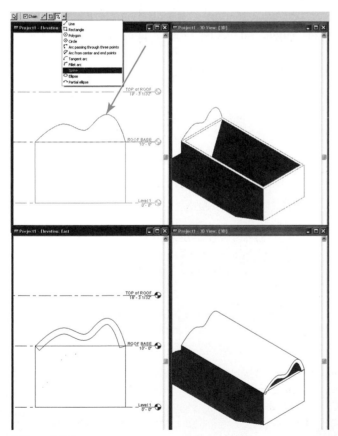

Figure 5-26

Exercise 5-9: The Join/Unjoin Roof Tool

1. Start a new drawing using the **RAC 2009\Imperial Templates\default.rte** template.
2. In the **Project browser**, double-click **Floor Plans > Level 1** to bring it up in the **Drawing Editor**.
3. Using the **Wall** tool in the **Basics** tab of the **Design Bar**, create **10′** high **Generic 8″** walls as shown in Figure 5-27.

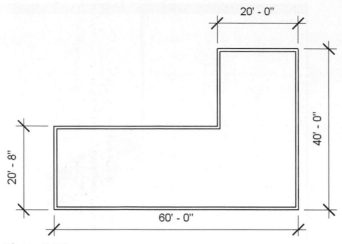

20' - 0"

40' - 0"

20' - 8"

60' - 0"

Figure 5-27

4. Select **Roof >> Roof by Footprint** from the **Basics** tab in the **Design Bar**.
5. Select **Yes** when asked if you want to move the **Roof** to **Level 2**.
6. Using the **Lines** command in the **Sketch** tab of the **Design Bar**, create the line shown in Figure 5-28.

Be sure that only the East wall has a **Slope Angle,** and that the Slope Angle is **6″**.

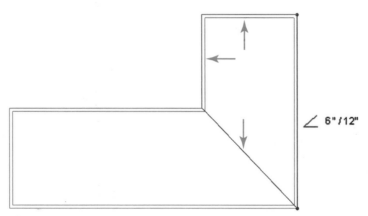

∠ 6" / 12"

Figure 5-28

7. Press the **Finish Sketch** tool in the **Sketch** tab, and select **NO** when the **Revit** dialog box asks you if you would like to attach the highlighted walls to the roof (see Figure 5-29).

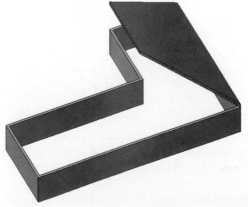

Figure 5-29

8. In the **Level 1** plan view, select the **Ref Plane** tool from the **Basics** tab of the **Design Bar**.
9. Select the **Pick Lines** tool from the **Options** toolbar.
10. Pick the **East** wall of the enclosure to place a **Reference Plane**.
11. Select the **Modify** tool from the **Basics** tab of the **Design Bar.**
12. Select the **Reference Plane** you just placed, **RMB**, and select **Element Properties** from the contextual menu that appears to bring up the **Element Properties** dialog box.
13. In the **Element Properties** dialog box, enter **EAST ROOF EDGE** in the **Name** field, and press the **OK** button to return to the **Drawing Editor**.
14. Select **Roof >> Roof by Extrusion** from the **Basics** tab in the **Design Bar** to bring up the **Work Plane** dialog box.
15. In the **Work Plane** dialog box, select the **Pick a plane** radio button, and **Reference Plane: EAST ROOF EDGE** from the **Specify a new Work Plane** drop-down list. Finally, press the **OK** button.
16. Because you are in a plan view, the **Go to View** dialog box will now appear.
17. In the **Go to View** dialog box, select **Elevation: East** and press the **Open View** button.
18. The view will now change to the **East Elevation,** and the **Roof Reference Level and Off-set** dialog box will appear.
19. In the **Roof Reference Level and Offset** dialog box, change to **Level 2** from the **Level** drop-down list and press the **OK** button.
20. Select **Lines** under the **Sketch** tab in the **Design Bar**.
21. Select **Line,** and with the **Snaps** (on) place a line as shown in Figure 5-30.

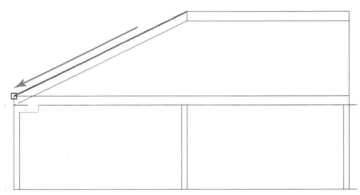

Figure 5-30

22. Press the **Finish Sketch** tool in the **Sketch** tab, and select **NO** when the **Revit** dialog box asks you if you would like to attach the highlighted walls to the roof.
23. Change to the **Default 3D View.**
24. Select the **Join/Unjoin Roof** tool from the **Edit** toolbar.
25. Select the edge of the roof you want to join, and then the existing roof you want to join with it (see Figure 5-31).
26. Save this file as **JOIN/UNJOIN ROOF**.

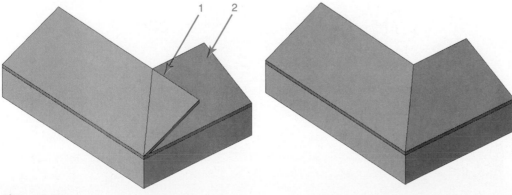

Figure 5-31

Exercise 5-10: Creating a Dormer

1. Start a new drawing using the **RAC 2009\Imperial Templates\default.rte** template.
2. Double-click on the **Level 1** floor plan in the **Project browser** to bring it up in the **Drawing Editor**.
3. Select the **Wall** tool from the **Basics** tab in the **Design Bar**, and create an enclosure **50′-0″** long by **30′-0″** wide and **10′-0″** high using the **Generic- 8″** wall (see Figure 5-32).

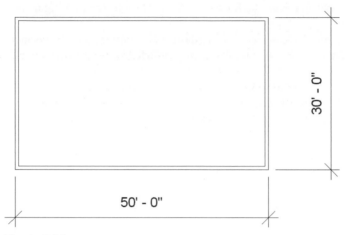

Figure 5-32

4. Select the **Wall** tool from the **Basics** tab in the **Design Bar**, and create an enclosure **50′-0″** long by **30′-0″** wide and **10′-0″** high using the **Generic- 8″** wall (see Figure 5-32).
5. Select the **Roof > Roof by Footprint** tool from the **Basics** tab in the **Design Bar**.

You will get a **Lowest Level Notice** dialog box. Select **Level 2** from the drop-down list and press the **Yes** button. You will now enter **Sketch** mode in the **Design Bar.**

6. In the **Design Bar**, select the **Pick Walls** icon, and enter **2′-0″** in the **Overhang** numeric field of the **Options** toolbar.
7. Select the outside of each wall until a continuous line appears around the enclosure.

Notice that a magenta-colored "angle" symbol appears opposite each side of the line you just created. These symbols indicate that that side of the roof will have a slope.

8. Select the left and right lines, and then uncheck the **Defines slope** check box in the **Options** toolbar.
9. Select the top and bottom lines, and enter **12** in the numeric field next to the "angle" symbol. This will create a **12″/ 12″** or **45 degree** slope (see Figure 5-33).

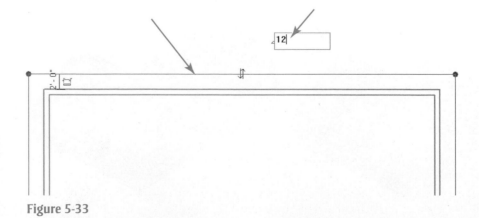

Figure 5-33

10. Press the **Finish Roof** icon in the **Sketch** tab to create the roof.

A **Revit** dialog box will appear asking if you would like to attach the highlighted walls to the roof. Press the **Yes** button, and select the **Default 3D** icon in the **View** toolbar to bring up a default 3D view (see Figure 5-34).

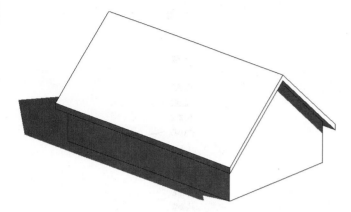

Figure 5-34

11. Double-click on the **Level 2** floor plan in the **Project browser** to bring it up in the **Drawing Editor**.
12. In the **Level 2** floor plan, select the roof, and then select the **Temporary Hide/Isolate** icon at the bottom of the **Drawing Editor**. Select **Hide Element** to hide the roof.
13. Select one of the walls of the enclosure, **RMB**, and select **Create Similar** from the contextual menu that appears.
14. In the **Options** toolbar, select **unconnected** from the **Height** drop-down list, and enter **6'-0"** in the adjacent numerical field, and **Loc Line = Finish Face Exterior** to create **6'-0"** high dormer walls.
15. Place walls as shown in Figure 5-35.

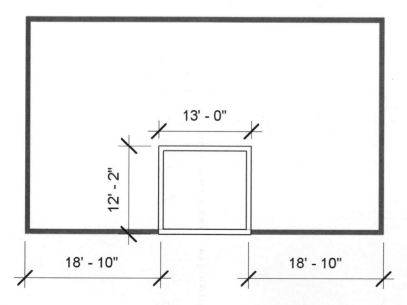

13' - 0"

12' - 2"

18' - 10"   18' - 10"

Figure 5-35

16. Again, select the **Default 3D** icon in the **View** toolbar to bring up a default 3D view (see Figure 5-36).
17. Double-click on the **East Elevation** in the **Project browser** to bring it up in the **Drawing Editor**.
18. Select the **Level** tool in the **Basics** tab of the **Design Bar**, and place a new level at the top of the dormer wall you just created (see Figure 5-37).

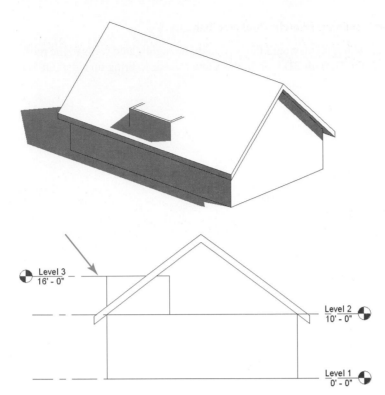

Figure 5-36

Figure 5-37

19. Double-click on the new floor plan level you created in the **Project browser** to bring that view into the **Drawing Editor**.
20. Select the **Roof > Roof by Footprint** tool from the **Basics** tab in the **Design Bar**.
21. In the **Design Bar**, select the **Pick Walls** icon, and enter **2′-0″** in the **Overhang** numeric field of the **Options** toolbar.
22. Select the outside of each wall until a continuous line appears around the enclosure.

Notice that a magenta-colored "angle" symbol appears opposite each side of the line you just created. These symbols indicate that that side of the roof will have a slope.

23. Select the top and bottom line, and then uncheck the **Defines Slope** check box in the **Options** toolbar.
24. Select the top and bottom lines, and enter **9** in the numeric field next to the "angle" symbol. This will create a **9″/ 12″** slope.
25. Press the **Finish Roof** icon in the **Sketch** tab to create the dormer roof.
26. Select the **Default 3D** icon in the **View** toolbar to bring up a default 3D view (see Figure 5-38).

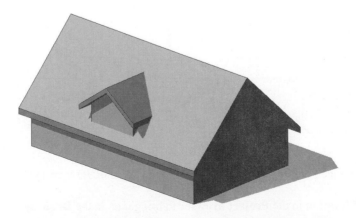

Figure 5-38

Now you must join the dormer roof to the main roof.

27. Select the **Model Graphics Style** icon at the bottom of the **Drawing Editor**, and select **Wireframe**.

28. Select the **Join/Unjoin Roof** icon from the **Tools** toolbar.
29. Select an edge of the dormer roof that touches the main roof, and then touch an edge of the roof that touches the dormer roof (see Figure 5-39).

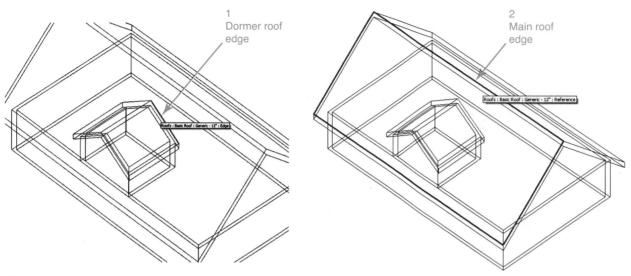

Figure 5-39

You will get a **Revit Architecture** dialog box telling you that the **Highlighted walls are attached to, but miss, the highlighted targets.** Press the **OK** button. The dormer roof will be cut to fit the main roof, and the rear and side walls that were attached to the dormer no longer are fully attached to the dormer roof (see Figure 5-40).

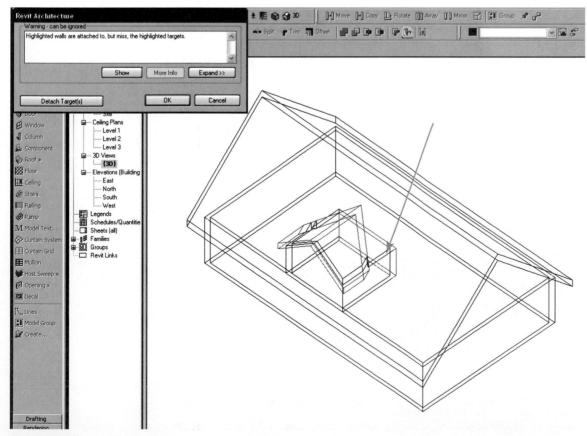

Figure 5-40

If you turn the model upside down, you will notice that the dormer has not cut through the roof (see Figure 5-41).

30. Return the model to its normal position.
31. Select **Opening > Dormer Opening** from the **Modeling** tab in the **Design Bar** (see Figure 5-42).
32. Select the main roof to bring up the **Pick Boundary** tab in the **Design Bar**.
33. In the **Pick Boundary** tab, select the **Pick** icon (see Figure 5-43).

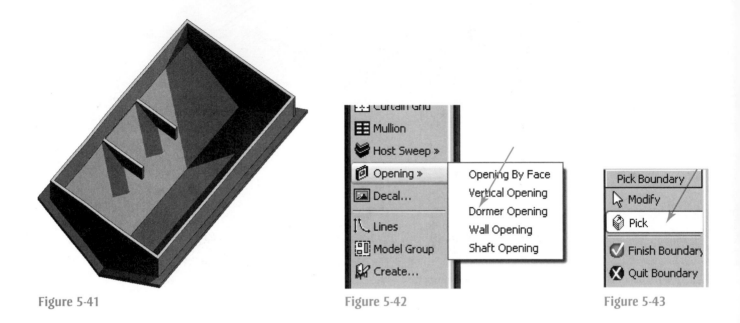

Figure 5-41   Figure 5-42   Figure 5-43

34. Pick and trim the boundary of the dormer that you wish to cut out of the main roof (see Figure 5-44).

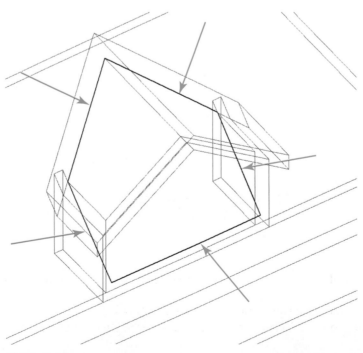

Figure 5-44

35. Select the **Finish Boundary** button in the **Pick Boundary** tab to create the opening (see Figure 5-45).

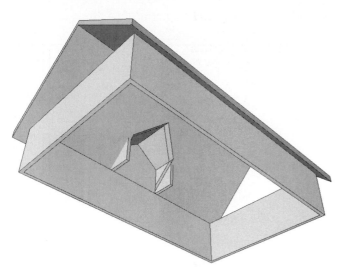

Figure 5-45

36. Select the **Window** tool from the **Basics** tab of the **Design Bar** and add a window (see Figure 5-46).

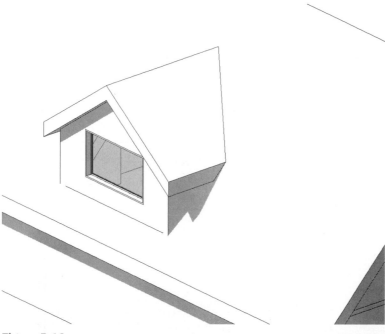

Figure 5-46

37. Double-click on the **Level 3** floor plan to bring up the **Level 3** view in the **Drawing Editor**.
38. Select the dormer walls, roof, and window and move them to the left.
39. Select the dormer walls, roof, and window again, and then select **Mirror** from the **Edit** toolbar.
40. Select the **Axis** button in the **Options** toolbar, and check the **Copy** check box.

41. Select the axis shown in Figure 5-47.

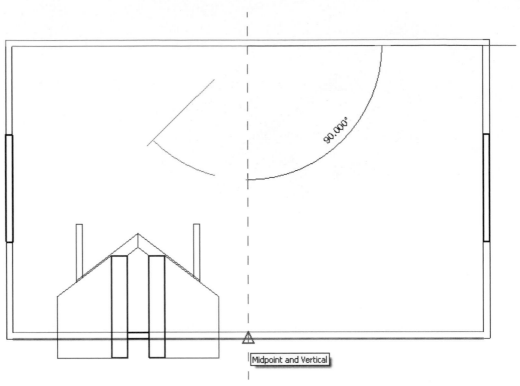

Figure 5-47

42. Click the second point of the axis to make a copy of the dormer (see Figures 5-48 and 5-49).
43. Save this file as **DORMERS**.

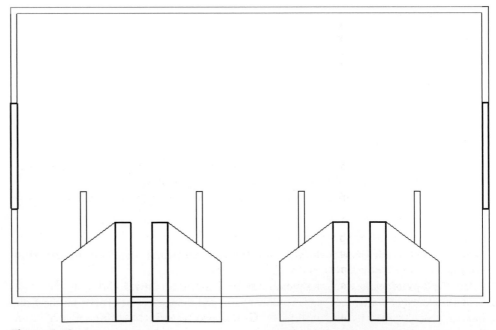

Figure 5-48

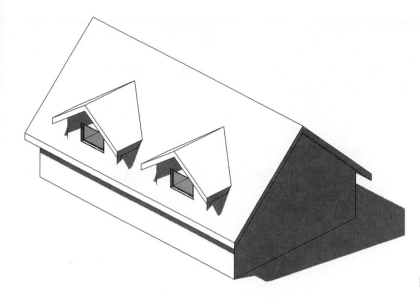

Figure 5-49

Exercise 5-11: Adding Gutters

1. Use the **JOIN/UNJOIN ROOF** file.
2. Change to the **Default 3D View.**
3. Select the **Modeling** tab in the **Design Bar**.
4. Select the **Host Sweep >> Roof Gutter** tool in the **Modeling** tab (see Figure 5-50).
5. Select the edge of the roof, and a gutter will appear (see Figure 5-51).

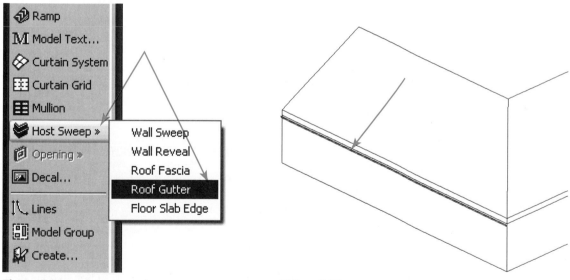

Figure 5-50   Figure 5-51

The default gutter is **Bevel 5′ × 5′**. If you expand **Families > Roofs > Gutter** in the **Project browser** you can see more gutters that have been included with the Revit template.

Gutters are created from profiles, and the profiles are located in the **Imperial Library > Families > Roofs** folder.

6. Change to the **East** view so that you can see the gutter in profile.
7. Select the gutter, **RMB**, and select **Element Properties** from the contextual menu to bring up the **Element Properties** dialog box.
8. In the **Element Properties** dialog box, press the **Edit/New** button to bring up the **Type Properties** dialog box.
9. In the **Type Properties** dialog box, select **Gutter profile – Rectangular : 6″ × 6″** from the profile drop-down list.

10. In the **Type Properties** dialog box, select the **Duplicate** button, and name the duplicate **Gutter – Rectangular 6″ × 6″**. Press the **Apply** button, and then press the **OK** button to return to the **Element Properties** dialog box.

11. In the **Element Properties** dialog box, change the **Vertical Profile Offset** to **1′-0″**, and watch the gutter move upward (see Figure 5-52).

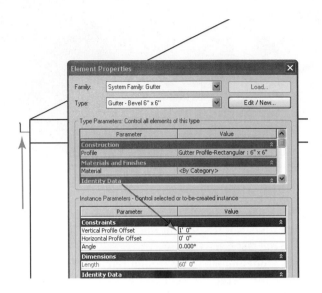

Figure 5-52

12. Experiment by changing profiles, and adjusting the **Vertical** and **Horizontal Profile Offsets**.

13. Save this file as **ROOF GUTTERS**.

Exercise 5-12: Creating a Roof Family

Revit ships with seven default Roofs. You create Roof structures in the same way you create wall types.

1. Open the **ROOF by FOOTPRINT** file.
2. Change to the **South Elevation** view.
3. Select the roof, **RMB**, and select **Element Properties** from the contextual menu to bring up the **Element Properties** dialog box.
4. In the **Element Properties** dialog box, select **Steel Truss – Insulation on Metal deck – EPDM** from the **Type** drop-down list.
5. In the **Element Properties** dialog box, press the **Edit/New** button to bring up the **Type Properties** dialog box.
6. In the **Type Properties** dialog box, press the **Edit** button in the **Structure** field to bring up the **Edit Assembly** dialog box.
7. In the **Edit Assembly** dialog box, at the lower left, press the **Preview** button to see a pre-view of the roof structure.

You can now see how the **Steel Truss – Insulation on Metal deck – EPDM** is structured.

The method for changing the structure is identical to that shown in Section 2 on Wall structures.

8. Experiment by changing the roof structure, and observe how the roof changes.
9. Save this file as **CREATING ROOF FAMILES.**

Exercise 5-13: Shape Editing: New Roof Slab Editing Options

1. Start a new drawing using the **RAC 2009\Imperial Templates\default.rte** template.
2. In the **Project browser**, double-click **Floor Plans > Level 1**.
3. In the **Design Bar**, under **Basics**, select the **Wall** tool.
4. Create **Basic 8″** walls **10′-0″** high as shown in Figure 5-53.

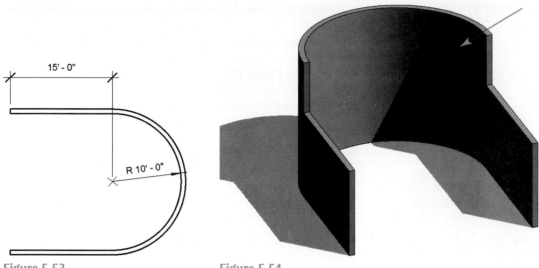

Figure 5-53   Figure 5-54

5. Change to the **Default 3D View**, and change the height of the arc wall to **16'-0"** (see Figure 5-54).
6. Change to the **East Elevation**, rename **Level 2** to **ROOF BASE**, and change its height to **8'-0"** (see Figure 5-55).

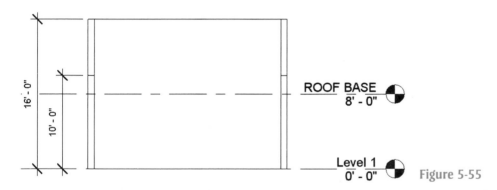

Figure 5-55

7. Double-click on the **ROOF BASE** floor plan in the **Project browser** to bring it up in the **Drawing Editor**.
8. In the **Design Bar**, **Basics** tab, select the **Roof > Roof by Footprint** tool to change into **Sketch** mode.
9. In the **Sketch** mode, select the **Pick Walls** button.
10. In the **Options** toolbar, uncheck the **Defines slope** check box.
11. Pick the inside of the three walls,
12. Next, in the **Sketch** mode, select the **Lines** button and complete the roof line (see Figures 5-56 and 5-57).

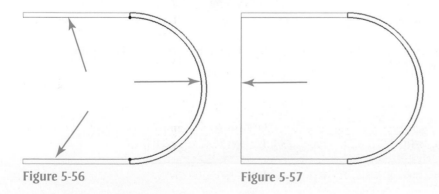

Figure 5-56   Figure 5-57

13. In **Sketch** mode, select the **Roof Properties** icon to bring up the **Element Properties** dialog box.
14. In the **Element Properties** dialog box, select **Generic -12″** for the **Type** and press the **OK** button.
15. Next, in the **Sketch** mode, select the **Finish Roof** button to create the roof.
16. Change to the **Default 3D View** (see Figure 5-58).
17. Select the roof, and choose the **Add new points to the slab shape** button from the **Options** toolbar (see Figure 5-59).

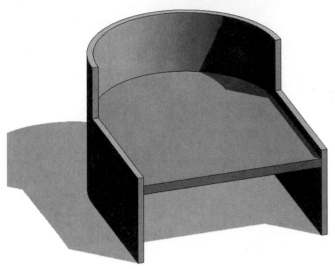

Figure 5-58

Figure 5-59

18. Select the middle of the curved section of roof to place a point (see Figure 5-60).

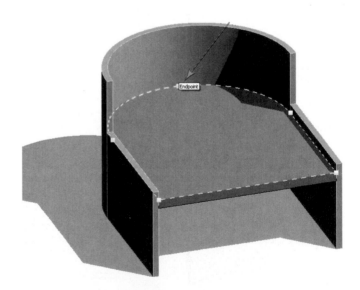

Figure 5-60

19. Next, choose the **Select and modify shapes** button from the **Options** toolbar (see Figure 5-61).

Figure 5-61

20. Select the point you just added (see Figure 5-62).

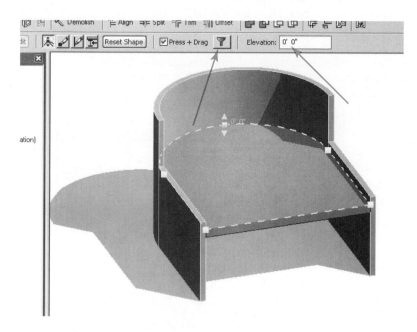

Figure 5-62

21. Select the point you just added, enter **3′-0″** in the **Options** toolbar, and then press the **<Enter>** key on your keyboard.
22. Pay attention to the warning, and then press the **<Esc>** key on your keyboard to complete the command (see Figure 5-63).

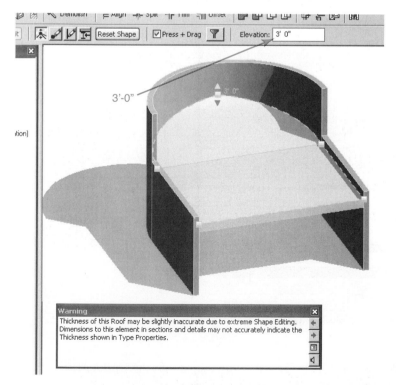

Figure 5-63

23. Select the roof, and press the **Element Properties** button on the **Options** toolbar to bring up the **Element Properties** dialog box (**1**).
24. Select the button opposite the **Curved Edge Condition** field (**2**).

25. Select the **Project to Side** radio button (**3**), and press the **OK** buttons to return to the **Drawing Editor** (see Figures 5-64 and 5-65).

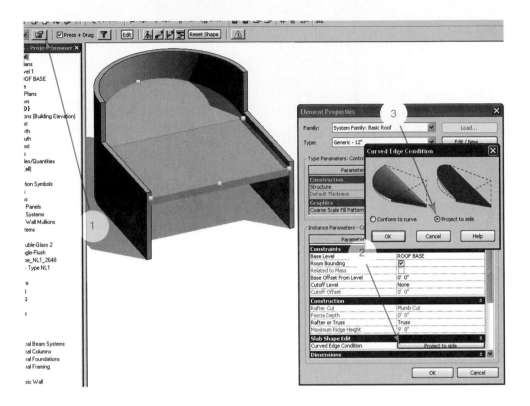

Figure 5-64

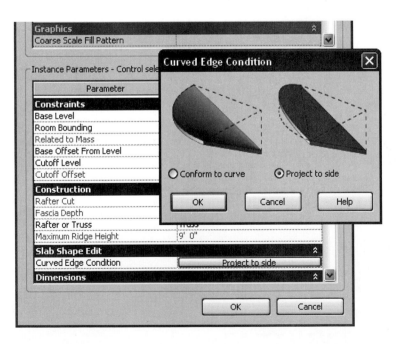

Figure 5-65

26. Again, select the **Add new points to the slab shape** button from the **Options** toolbar, and add a point at the midpoint of the slab.
27. Again, choose the **Select and modify shapes** button from the **Options** toolbar, and move the point downward **-4″** (see Figure 5-66).
28. Double-click on the **Site** in the **Project browser** to bring it up in the **Drawing Editor**.
29. Select the walls and roof, and then select the **Mirror** icon in the **Options** toolbar.

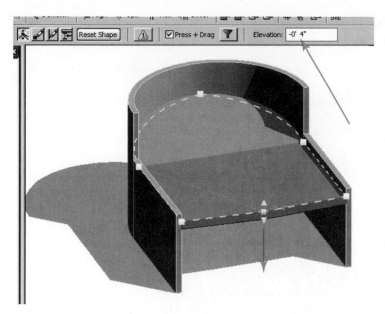

Figure 5-66

30. In the **Options** toolbar, select the **Pencil** tool, check the **Copy** check box, and drag an axis as shown in Figure 5-67.

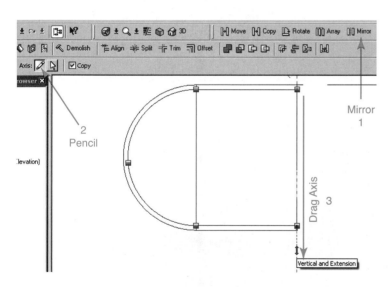

Figure 5-67

You will now have mirrored both sides of the building (see Figure 5-68).

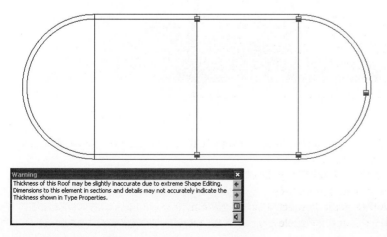

Figure 5-68

31. Change to the **Default 3D View** (see Figure 5-69).

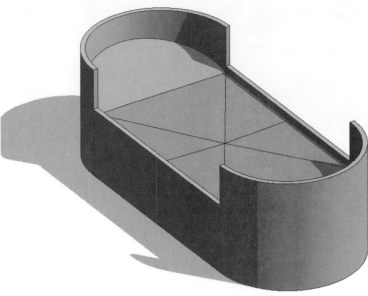

Figure 5-69

32. Adjust the wall heights and add windows, and you have a building with a Shape Edited roof (see Figure 5-70).
33. Save this file as **ROOF Shape Editing**.

Figure 5-70

SUMMARY

This section discussed the methods for creating and modifying roofs and dormers in Revit Architecture 2009.

Section Test Questions

True/false

1. True or False: Organic shaped roofs can be created in Revit.

2. True or False: Only rectangular openings can be created in Revit **Roofs.**

3. True or False: Revit allows you to change the materials and colors of the roof.

4. True or False: Revit has a tool for creating dormer openings in roofs.

Questions

1. What are the three methods for placing a roof?

2. What do you use **Sketch** mode for?

3. What is the **Slope Arrow** used for?

4. When do you use a **Roof by Extrusion**?

5. What is the purpose of **Shape Editing**?

6. What does the **Join/Unjoin Roof** tool do?

Floors

6

Section Objectives

- Learn how to create a floor by **Face**.
- Learn how to place a floor by **Walls**.
- Learn how to create a **Floor Family**.
- Learn how to add a floor slab edge.
- Learn how to use the Edit Cut Profile command.

In Revit Architecture, **Floors** are horizontal slabs. These slabs can be used for any horizontal purpose such as countertops, ceilings, and so on. As with Walls and Roofs, **Floors** can be configured with components such as structure, floor finishes, carpet, and so on.

You create floors by sketching them. You can sketch lines by picking walls or by using the **Lines** command in the sketch editor. You typically want to sketch a floor in a plan view, although you can sketch it in a 3D view, provided the work plane of the 3D view is set to the work plane of a plan view. Floors are automatically offset downward from the level on which they are sketched.

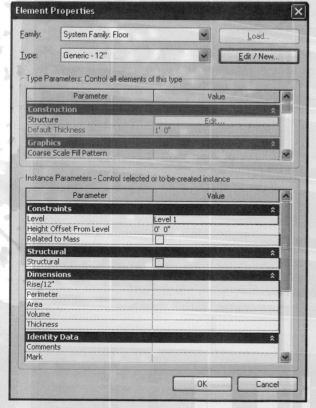

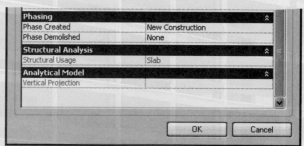

Constraints	
Level	The level with which the floor is associated.
Height Offset From Level	The height at which the floor is offset from the level.
Room Bounding	Bounding for room area and volume computations.
Related to Mass	Indicates that the element was created from a mass element. This is a read-only value.
Structural	
Structural	Indicates that the element has an analytical model. This is a read-only value.
Curved End Condition	**Conform to curve** or **Project to side.**
Dimensions	
Slope (Slope Angle; Rise/12" for Imperial; Rise/1,000 for metric)	Changes the value of slope-defining lines to the specified value, without the need to edit the sketch. The parameter initially displays a value if there is a slope-defining line. If there is no slope-defining line, the parameter is blank and disabled.
Perimeter	The perimeter of the floor. This is a read-only value.
Area	The area of the floor. This is a read-only value.
Volume	The volume of the floor. This is a read-only value.
Thickness	Indicates the thickness of the floor. This is a read-only value.
Identity Data	
Comments	Specific comments related to the floor that are not already covered in the description or type comments.
Mark	A user-specified label for the floor. This value must be unique for each floor in a project. Revit Architecture warns you if the number is already used, but allows you to continue using it. You can see the warning using the **REVIEW WARNINGS** command.
Phasing	
Phase Created	The phase when the floor was created.
Phase Demolished	The phase when the floor was demolished.
Structural Analysis	
Structural Usage	Sets the structural usage of the floor. This property is read-only before the floor is created. After you draw the floor, you can select it and then modify this property.
Analytical Model	
Vertical Projection	The plane of the floor used for analysis and design.

As with roofs, **Floors** can be created by three methods: by **Picking Walls,** by **Sketching with Lines,** or by selecting **Mass** faces.

FLOOR BY FACE

Floor by Face is used to place a floor on any horizontal face of a **Mass** model. The use of this feature is covered in Section 1 on Massing.

Exercise 6-1: Floor by Picking Walls

1. Start a new drawing using the **RAC 2009\Imperial Templates\default.rte** template.
2. In the **Project browser**, double-click **Floor Plans > Level 1** to bring it up into the **Drawing Editor**.
3. Using the **Wall** tool in the **Basics** tab of the **Design Bar**, select the **Basic Wall: Exterior – Brick on CMU wall** from the **Options** toolbar, and place a **15′-0″ × 30′-0″** rectangular enclosure **10′-0″** high.
4. Select **Medium** from the **Detail level** icon at the bottom of the Drawing Editor (see Figure 6-1).

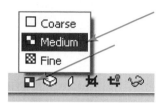

Figure 6-1

This will show all the detail in the wall in the plan view.

5. Select **Floor** from the **Basics** tab in the **Design Bar**.
6. Select **Pick Walls** from the **Sketch** tab (see Figure 6-2).
7. In the **Options** toolbar, check the **Extend into wall (to core)** check box.
8. Click on the northmost wall, and notice the sketch line appears at the outer face of the wall core.
9. Repeat, clicking on the remaining walls (see Figure 6-3).
10. When you have created all the floor edge lines, select the **Floor Properties** tool from the **Sketch** tab to bring up the **Element Properties** dialog box.

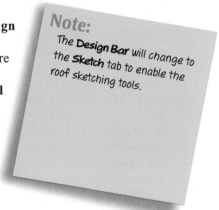

Note: The **Design Bar** will change to the **Sketch** tab to enable the roof sketching tools.

Figure 6-2

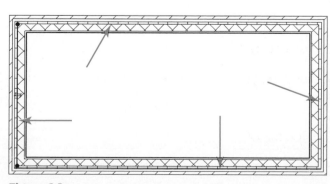

Figure 6-3

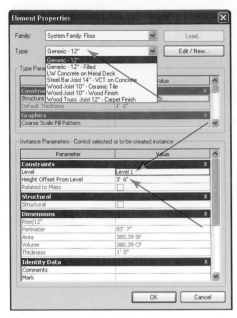

Figure 6-4

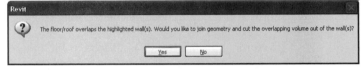

Figure 6-5

11. In the **Element Properties** dialog box, set the settings shown in Figure 6-4. (Make sure that the **Height Offset From Level** is set to **3′-0″**.)

12. Press the **Finish Sketch** tool in the **Sketch** tab, and select **Yes** when the **Revit** dialog box says **The floor/roof overlaps the highlighted wall(s). Would you like to join geometry and cut the overlapping volume out of the wall(s)?** (see Figure 6-5).

13. In the **Design Bar,** in the **Basics** tab, select the **Section** tool.

14. Place a section as shown in Figure 6-6.

15. Expand **Sections [Building section]** in the **Project browser**, and double-click on **Section 1** (the section you just created) to bring the section up in the **Drawing Editor**.

Note:
This will place the floor **3′-0″** above **Level 1.**

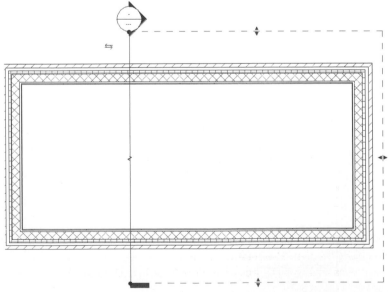

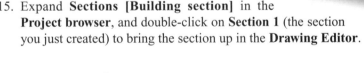

Figure 6-6

16. Select **Medium** from the **Detail level** icon at the bottom of the **Drawing Editor**.

Notice that the floor has been cut out of the wall. If you move the floor vertically in the section, the wall "heals" as the floor is moved (see Figure 6-7).

17. Save this file as **FLOOR by FOOTPRINT**.

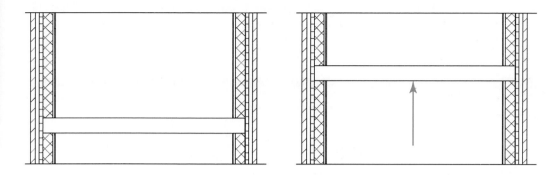

Figure 6-7

Exercise 6-2: Creating and Modifying a Floor Family

Revit ships with seven default **Floors**. A Floor type structure is created in the same manner as you create wall and roof types.

1. Using the previous exercise, make sure you are still in **Section 1**.
2. Select the floor, **RMB**, and select **Element Properties** from the contextual menu that appears to bring up the **Element Properties** dialog box.
3. In the **Element Properties** dialog box, set the **Level** to **1** and the **Height Offset From Level** to **0'-0"**.
4. In the **Element Properties** dialog box, select **Wood joist 10" – Wood Finish** from the **Type** drop-down list and press the **OK** button.
5. Set the scale to **1/2" = 1'-0"** , and press the **Thin Lines** icon on the **View** toolbar (see Figure 6-8).

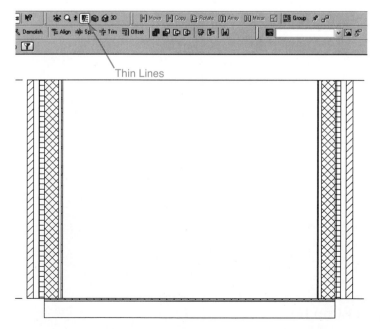

Figure 6-8

6. Again, select the floor, **RMB**, and select **Element Properties** from the contextual menu that appears to bring up the **Element Properties** dialog box.
7. In the **Element Properties** dialog box, press the **Edit/New** button to open the **Type Properties** dialog box.

8. In the **Type Properties** dialog box, press the **Edit** button in the **Structure** field to bring up the **Edit Assembly** dialog box.

9. In the **Edit Assembly** dialog box, at the lower left, press the **Preview** button to see a preview of the floor structure.

10. In the **Edit Assembly** dialog box, press the **Duplicate** button, and name the new floor **CONCRETE 6″ – Wood Finish**.

11. In the **Edit Assembly** dialog box, select **Layer 4 – Structure [1]** and change its **Material** from **Structure: Wood joist/Rafter Layer** to **Concrete - Cast-in-Place Concrete** (see Figure 6-9).

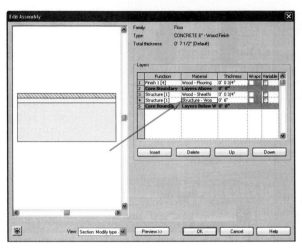
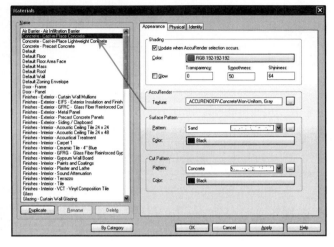

Figure 6-9

12. Change the thickness of **Layer 4 – Structure [1]** to **6″** and press the **OK** buttons to return to the **Drawing Editor**.

Floors by default automatically change their thickness from the level they are on—downwards (see Figure 6-10).

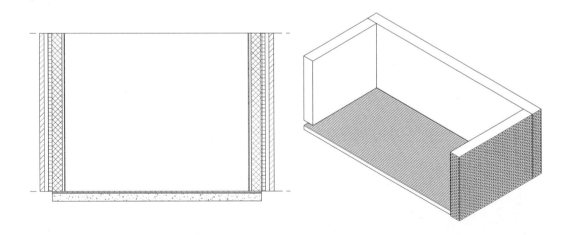

Figure 6-10

13. Experiment making changes in floor layer sizes and materials.

14. Save this file as **FLOOR FAMILIES**.

Exercise 6-3: Changing and Modifying a Floor Slab Edge

1. Using the previous exercise, make sure both the **Section 1** and **Default 3D** views are open in the **Drawing Editor**.

2. Hide one wall as shown previously in Figure 6-10.

3. Change to the **Modeling** tab in the **Design Bar**.
4. In the **Modeling** tab, select **Host Sweep > Floor Slab Edge** (see Figure 6-11).

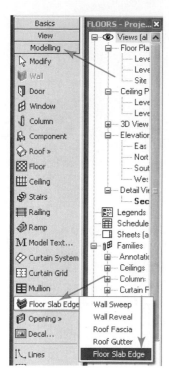

Figure 6-11

5. In the **Options** toolbar, select **Slab Edge: Thickened 24″ × 12″** from the drop-down list.
6. Select the lower edge of the floor (slab) in the **Default 3D View** or the lower left edge of the floor (slab) in the **Section 1** view.

The thickened slab edge will appear. This edge is created from a profile (see Figure 6-12).

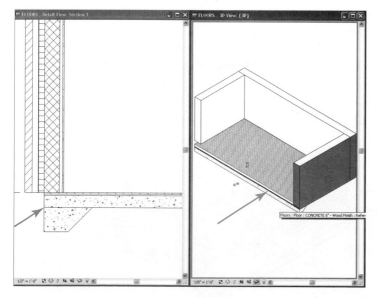

Figure 6-12

To change the shape of the edge, you will need to change the profile. The **Slab Edge Profiles** are located in the **Imperial** or **Metric** libraries.

7. Select **File > Open** from the **Main** menu to bring up the **Open** dialog box.
8. In the **Open** dialog box, select the **Imperial** (or Metric) **Library** at the left side of the dialog box to bring up the **Imperial Library**.

9. In the **Imperial Library**, open the **Profiles > Structural** folder.
10. In the **Structural** folder you will find the included **Slab Edge** profiles.
11. Double-click the **Slab Edge-Thickened** profile to bring it up in the **Drawing Editor**.
12. Using lines, change the **Slab Edge-Thickened** profile to that shown in Figure 6-13.
13. Select **File > Save As**, save the file as **Slab Edge – TEST** in the **Profiles > Structural** folder, and close the file.
14. Bring **Section 1** into the **Drawing Editor**.
15. Select **File > Load from library > Load Family** and locate the **Profiles > Structural** folder.

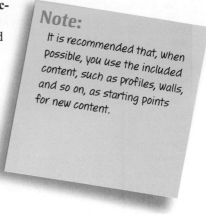

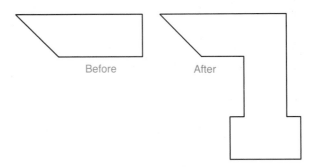

Figure 6-13

16. Double-click the **Slab Edge – TEST** file to load it into the session.
17. In the **Section 1** view, select the slab edge you previously placed, **RMB**, and select **Element Properties** from the contextual menu that appears to bring up the **Element Properties** dialog box.
18. In the **Element Properties** dialog box, press the **Edit/New** button to open the **Type Properties** dialog box.
19. In the **Type in Properties** dialog box, press the **Duplicate** button to bring up the **Name** dialog box. Type in **TEST EDGE with FOOTING,** and press the **OK** button to return to the **Type Properties** dialog box.
20. In the **Type Properties** dialog box, change the profile to **Slab Edge –TEST: 36″ × 12″**, and press the **OK** buttons to return to the **Drawing Editor** (see Figure 6-14).

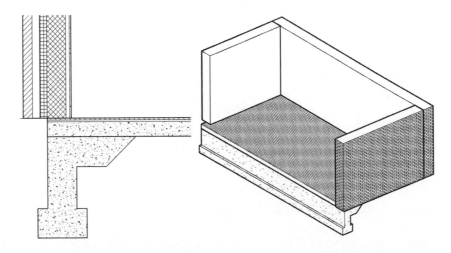

Figure 6-14

21. While in **Section 1**, select the **Join Geometry** icon from the **Tools** toolbar (see Figure 6-15).
22. Select the edge you just placed, and then select the slab itself—the two objects join as one (see Figure 6-16).

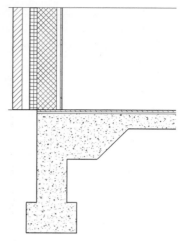

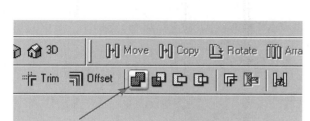

Figure 6-15   Figure 6-16

23. Experiment making changes in **Floor Slab Edges** and **Floor Slab Edge** profiles.
24. Save this file as **FLOOR SLAB EDGES**.

Exercise 6-4: Using the Edit Cut Profile Command

1. Using the previous exercise, make sure you are in the **Section 1** view.
2. Select the **Unjoin Geometry** icon from the **Tools** toolbar.
3. Select the floor slab edge you previously joined. It will unjoin into two elements.
4. Select the **Edit Cut Profile** icon from the **Tools** toolbar, and also select the **Boundary between faces** radio button in the **Options** toolbar (see Figure 6-17).

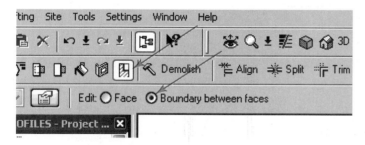

Figure 6-17

5. Select the floor slab edge. Its outline will change color, and the **Design Bar** will go into **Sketch** mode.
6. In the **Sketch** tab in the **Design Bar,** select the **Lines** tool and create the lines shown in Figure 6-18.
7. In the **Sketch** tab in the **Design Bar,** press the **Finish Sketch** button to complete the profile cut.

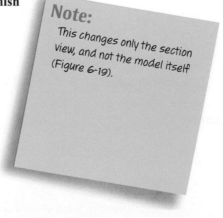

Note:
This changes only the section view, and not the model itself (Figure 6-19).

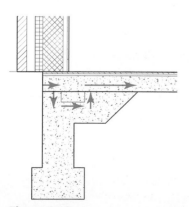

Figure 6-18

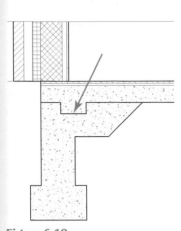

Figure 6-19

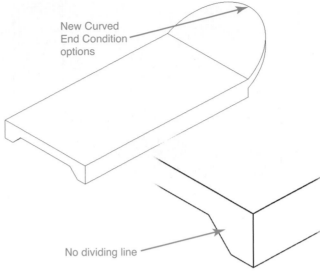

New Curved
End Condition
options

No dividing line

Figure 6-20

8. Save this file as **EDIT CUT PROFILE**.

The operations of modifying a **Floor** slope with the **Slope Arrow,** creating a hole in a **Floor Slab,** and modifying a **Floor Slab** by moving vertices are all done in the same manner as those shown in Section 5 on Roofs. Please refer to that section, and make sure you can use the commands presented there.

There are two new features for **Floor Slabs**:

Shape Editing new **Floor Curved End Condition** options. These are the same as the new **Roof Slab Curved End Condition** options (see Section 5).

Host Sweep > Floor Slab Edge now integrates with the slab, and leaves no line at the division (see Figure 6-20).

SUMMARY

This section discussed the methods for creating and modifying **Floor Slabs.** Included were methods for adding and modifying **Floor Slab Edges,** editing the floor by vertices, and using the **Edit Cut Profile** tool.

SECTION TEST QUESTIONS

Questions

1. What controls the shape of **Floor Slab Edges?**

2. What is the difference between **Floor Slabs** and **Roof Slabs** in Revit Architecture?

3. Under what conditions can you create floors by face?

4. Explain how you create floors by picking walls.

5. What does the **Extend into wall** check box do?

6. What does the **Edit Cut Profile** tool do?

7. Where in the interface is the **Floor Slab Edge** tool located?

8. In which direction—above or below the level—is the slab created?

Stairs, Railings, and Ramps

7

Section Objectives

- Know the definitions used in creating stairs.
- Know how to create and modify **Straight** stairs using the **Run** tool.
- Know how to create and modify **U-shaped** stairs using the **Run** tool.
- Learn how to add and delete risers.
- Learn how to create and modify stairs using the **Boundary** tool.
- Learn how to create **Multistory** stairs.
- Learn how to create **Monolithic** stairs.
- Know how to modify **Rail** objects.
- Learn how to host **Rail** objects.
- Learn how to create **Ramps**.

Stairs, railings, and ramps are an important part of almost every project, and it is here that designers often make mistakes. Revit Architecture 2009's stair and railing systems aid in the productivity and accuracy of these objects. Because of the complexity and variance of stairs, there are a multitude of settings. Once these settings are understood and preset, placing and modifying stairs is quite easy. By creating your own families, you can place stairs, railings, and ramps into a project quickly and efficiently.

Before you start these exercises, it is a good idea to understand stair concepts. Among these are **Rise and Run, Tread, Riser, Nosing,** and **Stringer.**

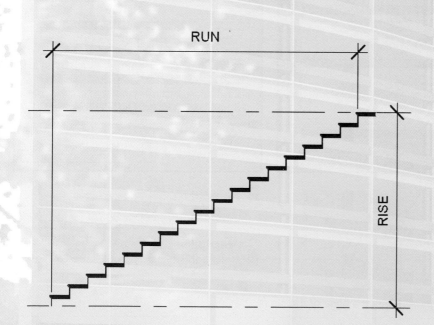

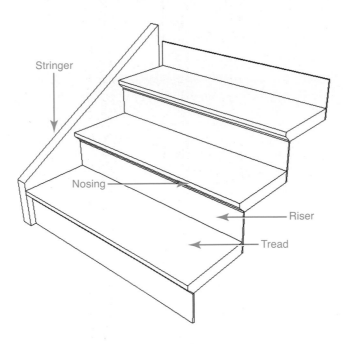

Stringer

Nosing

Riser

Tread

STAIR ELEMENT PROPERTIES

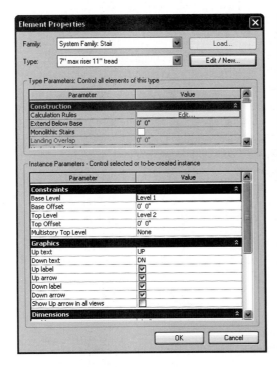

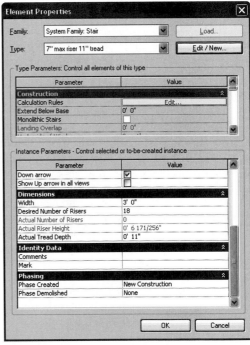

Name	Description
Constraints	
Base Level	Sets the base of the stairs.
Base Offset	Sets the stair's height from its base level.
Top Level	Sets the top of the stairs.

Name	Description
Top Offset	Sets the stair's offset from the top level.
Multistory Top Level	Sets the top of the stairs in a multistory building. The advantage to using this parameter (as opposed to sketching individual runs) is that if you change the railing on one run, that railing is changed on all the runs. Also, if you use this parameter, the Revit Architecture project file size does not change as significantly as it would if you sketched individual runs. **NOTE:** The levels in the multistory building should be a uniform distance apart.
Graphics	
Up Text	Sets the text for the Up symbol in plan. The default value is **UP**.
Down Text	Sets the text for the Down symbol in plan. The default value is **DN**.
Up Label	Displays or hides the Up label in plan.
Up Arrow	Displays or hides the Up arrow in plan.
Down Label	Displays or hides the Down label in plan.
Down Arrow	Displays or hides the Down arrow in plan.
Show Up arrow in all views	Displays the Up arrow in all project views.
Dimensions	
Width	Width of the stairs.
Desired Number of Risers	The number of risers is calculated based on the height between levels.
Actual Number of Risers	Normally, the same as **Desired Number of Risers**. However, it may be different if you do not complete adding the correct number of risers for the given run of the stairs. This is a read-only value.
Actual Riser Height	Displays the actual riser height. The value is equal to or less than the value specified in **Maximum Riser Height**. This is a read-only value.
Actual Tread Depth	You can set this value to change the tread depth without having to create a new stair type. Also, the **Stair Calculator** can change this value to satisfy the stair equation.
Identity Data	
Comments	Specific comments on the staircase.
Mark	A label created for the stairs. This value must be unique for each stairway in a project. Revit Architecture warns you if the number is already used but allows you to continue using it. (You can see the warning using the **REVIEW WARNINGS** command.)
Phasing	
Phase Created	The phase when the stairs were created.
Phase Demolished	The phase when the stairs were demolished.

There are basically two ways to create stairs: by **Run** or by **Boundary**. Both these methods ulti-mately are similar when you edit them.

Exercise 7-1: Creating and Modifying Stairs by the Run Method

Straight Stairs

1. Start a new drawing using the **RAC 2009\Imperial Templates\default.rte** template.
2. In the **Project browser**, double-click **Floor Plans > Level 1** to bring it up into the **Drawing Editor**.
3. Change to the **Modeling** tab in the **Design Bar**.
4. In the **Modeling** tab, select the **Stairs** tool.

The **Design Bar** will change to **Sketch** mode.

5. In the **Sketch** tab, select **Run** (see Figure 7-1).

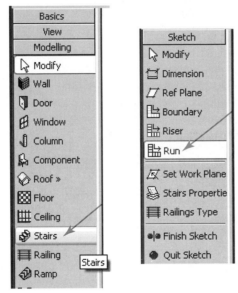

Figure 7-1

6. In the **Sketch** tab, select the **Railings Type** icon, select **Handrail-Rectangular** from the drop-down list, and press the **OK** button.
7. Select **Stairs Properties** in the **Sketch** tab to bring up the **Element Properties** dialog box.
8. In the **Element Properties** dialog box, set the **Base Level** to **Level 1**, **Top level** to **Level 2**, **Up text** to **UP**, **Down text** to **DN**, and check the **Up label**, **Up arrow**, **Down label**, and **Down arrow** check boxes.
9. **Uncheck** the **Show Up arrows in all views** check box. (You only want to see **Up** arrows in the Plan views.)
10. Still in the **Element Properties** dialog box, set the width to **4'-0"**.

You can change the **Desired Number of Risers**, but there is no need as Revit automatically calculates this for you based on the difference between the **Base Level** and **Top Level**.

11. Still in the **Element Properties** dialog box, set the **Phase Created** to **New Construction**.
12. A pencil cursor will appear. Click and drag your cursor to the right until you see **15'-7"** appear, and click again.

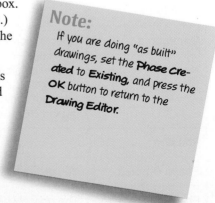

Note:
If you are doing "as built" drawings, set the **Phase Created** to **Existing**, and press the **OK** button to return to the **Drawing Editor**.

13. In the **Sketch** tab, press **Finish Sketch** to create the stair (see Figures 7-2 and 7-3).

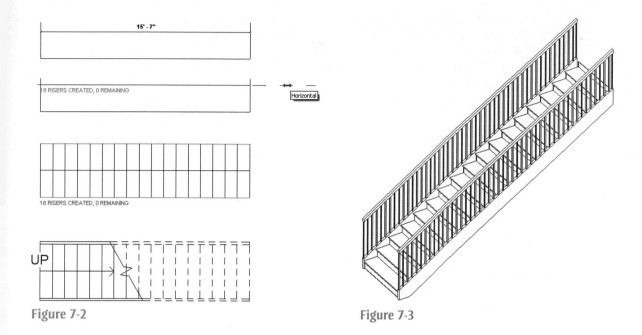

Figure 7-2   Figure 7-3

14. Be sure you are in the **Level 1** floor plan.
15. Select the stair. (Be sure to select the stair and not the railing by checking the drop-down list in the **Options** toolbar.)
16. Select the **Edit** button that appears in the **Options** toolbar to bring up the **Sketch** mode in the **Design Bar**.

The stair will return to **Sketch** mode.

17. Select the bottom left grip of the stair, and drag it downward.
18. In the **Sketch** tab, again press **Finish Sketch** to create the changed stair (see Figure 7-4).

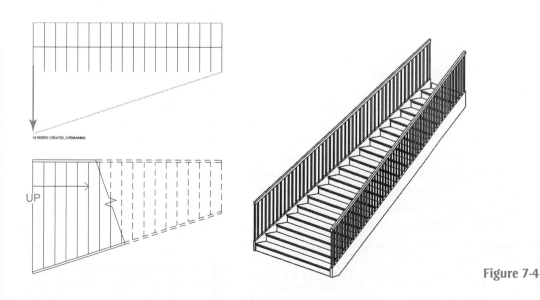

Figure 7-4

19. In the **Level 1** floor plan, select the stair again.
20. Again select the **Edit** button that appears in the **Options** toolbar to bring up the **Sketch** mode in the **Design Bar**.
21. Select the **Boundary** button in the **Sketch** tab.

The **Pick Lines** and **Draw** buttons as well as the drawing tools will appear on the **Options** toolbar.

22. Delete the line you moved in the previous exercise.
23. Pick the **Arc passing through three points** tool.
24. Place the line you just deleted with an arc.
25. In the **Sketch** tab, again press **Finish Sketch** to create the changed stair (see Figures 7-5 and 7-6).

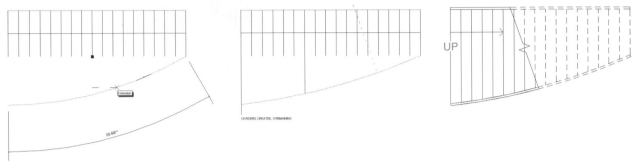

Figure 7-5

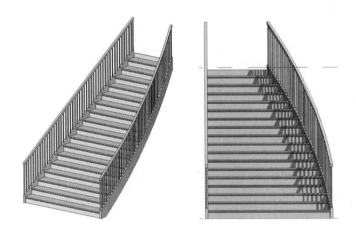

Figure 7-6

26. Save this file as **STRAIGHT STAIRS**.

Exercise 7-2: Creating and Modifying Stairs by the Run Method

"U"-shaped Stairs

1. Start a new drawing using the **RAC 2009\Imperial Templates\default.rte** template.
2. In the **Project browser**, double-click **Floor Plans > Level 1** to bring it up into the **Drawing Editor**.
3. Change to the **Modeling** tab in the **Design Bar**.
4. In the **Modeling** tab, select the **Stairs** tool.

The **Design Bar** will change to **Sketch** mode.

5. Select **Stair Properties** in the **Sketch** tab to bring up the **Element Properties** dialog box.
6. Set the parameters in the **Element Properties** dialog box to be the same as in the previous exercise.
7. In the **Sketch** tab, select **Run.**
8. Click and then drag your cursor to the right until the message **6 RISERS CREATED, 12 REMAINING** appears, and click again.
9. Drag your cursor downward, and click again.
10. Drag your cursor to the left, and click again to create the stair lines (see Figures 7-7 and 7-8).

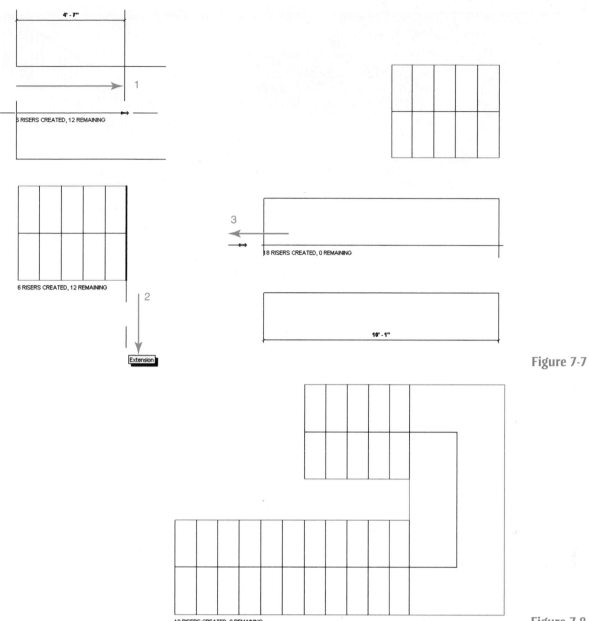

Figure 7-7

Figure 7-8

11. In the **Sketch** tab, again press **Finish Sketch** to create the changed stair (see Figures 7-9 and 7-10).

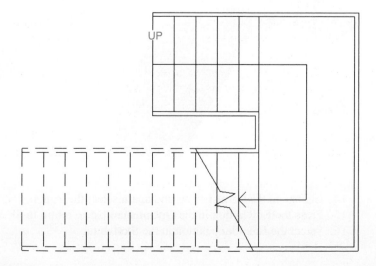

Figure 7-9

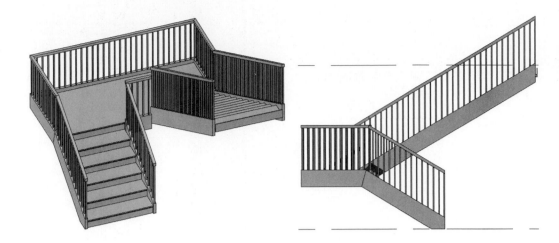

Figure 7-10

12. Return to the **Level 1** floor plan, and select the stair. Notice the small arrow shown in Figure 7-11.
13. Click the arrow to change the **Up/Down** direction of the stair, and change to the **Default 3D View** to see the change (see Figure 7-12).

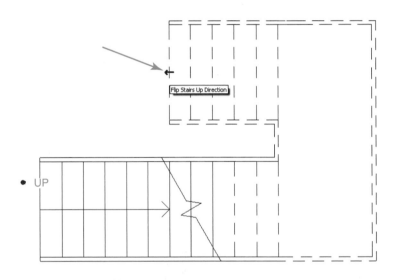

Figure 7-11

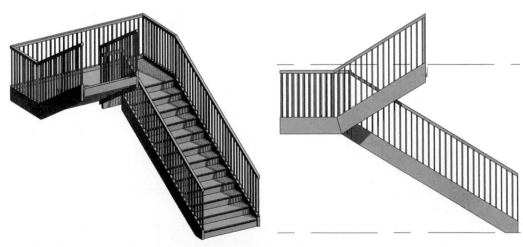

Figure 7-12

14. Change to the **Level 1** view, and again select the stair.
15. Press the **Edit** button in the **Options** toolbar to return to **Sketch** mode.
16. Select the **Boundary** button in the **Sketch** tab.

The **Pick Lines** and **Draw** buttons as well as the drawing tools will appear on the **Options** toolbar.

17. Select the **Rectangle** tool, and place a rectangle over the landing.
18. Using the **Split** tool in the **Tools** toolbar, adjust the landing as shown in Figure 7-13.

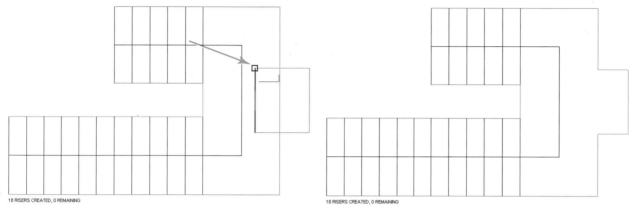

18 RISERS CREATED, 0 REMAINING   18 RISERS CREATED, 0 REMAINING

Figure 7-13

19. In the **Sketch** tab, again press **Finish Sketch** to create the changed stair (see Figure 7-14).

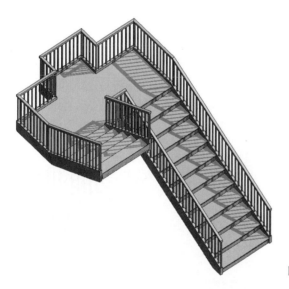

Figure 7-14

20. Save this file as **U SHAPED STAIRS**.

Exercise 7-3: Creating and Modifying Stairs by the Run Method

Adding and Deleting Risers

1. Return to the **Level 1** floor plan view.
2. Press the **Edit** button in the **Options** toolbar to return to **Sketch** mode.
3. Delete three risers from the long run.
4. Drag the centerline toward the right.
5. Drag the centerline of the short run to the left.
6. In the **Sketch** tab, again press **Finish Sketch** to create the changed stair (see Figures 7-15 and 7-16).
7. Experiment changing the stairs by returning to **Sketch** mode and using the **Boundary** tools.
8. Save this file as **CHANGING RISERS**.

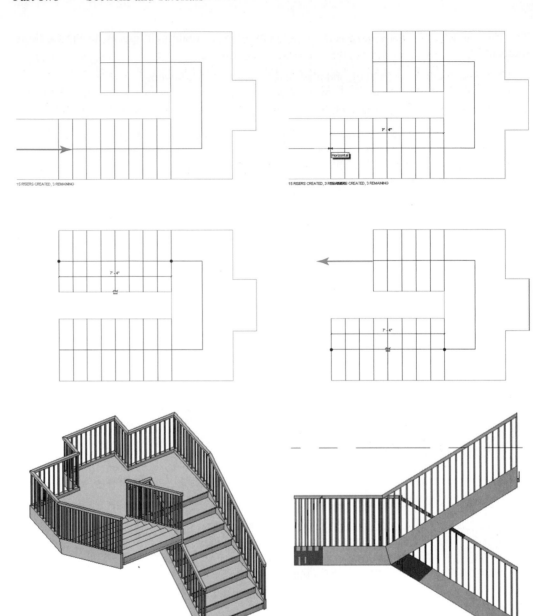

Figure 7-15

Figure 7-16

Exercise 7-4: Creating and Modifying Stairs Using Boundary Method

1. Start a new drawing using the **RAC 2009\ Imperial Templates\default.rte** template.
2. In the **Project browser**, double-click **Floor Plans > Level 1** to bring it up into the **Drawing Editor**.
3. Change to the **Modeling** tab in the **Design Bar**.
4. In the **Modeling** tab, select the **Stairs** tool.
5. Select **Stair Properties** in the **Sketch** tab to bring up the **Element Properties** dialog box.
6. Set the parameters in the **Element Properties** dialog box to be the same as in the previous exercises.

Note:

If you want to see or change the way the **Stair Calculator** calculates, do the following:

a. In the **Element Properties** dialog box, press the **Edit/New** button to open the **Type Properties** dialog box.

b. In the **Type Properties** dialog box, press the **Edit** button in the **Calculation Rules** field to bring up the **Stair Calculator** dialog box.

c. The calculator has been set for **IBC** and **BOCA** codes, so leave it alone.

d. Press the **OK** buttons to return to the **Drawing Editor**.

7. In the **Element Properties** dialog box, also notice that the **Desired Number of Risers** is **18** (automatically calculated by the **Stair Calculator**).
8. In the **Sketch** tab select the **Boundary** tool, select the **Line** tool from the **Options** toolbar, and place a line **10′-0″** long.

Notice that the statement below the lines reads **0 RISERS CREATED, 18 REMAINING.**

9. Select the **Boundary** tool again, and select the **Arc passing through three points** tool from the **Options** toolbar.
10. Select the **Riser** tool from the **Sketch** tab, and place a riser joining the two **Boundary** lines (see Figure 7-17).

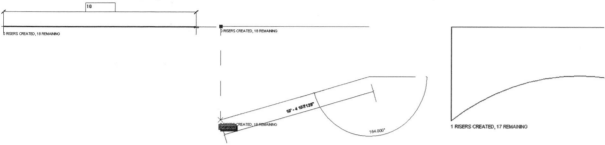

Figure 7-17

Notice that the readout below the bottom boundary tells you how many risers you have placed, and how many more need to be offset.

11. Select the **Offset** tool in the **Tools** toolbar, set it to **0′-11″**, and check the **Copy** check box (see Figure 7-18).

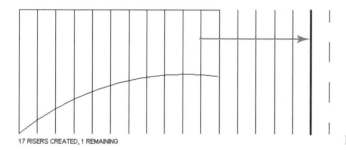

Figure 7-18

12. After you see that all the risers have been offset, drag the top boundary line to meet the last riser.
13. Select the **Boundary** tool again, and select the **Arc passing through three points** tool from the **Options** toolbar.
14. Add an additional arc line from the first arc to the last riser.
15. In the **Sketch** tab, again press **Finish Sketch** to create the changed stair (see Figures 7-19 and 7-20).

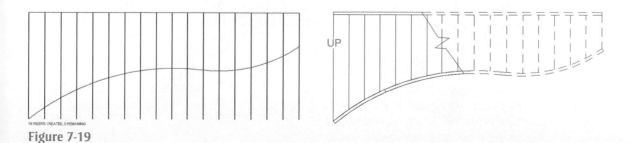

Figure 7-19

Figure 7-20

16. Experiment changing the stairs by returning to **Sketch** mode and using the **Boundary** tools.
17. Save this file as **BOUNDARY STAIRS**.

Exercise 7-5: Creating Multistory Stairs

Multistory buildings need repeating stairs or **Stair Towers**. Revit Architecture makes this process easy.

1. Start a new drawing using the **RAC 2009\Imperial Templates\default.rte** template.
2. In the **Project browser**, double-click **Floor Plans > Level 1** to bring it up into the **Drawing Editor**.
3. Using the information you have learned in the previous exercises, create a **3′-0″** wide **U Shaped** stair with even runs up and down (see Figure 7-21).

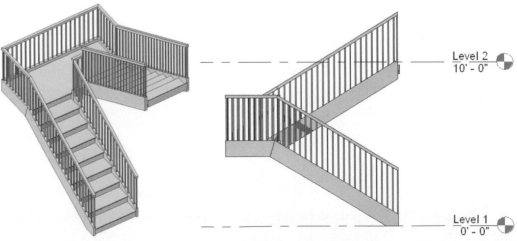

Figure 7-21

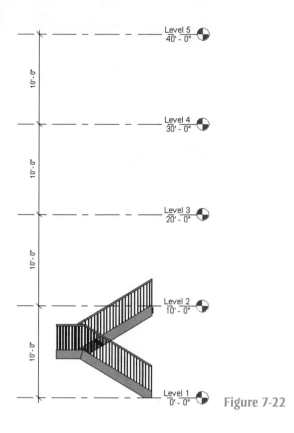

Figure 7-22

4. Change to the **North Elevation** and add three more levels—**10′-0″** from level to level (see Figure 7-22).
5. Select the stair, **RMB**, and select **Element Properties** from the contextual menu that appears to bring up the **Element Properties** dialog box.
6. In the **Element Properties** dialog box, select **Level 5** from the **Multistory Top Level** drop-down list (see Figure 7-23).

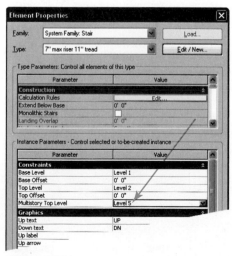

Figure 7-23

7. Press the **OK** button to finish the command and return to the **Drawing Editor** (see Figure 7-24).
8. Save this file as **MULTISTORY STAIRS**.

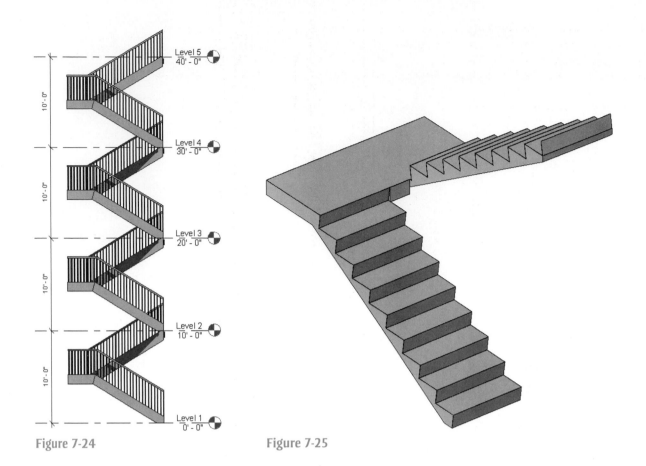

Figure 7-24

Figure 7-25

Exercise 7-6: Creating Monolithic Stairs

In Revit Architecture 2009, cast concrete stairs are called **Monolithic** stairs.

1. Start a new drawing using the **RAC 2009\Imperial Templates\default.rte** template.
2. In the **Project browser**, double-click **Floor Plans > Level 1** to bring it up into the **Drawing Editor**.
3. Using the information you have learned in the previous exercises, create a **3'-0"** wide **U Shaped** stair with even runs up and down.
4. Change to the **Default 3D View**.
5. Select the stair, **RMB**, and select **Element Properties** from the contextual menu that appears to bring up the **Element Properties** dialog box.
6. In the **Element Properties** dialog box, select the **Edit/New** button to bring up the **Type Properties** dialog box.
7. In the **Type Properties** dialog box, check the **Monolithic** check box, set the tread and riser thickness to **1/16"**, select **Slanted** from the **Riser** type drop-down list, and then press the **OK** buttons to return to the **Drawing Editor** (see Figure 7-25).
8. Save this file as **MONOLITHIC STAIRS**.

RAILINGS

You can add railings as free-standing components to levels, or attach them to hosts (such as floors, ramps, or stairs).

Exercise 7-7: Modifying Railings

1. Start a new drawing using the **RAC 2009\Imperial Templates\default.rte** template.
2. In the **Project browser**, double-click **Floor Plans > Level 1** to bring it up into the **Drawing Editor**.

3. Using the information you have learned in the previous exercises, again create a **3'-0"** wide **U Shaped** stair with even runs up and down.
4. Change to the **Default 3D View**.
5. Select one of the rails, and change the drop-down list to **Handrail – Pipe** in the **Options** toolbar.
6. Repeat the process for the other rail (see Figure 7-26).

Figure 7-26

7. Select the rail, **RMB**, and select **Element Properties** from the contextual menu that appears to bring up the **Element Properties** dialog box.
8. In the **Element Properties** dialog box, select the **Edit/New** button to bring up the **Type Properties** dialog box.
9. In the **Type Properties** dialog box, select the **Edit** button in the rail **Structure** field to bring up the **Edit Rails** dialog box (see Figure 7-27).

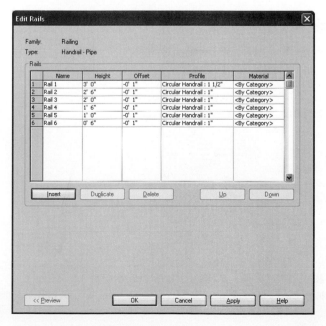

Figure 7-27

10. In the **Edit Rails** dialog box, change the **Rail 1 Profile** to **Rectangular Handrail: 2″ × 3″** from the **Profile** drop-down list, and then press the **OK** buttons to return to the **Drawing Editor** (see Figure 7-28).

11. Save this file as **MODIFYING RAILINGS**.

Note:
The rails and baluster shapes are controlled by profiles. As shown in previous sections, you can start with the default profiles and modify them to create new profiles. The rail profiles are contained in the **Profiles > Stairs** folder in either the **Imperial** or **Metric** libraries (see Figure 7-29).

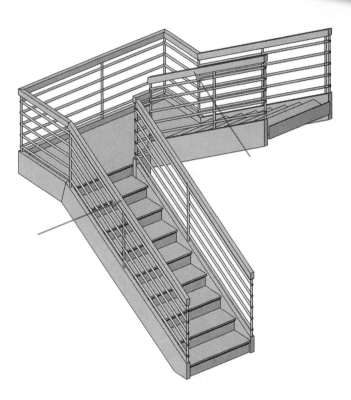

Figure 7-28

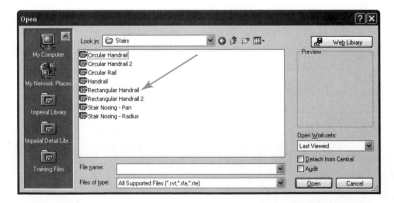

Figure 7-29

Exercise 7-8: Hosting Railings

Hosting allows you to attach railings to objects such as floors, slabs, and so on.

1. Start a new drawing using the **RAC 2009\Imperial Templates\default.rte** template.
2. In the **Project browser**, double-click **Floor Plans > Level 1** to bring it up into the **Drawing Editor**.

3. Select the **Floor** tool from the **Basics** tab in the **Design Bar** to enter **Sketch** mode.
4. In the **Sketch** tab in the **Design Bar**, select **Lines**.
5. Place a **10′ × 15′** rectangle in the **Drawing Editor**, and then press **Finish Sketch** in the **Sketch** tab to complete the floor.
6. Change to the **Modeling** tab in the **Design Bar**.
7. In the **Modeling** tab, select **Railing** to enter **Sketch** mode.
8. In the **Sketch** tab in the **Design Bar**, select **Set Host**, and select the floor you just created.
9. Change to the **Level 1** floor plan.
10. Select **Lines** from the **Sketch** tab in the **Design Bar**.
11. Place lines where you want a rail, and press **Finish Sketch** to create the railing (see Figure 7-30).
12. Save this file as **HOSTED RAILINGS**.

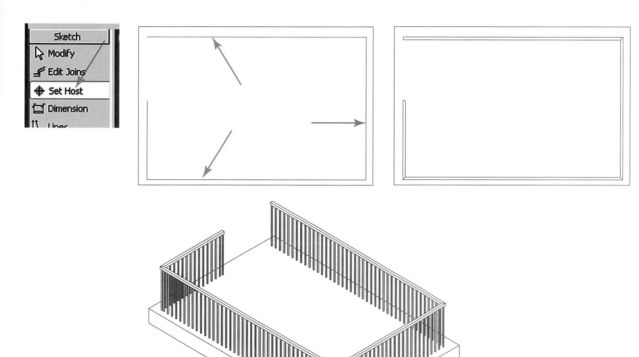

Figure 7-30

Exercise 7-9: Creating Ramps

With the inception of the handicap codes, ramps have become very important. Revit Architecture has a specialized routine specifically for ramps.

1. Start a new drawing using the **RAC 2009\Imperial Templates\default.rte** template.
2. In the **Project browser**, double-click **Floor Plans > Level 1** to bring it up into the **Drawing Editor**.
3. Change to the **Modeling** tab in the **Design Bar**.
4. In the **Design Bar,** select **Ramp** to enter **Sketch** mode.
5. In the **Sketch** tab, select **Ramp Properties** to bring up the **Element Properties** dialog box.
6. In the **Element Properties** dialog box, set the **Top Level** to none, and **Width** to **3′-0″**

You can alternately set the **Top Level** of the ramp to a level. If you prefer this method, be sure to name the level **TOP OF RAMP** and set its height appropriately.

7. In the **Element Properties** dialog box, select the **Edit/New** button to bring up the **Type Properties** dialog box.

8. In the **Type Properties** dialog box, set the **Thickness** to **4″**, **Maximum Incline Length** to **18′-0**, and **Ramp Max Slope (1/x)** to **6.0000**.

This means that you will create a **3″** thick ramp starting at **Level 1**, rising **1″** for every **6″** of run. Because you have set the run to **18′** (216″), the rise will be **3′-0″**. Let's check it.

9. Select **Run** from the **Sketch** tab, click in the **Drawing Editor**, drag to the right until the measurement reads **18′-0″**, and click again.

10. Press **Finish Sketch** to create the ramp (see Figure 7-31).

11. Save this file as **RAMPS**.

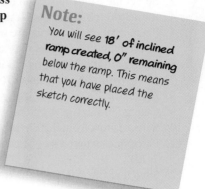

Note:
You will see **18′** of inclined ramp created, **0″** remaining below the ramp. This means that you have placed the sketch correctly.

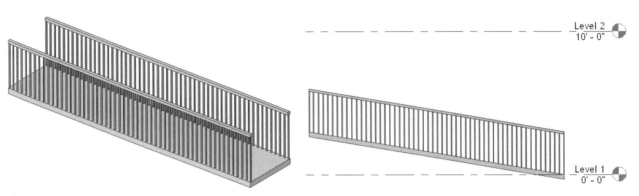

Figure 7-31

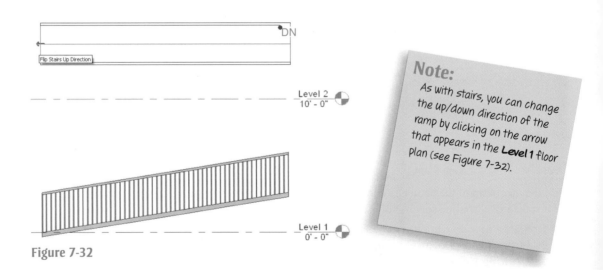

Figure 7-32

Note:
As with stairs, you can change the up/down direction of the ramp by clicking on the arrow that appears in the **Level 1** floor plan (see Figure 7-32).

SUMMARY

This section discussed the methods for creating and modifying **Stairs** and **Railings** in Revit Architecture 2009.

SECTION TEST QUESTIONS

True/false

1. True or False: Revit **Stairs** can only be straight stairs.

2. True or False: A stair rise is the distance between the treads.

3. True or False: Revit **Stairs** can be created without railings.

4. True or False: Revit's **Stair** nosing can be modified.

Questions

1. Examine a real stair and name its parts.

2. What are Revit's **Monolithic** stairs used for?

3. What is the purpose of Revit's **Hosted Railings**?

4. What type of stair do you use in a stair tower?

5. What is the purpose of the break mark in stairs going up?

6. Why do stairs going down have no break mark?

Curtain Walls and Glazing

8

Section *Objectives*

- Learn how to use **Curtain Wall 1**.
- Learn how to create **Curtain Walls** with lines.
- Learn how to create **Curtain Walls by Face**.
- Know how to configure the **Curtain Wall Grid**.
- Learn how to create sloped glazing.
- Learn how to create curved **Curtain Walls**.
- Know how to add doors and panels to **Curtain Walls**.

Curtain walls are very popular in contemporary commercial buildings. They are often called "store fronts" when used as entrance windows in malls and stores, and are never used as bearing components. In Revit Architecture, **Curtain Wall** objects are specialized versions of walls. Besides this, Revit Architecture contains several tools to create the curtain systems, create and change the curtain wall grids, and place and modify curtain wall mullions.

CURTAIN WALL ELEMENT PROPERTIES

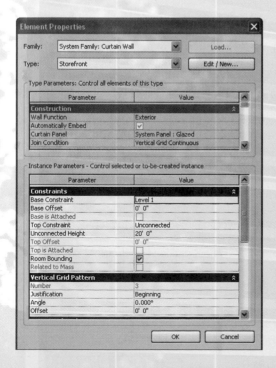

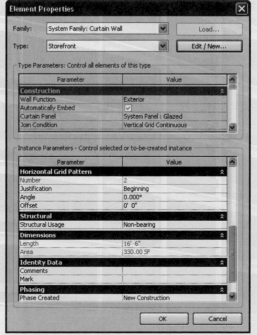

Name	Description
Construction	
Wall Function	Indicates the wall function.
Automatically Embed	Indicates whether the curtain wall automatically embeds into the wall.
Curtain Panel	Sets the curtain panel family type for the curtain element.
Join Condition	Controls which mullions break at intersections on a curtain element type. For example, this parameter makes all horizontal or vertical mullions on a curtain wall continuous, or it can make mullions on Grid 1 or Grid 2 continuous on a curtain system or sloped glazing.
Vertical/Horizontal Grid Pattern	
Layout	Sets an automatic vertical/horizontal layout for curtain grid lines along the length of a curtain wall. When set to a value other than None, Revit Architecture automatically adds vertical/horizontal grid lines to a curtain wall. **Fixed Distance** indicates that the curtain wall grids are placed at the exact value specified for **Vertical/Horizontal Spacing**. If the spacing is not an even factor of the wall's length, Revit Architecture inserts space at one or both ends of the wall, depending on the justification parameter. For example, if the wall is 46 feet and the vertical spacing is 5 feet and the justification is set to beginning, Revit Architecture adds 1 foot to the beginning of the wall before placing the first grid. See the Vertical/Horizontal Justification instance property description for more information on justification. **Fixed Number** indicates that you can set different numbers of curtain grids for different curtain wall instances. See the Vertical/Horizontal Number instance property description for more information. **Maximum Spacing** indicates that the curtain grids are placed at even intervals along the length of the curtain wall at a distance up to the value specified for **Vertical/Horizontal Spacing**.
Spacing	Enabled when **Layout** is set to **Fixed Distance** or **Maximum Spacing**. When the layout is set to a fixed distance, Revit Architecture uses the exact value for **Spacing**. When the layout is at a maximum spacing, Revit Architecture uses up to the specified value to lay out the grids.
Adjust for Mullion Size	Adjusts the position of type-driven gridlines to ensure that curtain wall panels are of equal size, whenever possible. Sometimes when mullions are placed, particularly on borders of curtain wall hosts, it can result in panels of unequal size, even if the **Layout** is set to **Fixed Distance**.
Vertical Mullions	
Interior Type	Specifies the mullion family for interior vertical mullions.
Border 1 Type	Specifies the mullion family for vertical mullions on the left border.
Border 2 Type	Specifies the mullion family for vertical mullions on the right border.
Horizontal Mullions	
Interior Type	Specifies the mullion family for interior horizontal mullions.
Border 1 Type	Specifies the mullion family for horizontal mullions on the left border.
Border 2 Type	Specifies the mullion family for horizontal mullions on the right border.

Name	Description
Identity Data	
Keynote	Add or edit the curtain wall keynote. Click in the value box to open the **Keynotes** dialog box.
Model	The model type for the curtain wall.
Manufacturer	Manufacturer for the stair materials.
Type Comments	Specific comments on the curtain wall type.
URL	A link to a web page for the manufacturer or other appropriate link.
Description	A description for the curtain wall.
Assembly Description	Description of the assembly based on the assembly code selection.
Assembly Code	Uniformat assembly code selected from hierarchical list.
Type Mark	A value to designate the particular curtain wall. Useful if you need to identify more than one curtain wall. This value must be unique for each curtain wall in a project. Revit Architecture warns you if the number is already used but allows you to continue using it.
Fire Rating	The fire rating of the curtain wall.
Cost	Material cost.
Constraints	
Base Constraint	The base level of the curtain wall. For example, **Level 1**.
Base Offset	Sets the curtain wall's height from its base constraint. This property is available only when the **Base Constraint** is set to a level.
Base is Attached	Indicates whether the base of the curtain wall is attached to another model component, such as a floor. This is a read-only value.
Top Constraint	Curtain wall height extends to the value specified in **Unconnected Height**.
Unconnected Height	The height of the curtain wall when it is sketched.
Top Offset	Sets the curtain wall's offset from the top level.
Top is Attached	Indicates whether the curtain wall top is attached to another model component, such as a roof or ceiling. This is a read-only value.
Room Bounding	If selected, the curtain wall is part of a room boundary. If not selected, the curtain wall is not part of a room boundary. This property is read-only before creating a curtain wall. After you draw the wall, you can select it and then modify this property.
Related to Mass	Indicates that the element was created from a mass element. This is a read-only value.

(continued)

Name	Description
Vertical/Horizontal Grid Pattern	
Number	If **Layout** (under **Vertical/Horizontal Grid Pattern**) is set to **Fixed Number**, enter a value here for the number of curtain grids on the curtain instance. The maximum value is **200**.
Justification	Determines how Revit Architecture adjusts the spacing of grids along the curtain element face, when the grid spacing does not divide evenly into the length of the face. Justification also determines which gridlines are first removed or added when gridlines are added or removed because of parameter changes or changes to the size of the face. **Beginning** adds space to the end of the face before placing the first grid. **Center** adds an even amount of space at both the beginning and end of the face. **End** adds space from the beginning of the face before placing the first grid.
Angle	Rotates the curtain wall grids to the specified angle. You can also specify this value for individual faces. If you specify this parameter for a face, then no value displays in this field. Valid values are between **89** and **−89**.
Offset	Starts grid placement at the specified distance from the justification point of the grids. For example, if **Justification** is specified as beginning and you enter a value of 5 feet here, Revit Architecture places the first grid 5 feet from the beginning of the face. Note that you can also set this value for individual faces. If you specify this parameter for a face, then no value displays in this field.
Structural	
Structural Usage	Sets the structural usage of the curtain wall. This property is read-only before creating a curtain wall. After you draw the curtain wall, you can select it and then modify this property.
Dimensions	
Length	The length of the curtain wall. This is a read-only value.
Area	The area of the curtain wall. This is a read-only value.
Identity Data	
Comments	Specific comments about the curtain wall.
Mark	Sets a label for the curtain wall. This value must be unique for each curtain wall in a project. Revit Architecture warns you if the number is already used, but allows you to continue using it.
Phasing	
Phase Created	The phase when the curtain wall was created.
Phase Demolished	The phase when the curtain wall was demolished.

Exercise 8-1: Using Curtain Wall 1

Curtain Walls are specialized walls. Revit Architecture ships with a default curtain wall labeled **Curtain Wall 1**.

1. Start a new drawing using the **RAC 2009\Imperial Templates\default.rte** template.
2. In the **Project browser**, double-click **Floor Plans > Level 1** to bring it up into the **Drawing Editor**.

3. Change to the **Basics** tab in the **Design Bar**.
4. In the **Basics** tab, select the **Wall** tool.
5. In the **Options** toolbar, select **Curtain Wall 1** (see Figure 8-1).
6. Place a **15′** long **10′-0″** high curtain wall in the **Drawing Editor**.
7. Change to the **Default 3D View**.

Notice that the curtain wall does not contain a grid or mullions.

8. Select the curtain wall you just placed, **RMB**, and select **Element Properties** from the contextual menu that appears to bring up the **Element Properties** dialog box.
9. In the **Element Properties** dialog box, press the **Edit/New** button to bring up the **Type Properties** dialog box.
10. In the **Type Properties** dialog box, set the **Vertical Mullions > Border 1 Type** to **Rectangular Mullion: 2.5″ × 5″**, and press the **OK** buttons to return to the **Drawing Editor** (see Figure 8-2).

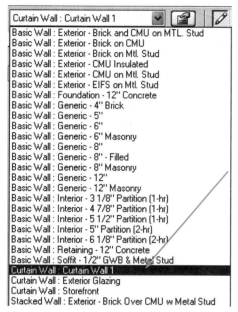

Figure 8-1

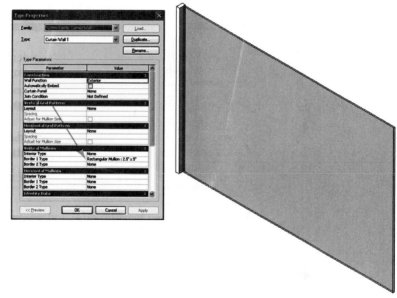

Figure 8-2

11. In the **Project browser**, expand the **Families > Curtain Wall Mullions > Rectangular Mullion** folder.
12. Select the **2.5″ × 5″ rectangular** mullion, **RMB**, and select **Properties** from the contextual menu that appears to bring up the **Type Properties** dialog box.
13. In the **Type Properties** dialog box, at the top right, press the **Duplicate** button, enter **8″ × 5″ Rectangular** in the name dialog box, and then press the **OK** button.
14. In the **Type Properties** dialog box, under **Dimensions**, set the **Width on side 2** to **8″**, **Width on side 1** to **5″**, and press the **OK** button to return to the **Drawing Editor**.
15. Select the curtain wall again, **RMB**, and select **Element Properties** from the contextual menu that appears to bring up the **Element Properties** dialog box.
16. In the **Element Properties** dialog box, press the **Edit/New** button to bring up the **Type Properties** dialog box.
17. In the **Type Properties** dialog box set the **Vertical Mullions > Border 2 Type** and **Horizontal Mullions > Border 2 Type** to **Rectangular Mullion: 2.5″ × 5″**.
18. In the **Type Properties** dialog box set the **Horizontal Mullions > Border 1 Type** to **Rectangular Mullion: 8″ × 5″** (the mullion **Type** you just created), and press the **OK** buttons to return to the **Drawing Editor** (see Figure 8-3).
19. In the **Modeling** tab in the **Design Bar**, select the **Curtain Grid** tool.
20. Select the curtain wall, and either a horizontal or vertical line will appear depending on where you move your cursor.

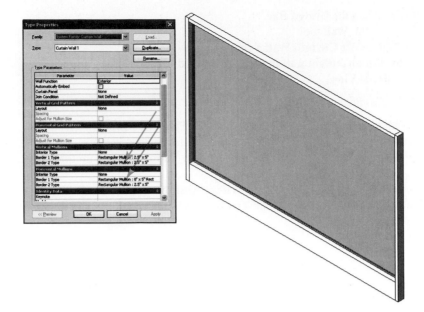

Figure 8-3

21. Adjust the grid lines by dragging and moving them, and then click.
22. After horizontal and vertical grid lines have been placed, select the **Mullion** tool from the **Modify** tab.
23. In the **Options** toolbar, select **Rectangular Mullion: 2.5″ × 5″**, and then select the vertical and horizontal curtain grid lines you just placed to create mullions (see Figure 8-4).
24. Change to the **South Elevation**.
25. Notice that the vertical mullions do not meet the horizontal mullions correctly.
26. Select a mullion.

Note:
You may have to "tap" the <Tab> key on your keyboard as you select the curtain wall to cycle through all the mullions.

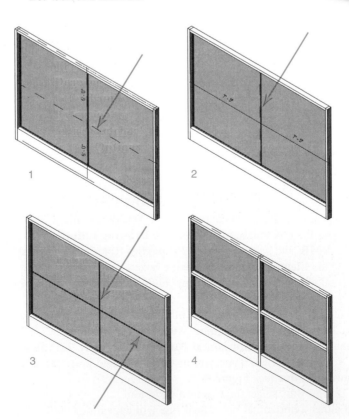

Figure 8-4

27. Select a mullion, and notice that two blue hatch marks appear at the ends of the mullion.

The blue hatch marks are toggles used to change the way one mullion meets another.

28. Click the toggle shown to make the bottom border mullion extend past the middle vertical mullion (see Figures 8-5 and 8-6).

29. Continue to individually select all the mullions and click their toggles to see the results
(see Figure 8-7).

30. Save this file as **USING CURTAIN WALL 1**.

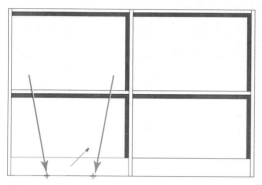
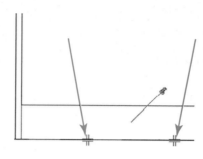

Figure 8-5

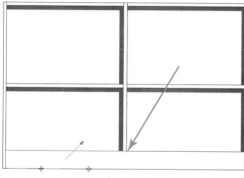

Figure 8-6

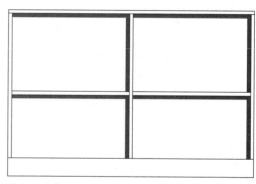

Figure 8-7

Exercise 8-2: Creating Curtain Walls with Lines

Curtain Walls can be created by selecting two polar lines. This is very useful for creating curtain
walls.

1. Start a new drawing using the **RAC 2009\Imperial Templates\default.rte** template.
2. In the **Project browser**, double-click **Floor Plans > Level 1** to bring it up into the
Drawing Editor.
3. Change to the **Basics** tab in the **Design Bar**.
4. In the **Basics** tab, select the **Wall** tool.
5. In the **Options** toolbar, select **Basics Wall: Generic - 8″** and create a **40′ × 20′** enclosure
15′-0″ high (see Figure 8-8).
6. In the **Basics** tab, select the **Lines** tool and create the lines shown in Figure 8-9.
7. In the **Project browser**, double-click **Floor Plans > Level 2** to bring it up into the
Drawing Editor.
8. In **Level 2**, draw the lines shown in Figure 8-10.
9. Change to the **Default 3D View**.
10. Change to the **Modeling** tab in the **Design Bar**.
11. In the **Modeling** tab, select the **Curtain System >> Curtain System by Lines** tool.

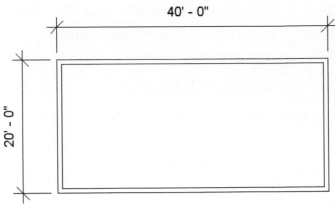

Figure 8-8

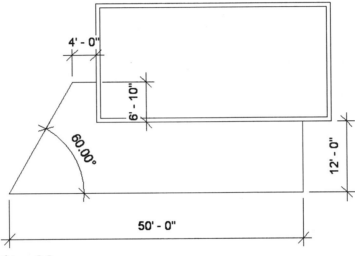

Figure 8-9

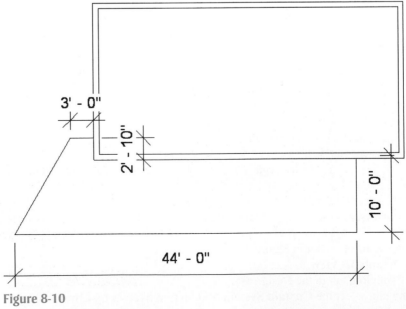

Figure 8-10

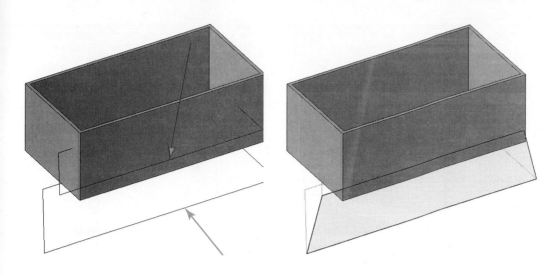

Figure 8-11

12. Pick the top and bottom lines you created to create a **Curtain System** (see Figure 8-11).
13. Continue creating **Curtain Systems** by selecting the rest of the top and bottom lines (see Figure 8-12).
14. Change to the **South Elevation** view.
15. Select the first **Curtain System** you created (south side), and then select the **Temporary Hide/Isolate** icon at the bottom of the **Drawing Editor**.
16. In the **Temporary Hide/Isolate** list, select **Isolate Element**.

This will temporarily isolate the **South** curtain system, and hide everything else in the **Drawing Editor** (see Figure 8-13).

17. Change to the **Basics** tab in the **Design Bar**.
18. In the **Basics** tab, select the **Ref** (Reference Plane) icon, and place a **Reference Plane** as shown in Figure 8-14.
19. Select the **Reference Plane** you just placed, and then select **Array** from the **Edit** toolbar.

Note:

Curtain System by Lines works only with two copular lines, and will not work with three lines such as those in a triangle.

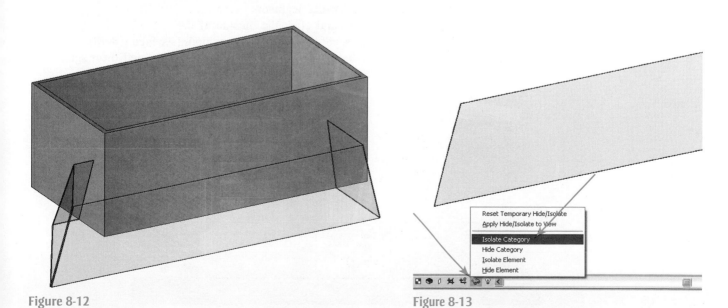

Figure 8-12

Figure 8-13

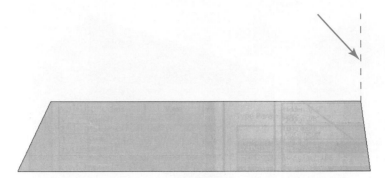

Figure 8-14

20. In the **Options** toolbar, select the **Linear** option, check the **Group And Associate** check box, enter **15** in the **Number** field, and select the **2nd** radio button (see Figure 8-15).

Linear

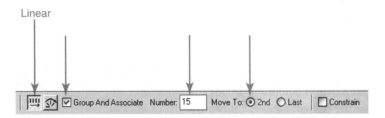

Figure 8-15

21. Click the top of the **Reference Plane** you just placed, and drag it to the left **3′-0″**, and click again to array the reference plane (see Figure 8-16).
22. Change to the **Modeling** tab in the **Design Bar**.
23. In the **Modeling** tab, select the **Curtain Grid** tool.
24. With the **Curtain Grid** tool, click on the point where the reference planes touch the **Curtain System** to place grid lines (see Figure 8-17).
25. When you are finished adding grid lines, delete the reference lines, and select the **Mullion** tool from the **Modeling** tab.
26. In the **Options** toolbar, select the **Rectangular Mullion: 2.5″ × 5″** and the **All Empty Segments** radio button, and then select and click the outside of the **Curtain System** and grid lines you created to place mullions (see Figure 8-18).
27. Select the **Temporary Hide/Isolate** icon at the bottom of the **Drawing Editor** again, and select **Reset Temporary Hide/Isolate** to unhide everything.

Note:
If you need more or fewer arrayed copies, you can change the number in the number field that appears below the arrayed reference planes.

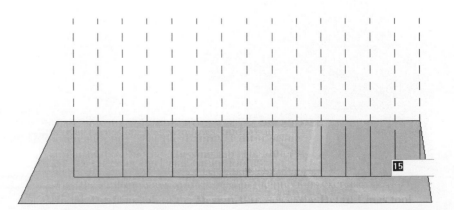

Figure 8-16

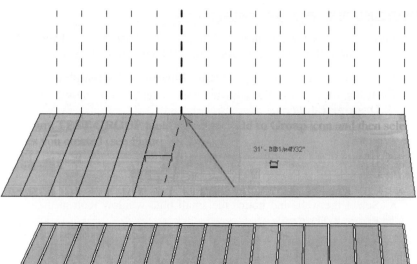

Figure 8-17

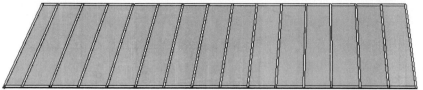

Figure 8-18

28. Using the information gleaned from this and the previous exercise, add **Curtain Grids** and **Mullions** to the rest of the curtain walls (see Figure 8-19).
29. Save this file as **CURTAIN WALLS WITH LINES**.

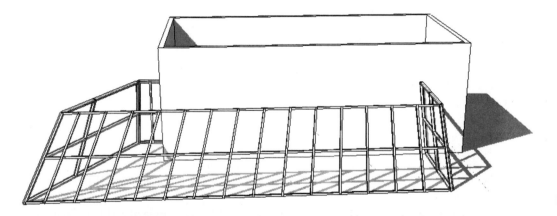

Figure 8-19

Exercise 8-3: Curtain Walls by Face

In Section 1 of this book, you are shown the **Curtain System by Face** option when creating a Mass Object. In Revit Architecture 2009, you have the option to place the **Curtain System by Face** in the **Modify** tab of the **Design Bar**. This may seem redundant, but the **Modify** tab has the **Curtain Grid** and **Mullion** controls that are not available in the **Massing** tab (see Figure 8-20).

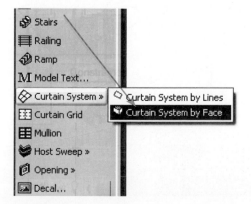

Figure 8-20

Exercise 8-4: Configuring the Curtain Wall Grid

You may want to have a curtain wall grid that is not horizontal and vertical, but rather at an angle. This is controlled by the **Curtain Wall Grid** icon on the face of the curtain wall.

1. Start a new drawing using the **RAC 2009\Imperial Templates\default.rte** template.
2. In the **Project browser**, double-click **Floor Plans > Level 1** to bring it up into the **Drawing Editor**.
3. Change to the **Basics** tab in the **Design Bar**.
4. Select the **Wall** tool.
5. In the **Options** toolbar, select **Curtain Wall 1**.
6. Place a **20′** long **15′-0″** high curtain wall in the **Drawing Editor**.
7. Change to the **Default 3D View**.
8. Select the wall, and notice the small blue window icon in the center of the wall (see Figure 8-21).
9. Select the icon, and a red grid with numbers will appear at the top and right quadrant.

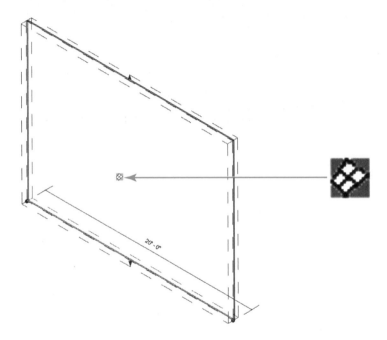

Figure 8-21

The numbers represent the vertical and horizontal grid offset and the degree of rotation of the grid.

10. Select the degree number, enter **25** (percent), and then press the **<Enter>** key on your keyboard (see Figure 8-22).

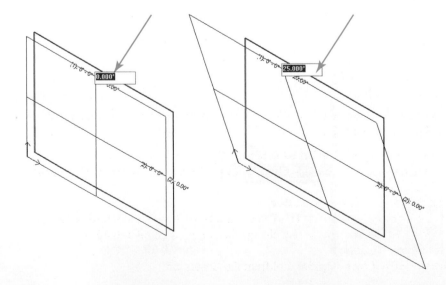

Figure 8-22

11. Repeat this process with the right-side numbers.
12. Select the **Curtain Grid** tool, and place grids (see Figure 8-23).

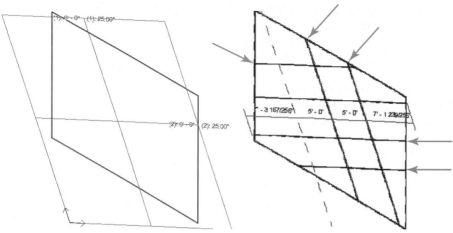

Figure 8-23

13. Select the **Mullion** tool from the **Modeling** tab.
14. In the **Options** toolbar, select **Rectangular Mullion: 2.5″ × 5″** and the **All Empty Segments** radio button, and then select and click the outside of the **Curtain System** and grid lines you rotated to place mullions (see Figure 8-24).
15. Save this file as **CONFIGURING THE GRID**.

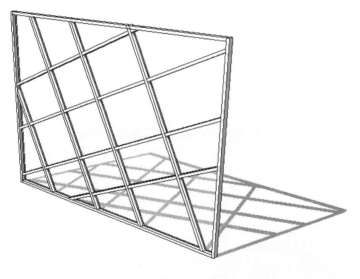

Figure 8-24

Exercise 8-5: Creating Sloped Glazing

Curtain Walls can also be used for canopies and sloped glass roofs. Revit Architecture has tools that make this process quick and painless.

1. Start a new drawing using the **RAC 2009\Imperial Templates\default.rte** template.
2. In the **Project browser**, double-click **Floor Plans > Level 1** to bring it up into the **Drawing Editor**.
3. Change to the **Basics** tab in the **Design Bar**.
4. Using the **Wall** tool, place an **18′-0″ × 18′-0″** enclosure **10′-0″** high in the **Drawing Editor**.
5. Change to the **South Elevation** view, and change the height of **Level 2** to **20′-0″**.
6. Change to the **Level 2** floor plan.
7. Select the **Roof >> Roof by Footprint** tool from the **Basics** tab.

8. You will now be in **Sketch** mode.
9. In the **Sketch** tab, select **Pick Walls**, and then uncheck the **Defines Slope** check box in the **Options** toolbar.
10. Pick all the walls, and then select the **Slope Arrow** tool from the **Sketch** tab.
11. Place an arrow as shown in Figure 8-25.
12. Select the arrow, **RMB**, and select **Element Properties** from the contextual menu that appears to bring up the **Element Properties** dialog box.
13. In the **Element Properties** dialog box, set the **Level at Tail** to **Default** (level you are now on).
14. Set the **Height Offset at Tail** to **0′-0″**.
15. Set the **Level at Head** to **Default**.
16. Set the **Height Offset at Head** to **Level 2 (10′-0″)** and press the **OK** button to create the roof.
17. Change to the **Default 3D View**.
18. Select all the walls, and press the **Attach** button in the **Options** toolbar.
19. Select the roof, and the walls will attach to the roof.
20. Select the roof, and then choose **Sloped Glazing** from the **Options** toolbar to create the sloped glazed roof (see Figures 8-26 and 8-27).

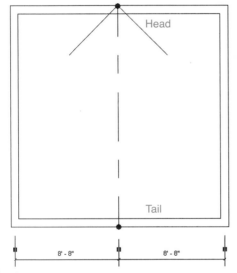

Figure 8-25

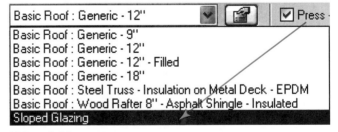

Figure 8-26

Figure 8-27

21. Select the **Curtain Grid** tool from the **Modeling** tab, and then select the **Mullion** tool and apply mullions (see Figure 8-28).
22. Save this file as **SLOPED GLAZING**.

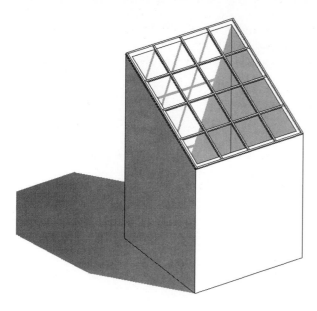

Figure 8-28

Exercise 8-6: Curved Curtain Walls

Any wall can be changed into a curtain wall by selecting it and choosing **Curtain Wall 1** from the **Options** toolbar. When you do this with **Curtain Wall 1**, the curved wall will become flat, but will automatically curve as you add segments (see Figure 8-29).

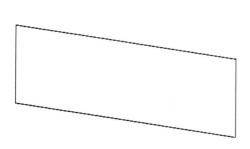
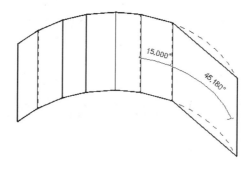

Figure 8-29

Exercise 8-7: Making Odd-Shaped Curtain Walls

1. Start a new drawing using the **RAC 2009\Imperial Templates\default.rte** template.
2. In the **Project browser**, double-click **Floor Plans > Level 1** to bring it up into the **Drawing Editor**.
3. Change to the **Basics** tab in the **Design Bar**.
4. Using the **Wall** tool, place a **40′-0″** long **Curtain wall 1**, **20′-0″** high in the **Drawing Editor**—starting from left to right.
5. Change to the **South Elevation** view.
6. Select the wall, and then select the **Edit Profile** button from the **Options** toolbar to enter **Sketch** mode.
7. Adjust the sketch lines of the wall that appear. You will get a message that **Constraints are not satisfied**. Press the **Remove Constraints** button in the message dialog box.

> **Note:**
> Walls always have their constraints set when you create them. You will always have to remove these constraints before you can change the profile shape of a wall for the first time.

8. While still in the **Sketch** tab, select **Lines** and add a circle to the wall.
9. In the **Sketch** tab, select **Finish Sketch** to modify the curtain wall (see Figure 8-30).

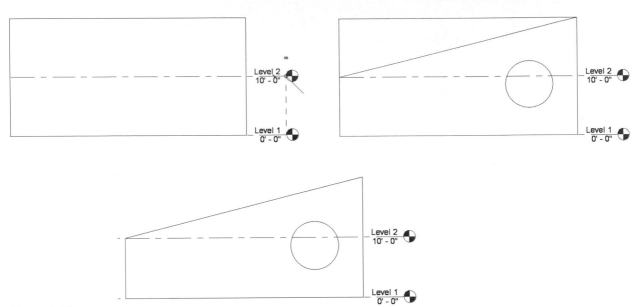

Figure 8-30

10. Change to the **Default 3D View**.
11. In the **Modeling** tab, select the **Curtain Grid** tool and add place grids.
12. Select the **Mullion** tool from the **Modeling** tab.
13. In the **Options** toolbar, select **Rectangular Mullion: 2.5″ × 5″** and the **All Empty Segments** radio button, and then select and click the outside of the curtain system and grid lines you created to place mullions (see Figure 8-31).
14. Save this file as **ODD SHAPED CURTAIN WALLS**.

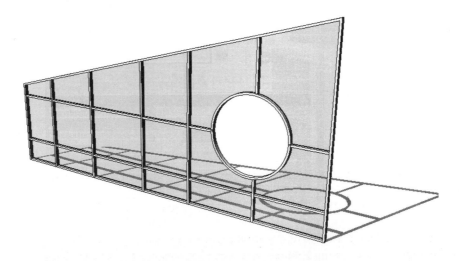

Figure 8-31

Exercise 8-8: Adding Doors and Panels to Curtain Walls

1. Start a new drawing using the **RAC 2009\Imperial Templates\default.rte** template.
2. In the **Project browser**, double-click **Floor Plans > Level 1** to bring it up into the **Drawing Editor**.
3. Change to the **Basics** tab in the **Design Bar**.
4. Using the **Wall** tool, place a **40′-0″** long, **20′-0″** high wall in the **Drawing Editor**—starting from left to right.
5. Select the wall, and select **Curtain Wall: Exterior Glazing** from the **Options** toolbar.

6. Apply mullions to all the gridlines in the **Curtain Wall: Exterior Glazing** wall you just created.

7. Change to the **Default 3D View** (see Figure 8-32).

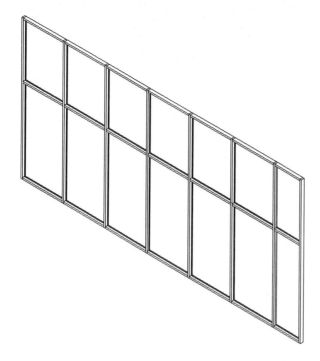

Figure 8-32

8. Place your cursor near one of the glazing panels, tap the **<Tab>** key on your computer until the glazing panel is highlighted, and then click your left mouse button to select it.

9. With the panel selected, **RMB**, and select **Element Properties** from the contextual menu that appears to bring up the **Element Properties** dialog box.

10. In the **Element Properties** dialog box, press the **Load** button (at the very top of the dialog box) to bring up the **Open** menu in the **Imperial** or **Metric Library**.

Note:
You can check to see if the **System Panel** is showing in the **Options** toolbar; this will indicate that the panel has been selected.

11. In the **Imperial Library** (or **Metric Library**), open the **Doors** folder.

12. In the **Doors** folder, select the **Curtain Wall Dbl Glass** door, then press the **Open** button to load the **Family**, and return to the **Drawing Editor**.

13. Repeat the previous step and load the **Curtain Wall Sgl Glass** door (see Figure 8-33).

14. Now that the doors are loaded, with the panel still selected, change the **Family** to **Curtain Wall Dbl Glass**.

15. Press the **OK** button in the **Element Properties** dialog box to return to the **Drawing Editor** and insert the door.

16. Repeat this process, placing the **Curtain Wall Sgl Glass** door (see Figure 8-34).

17. You can either create a new sill profile for the door sill mullions, or just delete the mullions below the doors. The base of the doors will elongate if you delete the sill mullions.

18. Again, with the **<Tab>** key, select the **Curtain Wall Dbl Glass** door you placed.

19. With the door selected, **RMB**, and select **Element Properties** from the contextual menu that appears to bring up the **Element Properties** dialog box.

20. In the **Element Properties** dialog box, press the **Edit/New** button to bring up the **Type Properties** dialog box.

21. In the **Type Properties** dialog box, select the **Duplicate** button, enter **WOOD CURTAIN WALL DOOR** in the **Name** field, and press the **OK** button to return to the **Type Properties** dialog box.

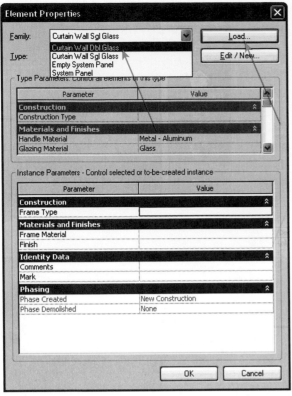

Figure 8-33

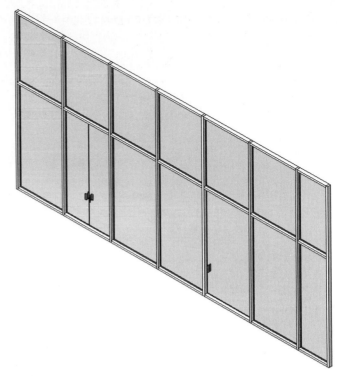

Figure 8-34

22. In the **Type Properties** dialog box, select the **Glazing Material** field to open the **Materials** dialog box.
23. In the **Materials** dialog box, select **Wood – Flooring** and press the **OK** buttons to return to the **Drawing Editor** (see Figure 8-35).
24. Using the **<Tab>** key on your computer, select the panel above the wood door you just created.

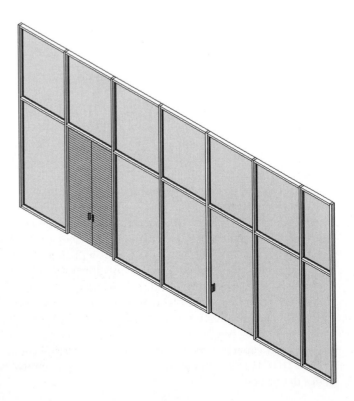

Figure 8-35

25. With the panel selected, select **Basic Wall: Generic - 4″ Brick** from the drop-down list in the **Options** toolbar.
26. Delete one of the horizontal mullions.
27. Select the horizontal curtain wall grid where the deleted mullion existed.
28. Click the "push pin" icon to turn off the constraint, then select the **Add or Remove Segments** button from the **Options** toolbar, and click the grid again to join the two glazing panels into one panel (see Figure 8-36).
29. Using the <**Tab**> key on your computer, select the single panel you just created, and again select **Basic Wall: Generic - 4″ Brick** from the drop-down list in the **Options** toolbar (see Figure 8-37).
30. Save this file as **CURTAIN WALL DOORS and PANELS**.

Note:
Curtain Wall panels will accept any wall, but only doors based on Curtain Wall doors.

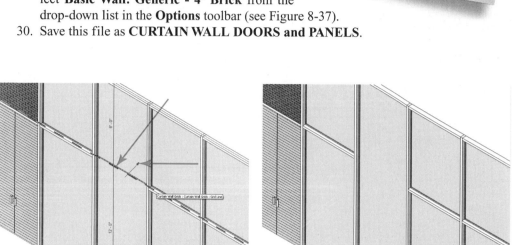

Figure 8-36

Figure 8-37

SUMMARY

This section discussed Revit Architecture 2009's methods for creating and modifying **Curtain Walls**. It also presented methods for creating sloped glazing and modifying curtain wall mullions.

SECTION TEST QUESTIONS

Exercise

Create a flat-topped pyramid with glass walls (see Figure 8-38).

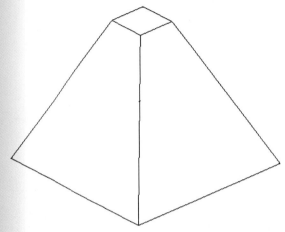

Figure 8-38

Questions

1. Where are the mullion families located?

2. What is a curtain wall?

3. What is the **Default Layer**?

4. What is the **Curtain Grid** used for?

Dimensions, Annotations, and Grids

9

Section Objectives

- Know how to set the **Dimension Style** variables and place dimension strings.
- Know how to use the **Spot Dimension** tool.
- Learn how to use the **Text** tool.
- Learn how to use the **Grid** tool.
- Learn how to use the **Scope Box**.
- Know how to use the **Tag** and the **Tag All Not Tagged** tools.
- Learn how to use the **Symbol** tool.

Dimensioning and annotation are the lifeblood of construction documents (drawings). In standard drawings, the dimension and text govern the picture. In nonintegrated systems, such as 2D CAD, the dimensions can differ from the picture, either intentionally (because one does not want to change the picture) or by mistake. In Revit Architecture, this is not possible because the dimensions are a function of the walls, doors, and other components; thus, the dimension strings and values always match the dimensions of the components.

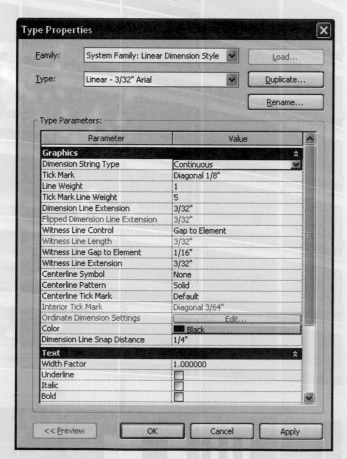

Grids are not necessary for residential structures, but are very important for commercial and large-scale projects, which usually are designed by relating everything to a set grid. Revit Architecture 2009 provides a complete set of automated dimensioning, annotation, and grid tools that fully enable users to document any construction project.

Name	Description
Graphics	
Dimension String Type	Continuous, Baseline, Ordinate options.
Tick Mark	The name of the tick mark style.
Line Weight	Sets the line weight number that designates thickness of the dimension line. You can choose from a list of values defined in Revit Architecture or define your own. You can change the definition of the line weights using the **Line Weights** command in the **Settings** menu. See **Line Weights**.
Tick Mark Line Weight	Sets the line weight that designates thickness of the tick mark. You can choose from a list of values defined in Revit Architecture or define your own.
Dimension Line Extension	Extends the dimension line beyond the intersection of the witness lines to the specified value. When you set this value, this is the size at which the dimension line plots if you are printing at 100 percent.
Flipped Dimension Line Extension	Controls the extent of the dimension line beyond the flipped arrow if the arrow flips on the ends of the dimension string. This parameter is enabled only when the tick mark type-parameter is set to an arrow type. See **Changing the Dimension Line Tick Mark**.
Witness Line Control	Switches between the fixed gap functionality and the fixed dimension line functionality.
Witness Line Length	If **Witness Line Control** is set to **Fixed to Dimension Line**, this parameter becomes available. Specifies the length of all witness lines in the dimensions. When you set this value, this is the size at which the witness line plots if you are printing at 100 percent.
Witness Line Gap to Element	If **Witness Line Control** is set to **Gap to Element**, this parameter sets the distance between the witness line and the element being dimensioned.
Witness Line Extension	Sets the extension of a witness line beyond the tick mark. When you set this value, this is the size at which the witness line plots if you are printing at 100 percent.
Centerline Symbol	You can select any of the annotation symbols loaded in the project. The centerline symbol appears above the witness lines that reference the centerlines of family instances and walls. If the witness line does not reference a center plane, you cannot place a centerline symbol above it.
Centerline Pattern	Changes the line pattern of the witness lines of the dimension, if the dimension references are the centerlines of family instances and walls. If the references are not at the centerline, this parameter does not affect the witness line pattern.

Name	Description
Centerline Tick Mark	Changes the tick mark at the ends of the centerline of a dimension.
Interior Tick Mark	Designates the tick mark display for inner witness lines when adjacent segments of a dimension line are too small for arrows to fit. When this occurs, the ends of the short-segment string flip, and the inner witness lines display the designated interior tick mark. This parameter is enabled only when the tick mark type parameter is set to an arrow type. See **Changing the Dimension Line Tick Mark**.
Ordinate Dimension Settings	Ordinate dimensions measure the perpendicular distance from an origin point called the datum to an element.
Color	Sets the color of dimension lines. You can choose from a list of colors defined in Revit Architecture or define your own. The default value is black.
Dimension Line Snap Distance	To use this parameter, set the **Witness Line Control** parameter to **Fixed to Dimension Line**. With this parameter set, additional snapping is available that aids in stacking linear dimensions at even intervals. The value of this parameter should be greater than the distance between the text and the dimension line, plus the height of the text. This parameter is used primarily in the European market.
Text	
Width Factor	**1.0** is the default for regular text width. The font width is scaled proportionately to the **Width Factor**. Height is not affected.
Underline	Check this box to underline text.
Italic	Check this box to italicize text.
Bold	Check this box to bold text.
Text Size	Specifies the size of the typeface for the dimension.
Text Offset	Specifies the offset of the text from the dimension line.
Read Convention	Specifies the read convention for the dimension text.
Text Font	Sets the Microsoft® True Type fonts for the dimensions.
Text Background	If you set the value to opaque, the dimension text is surrounded by a box that overlaps any geometry or text behind it in the view. If you set the value to transparent, the box disappears and everything not overlapped by the dimension text is visible.
Units Format	Click the button to open the **Format** dialog box. You can then set the format of the units with the dimension. (See **Formatting Parameters**.)
Show Opening Height	Place a dimension whose witness lines reference the same insert (window, door, or opening) in a plan view. If you select this parameter, the dimension includes a label that shows the height of the opening for the instance. The value appears below the dimension value you initially placed. Note: This parameter is used primarily in the German market.

The best way to understand what the dimension variables do is to place a dimension string, change the variables, and observe their effect.

Exercise 9-1: Setting the Dimension Style Variables

1. Start a new drawing using the **RAC 2009\Imperial Templates\default.rte** template.
2. In the **Project browser**, double-click **Floor Plans > Level 1** to bring it up into the **Drawing Editor**.
3. Set the Scale to **1/8″ = 1′-0″**
4. Change to the **Basics** tab in the **Design Bar**.
5. Select the **Wall** tool.
6. Create a **25′-0″ × 25′-0″ × 10′-0″** high enclosure using the **Basic wall: Exterior–Brick on CMU** wall type.
7. Change the **Detail Level** to **Medium** (see Figure 9-1).
8. Change to the **Drafting** tab in the **Design Bar**.
9. Select the **Dimension** tool.
10. In the **Options** toolbar, select the **Linear Dimension Style: Linear-3/32″ Arial**.
11. In the **Options** toolbar, select **Wall faces** from the **Prefer** field and **Individual References** from the **Pick** field (see Figure 9-2).

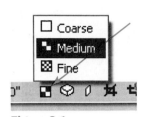

Figure 9-1

Figure 9-2

12. Select the left wall of the enclosure, then select the right wall. Finally, drag your cursor upward to locate the dimension string and click to place the dimension (see Figure 9-3).
13. Select **Settings > Annotations > Dimensions > Linear** from the **Main** menu to bring up the **Type Properties** dialog box (see Figure 9-5).
14. In the **Type Properties** dialog box, change each of the settings and observe the changes to the dimension string (see Figures 9-6 and 9-7).

Note:
The **Dimension Preference** option allows you to place the dimensions at **Wall centerlines, Wall faces, Center of core,** and **Faces of core.** You can also select placement by tapping the **<Tab>** key on your keyboard when selecting walls. This is very handy if you need to dimension from the studs (see Figure 9-4).

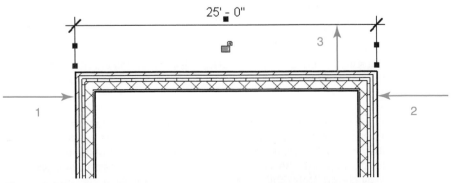

Figure 9-3

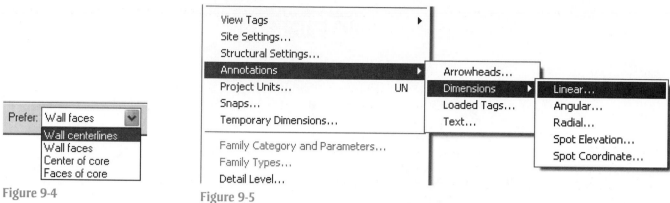

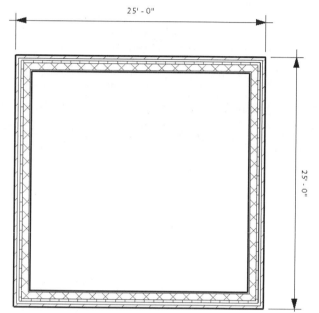

Figure 9-4

Figure 9-5

Figure 9-6

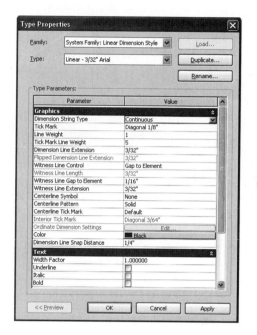

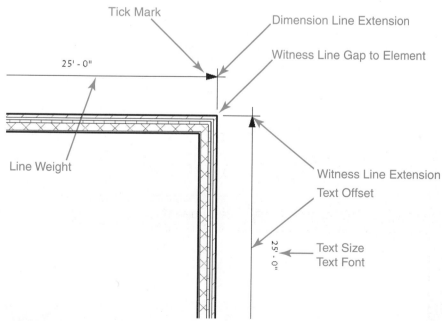

Figure 9-7

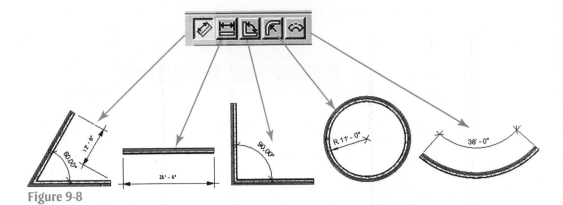

Figure 9-8

Note:
You can either select the **Dimension** families from the **Options** toolbar drop-down list, or select the icons shown in Figure 9-8; the results are the same.

15. Place walls, and select the different dimension placement options as shown in Figure 9-8.
16. Using the enclosure you made at the beginning of this exercise, delete all the dimensions.
17. This time, again select the **Dimension** tool and **Linear Dimension Style: Linear-3/32″ Arial** from the **Options** toolbar.
18. In the **Options** toolbar, select **Wall faces** from the **Prefer** field, but this time, select **Entire Walls** from the **Pick** drop-down list.
19. Select the edge of the wall, and drag and click to place the dimension (see Figure 9-9).
20. Select the **Dimension** tool again. With the **Entire Walls** pick chosen, press the **Options** button on the **Options** toolbar to bring up the **Auto Dimension Options** dialog box.

Note:
You might find that the **Entire Walls** placement method is often simpler and faster than the **Individual References** method because you use fewer mouse clicks.

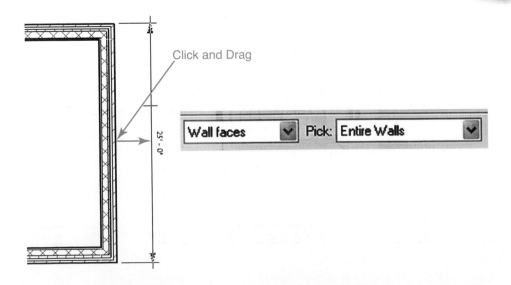

Click and Drag

Figure 9-9

21. In the **Auto Dimension Options** dialog box, select the **Centers** radio button.
22. Add a door to your enclosure, and place a dimension in the wall.
23. Add another door, select the **Dimension** tool, select the **Widths** radio button, and place a dimension (see Figure 9-10).
24. Select the dimension string you just placed for the **Openings Centers** of a door.
25. Notice the blue **EQ** symbol that has been crossed out.
26. Select the symbol to activate it—the door will become equally spaced between the end walls, and the dimension string will read **EQ** on both sides.

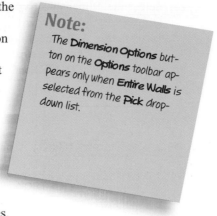

Note:

The **Dimension Options** button on the **Options** toolbar appears only when **Entire Walls** is selected from the **Pick** drop-down list.

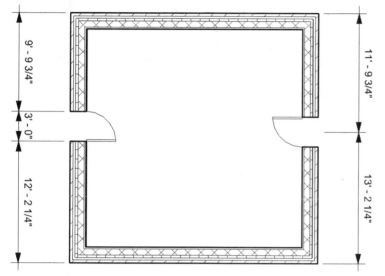

Figure 9-10

27. Select the blue **EQ** symbol again to deactivate it (remove the constraints); the dimension string will now read as dimensions (see Figure 9-11).

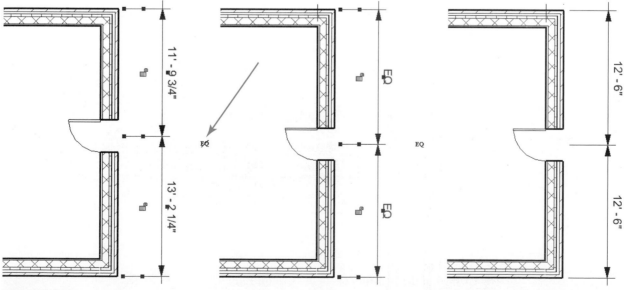

Figure 9-11

28. Select the **Dimension** tool again, activate the **Auto Dimension Options** dialog box, and check the **Intersecting Walls** check box.
29. Add another dimension string (see Figure 9-12).
30. Save this file as **DIMENSIONS**.

> **Note:**
> When you deactivate the **EQ**, you remove the automatic constraint. If you move the walls, the equality will no longer work.

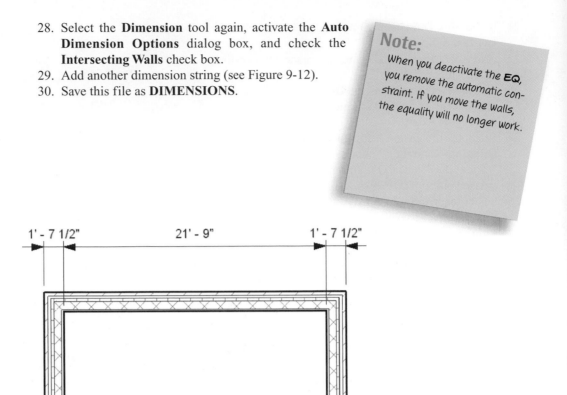

Figure 9-12

Spot Dimensions

Spot dimensions display the elevation of a selected point. You can place them in plan, elevation, and 3D views. They are typically used to obtain a point of elevation for ramps, roads, toposurfaces, and stair landings.

Exercise 9-2: Using the Spot Dimension Tool

1. Start a new drawing using the **RAC 2009\Imperial Templates\default.rte** template.
2. In the **Project browser**, double-click **Floor Plans > Level 1** to bring it up into the **Drawing Editor**.
3. Set the **Scale** to **1/8″ = 1′-0″**.
4. Change to the **Basics** tab in the **Design Bar**.
5. Place a **15′-0″** long, **20′-0″** high **Basic Wall: generic -8″** wall from left to right horizontally.
6. Add a stair run (settings do not matter), and delete the railing.
7. Change to the **South Elevation** view.
8. Set the **Model Graphics Style** to **Wireframe** (see Figure 9-13).

Figure 9-13

9. Add windows and doors as shown in Figure 9-14.
10. Change to the **Drafting** tab in the **Design Bar**.
11. Select the **Spot Dimension > Spot Elevation** tool.

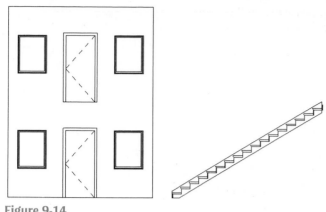

Figure 9-14

12. Select the top of the lower door, click, drag to the left, click again, drag horizontally, and click to place the **Spot Elevation**.
13. Select the **Spot Dimension > Spot Coordinate** tool.
14. Select the top of the upper left window, click, drag to the left, click again, drag horizontally, and click to place the **Spot Coordinate**.
15. Select the **Spot Dimension > Spot Elevation** tool.
16. Select one of the stair treads, click, drag to the left, click again, drag horizontally, and click to place the **Spot Elevation** (see Figure 9-15).

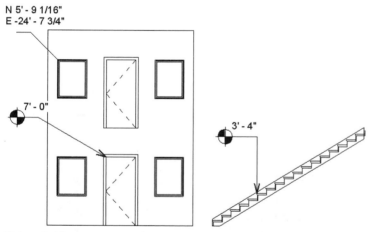

Figure 9-15

17. Select the spot elevation you placed for the door, **RMB**, and select **Element Properties** from the contextual menu to bring up the **Element Properties** dialog box.
18. In the **Element Properties** dialog box, press the **Edit/New** button at the top right of the dialog box to bring up the **Type Properties** dialog box.
19. In the **Type Properties** dialog box, put your name in the **Elevation Indicator** field, and press the **OK** buttons to return to the **Drawing Editor**. Notice that your name precedes the spot dimension. (You may have to select the dimension itself and move it upwards if it blocks the spot elevation symbol.)
20. Again, select the spot elevation you placed, and bring up the **Type Properties** dialog box.
21. This time change the **Indicator as Prefix/Suffix** field to **Suffix,** and press the **OK** buttons to return to the **Drawing Editor**. Again, notice that your name comes after the spot elevation.
22. Change to the **Default 3D View**.
23. Select the wall, and then select the **Rotate** tool from the **Edit** toolbar.
24. Rotate the walk, and notice that the **Spot Elevation > Coordinate** for the window changes (see Figure 9-16).

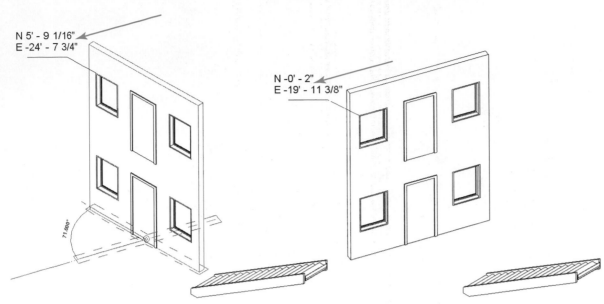

N 5' - 9 1/16"
E -24' - 7 3/4"

N -0' - 2"
E -19' - 11 3/8"

71.000"

Figure 9-16

25. Continue to select the spot dimensions you placed, and change their **Type Properties** to see their effects.
26. Save this file as **SPOT DIMENSIONS**.

Exercise 9-3: Baseline and Ordinate Dimensioning

Baseline dimensions are multiple dimensions measured from the same baseline.

1. Start a new drawing using the **RAC 2009\Imperial Templates\default.rte** template.
2. In the **Project browser**, double-click **Floor Plans > Level 1**.
3. In the **Design Bar**, under **Basic**, select the **Wall** icon.
4. Create the enclosure with **Basic wall: Generic 8″** walls as shown in Figure 9-17. (Do not dimension as shown in this figure.)

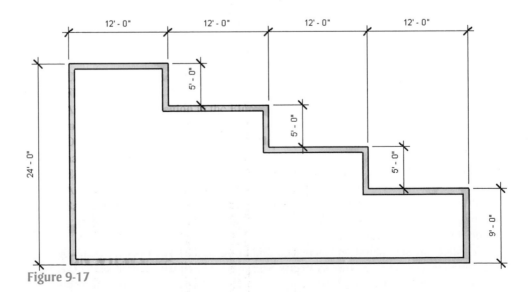

12' - 0"   12' - 0"   12' - 0"   12' - 0"

5' - 0"

5' - 0"

5' - 0"

24' - 0"

9' - 0"

Figure 9-17

5. Select the **Dimension** tool from the **Basics** tab in the **Design Bar**.
6. In the **Options** toolbar, select the **Aligned** button, then select **Linear Dimension Style: Linear - 3/32″ Arial** from the drop-down list, and, finally, press the **Element Properties** button to bring up the **Element Properties** dialog box (see Figure 9-18).

Figure 9-18

7. In the **Element Properties** dialog box, press the **Edit/New** button at the top right to bring up the **Type Properties** dialog box.
8. In the **Type Properties** dialog box, select **Baseline** from the **Dimension String Type** field, and press the **OK** buttons to return to the **Drawing Editor** (see Figure 9-19).

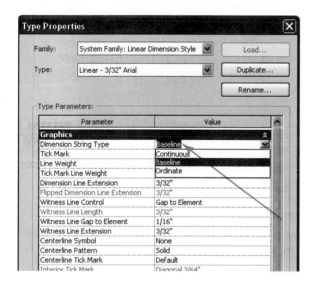

Figure 9-19

9. In the **Options** toolbar, select **Wall faces** from the **Prefer** drop-down list, and enter **1/4″** in the **Baseline Offset** field.
10. Select the walls in the order shown in Figure 9-20.

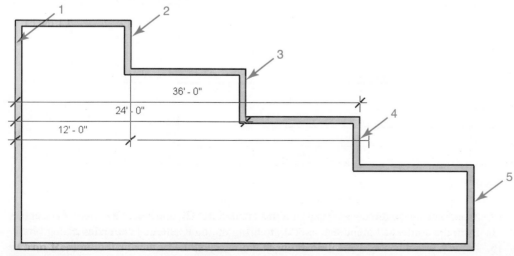

Figure 9-20

11. Move your cursor and click on the spot where you want to place the **Baseline** dimensions (see Figure 9-21).

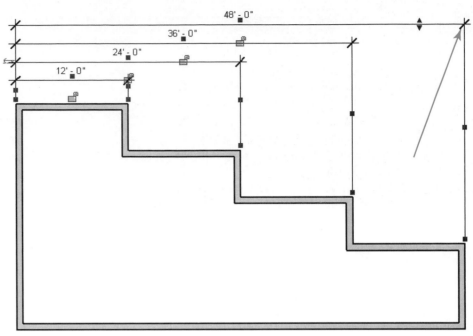

Figure 9-21

12. Select the **Modify** tool or press the **<Esc>** key twice on your keyboard.
13. Select the **12′-0″** dimension line, and drag it down as shown in Figure 9-22. Then click in an empty space in the **Drawing Editor** to place the line.

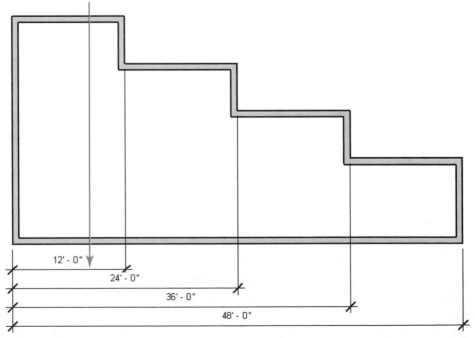

Figure 9-22

14. Select any of the dimension lines you just created, **RMB**, and select **Element Properties** from the contextual menu that appears to bring up the **Element Properties** dialog box.
15. In the **Element Properties** dialog box, you can adjust the distance between the **Baseline** dimension strings (see Figure 9-23).

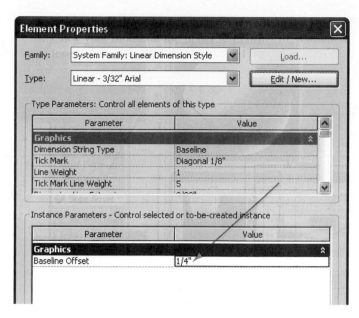

Figure 9-23

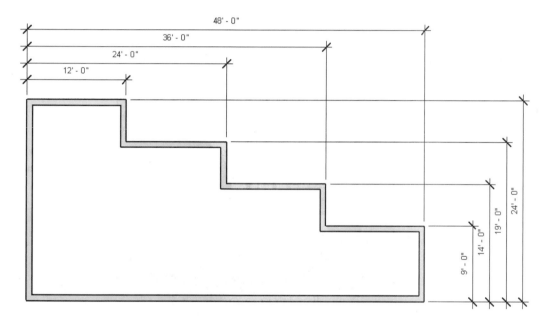

Figure 9-24

16. Continue to place dimensions (see Figure 9-24).
17. Save this file as **BASELINE DIMENSIONS**.

Ordinate Dimensioning

Ordinate dimensions measure the perpendicular distance from an origin point, called the datum, to an element. These dimensions prevent escalating errors by maintaining accurate offsets of the features from the datum.

1. Using the **BASELINE DIMENSIONS** file, delete all the dimensions you previously placed.
2. Select the **Dimension** tool from the **Basics** tab in the **Design Bar**.
3. In the **Options** toolbar, select the **Aligned** button, then select **Linear Dimension Style: Linear - 3/32″ Arial** from the drop-down list, and, finally, press the **Element Properties** button to bring up the **Element Properties** dialog box.
4. In the **Element Properties** dialog box, press the **Edit/New** button at the top right to bring up the **Type Properties** dialog box.
5. In the **Type Properties** dialog box, select **Ordinate** from the **Dimension String Type** field, and press the **OK** buttons to return to the **Drawing Editor**.

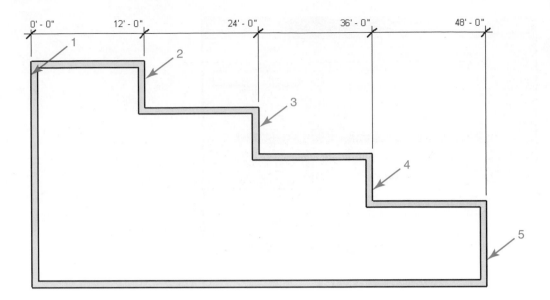

Figure 9-25

6. Select the walls in the order shown in Figure 9-25.
7. Select the dimension line you just created, **RMB**, and select **Element Properties** from the contextual menu that appears to bring up the **Element Properties** dialog box.
8. In the **Element Properties** dialog box, press the **Edit/New** button at the top right to bring up the **Type Properties** dialog box.
9. In the **Type Properties** dialog box, select the **Edit** button from the **Ordinate Dimension Settings** field to bring up the **Ordinate Dimension Settings** dialog box (see Figure 9-26).

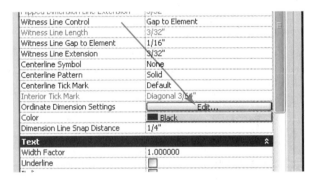

Figure 9-26

10. In the **Ordinate Dimension Settings** dialog box, select the **Parallel to Witness Line** and **End of Witness Line** radio buttons, and then press the **OK** buttons to return to the **Drawing Editor** (see Figures 9-27 and 9-28).
11. Save this file as **ORDINATE DIMENSIONING**.

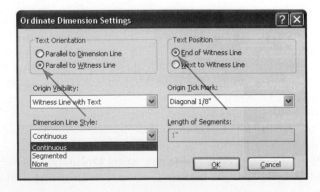

Figure 9-27

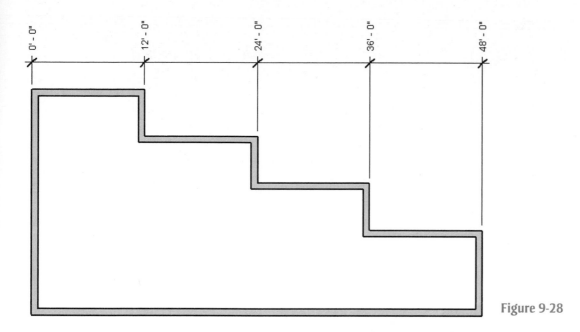

Figure 9-28

Exercise 9-4: Using the Text Tool

If you use a word processor such as Microsoft Word, Revit Architecture's **Text** tool should be quite easy to learn.

1. Start a new drawing using the **RAC 2009\Imperial Templates\default.rte** template.
2. Select **View > New > Drafting View** from the **Main** menu to bring up the **New Drafting View** dialog box.
3. In the **New Drafting View** dialog box, select the **1/8″ =1′-0″** from the **Scale** drop-down list, and press the **OK** button to bring the **Drafting View** into the **Drawing Editor**.
4. Change to the **Drafting** tab in the **Design Bar**.
5. Select the **Text** tool from the **Drafting** tab.
6. With the **Text** tool selected, choose **Text: 3/32″ Arial** from the **Options** toolbar drop-down list.
7. In the **Options** toolbar, select the **Left** justification button, and then select the **None Leader** button.
8. Click in the drafting view, drag diagonally to the right, and click again to create a word field.
9. Enter **Now is the time for all good drafts people to use Revit** in the text field. If this takes two lines, then the field needs to be stretched.
10. Drag the text field until your statement is on two lines (see Figure 9-29).

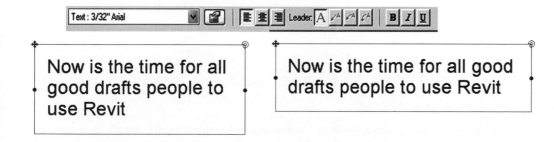

Figure 9-29

11. Select the **Rotate** icon and rotate the text field (see Figure 9-30).
12. Select the text field, and use the **B** (Bold), *I* (Italic), and <u>U</u> (Underline) buttons.
13. Again, select the **Text** tool from the **Drafting** tab.
14. With the **Text** tool selected, choose **Text: 3/32″ Arial** from the **Options** toolbar drop-down list.

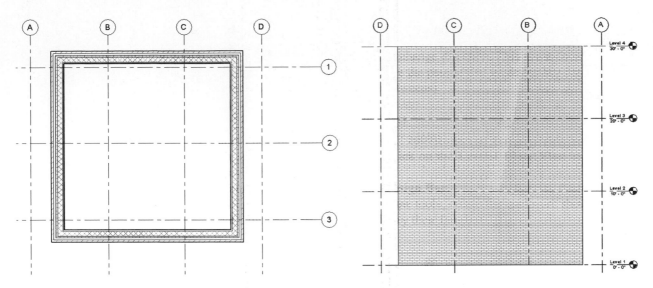

Figure 9-30

15. Select the other **Leader** tools and then place text again.
16. If you want to change the font or text size, select the outside outline of the text field you placed, **RMB**, and select **Element Properties** from the contextual menu that appears to bring up the **Element Properties** dialog box.
17. In the **Element Properties** dialog box, press the **Edit/New** button at the top right of the dialog box to bring up the **Type Properties** dialog box.

In the **Type Properties** dialog box, experiment by changing the properties and watching the effects (see Figure 9-31).

18. Save this file as **USING TEXT**.

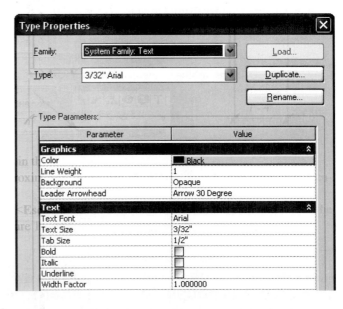

Figure 9-31

Exercise 9-5: Using the Grid Tool

1. Start a new drawing using the **RAC 2009\Imperial Templates\default.rte** template.
2. In the **Project browser**, double-click the **East Elevation** to bring it up into the **Drawing Editor**.
3. In the **East Elevation**, select the left end of the **Level 2** datum line, **RMB**, and select **Create Similar** from the contextual menu that appears.
4. Drag your cursor upward and click to place a new level datum line.
5. Drag to the right until the right point of the level datum line aligns with the right point of **Level 2**, and click to set the point.

6. Select the height number and set it to **20′-0″**
7. Repeat steps 3–6 creating another level datum line at **30′-0″** (see Figure 9-32).

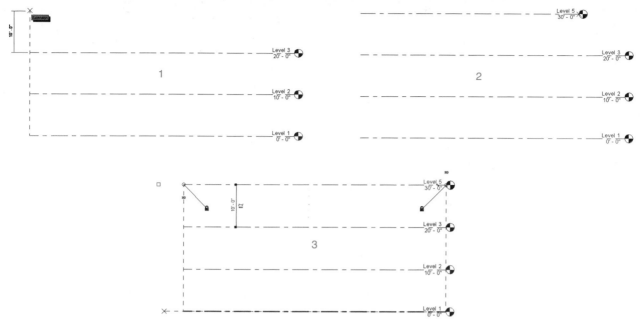

Figure 9-32

8. Select one of the level datum lines, and notice the check box at the end that does not have a bullet marker.
9. Check the check box to turn the level datum line markers on and off (see Figure 9-33).

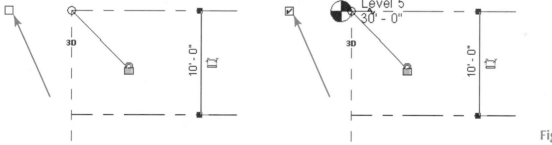

Figure 9-33

10. In the **Project browser**, double-click the **Level 1** floor plan to bring it up into the **Drawing Editor**.
11. Change to the **Drafting** tab in the **Design Bar**.
12. Select the **Grid** tool.
13. Click in the **Drawing Editor**, drag upwards, and click again to place the grid line and bubble.
14. Select the number in the grid bubble, and enter the letter **A**.
15. Select the bottom of the grid line, **RMB**, and select **Create Similar** from the contextual menu that appears.
16. Drag your cursor to the right **10′-0″** and click to place a new grid line.
17. Drag your cursor upwards until it aligns with the top of the previous grid bubble.

Notice that the new grid bubble is labeled **B**.

18. Repeat the previous steps creating grid lines **C** and **D**.
19. Click in the **Drawing Editor**, drag to the right (horizontal), and click again to place the grid line and bubble.

20. This time label the grid bubble **1**.
21. Create two more horizontal grids.

Notice that the new grid bubbles are labeled **2** and **3** (see Figure 9-34).

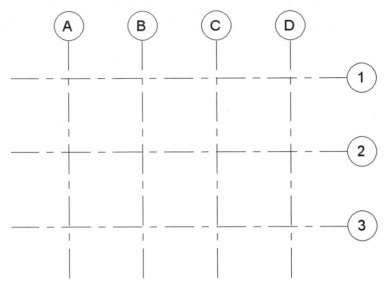

Figure 9-34

As with level datum line markers, you can check and uncheck the grid bubbles to make them visible or invisible.

22. In the **Project browser**, double-click on the rest of the floor plan levels to bring them into the **Drawing Editor**.
23. Close any other views.
24. Select **Window > Tile** from the **Main** menu.
25. Select the **1** gridline, drag it to the right, and notice that it moves in all the levels.
26. Click on the blue 3D text to change it to 2D. (Notice the small circle near the 3D mark fills in (see Figure 9-35).)

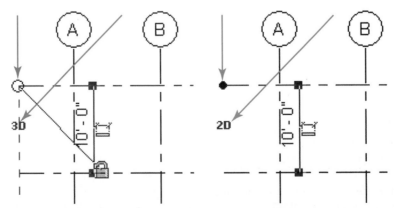

Figure 9-35

27. With the **2D** activated, again drag the **1** gridline to the right, and notice that the grid does not change in the other floor levels (see Figure 9-36).
28. Select the gridline you moved in Level 1, and then press the **Propagate Extents** button in the **Options** toolbar to bring up the **Propagate datum extents** dialog box.
29. In the **Propagate datum extents** dialog box, check the **Floor Plan: Level 2** and **Floor Plan: Level 3** check boxes (see Figure 9-37).

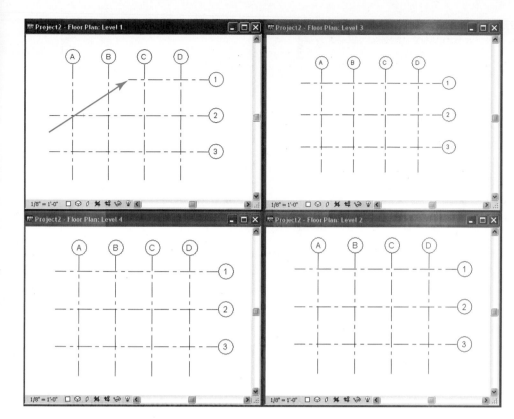

Figure 9-36

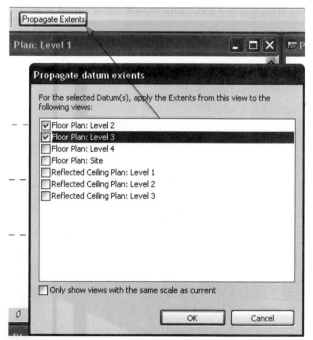

Figure 9-37

Grid lines for **Floor Plan: Level 2** and **Floor Plan: Level 3** will now match the grid lines in **Floor Plan: Level 1**, but not in **Floor Plan: Level 4** (see Figure 9-38).

30. In the **Project browser**, double-click the **East Elevation** to bring it up into the **Drawing Editor**.

31. In the **East Elevation**, unlock and then move the grid bubble below the **Level 2** datum line (see Figure 9-39).

Note:
The 3D extents (the 3D-2D text) allow you to have the grid-lines linked in all floor plans, or just one floor plan. Experiment in all the views by turning the 3D extents on and off and moving grid lines.

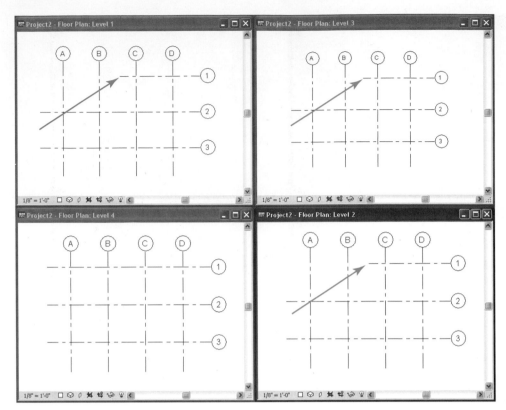

Figure 9-38

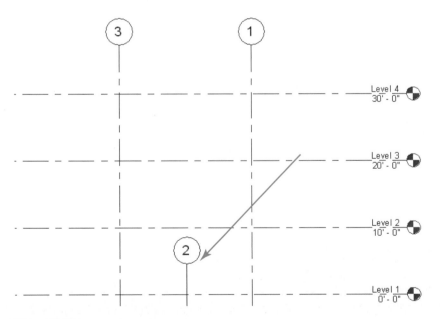

Figure 9-39

Notice that the grid lines for **Floor Plan: Level 2, Floor Plan: Level 3**, and **Floor Plan: Level 4** don't display grid line **2** because it is below those levels in the **East Elevation** (see Figure 9-40).

32. In **Floor Plan: Level 1**, select the **1** gridline and click the **Z** icon to allow you to move the grid bubble. (This is important if you have many grid lines close to each other (see Figure 9-41).)

33. Save this file as **GRID TOOL**.

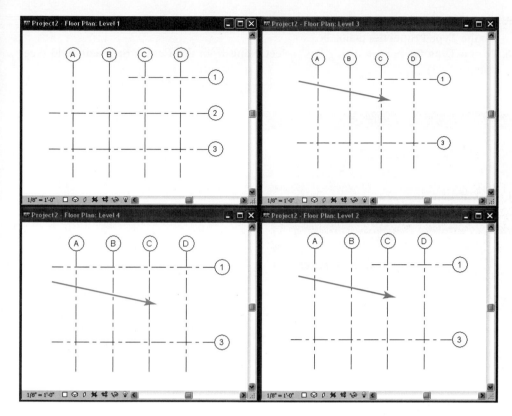

Figure 9-40

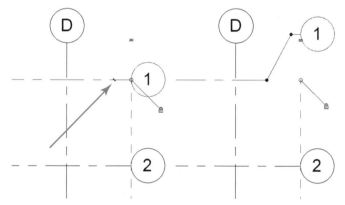

Figure 9-41

Exercise 9-6: New Grid Controls

Split Grid Lines (None)

1. Start a new drawing using the **RAC 2009\Imperial Templates\default.rte** template.
2. In the **Project browser**, double-click **Floor Plans > Level 1**.
3. In the **Design Bar**, under **Basic**, select the **Grid** tool.
4. In the **Options** toolbar, select **Grid: 1/4″ Bubble** from the drop-down list, and press the **Element Properties** button to bring up the **Element Properties** dialog box (see Figure 9-42).

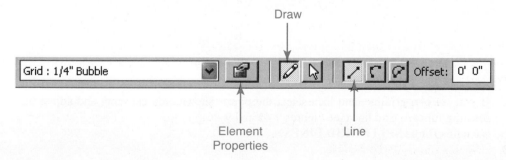

Figure 9-42

5. In the **Element Properties** dialog box, press the **Edit/New** button at the top right to bring up the **Type Properties** dialog box.

6. In the **Type Properties** dialog box, select **None** from the **Center Segment** field (see Figure 9-43).

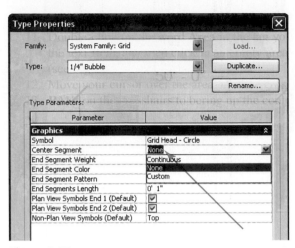

Figure 9-43

7. Select the **Dimension** tool from the **Basics** tab in the **Design Bar**, and place four gridlines. Notice that the grid lines are broken at their centers (see Figure 9-44).

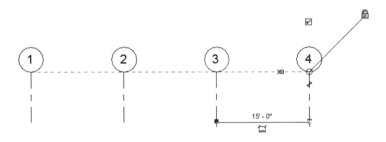

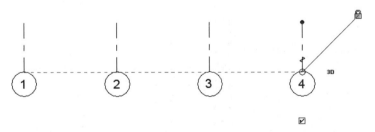

Figure 9-44

8. If you select a gridline, and then select the points shown, you can drag and adjust the opening for each grid line (see Figures 9-45 and 9-46).

9. Save this file as **SPLIT GRID LINES**.

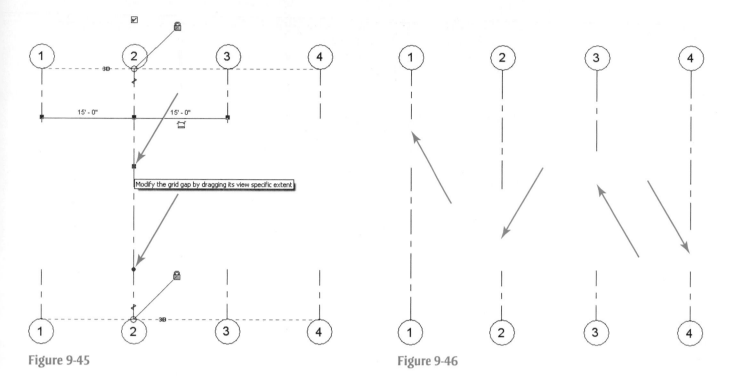

Figure 9-45   Figure 9-46

Custom Grid Lines

1. Using the previous file, select one of the grid lines, and then select the **Element Proper-ties** icon in the **Options** toolbar to bring up the **Element Properties** dialog box.
2. In the **Element Properties** dialog box, set the following:
    a. **Center Segment** to **Custom**
    b. **Center Segment Pattern** to **Hidden 1/8″**
    c. **Center Segment Weight** to **1**
    d. **End Segment Weight** to **8**
    e. **End Segment Pattern** to **Double Dash 5/8″** (see Figure 9-47)

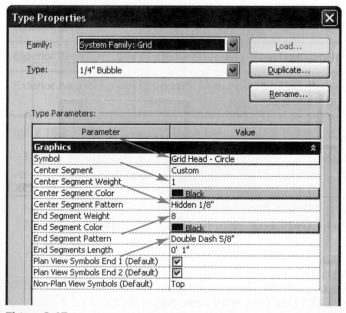

Figure 9-47

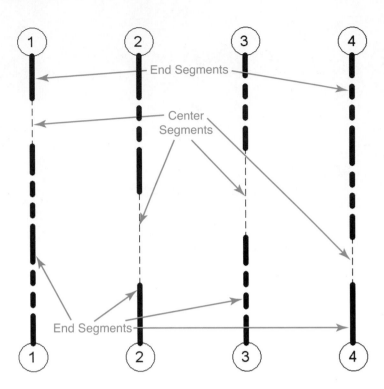

Figure 9-48

3. Press the **OK** buttons to return to the **Drawing Editor**.

Notice the changes that happen to the grid lines. If you select the points that you moved in the previous exercise, you can adjust the segments (see Figure 9-48).

4. Continue making changes in the **Type Properties** dialog box and observe the results.
5. Save this file as **Custom Grid lines**.

SCOPE BOX TOOL

Scope boxes control the visibility of datum planes (levels, reference planes, and grids) in views whose cutting plane intersects the scope box. Scope boxes are particularly useful for controlling the visibility of datums that are not parallel or orthogonal to a view.

Adding grids, levels, and reference lines to a project can display them in more views than you may want. For example, if you add grid lines to a plan view, the grid lines appear in all plan views of the model. You may not want this effect. Instead, you may want to localize the appearance of the datums to certain views. This is exactly what a scope box is for: to limit the range in which the datums appear.

Exercise 9-7: Using the Scope Box Tool

1. Open the **GRID TOOL** file.
2. In the **Project browser**, double-click **Floor Plans > Level 1** to bring it up into the **Drawing Editor**.
3. Change to the **Basics** tab in the **Design Bar**.
4. Select the **Wall** tool and place a **25′-0″ × 25′-0″ × 40′-0″** high enclosure within the gridlines you created.
5. Change the scale to **1/4″ = 1′-0″** (see Figure 9-49).
6. Change to the **Drafting** tab in the **Design Bar**.
7. Select the **Scope Box** tool.
8. In the **Options** toolbar, enter **TEST SCOPE BOX** in the **Name** field, and set the **Height** to **30′-0″**.
9. Create a scope box as shown in Figure 9-50.

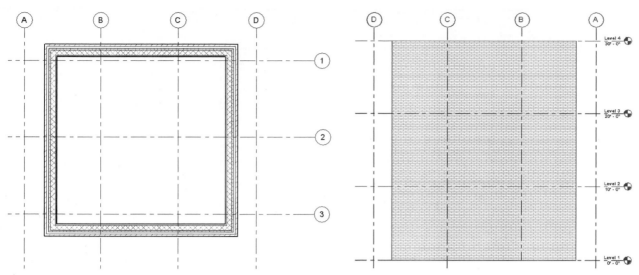

Figure 9-49

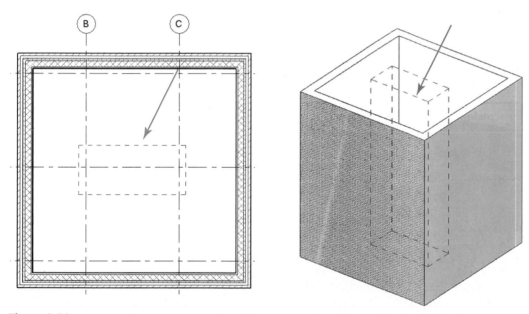

Figure 9-50

10. Change to the **Basics** tab in the **Design Bar**.
11. In the **Basics** tab, select the **Section** tool.
12. In the **Floor 1** view, place two section marks as shown in Figure 9-51.
13. Be sure to flip the sections (if necessary) by selecting the small blue arrows (Figure 9-52).
14. Select grid line **C**, **RMB**, and select **Element Properties** from the contextual menu to bring up the **Element Properties** dialog box.
15. In the **Element Properties** dialog box, select **TEST SCOPE BOX** from the **Scope Box** drop-down list (see Figure 9-53).
16. Double-click on the section mark to open the section view (see Figure 9-54).
17. Close all the views except the **Level 1** and **Section** views.
18. Select **Window > Tile** from the **Main** menu.
19. Move the section mark in the **Level 1** view, and watch the grid appear and disappear in the **Section** view as the section mark touches the scope box.
20. Add more scope boxes and attach grid lines to them; move the section marks and observe the results (see Figure 9-55).

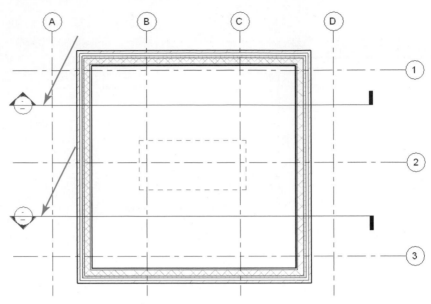

Figure 9-51

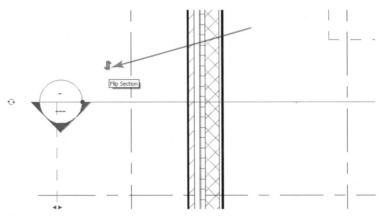

Figure 9-52

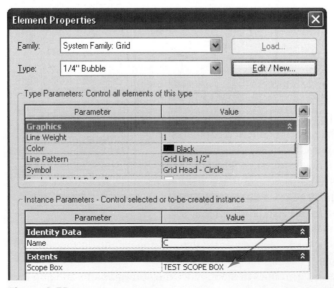

Figure 9-53

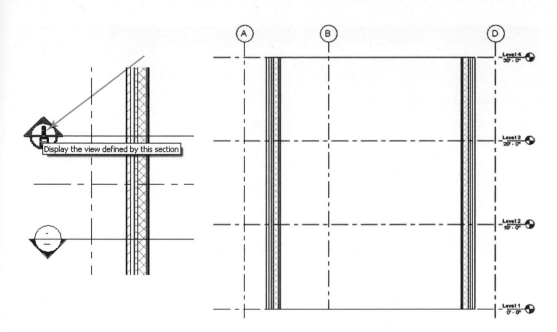

Figure 9-54

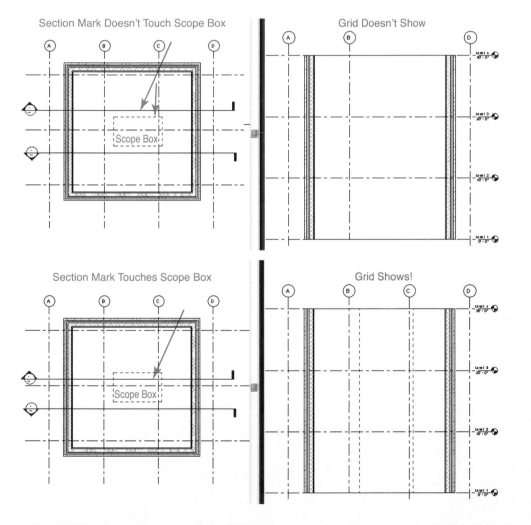

Figure 9-55

21. To hide the scope box itself in different views, select the scope box, **RMB**, and select **Element Properties** from the contextual menu to bring up the **Element Properties** dialog box.

22. In the **Element Properties** dialog box, select the **Views Visible** dialog box to bring up the **Scope Box Views Visible** dialog box.

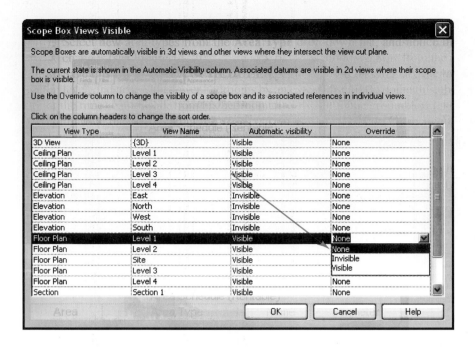

Scope Box Views Visible

Scope Boxes are automatically visible in 3d views and other views where they intersect the view cut plane.

The current state is shown in the Automatic Visibility column. Associated datums are visible in 2d views where their scope box is visible.

Use the Override column to change the visiblity of a scope box and its associated references in individual views.

Click on the column headers to change the sort order.

View Type	View Name	Automatic visibility	Override
3D View	{3D}	Visible	None
Ceiling Plan	Level 1	Visible	None
Ceiling Plan	Level 2	Visible	None
Ceiling Plan	Level 3	Visible	None
Ceiling Plan	Level 4	Visible	None
Elevation	East	Invisible	None
Elevation	North	Invisible	None
Elevation	West	Invisible	None
Elevation	South	Invisible	None
Floor Plan	Level 1	Visible	None
Floor Plan	Level 2	Visible	None None / Invisible / Visible
Floor Plan	Site	Visible	Invisible
Floor Plan	Level 3	Visible	Visible
Floor Plan	Level 4	Visible	None
Section	Section 1	Visible	None

[OK] [Cancel] [Help]

Figure 9-56

23. In the **Scope Box Views Visible** dialog box, select **Invisible** from the **Override** drop-down list for the view that you do not want to show the scope box (see Figure 9-56).
24. Save this file as **SCOPE BOXES**.

Exercise 9-8: How to Use the Tag and Tag All Not Tagged Tools

1. Start a new drawing using the **RAC 2009\Imperial Templates\default.rte** template.
2. In the **Project browser**, double-click **Floor Plans > Level 1** to bring it up into the **Drawing Editor**.
3. Set the **Scale** to **1/4″ = 1′-0″**
4. Change to the **Basics** tab in the **Design Bar**.
5. Select the **Wall** tool.
6. Create a **25′-0″ × 25′-0″ × 10′-0″** high enclosure using the **Basic wall: Exterior – Brick on CMU** wall type.
7. Change the **Detail Level** to **Medium**.
8. Select the **Door** and **Window** tools and add doors and windows as shown in Figure 9-57.
9. Change to the **Drafting** tab in the **Design Bar**.
10. Select the **Tag >> By Category** tool.

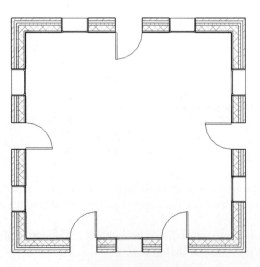

Figure 9-57

11. In the **Options** toolbar, select **Horizontal** from the drop-down list and uncheck the **Leader** check box.
12. Click on one window and one door to place their tags.
13. Select the **Tag All Not Tagged** tool to bring up the **Tag All Not Tagged** dialog box.
14. In the **Tag All Not Tagged** dialog box, select the **Door Tag** field and press the **Apply** button.
15. Repeat the process for the **Window Tag**, press the **Apply** button again, and then press the **OK** button to return to the **Drawing Editor** (see Figure 9-58).

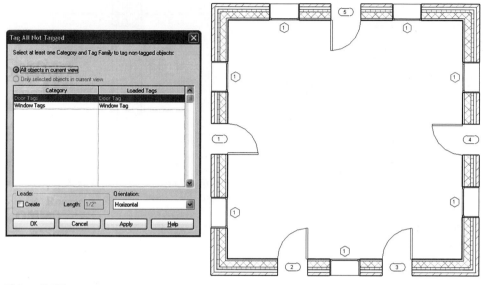

Figure 9-58

16. Select the **Tag >> By Material** tool.
17. In the **Options** toolbar, select **Horizontal** from the drop-down list, and check the **Leader** check box.
18. In the **Options** toolbar, select the **Element Properties** button to bring up the **Element Properties** dialog box.
19. In the **Element Properties** dialog box, select the **Edit/New** button to bring up the **Type Properties** dialog box.
20. In the **Type Properties** dialog box, select **Arrow Filled 30 Degree** from the **Leader Arrowhead** drop-down list, and then press the **OK** buttons to return to the **Drawing Editor** (see Figure 9-59).

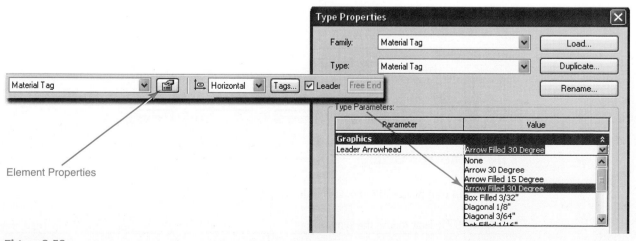

Figure 9-59

21. Move your cursor over the wall, and the wall materials will appear.
22. When you see **Brick** appear, click your mouse, drag it to the right, click, and then move the cursor and click to place the tag (see Figure 9-60).

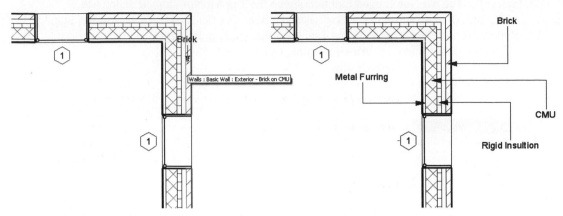

Figure 9-60

23. Select the **Tag >> By Category** tool again.
24. In the **Options** toolbar, select the **Tags** button to bring up the **Tags** dialog box.
25. In the **Tags** dialog box, press the **Load** button and load the **Wall** tag from the **Annotations** folder of the **Imperial Library**.
26. In the **Options** toolbar, check the **Leader** check box, select **Attached End** from the drop-down list, and enter **1/2″** in the number field.
27. Select each wall, and place a wall tag.

The tag will be empty. This is because the walls have not been given a type letter or number.

28. Select a wall, **RMB**, and select **Element Properties** to bring up the **Element Properties** dialog box.
29. In the **Element Properties** dialog box, press the **Edit/New** button to bring up the **Type Properties** dialog box.
30. In the **Type Properties** dialog box, enter **A** in the **Type Mark** field, and press the **OK** buttons to return to the **Drawing Editor** (see Figure 9-61).
31. Save this file as **REVIT TAGS**.

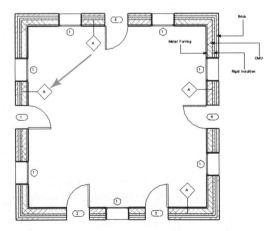

Figure 9-61

THE SYMBOL TOOL

The **Symbol** tool places 2D annotation drawing symbols into the project.

EXERCISE 9-9: How to Use the Symbol Tool

1. Start a new drawing using the **RAC 2009\Imperial Templates\default.rte** template.
2. Change to the **View** tab in the **Design Bar**.

3. In the **Design Bar**, select the **Drafting View** tool to bring up the **New Drafting View** dialog box.
4. In the **New Drafting View** dialog box, select **1/4″ = 1′-0″** from the **Scale** drop-down list and press the **OK** button to bring the **Drafting View** into the **Drawing Editor**.
5. Change to the **Drafting** tab in the **Design Bar**.
6. Select the **Symbol** tool.
7. In the **Options** toolbar, press the **Load** button and select **North Arrow 1** from the **Annotations** folder in the **Imperial library**.
8. In the **Options** toolbar, select the **Element Properties** button to bring up the **Element Properties** dialog box.
9. In the **Element Properties** dialog box, select the **Edit/New** button to bring up the **Type Properties** dialog box.
10. In the **Type Properties** dialog box, select **Arrow Filled 30 Degree** from the **Leader Arrowhead** drop-down list, and then press the **OK** buttons to return to the **Drawing Editor**.
11. In the **Options** toolbar, select **3** from the **Number of Leaders** field, and check the **Rotate after placement** check box.
12. Click in the drafting view to place the **North Arrow 1** symbol.
13. Because you selected three leaders in the **Options** toolbar, three leaders appear with the symbol.
14. Rotate the symbol and adjust the leaders.
15. If you want to add or remove a leader, press the **Add a Leader** or **Remove a Leader** button on the **Options** toolbar (see Figure 9-62).
16. Select the **Edit Family** button in the **Options** toolbar to bring up the **Revit** dialog box that asks if you want to **Open "North arrow 1" for editing.**
17. Select the **Yes** button to open the **Family** tab in the **Design Bar**.
18. In the **Family** tab, select the **Filled Region** tool to enter **Sketch** mode.
19. In the **Sketch** tab, select the **Lines** tool, and then trace the arrow head (see Figure 9-63).
20. In the **Sketch** tab, press the **Region Properties** button to bring up the **Element Properties** dialog box.

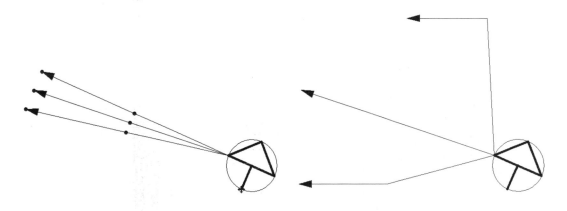

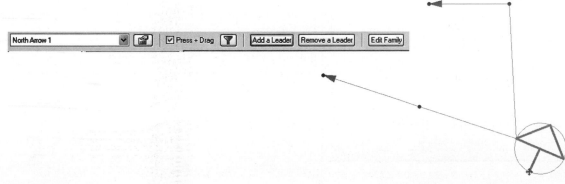

Figure 9-62

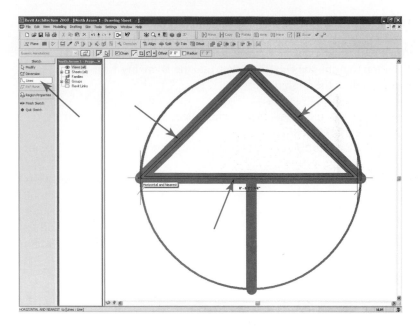

Figure 9-63

21. In the **Element Properties** dialog box, select the **Edit/New** button to bring up the **Type Properties** dialog box.
22. In the **Type Properties** dialog box, select the **Diagonal crosshatch** in the **Cut fill pattern** field to open the **Fill Patterns** dialog box.
23. In the **Fill Patterns** dialog box, select the **Solid fill** pattern and press the **OK** buttons to return to the **Drawing Editor** (see Figure 9-64).

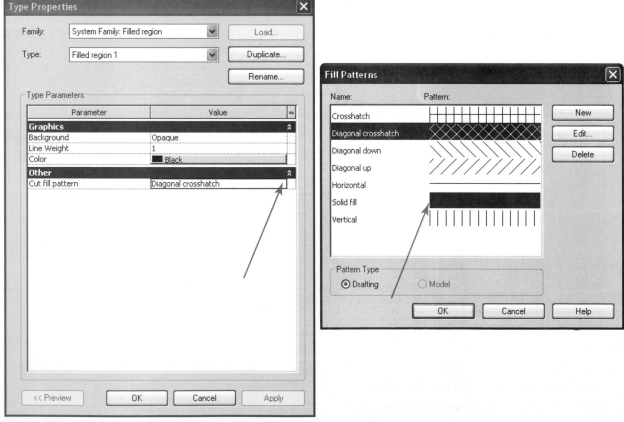

Figure 9-64

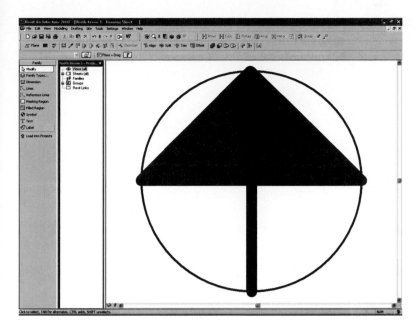

Figure 9-65

24. In the **Sketch** tab, press the **Finish Sketch** button to return to the **Family** tab in the **Design Bar** (see Figure 9-65).
25. In the **Family** tab, press the **Load into Projects** button to bring up the **Reload Family** dialog box.
26. In the **Reload Family** dialog box, press the **Yes** button when asked **Family North arrow 1 is already in use in this project. Overwrite the existing version?**

You will now be returned to the **Drafting View** in the **Drawing Editor**, and the arrow will be filled.

27. Repeat steps 16–26 and experiment creating new symbols with different names.
28. Save this file as **REVIT SYMBOLS**.

SUMMARY

This section discussed dimensioning, grids, and annotation using Revit Architecture 2009. In the discussion of dimensioning, spot dimensions and baseline and ordinate dimensioning were shown. In the discussion of grids, the methods for placing and modifying grids were illustrated. These methods included Revit 2009's ability to control the grid line itself. Finally, this section examined the locating, placing, and modifying of Revit's **Annotation** families.

SECTION TEST QUESTIONS

Exercise

Create a **40′ × 60′** grid **10′-0″** on center in both directions. Place walls inside this grid. Dimension and annotate the plan.

Questions

1. What is the purpose of the scope box?
2. What is the definition of ordinate dimensioning?
3. What is the definition of baseline dimensioning?
4. Is there a spline dimensioning tool?
5. What is the purpose of the symbol in the **Drafting** tab tool?
6. What turns the bubbles on and off at the ends of the grid lines?

Drafting and Detail Components

10

Section Objectives

- Understand the **Drafting View**.
- Know how to set **Line Styles, Line Weights,** and **Line Patterns**.
- Learn how to use the **Detail Group** tool.
- Know how to create **Details** in Revit Architecture 2009.
- Learn how to use the **Repeating Detail** tool.
- Learn how to use the **Detail Component** tool.
- Learn how to use the **Masking Region** tool.
- Know how to use the **Insulation** tool.
- Know how to use the **Break Line** tool.

Drafting and detailing tools are essential to the development of a set of construction documents (CDs). These tools are generally used to explain, in finer detail, parts and details of a building that cannot be explained either in 3D or in larger plan or section views. For these purposes, Revit Architecture 2009 utilizes standard electronic drafting tools plus automated detailing tools. Among these automated detailing tools are the **Detail Components**, which are contained in the **Family** libraries. These **Detail Components** speed up the 2D drafting process by adding parametric controls to these tools.

Although this section illustrates the methodology for using the drafting tools and **Detail Components**, every tool is not explored. To this end, it is highly recommended that you open all the tools and **Detail Components** and then experiment with each one to understand each tool's idiosyncrasies.

Exercise 10-1: The Drafting View

1. Start a new drawing using the **RAC 2009\Imperial Templates\default.rte** template.
2. In the **Project browser**, double-click **Floor Plans > Level 1** to bring it up into the **Drawing Editor**.
3. Change to the **Drafting** tab in the **Design Bar**.
4. Select **View > New > Drafting View** from the **Main** menu to bring up the **New Drafting View** dialog box (see Figure 10-1).
5. In the **New Drafting View** dialog box, enter **TEST DRAFTING VIEW** in the **Name** field and select **1 1/2″ = 1′-0″** from the **Scale** field.
6. Press the **OK** button to create the **TEST DRAFTING VIEW**, and bring it into the **Drawing Editor**.
7. Save this file as **DRAFTING VIEWS**.

> **Note:**
> Notice that some of the tools in the **Drafting** tab (**Spot Dimension, Grid, Level,** etc.) have become gray, and cannot be selected. This is because the **Drafting View** is strictly a 2D view, and is not linked to the model. Please refer to Section 9 on dimensioning and annotation for information on the use of the tools that are available for the **Drafting View**.

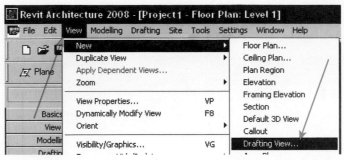

Figure 10-1

Exercise 10-2: Setting Line Styles, Line Weights, and Line Patterns

1. Use the drafting view you created in the previous exercise.
2. Select **Settings < Line Styles** from the **Main** menu to bring up the **Line Styles** dialog box (see Figure 10-2).
3. In the **Line Styles** dialog box, press the **OK** button to return to the drafting view.
4. Select the **Detail Lines** tool from the **Drafting** tab of the **Design Bar**.
5. Select a line style from the **Options** toolbar drop-down list.
6. Place four **1'-0"** long lines with the line styles shown in Figure 10-3.
7. Select **Settings > Line Styles** to open the **Line Styles** dialog box again.

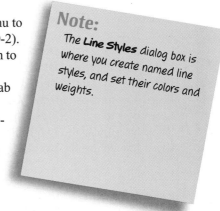

> **Note:**
> The **Line Styles** dialog box is where you create named line styles, and set their colors and weights.

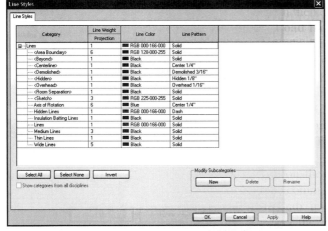

Figure 10-2

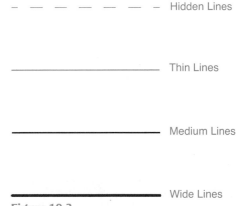

Figure 10-3

8. In the **Line Styles** dialog box, for **Wide Lines**, select **8** from the drop-down list in the **Line Weight/Projection** column and press the **OK** button.

Notice that the line increases in weight.

9. Select **Settings > Line Styles** to open the **Line Styles** dialog box again.
10. In the **Line Styles** dialog box, for **Wide Lines**, select **Center 1/4"** from the drop-down list in the **Line Pattern** column and press the **OK** button.
11. Repeat this process, changing the various settings for the **Hidden**, **Thin,** and **Medium** lines (see Figure 10-4).
12. Select **Settings > Line Weights** to open the **Line Weights** dialog box (see Figure 10-5).

Hidden Lines

Thin Lines

Medium Lines

Wide Lines

Figure 10-4

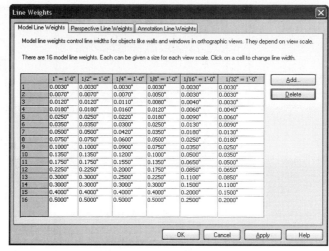

Figure 10-5

13. In the **Line Weights** dialog box, select the **Perspective**, and then the **Annotation Line Weights** tabs.

These tabs allow you to have unlimited line weight control over different types of views and annotations.

14. Select the **Model Line Weights** tab.
15. Select the **Add** button at the top right of the dialog box to bring up the **Add Scale** dialog box.
16. In the **Add Scale** dialog box, select **1 1/2″ = 1′-0″** from the drop-down list and press the **OK** button to return to the **Line Weights** dialog box.

Here you can change the line weight for each of the 16 numbered lines, specifically for the 1 1/2″ = 1′-0″ scale.

17. Select **Settings > Line Patterns** to open the **Line Patterns** dialog box (see Figure 10-6).
18. In the **Line Patterns** dialog box, select the **New** button to bring up the **Line Pattern Properties** dialog box.
19. In the **Line Pattern Properties** dialog box, enter **TEST LINE PATTERN**.
20. Enter the dash/dot **Types** and **Values** shown in Figure 10-7.
21. Press the **OK** button in the **Line Pattern Properties** dialog box to return to the **Line Patterns** dialog box (see Figure 10-8).

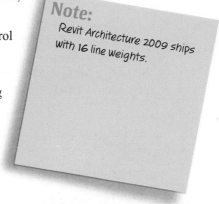

Note:
Revit Architecture 2009 ships with 16 line weights.

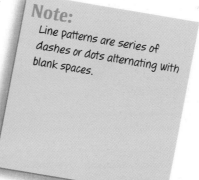

Note:
Line patterns are series of dashes or dots alternating with blank spaces.

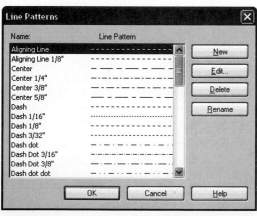

Figure 10-6

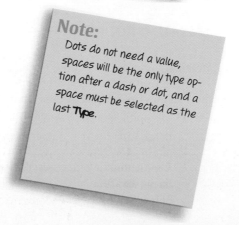

Note:
Dots do not need a value, spaces will be the only type option after a dash or dot, and a space must be selected as the last **Type**.

Figure 10-7

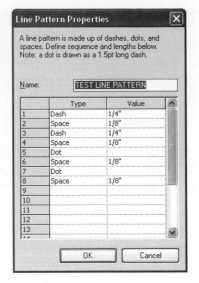

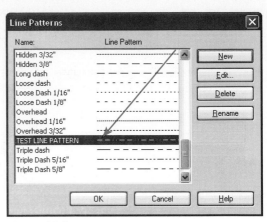

Figure 10-8

22. Select **Settings > Line Styles** from the **Main** menu again, and set the **Line Pattern** for the **Medium Lines** to the **TEST LINE PATTERN** that you just created (see Figure 10-9).
23. Press the **OK** button in the **Line Styles** dialog box to return to the **Drawing Editor**, and then place a **2′-0″** long **Medium** line (see Figure 10-10).
24. Save this file as **LINE SETTINGS**.

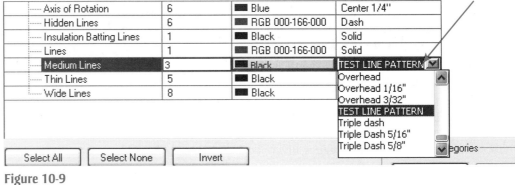

Figure 10-9

Figure 10-10

DETAIL GROUPS

Detail Groups are collections of elements such as detail lines that can be placed as copies in the **Drawing Editor**. Because groups are linked copies, changes to one of the elements in a group affects all the copies in that group. **Detail Groups** are particularly useful for automatically making changes over copies such as windows, and so on.

Exercise 10-3: Using the Detail Group Tool

1. Use the drafting view you created in the previous exercise.
2. In the **Drafting** tab of the **Design Bar**, select the **Detail Lines** tool.

3. Using the **Detail Lines** tool, place a circle and rectangle in the **Drawing Editor** (see Figure 10-11).

4. Select the **Group** tool from the **Edit** toolbar, or select **Edit > Group > Create Group** from the **Main** menu to bring up the **Create Group** dialog box.

5. In the **Create Group** dialog box, enter **TEST GROUP,** select the detail radio button, press the **OK** button to "yellow" the screen, and bring up the **Detail Group: TEST GROUP** tools.

6. In the **Detail Group: TEST GROUP** tools, select the **Add to Group** icon and then select all the detail lines you created (see Figure 10-12).

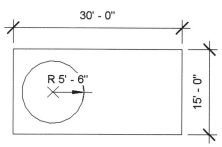

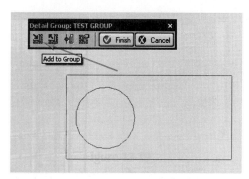

Figure 10-11   Figure 10-12

7. After you have selected all the lines, press the **Finish** button to return to the **Drawing Editor**.

8. Select the **Detail Group** tool from the **Drafting** tab in the **Design Bar**.

9. With the **Detail Group** tool selected, select **Detail Group: TEST GROUP** from the **Options** toolbar drop-down list and **check** the **Constrain** check box.

10. Place two copies of the **TEST GROUP**, re-checking the **Constrain** check box before placing each copy.

11. Select the first group object used to create the group (the left-hand object).

Note:

Checking the **Detail Group Constrain** check box constrains the group copies to horizontal and vertical. With the **Detail Group Constrain** check box unchecked, your group copies can be placed at any angle (see Figure 10-13).

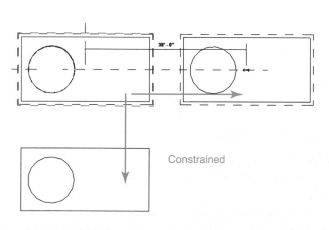

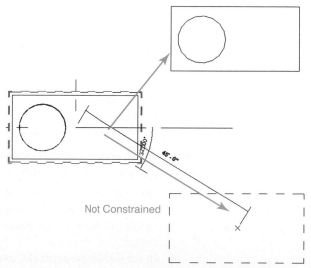

Constrained

Not Constrained

Figure 10-13

12. In the **Options** toolbar, select the **Edit Group** button to yellow the screen, and bring up the **Detail Group: TEST GROUP** tools.
13. Delete the circle, and then press the **Finish** button.
14. Using the **Detail Lines** tool, place a rectangle inside the original rectangle you created.
15. Select the first group object used to create the group again.
16. In the **Options** toolbar, again, select the **Edit Group** button to yellow the screen, and bring up the **Detail Group: TEST GROUP** tools.
17. In the **Detail Group: TEST GROUP** tools, select the **Add to Group** icon, select the lines for the internal rectangle you just placed, and then press the **Finish** button to return to the **Drawing Editor**.

All the copies of the original group change to match the original detail lines.

18. Repeat the above process, adding text to the first group object.

All the copies of the original group change to match the original detail lines (see Figure 10-14).

19. Experiment creating, editing, adding, and deleting groups.
20. Save this file as **DETAIL GROUPS**.

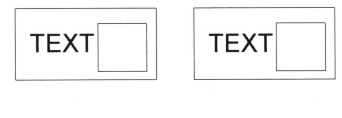

Figure 10-14

CREATING DETAILS IN REVIT ARCHITECTURE 2009

Detail Components

Detail Components are predrawn line-based 2D elements that you can add to detail or drafting views. They are visible only in those views. They scale with the model rather than with the sheet.

Exercise 10-4: Using the Detail Component Tool

1. Create a new drafting view as shown in the previous exercises.
2. Name the drafting view **DETAIL COMPONENTS VIEW**.
3. Set the scale to **1 1/2″ = 1′-0″**.
4. In the **Drafting** tab of the **Design Bar**, select the **Detail Component** tool.
5. In the **Options** toolbar, press the **Load** button to bring up the **Library** (Imperial or Metric).
6. In the **Library**, locate and open the **Detail Components** folder.

The **Detail Components** folder contains 16 folders corresponding to the CSI (Construction Specification Institute) MasterFormat 16-division list (see Figure 10-15).

7. Open the **Div 03-Concrete** folder.
8. In the **Div 03-Concrete** folder, open the **03300-Cast-in-Place Concrete** folder.
9. In the **03300-Cast-in-Place Concrete** folder, open the **03310-Structural Concrete** folder.
10. In the **03310-Structural Concrete** folder, select the **Double Tee Joist-Section**, and press the **Open** button to load the family and return to the **Drawing Editor** (see Figure 10-16).

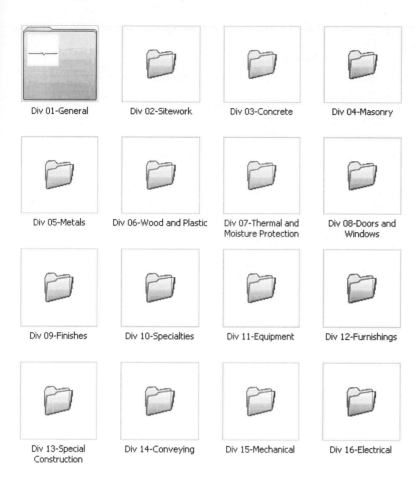

Figure 10-15

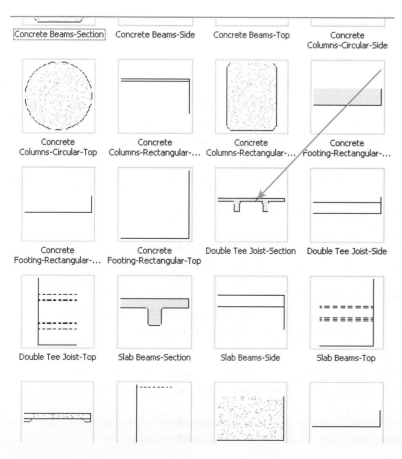

Figure 10-16

11. Click in the **Drawing Editor** to place the **Double Tee Joist-Section** (see Figure 10-17).

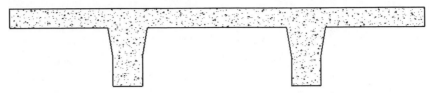

Figure 10-17

As with all detail components, the **Double Tee Joist-Section** is parametric.

12. Select the **Double Tee Joist-Section** you placed, **RMB**, and select **Element Properties** from the contextual menu that appears to bring up the **Element Properties** dialog box.
13. In the **Element Properties** dialog box, select the **Edit/New** button to bring up the **Type Properties** dialog box.
14. In the **Type Properties** dialog box, change the **Rib_Width** to **3″**, **Thickness** (slab) to **3″**, and **Rib_Dist** to **5′-0″**, and press the **OK** button to return to the **Drawing Editor.**
15. In the **Drafting** tab of the **Design Bar**, again, select the **Detail Component** tool.

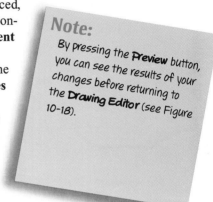

Note:

By pressing the **Preview** button, you can see the results of your changes before returning to the **Drawing Editor** (see Figure 10-18).

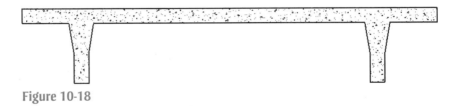

Figure 10-18

16. In the **Library**, select and open the **Div 04-Masonry** folder.
17. In the **Div 04-Masonry** folder, select and open the **04220-Concrete Masonry Units** folder.
18. In the **04200-Clay Masonry Units** folder, select the **CMU-2 Core-Section** family, and press the **Open** button to load it and return to the **Drawing Editor**.
19. In the **Options** toolbar, select **CMU-2 Core-Section: -8″ × 8″ × 16″** from the dropdown list.
20. A CMU block will appear at your cursor. With the **End Point** snap (on), snap to the left edge of the **Double Tee Joist-Section** you placed.
21. Select the **Detail Component** tool again, press the **Load** button in the **Options** toolbar, and select the **Div 05- Metals >05090-Metal Fastenings** folder.
22. In the **05090-Metal Fastenings** folder, select the **Steel Base Plate-Side-Width** and **Anchor Bolts hook-Side** families, and open them.
23. Again, select the **Detail Component** tool.
24. In the **Options** toolbar, select **Steel Base Plate-Side-Width: 1″** from the drop-down list and place it on top of the CMU.
25. Select the **Detail Component** tool, select the **Anchor Bolts hook-Side: 3/4″** from the **Options** toolbar drop-down list, and then place it in the base plate.

Note:

You will now need to make 14 copies vertically of the CMU. This can be done in several ways. One way is to **Array** the CMU vertically; but the best way is to use the **Repeating Detail** tool from the **Drafting** tab in the **Design Bar.**

Using the **Array** tool:

a. Select the **CMU** you placed, and then select the **Array** tool from the **Edit** toolbar.

b. In the **Options** toolbar, select the **Linear** button, uncheck **Group And Associate,** enter **14** in the **Number** field, check the **Constrain** check box, and press the **Activate Dimensions** button.

c. Select the lower left corner of the CMU, move your cursor upward until the dimension reads **8",** and click again to create **14** vertical copies of the CMU (see Figures 10-19, 10-20, and 10-21).

Using the **Repeating Detail** tool:

a. Select the **Repeating Detail** tool from the **Drafting** tab (see Figure 10-22).

b. In the **Options** toolbar, select the **Element Properties** button to bring up the **Element Proper-ties** dialog box.

c. In the **Element Properties** dialog box, select the **Edit/New** button to bring up the **Type Prop-erties** dialog box.

d. In the **Type Properties** dialog box, select the **Duplicate** button to bring up the **Name** dialog box.

e. Enter **REPEATING CMU** in the **Name** field, and press the **OK** button to return to the **Type Properties** dialog box.

f. In the **Type Properties** dialog box, select **CMU-2 Core-Section: 8" × 8" × 16"** from the **Detail** drop-down list.

g. In the **Type Properties** dialog box, select **Fixed Distance** from the **Layout** drop-down list, set the **Spacing** to **8",** and press the **OK** buttons to return to the **Drawing Editor** (see Figure 10-23).

h. Click your cursor at the top of the CMU you placed in step 20, drag your cursor upward, enter **9'4 (9'-4")** in the number field, and press the **<Enter>** key on your keyboard to create the 14 CMU copies (see Figure 10-24).

Figure 10-19

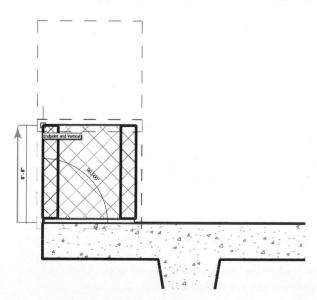

Figure 10-20

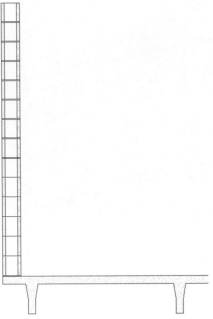

Figure 10-21

Figure 10-22

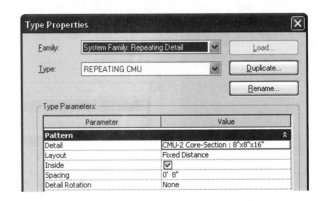

Figure 10-23

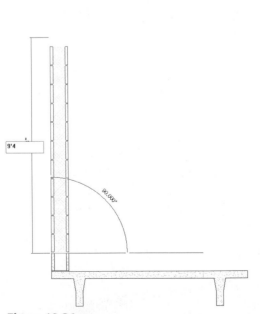

Figure 10-24

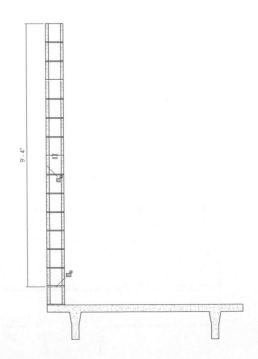

26. Select the **Detail Component** tool again, press the **Load** button in the **Options** toolbar, and select the **Div 05- Metals >05200-Metal Fastenings > 05210-Steel Joists** folder.

Note: You will have to use the **Mirror** tool in the **Edit** toolbar, and will have to adjust the length and hook length of the J bolt by selecting the J bolt and moving the small adjustment arrows that appear (see Figure 10-25).

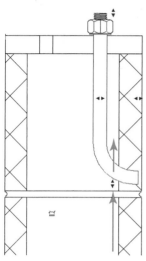
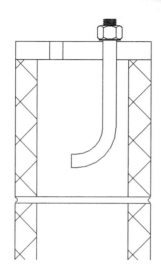

Figure 10-25

Note: If the J bolt body does not appear, it may be behind the CMU and plate. To correct this, select the J bolt head and select the **Bring to Front** button in the **Options** toolbar (see Figure 10-26).

Bring to Front

Figure 10-26

27. In the **05210-Steel Joists** folder, select the **K-Series Bar Joist-Side** family, select the **18K3 Joist** from the list, and then open it.
28. Select the **Detail Component** tool, select the **K-Series Bar Joist-Side: 18K3 Joist** from the **Options** toolbar drop-down list, and then place it on top of the base plate.
29. Select the joist you just placed and move the top and bottom joist cord adjustment arrows (see Figure 10-28).
30. Select the **Detail Component** tool again, press the **Load** button in the **Options** toolbar, and select the **Div 05- Metals >05300-Metal Deck > 05310-Steel Deck** folder.
31. In the **05310-Steel Deck** folder, select the **Roof Deck-Section** family and then open it.
32. Select the **Repeating Detail** tool in the **Drafting** tab of the **Design Bar**.
33. In the **Options** toolbar, select the **Element Properties** button to bring up the **Element Properties** dialog box.
34. In the **Element Properties** dialog box, select the **Edit/New** button to bring up the **Type Properties** dialog box.

Note: Some of the **Detail Components** will have a list of types in the folder. **Metal Joists** is an example of this (see Figure 10-27).

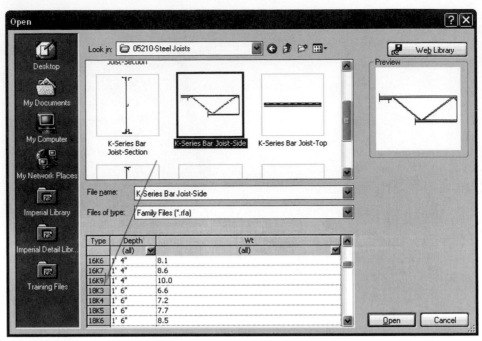

Figure 10-27

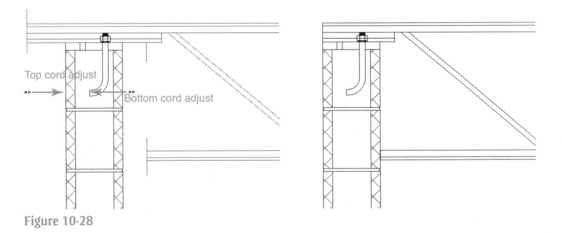

Figure 10-28

35. In the **Type Properties** dialog box, select the **Duplicate** button to bring up the **Name** dialog box.
36. Enter **REPEATING ROOF DECKING** in the **Name** field and press the **OK** button to return to the **Type Properties** dialog box.
37. In the **Type Properties** dialog box, select **Roof Decking Section: 1.5 NR 18** from the **Detail** drop-down list.
38. In the **Type Properties** dialog box, select **Fixed Distance** from the **Layout** drop-down list, set

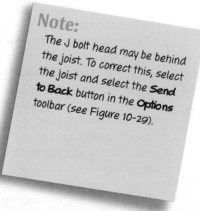

Note:

The J bolt head may be behind the joist. To correct this, select the joist and select the **Send to Back** button in the **Options** toolbar (see Figure 10-29).

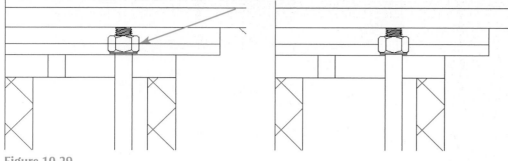

Figure 10-29

the **Spacing** to **6″**, **Detail Rotation** to **90 Counterclockwise**, and press the **OK** buttons to return to the **Drawing Editor**.

39. Click at the top left corner of the joist top cord, drag your cursor to the right **5′-0″**, and then click again to create the roof decking detail (see Figure 10-30).

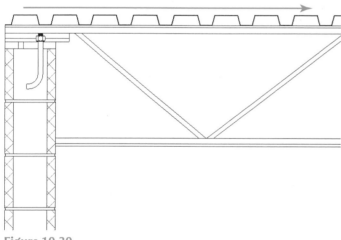

Figure 10-30

Exercise 10-5: Creating the Gravel and Earth with the Filled Region Tool

1. Select the **Filled Region** tool in the **Drafting** tab of the **Design Bar** to bring up the **Sketch** tab in the **Design Bar**.
2. In the **Sketch** tab, select the **Lines** tool and place a **4″** wide enclosure below the slab.
3. Select **Region Properties** from the **Sketch** tab to bring up the **Element Properties** dialog box.
4. In the **Element Properties** dialog box, select the **Edit/New** button to bring up the **Type Properties** dialog box.
5. In the **Type Properties** dialog box, select the **Duplicate** button to bring up the **Name** dialog box.
6. Enter **GRAVEL PATTERN** in the **Name** field and press the **OK** button to return to the **Type Properties** dialog box.
7. In the **Type Properties** dialog box, select the **Fill Pattern Value** to bring up the **Fill Patterns** dialog box.

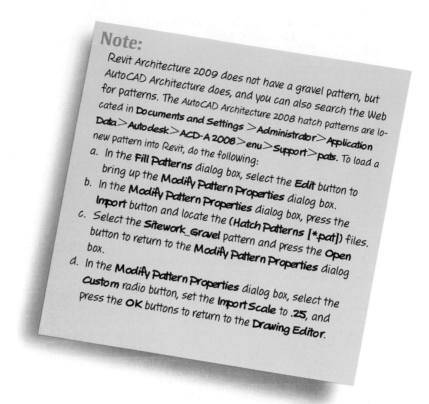

Note:

Revit Architecture 2009 does not have a gravel pattern, but AutoCAD Architecture does, and you can also search the Web for patterns. The AutoCAD Architecture 2008 hatch patterns are located in **Documents and Settings** > **Administrator** > **Application Data** > **Autodesk** > **ACD-A 2008** > **enu** > **Support** > **pats**. To load a new pattern into Revit, do the following:

a. In the **Fill Patterns** dialog box, select the **Edit** button to bring up the **Modify Pattern Properties** dialog box.

b. In the **Modify Pattern Properties** dialog box, press the **Import** button and locate the **(Hatch Patterns [*.pat])** files.

c. Select the **Sitework_Gravel** pattern and press the **Open** button to return to the **Modify Pattern Properties** dialog box.

d. In the **Modify Pattern Properties** dialog box, select the **Custom** radio button, set the **Import Scale** to **.25**, and press the **OK** buttons to return to the **Drawing Editor**.

8. In the **Sketch** tab, press **Finish Sketch** to create the **Filled Region** with **Gravel**. (Remember to press the **Send to Back** button if the gravel is in front of the slab.) (See Figure 10-31.)

Figure 10-31

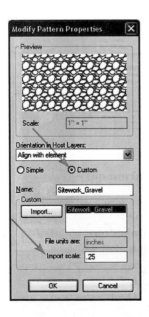

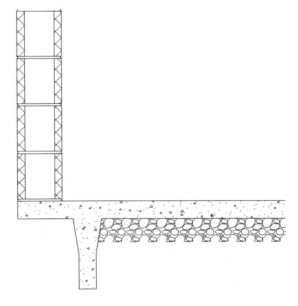

Exercise 10-6: Using the Masking Region Tool

The **Masking Region** is used to cover objects.

1. Finish the previous exercise placing **Filled Regions,** moving them to the front and back to get the effect you need.

2. Select the **Masking Region** tool from the **Drafting** tab to enter **Sketch** mode.
3. In the **Sketch** tab, select the **Lines** tool, and then select **Wide** from the drop-down list and **Circle** from the **Options** toolbar.
4. Place a circle, and it will mask the gravel (see Figure 10-32).

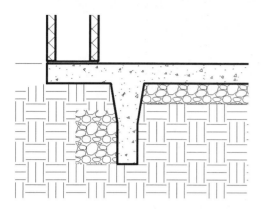 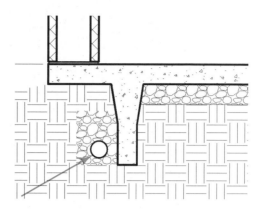

Figure 10-32

Exercise 10-7: Using the Insulation Tool

1. Using the information you have learned in the previous exercises, select the **Detail Component** tool and place **1/2″** sheathing, **3-1/2″** metal stud, and **1/2″** gypsum board in your detail.
2. Select the **Insulation** tool from the **Drafting** tab.
3. Select the **Pencil**, enter **3-1/2″** in the **Width** field, and select **to center** from the drop-down list (see Figure 10-33).
4. With the **Midpoint** snap (on), click at the midpoint of the stud at its base, and then drag and snap to the top of the stud to place the insulation. If you change your mind about the size of the insulation, select the insulation and change the **Width** field (see Figure 10-34).

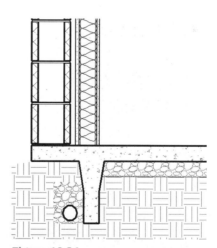

Figure 10-33

Figure 10-34

Exercise 10-8: Using the Break Line

Designers often use break lines to isolate parts of a drawing.

1. Select the **Detail Component** tool from the **Drafting** tab.
2. In the **Options** toolbar, press the **Load** button to bring up the **Library** (Imperial or Metric).
3. In the **Library**, locate and open the **Detail Components** folder.
4. In the **Detail Components** folder, locate and open the **Div 01-General** folder.
5. In the **Div 01-General** folder, select the **Break Line** family and **Open** it.

6. Select the **Detail Component** tool from the **Drafting** tab, select **Break Line** from the **Options** toolbar drop/down list, and check the **Rotate after placement** check box.
7. Place the break line and use the adjustment arrows to stretch it to cover the right side of the detail (see Figure 10-35).

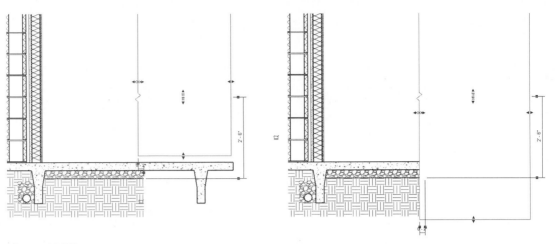

Figure 10-35

Using the information you have now learned, complete the detail by adding components. Add more break lines and annotations. Through the **Drafting** tab, Revit Architecture 2009 has full detailing and drafting capability (see Figures 10-36 and 10-37).

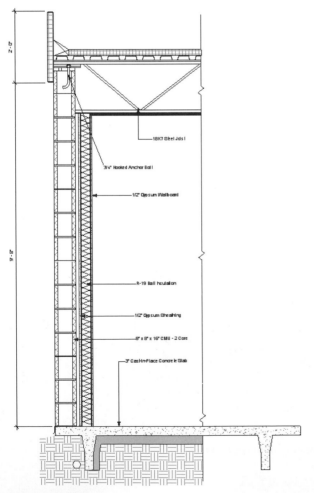

Figure 10-36

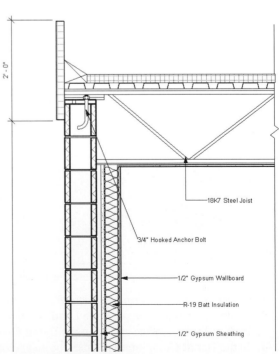

Figure 10-37

Summary

This section demonstrated the drafting capabilities of Revit Architecture 2009. Included in this demonstration were the methodology and use of **Detail Components** to aid in automating the drafting process.

Section Test Questions

Exercise

Create a wall section of one floor of the building that you are in now.

Questions

1. From where do you open the **Line Styles** dialog box?

2. What are **Detail Groups?**

3. What are **Detail Components?**

4. What is the purpose of the **Repeating Detail** tool?

5. What is the purpose of the **Masking Region** tool?

6. Revit Architecture 2009 ships with how many lineweights?

7. What is the purpose of the **Filled Region** tool?

8. From where do you get the **Break Line** tool?

Views

11

Section Objectives

- Understand **Floor Plan** and **Reflected Ceiling Plan** (RFC) **Views**.
- Learn how to use **Elevation Views**.
- Learn how to use **Section Views**.
- Learn how to use **Callout Views**.
- Learn how to use **Drafting Views**.
- Learn how to use **Camera Views**.
- Learn how to use **Walkthrough Views**.
- Know how to use **Legend Views** and **Legend Components**.
- Learn how to use **Matchline Views**.
- Learn how to use **Schedule Views**.

VIEWS

Although Revit Architecture is 3D BIM modeling software, it represents the model in **Views**. A Revit Architecture 2009 project file contains a database of information about a building model. A project view or **View** is one way of looking at that information. The views of the model can be represented on the screen or in print as either 2D or 3D representations. The **Project browser** lists the views available for a project. As new views are created, they are added to the browser. The default Revit Architecture 2009 software comes out of the box with two floor plan views, two matching ceiling plan views, and four elevation views. These views, as well as new views that you create during a project are located in the **Project browser**. These can include floor plans, ceiling plans, elevations, sections, detail views, drafting views, 3D views, walkthrough views, legend views, schedules, renderings, and plot sheets.

In this section, we explore the creation and modification of Revit Architecture's **Views** as well as the methodology of their use.

PLAN VIEWS

Floor Plans and Reflected Ceiling Plans

The **Floor Plan** view is the default view in a new project. Most projects include at least one floor plan. **Floor Plan** views are created automatically as you add new levels to your project. **Reflected Ceiling** plan views are also created automatically as you add new levels to your project.

The default Revit Architecture 2009 template ships with two **Floor Plans** and **Ceiling Plans** labeled **Level 1** and **Level 2** within the **Project browser** (see Figure 11-1).

Floor Plans and **Reflected Ceiling Plans** are connected to and interactive with the levels in **Elevation**.

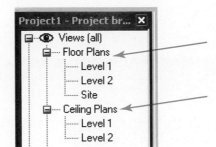

Figure 11-1

Exercise 11-1: Creating New Levels and Floor Plan Views

1. Start a new drawing using the **RAC 2009\Imperial Templates\default.rte** template.
2. In the **Project browser**, double-click on the **East Elevation** to bring it up into the **Drawing Editor**.
3. Change to the **Basics** tab in the **Design Bar**.
4. In the **Basics** tab, select the **Level** tool, and add two more levels.

Notice that the levels show up as new levels in the **Project browser**. If you change the name of the levels in the **Elevation**, the levels change name in the **Project browser** (see Figures 11-2 and 11-3).

5. Save this file as **FLOOR PLAN VIEWS**.

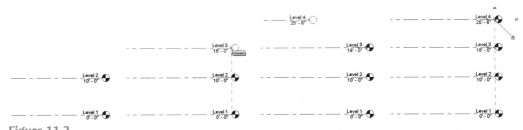

Figure 11-2

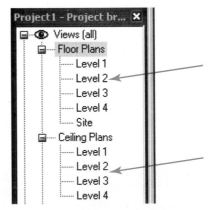

Figure 11-3

ELEVATION VIEWS

Elevation Views are part of the default template in Revit Architecture. When you create a project with the template, four elevation views are included: north, south, east, and west. Elevation views are where you sketch level lines. For each level line that you sketch, a corresponding plan view is created.

You can create additional exterior elevation views and interior elevation views. Interior elevation views depict detailed views of interior walls and show how the features of the wall should be built.

The **Floor Plans** in the default Revit Architecture 2009 template contain four **Elevation View** cameras labeled **North**, **East**, **South**, and **West**. They correspond to the **North**, **East**, **South**, and **West Elevations** in the **Project browser** (see Figure 11-4).

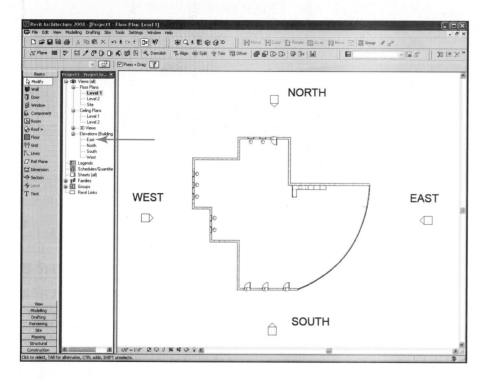

Figure 11-4

Double-clicking on any **Elevation View** in the **Project browser** will bring up that view in the **Drawing Editor**. If you click on several views and then select **Window > Tile** from the **Main** menu, you will get the result in Figure 11-5.

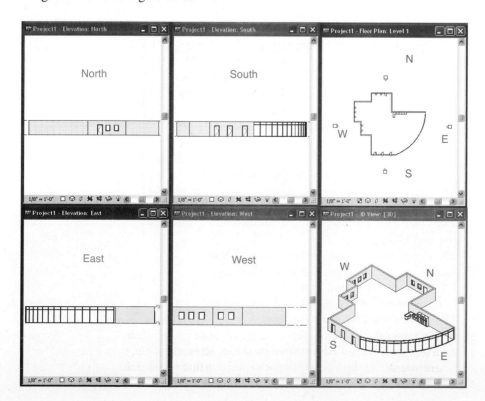

Figure 11-5

INTERIOR ELEVATION VIEWS

Exercise 11-2: Creating New Interior Elevation Views

1. Start a new drawing using the **RAC 2009\Imperial Templates\default.rte** template.
2. Double-click on **Level 1** in the **Project browser** to bring it up in the **Drawing Editor**.
3. Select the **Wall** tool from the **Basics** tab of the **Design Bar**.
4. Select **Basic Wall: Generic – 8″** and the **Draw** (pencil) tool from the **Options** toolbar.
5. Make the walls **10″-0′** high, set the **Loc Line:** to **Finish Line Exterior**, and create the enclosure shown in Figure 11-6.

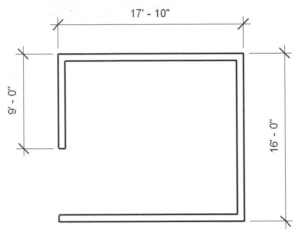

Figure 11-6

6. Place the walls in a counterclockwise direction.
7. Select the **Component** tool from the **Basics** tab of the **Design Bar**.
8. In the **Options** toolbar, press the **Load** button to open the **Imperial Library**.
9. In the **Imperial Library**, open the **Casework** folder.
10. In the **Casework** folder, open the **Domestic Kitchen** folder.
11. Select all the families in the **Domestic Kitchen** folder, and press the **Open** button to load the families and return to the **Drawing Editor**.
12. Select the **Component** tool from the **Basics** tab again, select base cabinets, countertops, and upper cabinets from the drop-down list in the **Options** toolbar, and place them in the enclosure you made.
13. Repeat the **Component** loading and placing process, loading chairs and a table from the **Furniture** folder.
14. Place two windows in the enclosure walls (see Figure 11-7).
15. Change to the **View** tab in the **Design Bar**.
16. Select the **Elevation** tool in the **View** tab.
17. Place the **Elevation marker** in the middle of your enclosure with the pointer pointing upward.
18. Notice that **Elevation 1-a** appears in the **Project browser** (see Figure 11-8).
19. Double-click on **Elevation 1-a** in the **Project browser** to bring up the elevation in the **Drawing Editor**.

Note:
Section 13 covers *Components* in more detail.

Note:
When the elevation comes up, you may notice that it is surrounded by a rectangle. This is the *Crop View*, and dictates what will be shown on the *Drawing* sheet when you drag the view to that sheet.

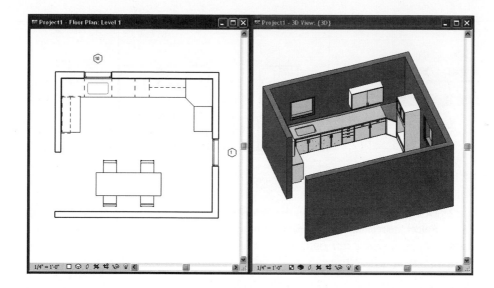

Figure 11-7

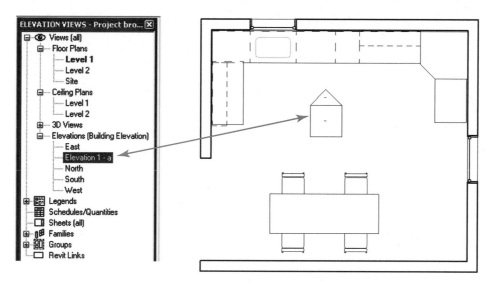

Figure 11-8

To control the **Crop View**, do the following:

20. Select the crop rectangle and move the arrows that appear to crop the view.
21. After cropping the view, select the **Hide Crop Region** button to hide the crop rectangle (see Figures 11-9 and 11-10).

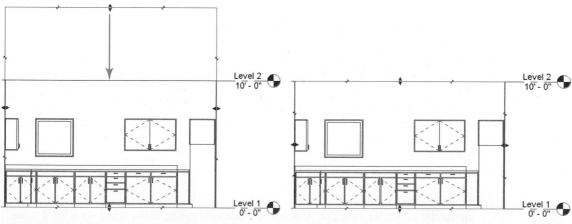

Figure 11-9

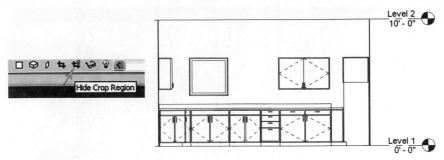

Figure 11-10

22. Double-click on **Level 1** in the **Project browser** to bring it up in the **Drawing Editor**.
23. Select the rectangle of the **Elevation marker** you placed in step 16 to activate its adjustment.
24. Check the check box opposite the **Elevation direction** you wish to add, and then press the <Esc> key on your keyboard to create the new **Elevation view**.

Notice that **Elevation 1-b** appears in the **Project browser**.

25. Repeat steps 22 and 23 to create all four views (see Figure 11-11).

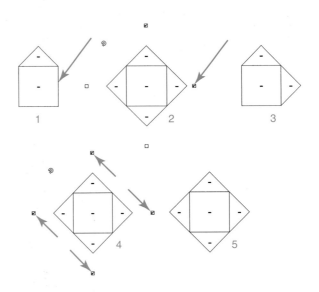

Figure 11-11

26. Click on one of the arrows in the **Elevation marker** to show the **Crop Region** in the **Floor Plan** view.
27. Adjust the **Crop Region** in the **Floor Plan** view to encompass the objects you wish to see in elevation, and press the <Esc> key on your keyboard to complete the adjustment.
28. Double-click on the **Elevation 1-a**, **Elevation 1-b**, **Elevation 1-c**, and **Elevation 1-d** that have been automatically created in the **Project browser** to bring them up in the **Drawing Editor**.
29. Adjust the **Crop Region** for each elevation you created.
30. Save this file as **INTERIOR ELEVATION VIEWS** (see Figure 11-12).

SECTION VIEWS

Exercise 11-3: Creating New Section Views

1. Using the previous exercise, double-click on **Level 1** in the **Project browser** to bring it up in the **Drawing Editor**.
2. Delete the **Elevation marker**, or delete **Elevation 1-a**, **Elevation 1-b**, **Elevation 1-c**, and **Elevation 1-d** from the **Project browser**.

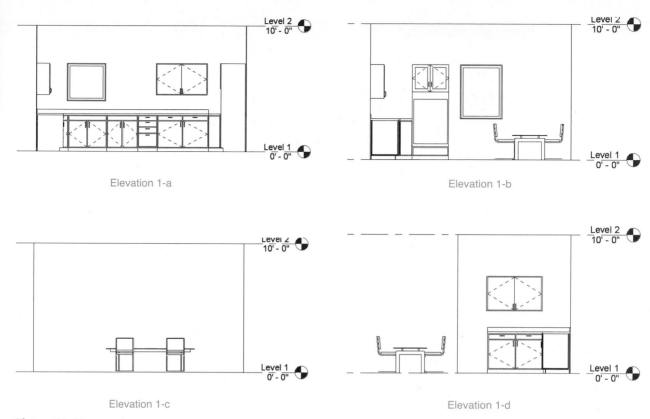

Elevation 1-a

Elevation 1-b

Elevation 1-c

Elevation 1-d

Figure 11-12

3. Select the **Section** tool from the **View** tab in the **Design Bar.**
4. Place a **Section marker** by clicking at the left of the enclosure, dragging to the right of the enclosure, and clicking again. Make sure the marker bisects the cabinets and counter (see Figure 11-13).

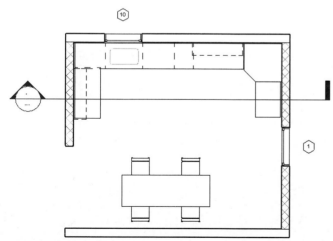

Figure 11-13

5. Select the **Modify** arrow in the **View** tab of the **Design Bar**, and click the dashes in the head of the **Section marker**, or double-click **Section 1** that has appeared in the **Sections [Building Section]** tree in the **Project browser**. This will bring the section up in the **Drawing Editor** (see Figure 11-14).

A **Crop Region** will appear around the section. Using the information you learned in the previous exercise, adjust and hide the **Crop Region**.

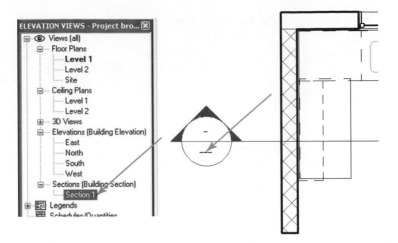

Figure 11-14

6. Close all views except **Level 1** and **Section 1**.
7. Select **Windows > Tile** from the **Main** menu to tile the views side by side (see Figure 11-15).
8. Select and move the **Section** marker in the **Level 1** view and notice how the **Section** view changes (see Figure 11-16).
9. Save this file as **SECTION VIEWS**.

Figure 11-15

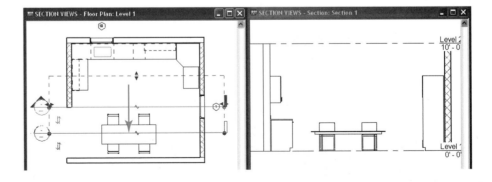

Figure 11-16

CALLOUT VIEWS

Callout views are used to show special areas in more detail.

Exercise 11-4: Creating New Callout Views

1. Using the previous exercise, double-click on **Level 1** in the **Project browser** to bring it up in the **Drawing Editor**.
2. Delete the **Section marker**, or delete **Section 1** from the **Project browser**.

3. Select the **Callout** tool from the **View** tab in the **Design Bar**.

4. Click your mouse at the upper left corner of your enclosure; drag and click again at the lower left location shown in Figure 11-17.

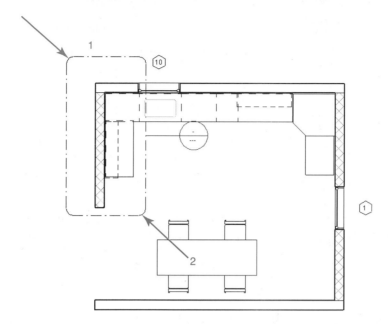

Figure 11-17

5. Double-click on the dashes in the head of the **Callout marker**, or double-click on the **Callout of Level 1** that has appeared in the **Floor Plans** tree in the **Project browser**. This will bring the callout up in the **Drawing Editor**.

A **Crop Region** will appear around the section. Using the information you learned in the previous exercise, adjust and hide the **Crop Region**.

6. Finally, you can change scale, add dimensions, put in extra insulation, and so on (see Figure 11-18).

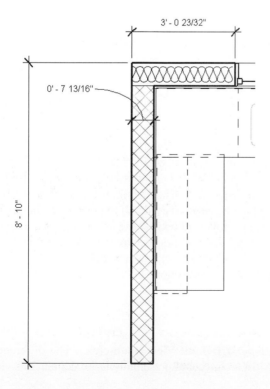

Figure 11-18

7. Delete the callout marker, or delete the **Callout of Level 1** that has appeared in the **Floor Plans** tree of the **Project browser**.
8. Again, select the **Callout** tool from the **View** tab in the **Design Bar.**
9. Before you place the callout, check the **Reference other view** check box in the **Options toolbar**.
10. Again, place a callout as you did in step 4 of this exercise.

Notice that the **Callout of Level 1** now appears under **Drafting Views** in the **Project browser**. If you double-click on this callout in the **Project browser**, you get a sheet on which to draw 2D details, and referenced to the callout. Notice also that the callout has the word **Sim** next to the callout marker, letting you know that this callout is a drafting view (see Figure 11-19).

11. Select the callout marker line, and select the round grip to move the marker as shown in Figure 11-20.
12. Select the other round grips to move and adjust the placement of the marker (see Figure 11-21).
13. Save this file as **CALLOUT VIEWS**.

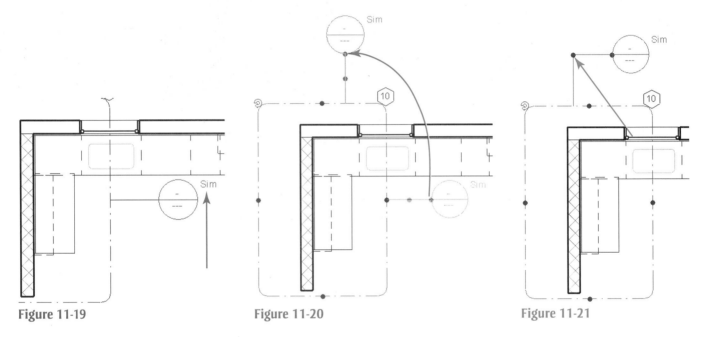

Figure 11-19   **Figure 11-20**   **Figure 11-21**

DRAFTING VIEWS

During the course of a project, you may want to create details in a view that are not directly associated with the model. Rather than creating a callout and then adding details to it, you may want to create detail conditions where the model is not needed (for example, a carpet-transition detail that shows where carpet switches to tile, or roof-drain details not based on a callout on the roof).

You create this unassociated, view-specific detail in a drafting view. The drafting view is not associated with the model. In a drafting view, you create details at differing view scales (coarse, medium, or fine) and use 2D detailing tools: detail lines, detail regions, detail components, insulation, reference planes, dimensions, symbols, and text. These are the exact same tools used in creating a detail view. However, drafting views do not display any model elements. When you create a drafting view in a project, the view is saved with the project.

The use of the drafting view is illustrated in Section 10, "Drafting and Detail Components."

CAMERA VIEWS

Camera views are a variation of the **3D Default View (Isometric)**. The difference is that a **Camera** view is true perspective. Most architectural presentations are done in this view.

Exercise 11-5: Creating New Camera Views

1. Using the previous exercise, double-click on **Level 1** in the **Project browser** to bring it up in the **Drawing Editor**.
2. Delete the callout marker, or delete **Callout of Level 1** in the **Project browser**.
3. Select the **Camera** tool from the **View** tab in the **Design Bar.**
4. Place a camera by clicking at the left of the enclosure, dragging to the right of the enclosure, and clicking again in the center of the enclosure to bring up the **Camera** view that you have created as shown in Figure 11-22.

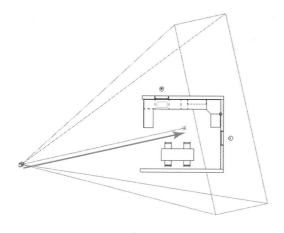
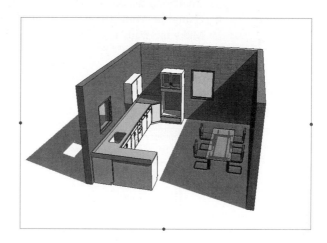

Figure 11-22

5. In the **Project browser**, expand the **3D Views** tree, select **3D View 1** (the camera view you just created), **RMB**, and select **Rename** from the contextual menu that appears.
6. Change the name of **3D View 1** to **CAMERA**.
7. Close all views except **Level 1** and **CAMERA**.
8. Select **Windows > Tile** from the **Main** menu to tile the views side by side.
9. Select **Shading with Edges**, and **Shadows On** from the **Model: Graphic Style** and **Shadows** icons at the bottom of the **Drawing Editor** (see Figure 11-22).
10. In the **CAMERA** view, select the **Crop Region**.
11. With the **Crop Region** in the **CAMERA** view selected, the camera will appear in the **Level 1 view**.
12. Select the **Level 1 view**.
13. Move the camera, and the **CAMERA** view will change.
14. Change to the **CAMERA** view.
15. Place your cursor within the **Crop Region**, hold the <Shift> key on your keyboard, and depress the middle (roll) button on your mouse.
16. While holding these buttons, move your mouse to change the **CAMERA** view, and also move the camera in the **Level 1 view**.
17. Save this file as **CAMERA VIEWS**.

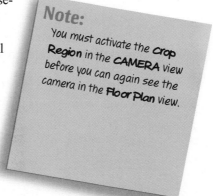

Note:
You must activate the Crop Region in the CAMERA view before you can again see the camera in the Floor Plan view.

WALKTHROUGH VIEWS

A walkthrough is a camera that follows a path that you define. The path comprises frames and key frames. A key frame is a modifiable frame in which you can change the direction and position of the camera.

In Revit Architecture 2009, the default **Walkthroughs** run at 15 frames per second. The default **Walkthrough** in Revit Architecture is 300 frames (pictures) or 10 seconds of playback. The key frame is a point at which you click to change direction. This name comes from the fact that the main animators (in Disney's time) were the people that made the key (or main) pictures, and their aides made the in-between pictures (tweens).

Exercise 11-6: Creating Walkthrough Views

1. Start a new drawing using the **RAC 2009\Imperial Templates\default.rte** template.
2. In the **Project browser**, double-click on the **Level 1 Floor Plan** to bring it up into the **Drawing Editor**.
3. Change to the **Basics** tab in the **Design Bar**.
4. Using the **Wall**, **Door**, and **Window** tools, create the enclosure shown in Figure 11-23. Make the walls **10′-0″** high and vary their families.

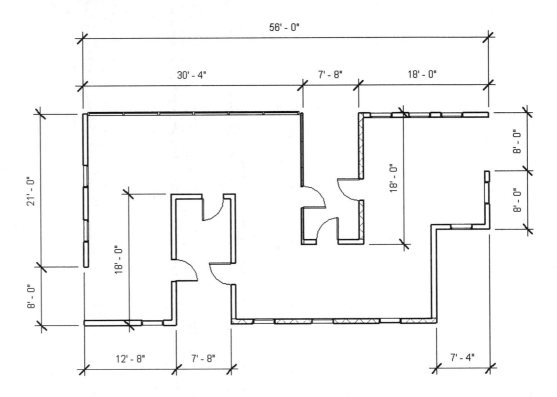

Figure 11-23

5. Select the **Walkthrough** tool in the **View** tab of the **Design Bar**.
6. Starting at the left, click approximately every **10′-0″** as you trace a path through the enclosure.
7. After the last click, press the **<Esc>** key on your keyboard to stop the path and create the walkthrough as shown in Figure 11-24.

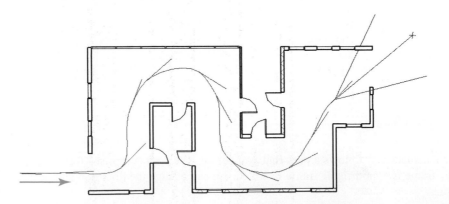

Figure 11-24

8. Select the walkthrough path you just created, **RMB**, and select **Element Properties** from the contextual menu to bring up the **Element Properties** dialog box.

9. At the bottom of the **Element Properties** dialog box, select the **300** button in the **Walkthrough Frames** field to bring up the **Walkthrough Frames** dialog box.

10. In the **Walkthrough Frames** dialog box, **check** the **Indicators** check box, leave the **Frame increment** at **5**, and press the **OK** buttons to return to the **Drawing Editor** (see Figure 11-25).

You can now see 20 of the frames in the **Level 1 Floor Plan** (see Figure 11-26).

11. With the walkthrough path selected, select the **Edit Walkthrough** button in the **Options** toolbar.

12. The **Options** toolbar will change to the **Walkthrough** options.

13. In the **Options** toolbar, select **Path** from the **Controls** drop-down list (see Figure 11-27).

Note: If your camera path disappears from view, **RMB** on **TEST WALKTHROUGH** in the Project browser, and select **Show Camera** from the contextual menu that appears.

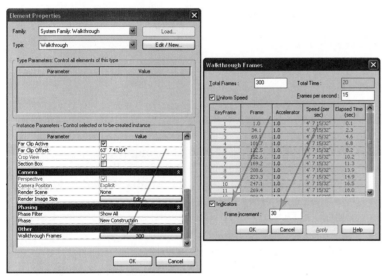

Figure 11-25

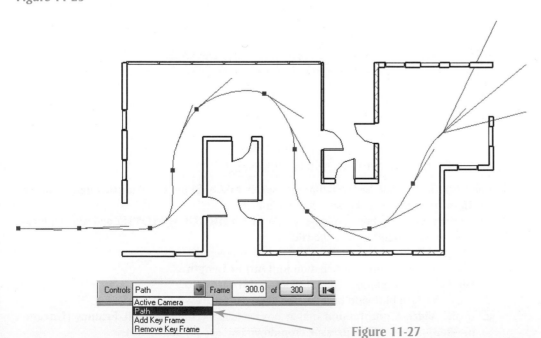

Figure 11-26

Figure 11-27

The key frames will now appear, and you can drag them to change the path. You can experiment with **Add Key Frame** and **Remove Key Frame** if you wish. Adding more key frames increases your control, while decreasing key frames gives the program more control.

14. In the **Options** toolbar select the **Element Properties** button to bring up the **Element Properties** dialog box.

        In the **Element Properties** dialog box, **uncheck** the **Far Clip Active** check box.

Far Clip "clips" the picture in the distance from the camera target, and can be set to a distance. TURN THIS OFF (see Figure 11-28).

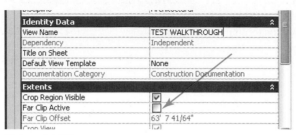

Figure 11-28

15. Select **Active Camera** from the **Controls** drop-down list.
16. Set the **Frame** to **0** and leave everything else alone.
17. Click in an empty space in the **Drawing Editor**, and the Revit message **Do you want to quit editing the walkthrough** will appear. Press the **Yes** button to return to the **Drawing Editor**.
18. Double-click on **TEST WALKTHROUGH** in the **Walkthroughs** tree in the **Project browser** to bring up the perspective walkthrough in the **Drawing Editor**.
19. Select **Shading with Edges** and **Shadows On** from the **Model: Graphic Style** and **Shadows** icons at the bottom of the **Drawing Editor**.
20. In the **Project browser**, RMB on **TEST WALKTHROUGH**, and select **Show Camera** from the contextual menu to activate the **Walkthrough** controls.
21. Select the **Edit Walkthrough** button in the **Options** toolbar.
22. The **Options** toolbar will change to the **Walkthrough** options.
23. In the **Options** toolbar, select the **Play** button to view the walkthrough animation (see Figure 11-29).

Play

Figure 11-29

Exercise 11-7: Making an AVI Movie from the Walkthrough

1. Once you have made the walkthrough, select **File > Export > Walkthrough** from the **Main** menu to bring up the **Save As** dialog box.
2. In the **Save As** dialog box, name the file **WALKTHROUGH MOVIE**, and select a location on your computer to save the file.
   a. Select **AVI Files** from the **Save as type** drop-down list.
   b. Select the **All frames** radio button for **Output Length.**
   c. Set the **Model Graphics Style** to **Shading with Edges.**
   d. Press the **Save** button to bring up the **Video Compression** dialog box.
   e. In the **Video Compression** dialog box, select the default, **Full Frames [Uncompressed]** from the **Compressor** drop-down list (see Figure 11-30).

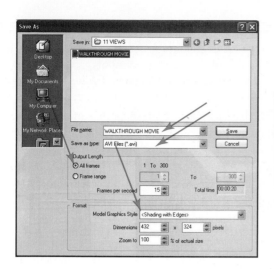

Figure 11-30

3. Press the **OK** button in the **Video Compression** dialog box to start the movie making process; this should take about **3** minutes.
4. Go to the **Windows Desktop** and open **My Computer**.
5. Go to the location where you saved the walkthrough avi.
6. Double-click on the **WALKTHROUGH MOVIE.avi** file.

The Windows Media Player will open, and your movie will play (see Figure 11-31).

7. Save this file as **WALKTHROUGH VIEWS**.

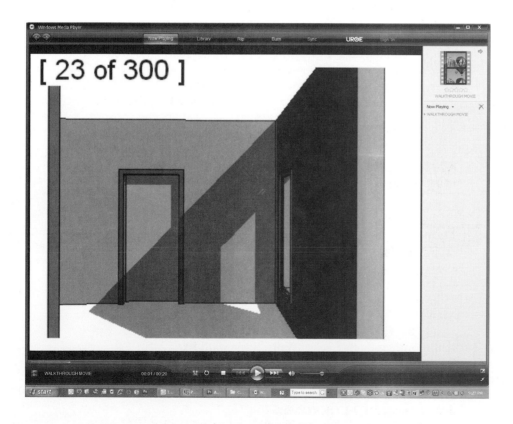

Figure 11-31

LEGEND VIEWS AND LEGEND COMPONENTS

Every good architectural documentation set includes a legend. A legend lists the various building components and annotations used in a project, and makes it easy for someone to understand what the various annotations mean.

Some typical legends include:

- **Annotation Legend:** Displays sheet annotations such as section heads, level markers, spot elevation marks, elevation symbols, keynote symbols, revision tags, element tags, and other symbols that do not represent model objects. Each symbol has an associated piece of descriptive text. All symbols are shown at printed size.

- **Model Symbol Legend:** Displays symbolic representations of model objects with some descriptive text. Typical elements are electrical fixtures, plumbing fixtures, mechanical equipment, and site objects.

- **Line Styles Legend:** Displays a line in a selected line style and text identifying what that line style represents on drawings. Among the uses are fire rating lines, property lines, setback lines, electric wiring, plumbing, utilities, and centerlines.

Exercise 11-8: Creating a Legend View

1. Start a new drawing using the **RAC 2009\Imperial Templates\default.rte** template.
2. Change to the **View** tab in the **Design Bar**.
3. In the **View** tab, select the **Legend** tool to bring up the **New Legend View** dialog box.
4. In the **New Legend View** dialog box, enter **TEST LEGEND** in the **Name** field, select **1/4″ = 1′-0″** from the **Scale** drop-down list, and press the **OK** button to bring up the **TEST LEGEND** view (see Figure 11-32).

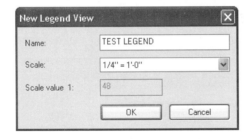

Figure 11-32

Notice that **TEST LEGEND** now also appears under **Legends** in the **Project browser** (see Figure 11-33).

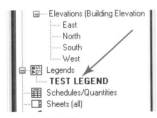

Figure 11-33

5. Change to the **Drafting** tab in the **Design Bar**.
6. In the **Drafting** tab, select the **Legend Component** tool that is now available (see Figure 11-34).
7. In the **Options** toolbar, select **Doors: Single-Flush: 32″ × 84″** and **Floor Plan** from the **View** drop-down list.
8. Place the door in the **TEST LEGEND** view that is in the **Drawing Editor**.
9. Repeat step 7, selecting **Elevation: Front** from the **View** drop-down list and placing the door elevation next to the **Floor Plan** view.
10. In the **Options** toolbar, select **Walls: Basic wall: Exterior – Brick and CMU on MTL Stud**.
11. Select **Section** from the **View** drop-down list.
12. Enter **8′-0″** in the **Host Length** field, and place the wall in the **TEST LEGEND** view.

Figure 11-34

13. In the **Drafting** tab of the **Design Bar**, select the **Symbol** tool.
14. Select symbols from the **Options** toolbar drop-down list and place them in the **TEST LEGEND** view.
15. Save this file as **LEGEND VIEWS**.

Note:
When you select the **Legend Component** tool, the **Options** toolbar also will appear with **Families** and **View** options. All the **Families**, such as doors, windows, walls, annotations, and so on, that have been loaded in the project are available here (see Figure 11-35).

Note:
You can dimension doors and windows in the **Legend** view, but not walls. If you change the parameters of an object in your project, its 2D view in the **Legend** view will also change (see Figure 11-36).

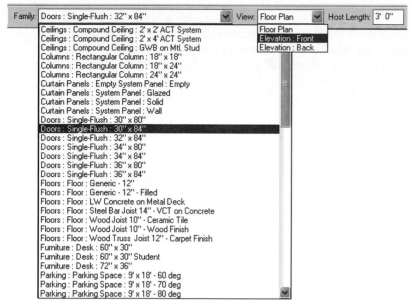

Figure 11-35

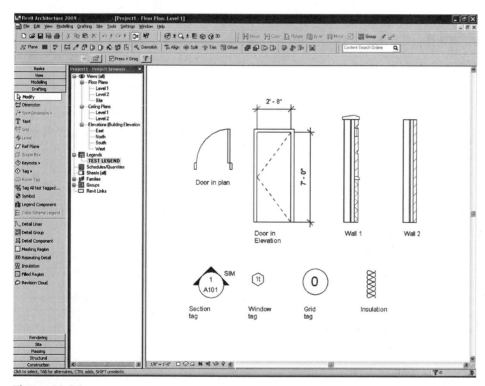

Figure 11-36

MATCHLINES

Matchlines are used when buildings are too big to be shown on one plot sheet. Using a **Matchline**, you can separate a building into several parts and spread the plans over several plot sheets.

In Revit Architecture 2009, **Matchlines** can be used in **Floor Plans**, **Callouts**, **Elevations**, and **Sections**. **Matchlines** have properties that can specify the top and bottom line constraints, thus giving them the ability to match different levels. These properties, though, are not available in elevations and sections because these properties do not apply in these views.

Exercise 11-9: Creating a Matchline View

1. Start a new drawing using the **RAC 2009\Imperial Templates\default.rte** template.
2. Set the **Scale** to **1/4″ = 1′-0″**, and **Detail Level** to **Medium**.
3. Change to the **Basics** tab in the **Design Bar**.
4. Select the **Wall** tool.
5. Place **Basic Wall: Exterior – brick on CMU 10′-0″** high to create the enclosure shown in Figure 11-37.

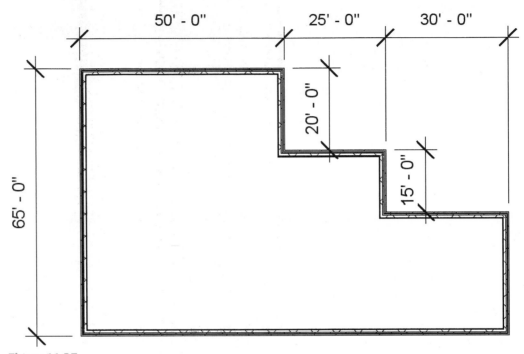

Figure 11-37

At 1/4″ = 1′0″ scale, this drawing might be too big to be contained on one 22″ × 34″ plot sheet. In the following steps, you will divide the floor plan into two sections that are electronically connected.

6. Change to the **View** tab in the **Design Bar**.
7. In the **View** tab, select the **Matchline** tool.
8. You are now in **Sketch** mode. Using the **Lines** tool from the **Sketch** tab, create a matchline, and then press the **Finish Sketch** button to return to the **Drawing Editor** (see Figure 11-38).

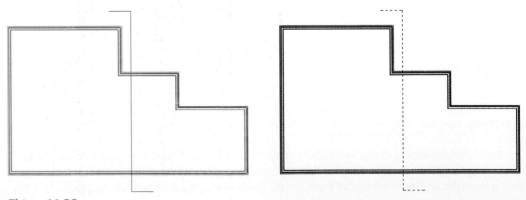

Figure 11-38

9. **RMB** on **Level 1** in the **Project browser**, and select **Duplicate View > Duplicate as Dependent** from the contextual menu that appears.

This new view will appear in the **Project browser** as **Dependent on Level 1** (see Figure 11-39).

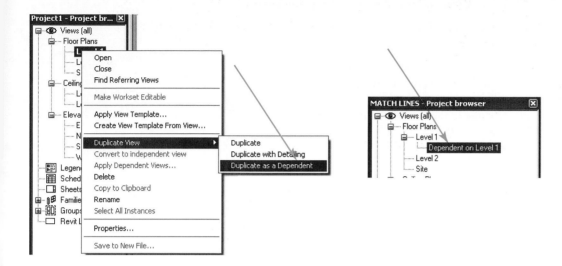

Figure 11-39

You now have two views of **Level 1**. Using the **Crop Regions**, you will crop opposite portions of the building on each view, and assign them sheet numbers.

10. Select the **Show Crop Region** button at the bottom of **Drawing Editor** to turn the **Crop Region** on. (If the **Crop Region** is already on, the button will read **Hide Crop Region**.)

11. Select the **Crop Region** in the **Drawing Editor**, and move the arrow grips on the right side of the drawing to the left so that only the left portion of the floor plan is showing (see Figure 11-40).

12. Double-click on **Dependent on Level 1** in the **Project browser** to bring it up in **Drawing Editor**.

13. Select the **Show Crop Region** button at the bottom of the **Drawing Editor** to turn the **Crop Region** on. (If the **Crop Region** is already on, the button will read **Hide Crop Region**.)

14. Select the **Crop Region** in the **Drawing Editor**, and move the arrow grips on the left side of the drawing to the right so that only the right portion of the floor plan is showing (see Figure 11-41).

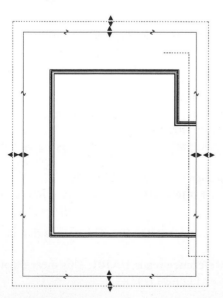

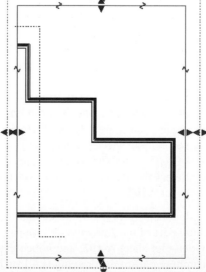

Figure 11-40   Figure 11-41

15. Select the **Hide Crop Region** button at the bottom of the **Drawing Editor** to turn the **Crop Region** off.
16. Bring the **Level 1** floor plan view up into the **Drawing Editor**.
17. Select the **Hide Crop Region** button at the bottom of the **Drawing Editor** to turn the **Crop Region** off.

Now you must add a **View Reference** tag.

18. In the **View** tab, select the **View Reference** tool.
19. Place **View References** at the top and bottom of the matchline you created. You may have to zoom up to see the placement.
20. Change to the **Basics** tab in the **Design Bar**.
21. Place the text **Match Line** above the **View References** you placed.
22. Repeat this process for the **Dependent on Level 1** view (see Figure 11-42).
23. In the **View** tab of the **Design Bar**, select the **Sheet** tool to bring up the **Select a Titleblock** dialog box.

> **Note:**
> When placed on a matchline, a **View Reference** will show which plot page contains the dependent view.

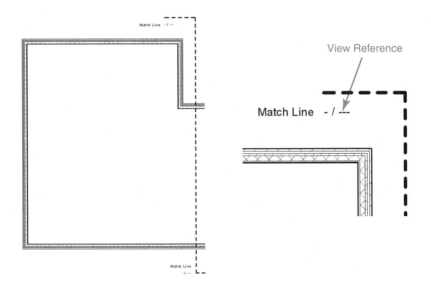

Figure 11-42

24. In the **Select a Titleblock** dialog box, press the **Load** button to go to the **Imperial Library** (or **Metric** if you desire).
25. In the **Library**, open the **Titleblocks** folder, and open the **C17 × 22 Horizontal** family. You will then return to the **Select a Titleblock** dialog box.
26. In the **Select a Titleblock** dialog box, select the **C17 × 22 Horizontal** family and press the **OK** button to bring up the first plot sheet.
27. Make sure the sheet number is **A101**; select and change it if necessary.
28. Select the **Level 1** view from the **Project browser** and drag it into plot sheet **A101**.
29. Again, select the **Sheet** tool to bring up the **Select a Titleblock** dialog box.
30. Again, select the **C17 × 22 Horizontal** family and press the **OK** button to bring up the second plot sheet.
31. Make sure the sheet number is **A102**; select and change it if necessary.
32. Select the **Dependent on Level 1** view from the **Project browser**, and drag it into plot sheet **A102**.

Open plot sheet **A-101**, and notice that the **View Reference** reads **1/A102**. This means that the matching part of the drawing is # 1 on page A102.

Open plot sheet **A-102**, and notice that the **View Reference** reads **1/A101**. This means that the matching part of the drawing is # 1 on page A101 (see Figure 11-43).

33. Save this file as **MATCHLINES**.

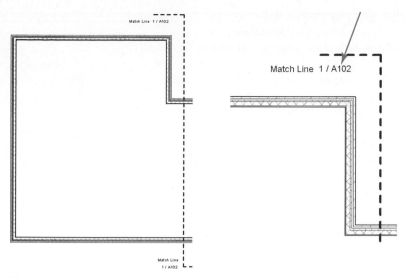

Figure 11-43

SCHEDULE VIEWS

A schedule is a display of information, extracted from the properties of elements in a project. A Revit Architecture schedule can list every instance of the type of element you have placed in the project.

Exercise 11-10: Creating a Schedule View

1. Start a new drawing using the **RAC 2009\Imperial Templates\default.rte** template.
2. Set the **Scale** to **1/4″ = 1′-0″**, and **Detail Level** to **Medium**.
3. Change to the **Basics** tab in the **Design Bar**.
4. Select the **Wall**, **Door**, and **Window** tools. (Load several different doors and windows.)
5. Place **Basic Wall: Generic-8″ 10′-0″** high and several doors and windows to create the enclosure shown in Figure 11-44.

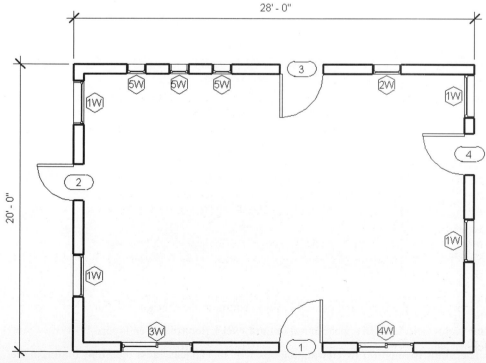

Figure 11-44

6. Change to the **View** tab in the **Design Bar**.
7. In the **View** tab, select the **Schedule/Quantities** tool to bring up the **New Schedule** dialog box (see Figure 11-45).
8. In the **New Schedule** dialog box, scroll down, select the **Windows** category, and press the **OK** button to bring up the **Schedule Properties** dialog box.
9. In the **Schedule Properties** dialog box, change to the **Fields** tab.
10. In the **Fields** tab, select **Count** and press the **Add** button.

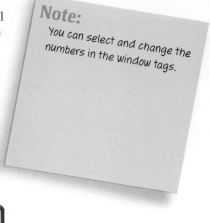

Note:
You can select and change the numbers in the window tags.

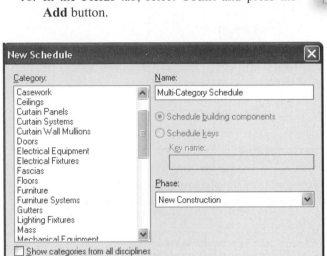

Figure 11-45

11. Repeat the **Add** process with **Type**, **Height**, **Width**, and **Type Mark**.
12. Press the **OK** button, and the schedule will appear in the **Drawing Editor** (see Figure 11-46).

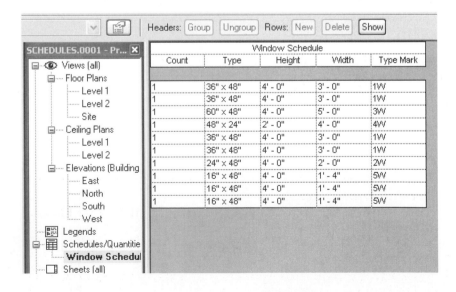

Figure 11-46

13. Select one of the fields and press the **Show** button in the **Options** toolbar.

The window you selected will appear in red in the **Level 1** floor plan (see Figure 11-47).

14. The **Show Element(s) In View** dialog box will also appear. Press the **Show** button in the dialog box to show the window in other views.

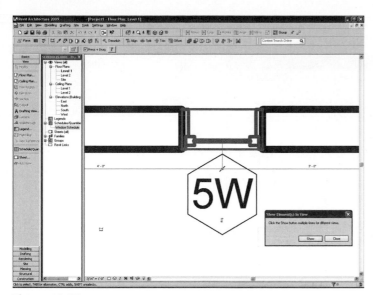

Figure 11-47

15. Double-click **Window Schedule** under **Schedules/Quantities** in the **Project browser** to bring it up again in the **Drawing Editor**.
16. Select a different window size from the **Type** drop-down list and press the **Show** button again.

The window will change in the **Level 1** floor plan, and add a new type mark number (see Figure 11-48).

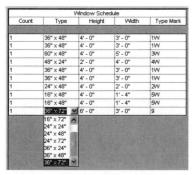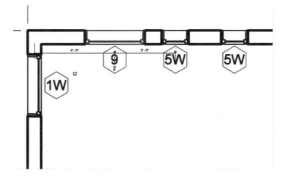

Figure 11-48

17. Double-click **Window Schedule** under **Schedules/Quantities** in the **Project browser** to bring it up again in the **Drawing Editor**.
18. **RMB** and select **View Properties** from the contextual menu to bring up the **Element Properties** dialog box.
19. In the **Element Properties** dialog box, press the **Sorting/Grouping** button to bring up the **Sorting/Grouping** tab in the **Schedule Properties** dialog box.
20. In the **Sorting/Grouping** tab, check the **Grand totals** and **Itemize every instance** check boxes (see Figure 11-49).
21. Press the **OK** buttons to return to the **Window Schedule**. The schedule will now show **Grand Total** plus the total count of windows.
22. Continue to change parameters in the different **Element Properties** tabs and observe the changes in the schedule.
23. Save this file as **SCHEDULES**.

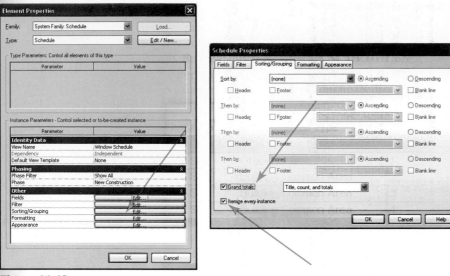

Figure 11-49

SUMMARY

This section explained and demonstrated the different **Views** available in Revit Architecture 2009. Also included in this sec-tion was a demonstration of how to create an animated walk-through and a **Matchline** view.

SECTION TEST QUESTIONS

Exercise

Create the following schedules.

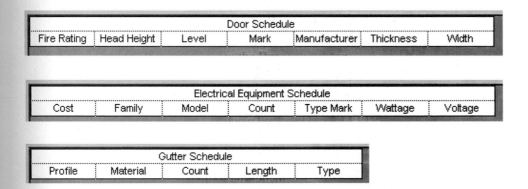

Door Schedule						
Fire Rating	Head Height	Level	Mark	Manufacturer	Thickness	Width

Electrical Equipment Schedule						
Cost	Family	Model	Count	Type Mark	Wattage	Voltage

Gutter Schedule				
Profile	Material	Count	Length	Type

Questions

1. What are Revit Architecture 2009 **Views**?

2. What is a **Callout View** used for?

3. What is a **Legend View** used for?

4. What is the difference between a **Floor Plan** and a **Reflected Ceiling Plan**?

5. What is the relationship between **Levels** and **Views**?

Components and Families

12

Section
Objectives

- Know how to add and modify **Components** in your project.
- Learn how to use **System Families**.
- Learn how to use **In-Place Families**.
- Know how to use **Loadable Families** and the **Family Editor**.

COMPONENT

A component is a building element that is usually delivered and installed on site, rather than built in place. Windows, doors, and furniture are components. In contrast, walls, floors, and roofs are built in place; these are called *hosts* or *host elements*. A hosted component is a component that requires a host. For example, a window is hosted by a wall. A desk is hosted by a floor or level. Doors, windows, model lines, and components (e.g., furniture) are all hosted components. After you place a hosted component onto a host, you can rehost it (change its host).

FAMILY

A family is a class of elements in a category. A family groups elements with a common set of parameters (properties), identical uses, and similar graphical representations. Different elements in a family may have different values for some or all properties, but the set of properties (their names and meanings) is the same. For example, families of double-hung windows all contain a similar type of double-hung window, but of different sizes. Each window size is a type within the double-hung windows family.

In this section you will explore the creation, use, and modification of Revit Architecture 2009 **Components** and **Families**.

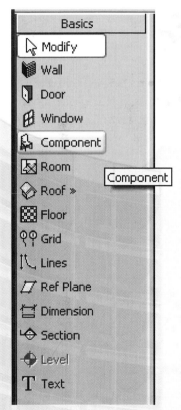

Exercise 12-1: Adding and Modifying Components

1. Start a new drawing using the **RAC 2009\Imperial Templates\default.rte** template.
2. In the **Project browser**, double-click on the **LEVEL 1** floor plan to bring it up into the **Drawing Editor**.
3. Change to the **Basics** tab in the **Design Bar**.
4. In the **Basics** tab, select the **Component** tool.
5. In the **Type Selector**, select **Desk: 60″ × 30″** from the drop-down list.
6. Click in the **Drawing Editor** to place the desk.
7. Change to the **Default 3D View** and hold down the <Shift> key on your keyboard while holding down the middle mouse button to orient the desk as shown in Figure 12-1.
8. Change back to the **LEVEL 1** floor plan view.
9. Again in the **Basics** tab, select the **Component** tool.
10. In the **Options** toolbar, press the **Load** button to bring up the **Open** dialog box for the **Imperial** or **Metric Library**.

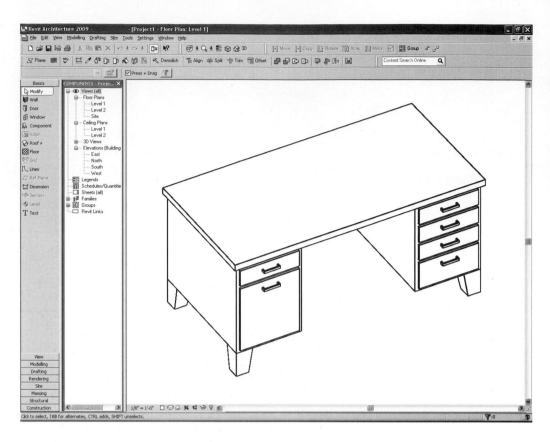

Figure 12-1

11. In the **Library**, select the **Furniture** folder.
12. In the **Furniture** folder, select **Chair-Breuer**, and press the **Open** button to return to the **Drawing Editor**.
13. Press the <**Space bar**> key on your keyboard to rotate the chair, and then click in the **Drawing Editor** to place the chair (see Figure 12-2).

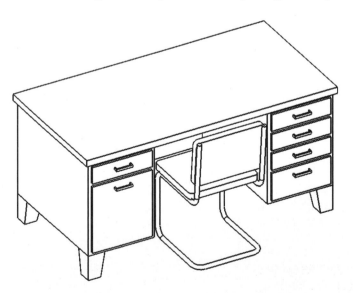

Figure 12-2

14. Select the desk, **RMB**, and select **Element Properties** from the contextual menu to bring up the **Element Properties** dialog box.
15. In the **Element Properties** dialog box, select the **Edit/New** button to bring up the **Type Properties** dialog box.
16. In the **Type Properties** dialog box, press the **Duplicate** button to bring up the **Name** dialog box.
17. In the **Name** dialog box, enter **TEST DESK** and press the **OK** button to return to the **Type Properties** dialog box.

18. In the **Type Properties** dialog box, enter **4′-0″** in the **Depth** field and **8′-0″** in the **Width** field, and then press the **OK** buttons to return to the **Drawing Editor** (see Figure 12-3).

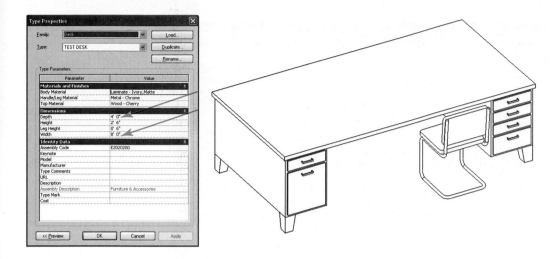

Figure 12-3

Most components have parameters that can be changed. Add more components and experiment with changing their **Type** parameters.

You can locate components on the Internet by Googling on "Revit Components" or "Revit Component Families." Some of the sites you will find will offer components for sale, and others will offer free components. BIM World http://www.bimworld.com is an excellent source for content. They will also create content for you for a price (see Figure 12-4).

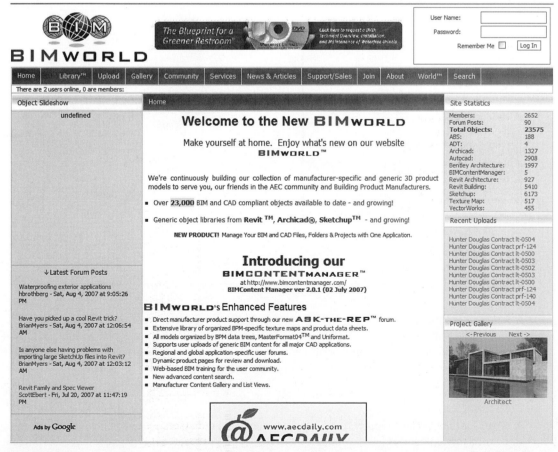

Figure 12-4

You can also download components from the Revit Content Distribution Center (http://revit.autodesk.com/libraryhtml/index.html) (see Figure 12-5).

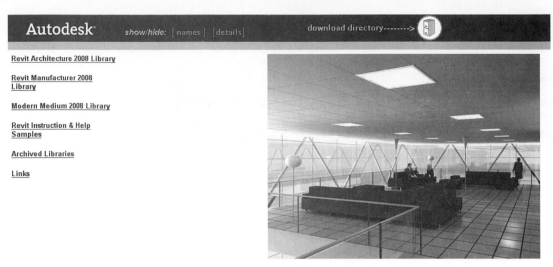

This site requires Internet Explorer 5+ or Netscape Navigator 6+.

Figure 12-5

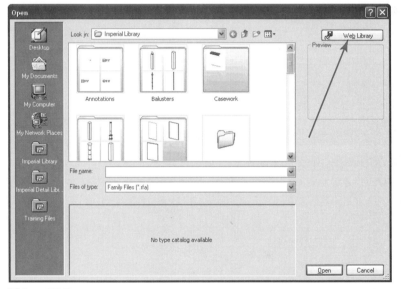

Figure 12-6

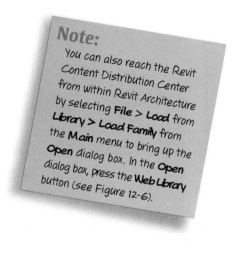

Note:
You can also reach the Revit Content Distribution Center from within Revit Architecture by selecting **File > Load** from **Library > Load Family** from the **Main** menu to bring up the **Open** dialog box. In the **Open** dialog box, press the **Web Library** button (see Figure 12-6).

FAMILIES

A family is a collection of objects called types. A family groups elements with a common set of parameters, identical use, and similar graphical representation. Different types within a family may have different values of some or all parameters, but the set of parameters—their names and their meaning—are the same. All elements in Revit Architecture are family-based.

Type

A type is a member of a family. Each type has specific parameters that are constant for all instances of the type that exist in a model; these are **Type Parameters**. Types also have **Instance Parameters**, which may vary for each instance of a type in the model.

Revit Architecture provides a large number of predefined families for use in your project. If you need to create families for a certain project, Revit Architecture gives you that facility. Creating a new family is easy, because Revit Architecture provides many templates, including templates for doors, structural members, windows, furniture, and electrical fixtures, and lets you graphically draw the new family.

There are three types of families in Revit Architecture: **System Families**, **In-Place Families**, and **Loadable Families**.

Exercise 12-2: System Families

System Families are the basic building blocks of Revit Architecture. An example would be **Wall** and **Floor Families**.

1. Start a new drawing using the **RAC 2009\Imperial Templates\default.rte** template.
2. In the **Project browser**, double-click on the **LEVEL 1** floor plan to bring it up into the **Drawing Editor**.
3. Change to the **Basics** tab in the **Design Bar**.
4. Select the **Wall** tool and place a wall in the **Drawing Editor**.
5. Select the **Lines** tool and place a line in the **Drawing Editor**.
6. Select the **Floor** tool and create a floor object in the **Drawing Editor**.
7. Select each of these objects, **RMB**, and select **Element Properties** from the contextual menu to bring up the **Element Properties** dialog box.
8. In the **Element Properties** dialog box, notice that the **Family** name begins with **System Family** (see Figure 12-7).

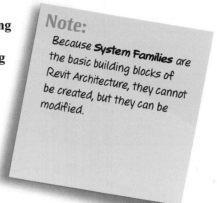

Note:
Because **System Families** are the basic building blocks of Revit Architecture, they cannot be created, but they can be modified.

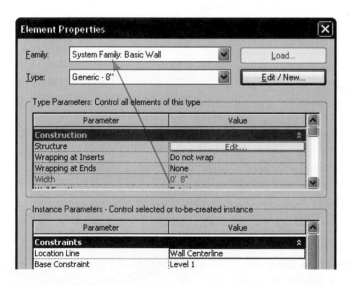

Figure 12-7

Exercise 12-3: In-Place Families

An **In-Place Family** is a family created within the context of the current project. The family exists only in the project and cannot be loaded into other projects. By creating In-Place Families, you create components unique to a project or components that reference geometry within the project.

1. Start a new drawing using the **RAC 2009\Imperial Templates\default.rte** template.
2. In the **Project browser**, double-click on the **LEVEL 1** floor plan to bring it up into the **Drawing Editor**.

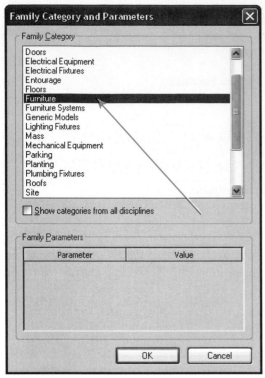

Figure 12-8

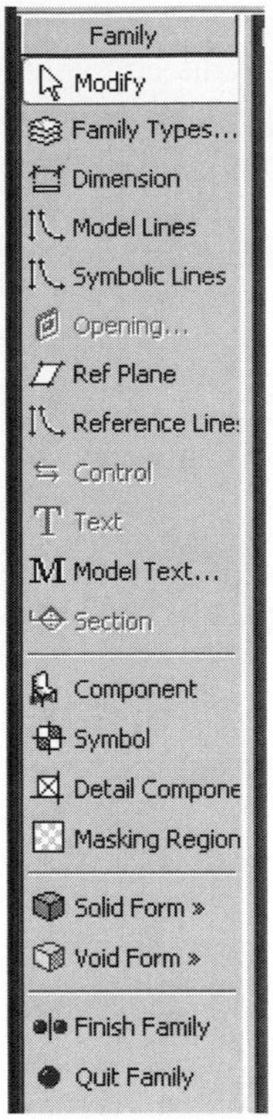

Figure 12-10

Figure 12-9

Note:
The **Design Bar** has changed to the **Family** tab (see Figure 12-9).

Note:
The **Family** tab will change to the **Sketch** tab (see Figure 12-10).

Note:
There will already be a button at the end of the field, but when you select **<By Category>** another button will appear—thus you will have two buttons.

3. Change to the **Modeling** tab in the **Design Bar**.
4. Select the **Create** tool to bring up the **Family Category and Parameters** dialog box.
5. In the **Family Category and Parameters** dialog box, select **Furniture** and press the **OK** button to bring up the **Name** dialog box (see Figure 12-8).
6. In the **Name** dialog box, enter **IN PLACE FAMILY TEST**, and press the **OK** button to return to the **Drawing Editor**.
7. In the **Family** tab, select the **Solid Form >> Solid Extrusion** tool.
8. In the **Sketch** tab, select the **Lines** tool.
9. In the **Options** toolbar, select the **Rectangle** tool.
10. Place a **4′ × 8′** rectangle in the **Drawing Editor** (see Figure 12-11).
11. In the **Sketch** tab, select the **Extrusion Properties** tool to bring up the **Element Properties** dialog box.
12. In the **Element Properties** dialog box, set the **Extrusion End** to **4″**.
13. In the **Element Properties** dialog box, select the **<By Category>** button in the **Material** field to create a button at the end of the field.
14. Pick the leftmost button that appears in the **Material** field to bring up the **Materials** dialog box (see Figures 12-12 and 12-13).
15. In the **Materials** dialog box, select **Masonry-Brick**; press the **OK** button to return to the **Element Properties** dialog box.

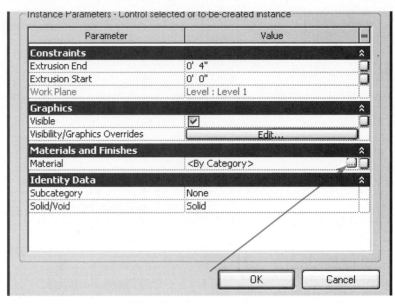

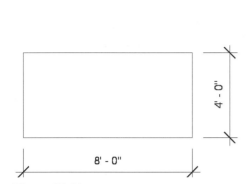

Figure 12-11   Figure 12-12

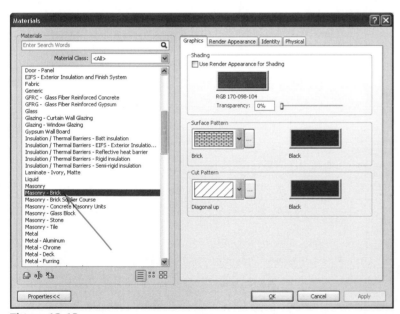

Figure 12-13

16. In the **Element Properties** dialog box, select the rightmost button in the **Materials** field to bring up the **Associate Family Parameter** dialog box (see Figure 12-14).

17. In the **Associate Family Parameter** dialog box, press the **Add parameter** button to bring up the **Parameter Properties** dialog box.

18. In the **Parameter Properties** dialog box, select the **Family parameter** radio button, enter **TABLE TOP** in the **Name** field, select **Materials and Finishes** from **Group parameter under**, and select the **Type** radio button (see Figure 12-15).

19. Press the **OK** buttons to return to the **Drawing Editor**.

20. In the **Sketch** tab, press the **Finish Sketch** button to return to the **Family** tab in the **Design Bar**.

21. In the **Family** tab, again select the **Solid Form >> Solid Extrusion** tool.

22. In the **Sketch** tab, select the **Model Lines** tool.

23. In the **Options** toolbar, select the **Rectangle** tool.

24. Place a **6′ × 8″** rectangle in the center of the table top (see Figure 12-16).

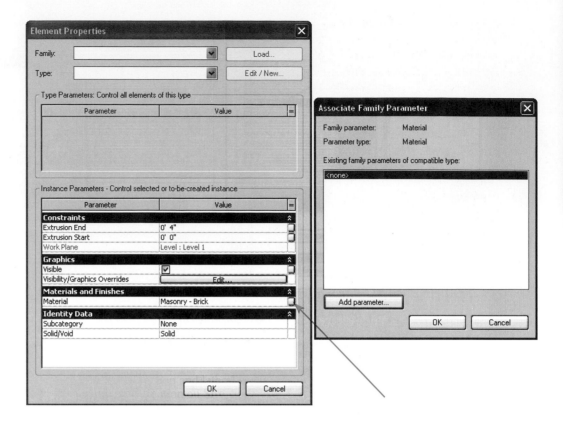

Figure 12-14

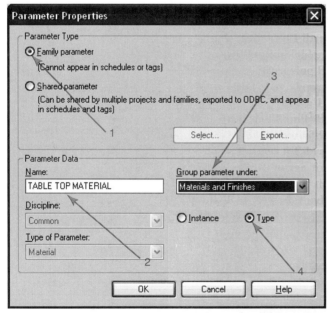

Figure 12-15

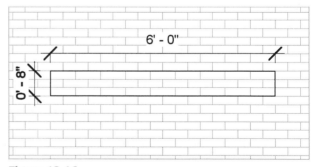

Figure 12-16

25. In the **Sketch** tab, select the **Extrusion Properties** tool to bring up the **Element Properties** dialog box.

26. In the **Element Properties** dialog box, set the **Extrusion End** to **–3′ 4″**.

27. In the **Element Properties** dialog box, select the **Masonry-Brick** button in the **Material** field to create a button at the end of the field.

28. Pick the leftmost button that appears in the **Material** field to bring up the **Materials** dialog box.

29. In the **Materials** dialog box, select **Finishes—Exterior—Siding/Clapboard** and press the **OK** button to return to the **Element Properties** dialog box.

30. In the **Element Properties** dialog box, select the right-most button in the **Materials** field to bring up the **Associate Family Parameter** dialog box.

31. In the **Associate Family Parameter** dialog box, select the **Add parameter** button to bring up the **Parameter properties** dialog box.

32. In the **Parameter Properties** dialog box, select the **Family parameter** radio button, enter **LEG** in the **Name** field, select **Materials and Finishes** from **Group parameter under**, and select the **Type** radio button.

33. Press the **OK** buttons to return to the **Drawing Editor**.

34. In the **Sketch** tab, press the **Finish Sketch** button.

35. In the **Family** tab, press the **Finish Family** button.

36. Change to the **Default 3D View**.

37. Select the table, **RMB**, and select **Element Properties** to bring up the **Element Properties** dialog box.

38. In the **Properties** dialog box, select the buttons at the right side of the **TABLE TOP** and **LEG Materials and Finishes**.

39. Change the materials (see Figures 12-17 and 12-18).

40. Save the file as **IN PLACE FAMILIES**.

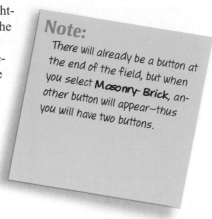

Note:
There will already be a button at the end of the field, but when you select **Masonry-Brick**, another button will appear—thus you will have two buttons.

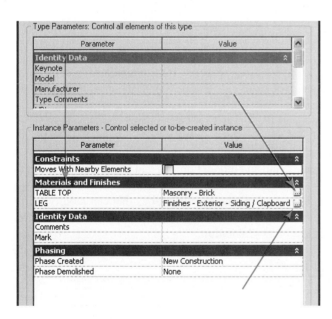

Figure 12-17

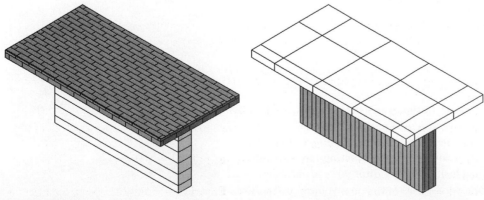

Figure 12-18

When you create a family, Revit Architecture provides you with a template that serves as a building block and contains most of the information needed by Revit Architecture to place the family in the project. Among other elements, the template can include reference planes, dimensions, and predefined geometry, such as window trim.

The following are the basic kinds of family templates:

- wall-based
- ceiling-based
- floor-based
- roof-based
- standalone
- line-based
- face-based

Wall-based, ceiling-based, floor-based, and roof-based templates are known as host-based templates. A host-based family can be placed in a project only if an element of its host type is present.

The wall-based template is for components inserted into walls. Wall components can include openings, such that placing the component on a wall also cuts an opening in the wall. Some examples of wall-based components include doors, windows, and lighting fixtures. Each template includes a wall; the wall is necessary for showing how the component fits in a wall.

The ceiling-based template is for components inserted into ceilings. Ceiling components can include openings, so that placing the component on a ceiling also cuts an opening in the ceiling. Examples of ceiling-based families include sprinklers and recessed lighting fixtures.

The floor-based template is for components inserted into floors. Floor components can include openings, so that placing the component on a floor also cuts an opening in the floor. An example of a floor-based family is a heating register.

The roof-based template is for components inserted into roofs. Roof components can include openings, so that placing the component on a roof also cuts an opening in the roof. Examples of roof-based families include soffits and fans.

The standalone template is for components that are not host-dependent. A standalone component can appear anywhere in a model and can be dimensioned to other standalone or host-based components. Examples of standalone families include columns, furniture, and appliances.

The line-based template is used to create detail and model families that use 2-pick placement similar to structural beams.

The face-based template is used to create work plane–based families that can modify their hosts. Families created from the template can make complex cuts in hosts. Instances of these families can be placed on any surface, regardless of its orientation.

Exercise 12-4: Loadable Families and the Family Editor

Loadable Families can be used in any project.

1. Start a new drawing using the **RAC 2009\Imperial Templates\default.rte** template.
2. Select **File > New > Family** from the **Main** menu to bring up the **New** dialog box.
3. Select the **Imperial** templates folder (or **Metric** folder).
4. In the **Imperial** templates folder, select **Door.rft** (see Figure 12-19).

Notice that the **Design Bar** has changed to the **Family** tab. You are now in the **Family Editor**.

You create objects in the **Family Editor** using tools similar to those in the **Massing** tab. The difference is that in the **Family Editor** you can make the object "parametric." This means that you can make the objects modifiable through the **Element Properties** dialog box.

Note:
If you are not automatically taken to this folder, search to **Local Disk** **[c:] > Documents and Settings > All Users > Application Data > Autodesk > RAC 2009 > Imperial Templates**. Notice that there are many different templates. Each template has been created by Autodesk to aid you in creating components and content.

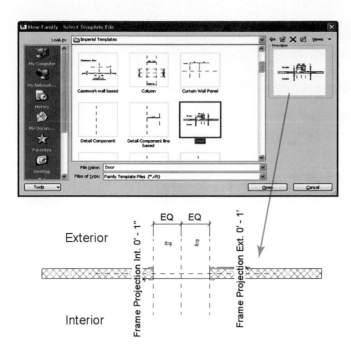

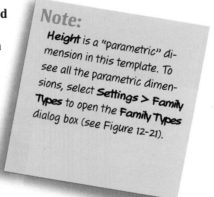

Figure 12-19

5. Make sure you are in the **Ref. Level** floor plan. (Double-click in the **Project browser** if you are not.)
6. Change to **1″ = 1′-0″** scale so that the text becomes smaller.
7. In the **Family** tab of the **Design Bar**, select **Solid Form >> Solid Extrusion**.
8. In the **Sketch** tab that now appears in the **Design Bar**, select the **Lines** tool.
9. Select the rectangle tool from the **Options** toolbar, and place a **3′-0″ × 1 3/4″** rectangle as shown in Figure 12-20.
10. Change to the **Exterior Elevation**, and notice that the door height is dimensioned to **7′-0″** and labeled **Height**.
11. In the **Sketch** tab, select the **Extrusion Properties** tool to open the **Extrusion Properties** dialog box.

> **Note:**
> **Height** is a "parametric" dimension in this template. To see all the parametric dimensions, select **Settings > Family Types** to open the **Family Types** dialog box (see Figure 12-21).

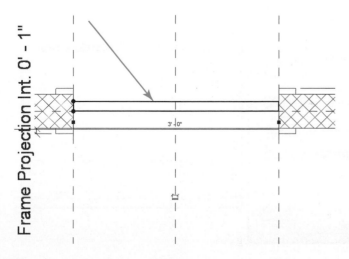

Figure 12-20

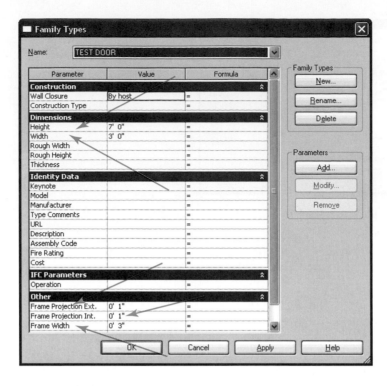

Figure 12-21

12. In the **Extrusion Properties** dialog box, select the right-side button in the **Extrusion End** field to bring up the **Associate Family Parameter** dialog box.
13. In the **Associate Family Parameter** dialog box, pick the **Height** parameter.

This will make the height of the extrusion (door you are creating) match the **Height** of the door opening (see Figure 12-22).

14. Press the **OK** buttons to return to the **Drawing Editor**.
15. In the **Sketch** tab, press the **Finish Sketch** button.

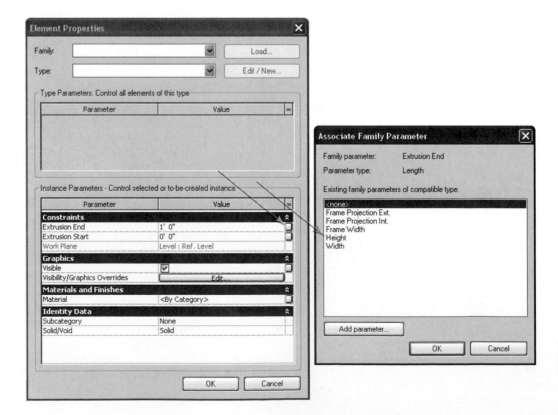

Figure 12-22

You have now extruded a 3D door and opening whose heights are controlled by the **Height** parameter.

16. In the **Family** tab of the **Design Bar**, select **Void Form >> Solid Extrusion**.
17. In the **Sketch** tab that now appears in the **Design Bar**, select the **Model Lines** tool.
18. Change the **Drawing Scale** to **1″ = 1′-0″** (so the text becomes smaller).
19. Select the rectangle tool from the **Options** toolbar, and place a **2′-0″ × 2′-0″** rectangle as shown in Figure 12-23.

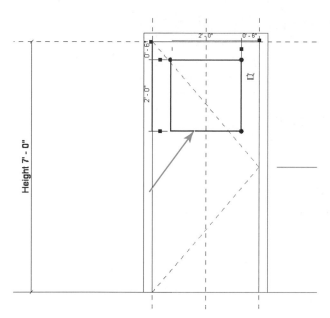

Figure 12-23

20. Change to the **Default 3D Wiew**.
21. In the **Sketch** tab, press the **Extrusion Properties** tool to open the **Element Properties** dialog box.
22. In the **Element Properties** dialog box, set the **Extrusion End** to **1′-0″** and **Extrusion Start** to **−1′−0″**, and then press the **OK** button to return to the **Drawing Editor**.
23. In the **Sketch** tab, press the **Finish Sketch** button to return to the **Family Editor**.

Notice that the door has a 2′ × 2′ opening (see Figure 12-24).

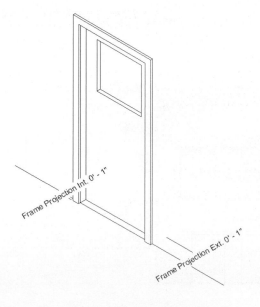

Figure 12-24

24. Return to the **Exterior Elevation**.
25. Select the **Dimensions** tool from the **Family** tab.
26. Dimension the opening (see Figure 12-25).

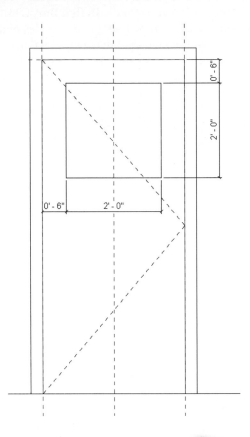

Figure 12-25

27. Select the **2'-0″** dimension at the right side of the opening.
28. In the **Options** toolbar, select **<Add parameter...>** from the **Label** drop-down list to bring up the **Parameter Properties** dialog box (see Figure 12-26).
29. In the **Parameter Properties** dialog box, select the **Family parameter** radio button, enter **OPENING HEIGHT** in the **Name** field, select **Dimensions** from **Group parameters under**, select the **Type** radio button, and then press the **OK** button (see Figure 12-27).

Note:
The other parameters you see in the **Label** list control different dimensions in the **Family**—thus controlling the size of different components in the **Family** object. You will be adding a new controllable parameter to the object.

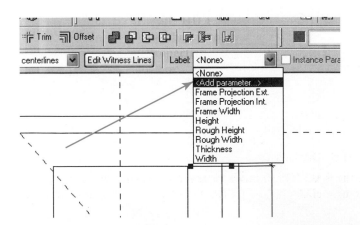

Figure 12-26

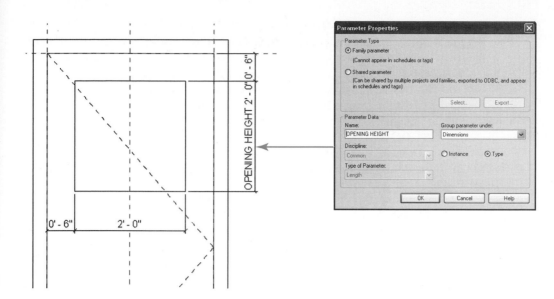

Figure 12-27

30. Repeat step 29 creating the **OPENING WIDTH**, **LEFT STILE**, and **TOP STYLE** parameters.
31. Select **Settings > Family Types** from the **Main** menu to bring up the **Family Types** dialog box.

Notice that the new parameters you just created are in the **Family Types** dialog box (see Figure 12-28).

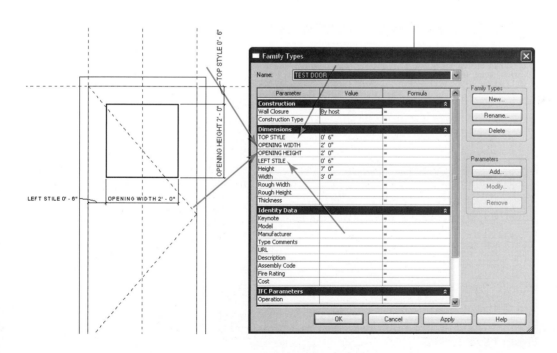

Figure 12-28

32. Select **File > Save As > TEST DOOR**.

Exercise 12-5: Using the New TEST DOOR Family

1. Start a new drawing using the **RAC 2009\Imperial Templates\default.rte** template.
2. In the **Project browser**, double-click on the **LEVEL 1** floor plan to bring it up into the **Drawing Editor**.

3. Change to the **Basics** tab in the **Design Bar**.
4. Select the **Wall** tool and place a **Basic Wall: Generic-8″** wall **10′-0″** high and **10′-0″** long in the **Drawing Editor**.
5. Select **File Load from Library > Load Family** from the **Main** menu.
6. Locate the **TEST DOOR** family you created in the previous exercise.
7. In the **Basics** tab of the **Design Bar**, select the **Door** tool.
8. In the **Options** toolbar, select the **TEST DOOR**.
9. Place the **TEST DOOR** into the wall.
10. Change to the **Default 3D View**.
11. Select the door, **RMB**, and select **Element Properties** to bring up the **Element Properties** dialog box.
12. In the **Element Properties** dialog box, select the **Edit/New** button near the top right to bring up the **Type Properties** dialog box.
13. In the **Type Properties** dialog box, change the **OPENING WIDTH** to **2′-6″**, the **OPENING HEIGHT** to **5′-0″**, the **LEFT STYLE** to **3″**, and then press the **OK** button to return to the **Drawing Editor** (see Figure 12-29).

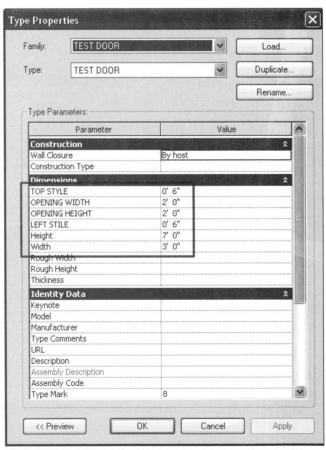

Figure 12-29

The door opening changes because it is "parametrically" controlled from the **Type Properties** dialog box (see Figure 12-30).

14. Save the file as **FAMILY EDITOR**.

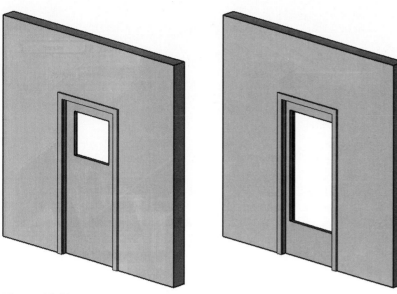

Figure 12-30

SUMMARY

This section explained how to use and modify **Components** and **Families** in Revit Architecture 2009. Among the subjects discussed were **System Families**, **In-Place Families Load-able Families**, and the **Family Editor**. Also shown were methods for downloading and importing **Families** from the Internet.

SECTION TEST QUESTIONS

True/False

1. True or False: A floor is not a host object.

2. True or False: Family parameters cannot be modified.

3. True or False: The standalone **Family** template is for components that are not host-dependent.

4. True or False: There are four types of **Families** in Revit Architecture.

5. True or False: You create objects in the **Family Editor** using tools similar to those in the **Massing** tab. The difference in the **Family Editor** is that you can make the objects parametric.

Questions

1. What is the definition of a Revit Architecture 2009 **Family**?

2. What is definition of a Revit Architecture 2009 **Component**?

3. What is an **In-Place Family** used for?

4. What is a **Loadable Family**?

5. Where do you find the **Add parameter** drop-down list?

Site

13

Section Objectives

Most architectural projects include site drawings. Revit Architecture 2009 has an excellent site creation tool called the **Toposurface** tool. This tool allows you to develop the site manually by entering elevation points, or automatically by importing point data from your civil engineer's or surveyor's 3D files.

- Learn how to use the **Toposurface** tool.
- Know how to use the **Pad** tool with the **Toposurface**.
- Learn how to create a **Toposurface** base.
- Know how to create a **Toposurface** with **Points**.
- Know how to use the **Split Surface** tool.
- Learn how to add **Site Components**.
- Learn how to label **Contours**.

Exercise 13-1: Using the Toposurface Tool

The **Toposurface** tool is used to create a Revit 3D ground model when you have a 3D CAD topo file from your civil engineer.

1. Download the TEST SITE 1 CAD file from the Internet at http://www.hergra.org//REVIT_BOOK_PRACTICE_FILES.html, and place it in a new directory on your computer called SITE.
2. Start a new drawing using the **RAC 2009\Imperial Templates\default.rte** template.
3. In the **Project browser**, double-click on the **Site** floor plan to bring it up into the **Drawing Editor**.
4. Change to the **Site** tab in the **Design Bar**.
5. Select **File > Import/Link** from the **Main** menu to bring up the **Import/Link** dialog box.
6. In the **Import/Link** dialog box, search for the **TEST SITE 1** file on the CD.
7. In the **Import/Link** dialog box, set the **Layer/Level Colors** to **Black and white**, select the **Manually place** radio button, select the **Cursor at origin** radio button, set **Place at level** to **Level 1**, and then press the **Open** button and place the CAD file (see Figure 13-1).
8. Select **Settings > Site Settings** from the **Main** menu to bring up the **Site Settings** dialog box.
9. In the **Site Settings** dialog box, check the **At Intervals of** check box, and set the **Contour Line Display** to **2'-0"** (to display contours at 2'-0" heights).
10. Change to the **Site** tab in the **Design Bar**.
11. In the **Site** tab, select the **Toposurface** tool to bring the **Toposurface** tab into the **Design Bar**.

Note:
If you want to change the pattern that displays when you cut a section through the **Toposurface**, or change the rendering color of the surface, you can select the **Section cut material** button to bring up the **Materials** dialog box (see Figure 13-2).

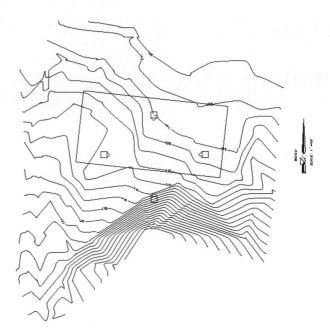

Figure 13-1

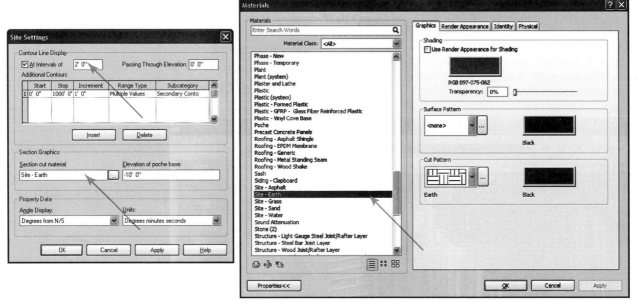

Figure 13-2

12. In the **Toposurface** tab, select **Use Imported >> Import Instance** and select the **TEST SITE 1** file you placed in the **Site** view.

The **Add Points from Selected Layers** dialog box will appear.

13. In the **Add Points from Selected Layers** dialog box, press the **Select Check None** button to clear all the check boxes, and then check the **EG-EX** check box.

14. In the **Add Points from Selected Layers** dialog box, press the **OK** button to return to the **Site** view, and create the **Toposurface**.

15. In the **Toposurface** tab, select the **Finish Surface** tool to complete the toposurface, and return to the **Site** tab in the **Design Bar**.

16. Enter **VG** on your keyboard to bring up the **Visibility/Graphic Overrides for Floor Plan: Site** dialog box.

Note:
In the file sent by the civil engineer, all the intervals are placed on the **EG-EX** layer.

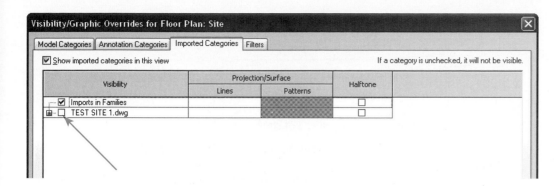

Figure 13-3

17. In the **Visibility/Graphic Overrides for Floor Plan: Site** dialog box, select the **Imported Categories** tab.
18. In the **Imported Categories** tab, uncheck the **TEST SITE 1** drawing, and press the **OK** button to return to the **Drawing Editor** (see Figure 13-3).
19. Change to the **East Elevation** view.
20. Enter **VG** on your keyboard to bring up the **Visibility/Graphic Overrides for Floor Plan: Site** dialog box.
21. In the **Visibility/Graphic Overrides for Floor Plan: Site** dialog box, select the **Imported Categories** tab.
22. In the **Imported Categories** tab, uncheck the **TEST SITE 1** drawing and press the **OK** button to return to the **Drawing Editor**.
23. Change the scale to **1″ = 40′**
24. Save this file as **TOPOSURFACE TOOL**.

Note:
Unchecking the **TEST SITE 1** drawing will hide the CAD drawing in the **Site** view (see Figure 13-4).

Figure 13-4

Exercise 13-2: Using the Pad Tool with the Toposurface

The **Pad** tool is used to create a building pad for a building.

1. Using the previous exercise, change to the **Level 1** floor plan.
2. Drag **Level 1** to the lowest point on the toposurface **(102′-0″)**.
3. Drag **Level 2** to the highest point on the toposurface **(146′-0″)** (Figure 13-5).
4. Change to the **Level 1** floor plan.

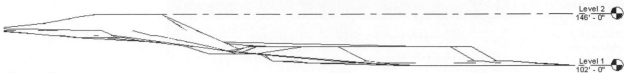

Figure 13-5

Notice that the toposurface you created does not show in the **Level 1** floor plan.

5. Enter **VG** on your keyboard to bring up the **Visibility/Graphic Overrides for Floor Plan: Site** dialog box.
6. In the **Visibility/Graphic Overrides for Floor Plan: Site** dialog box, select the **Model Categories** tab.
7. In the **Model Categories** tab, check the **Topography** check box.
8. Change to the **Basics** tab.
9. In the **Basics** tab, select the **Wall** tool.
10. In the **Options** toolbar, select **Basic Wall: Generic -8″**.
11. In the **Options** toolbar, select the **Pick Lines** tool (pointer), and set the **Level** to **Level 1**, the **Height** to **level 2**, and **Loc Line** to **Finish Face: Exterior**.
12. Pick on the lines of the rectangle in the **TEST SITE 1** CAD drawing to create a **40′** high enclosure.
13. Change to the **Site** tab in the **Design Bar**.
14. Select the **Pad** tool to change to **Sketch** mode.
15. In the **Sketch** tab, select the **Pick Walls** tool.
16. Pick the outside walls of the enclosure you previously created.
17. In the **Sketch** tab, select the **Pad Properties** tool to bring up the **Element Properties** dialog box.
18. In the **Element Properties** dialog box, set the **Height Offset From Level** to **1′-0″** and then press the **OK** button to return to the **Drawing Editor**.
19. Select **Finish Sketch** to create the building pad (see Figure 13-6).

Figure 13-6

You have now created the walls and building pad (see Figure 13-7).

20. Change to **Level 2**.
21. Change to the **Basics** tab in the **Design Bar**.
22. In the **Basics** tab, select **Roof > Roof by Footprint** to change to **Sketch** mode.
23. In the **Sketch** tab, select the **Pick Walls** tool.

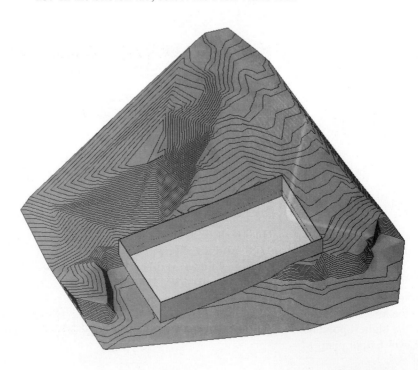

Figure 13-7

24. In the **Options** toolbar, check the **Defines Slope** check box, and enter **2'-0"** in the **Overhang** field.
25. Pick the outside walls of the enclosure you previously created.
26. Select **Finish Roof** to create the roof (see Figure 13-8).
27. Save this file as **TOPOSURFACE**.

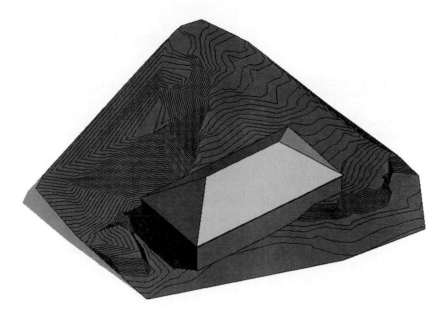

Figure 13-8

Exercise 13-3: Creating the Toposurface Base

You have created a **Toposurface**, but it is not sitting on a base.

1. Select **Settings > Site Settings** from the **Main** menu to bring up the **Site Settings** dialog box.
2. In the **Site Settings** dialog box, select the **Section cut material** button to bring up the **Materials** dialog box.
3. In the **Materials** dialog box, select the **Cut Pattern** button to bring up the **Fill Patterns** dialog box.
4. In the **Fill Patterns** dialog box, select the **No Pattern** button, and then press the **OK** buttons to return to the **Drawing Editor** (see Figures 13-9 and 13-10).

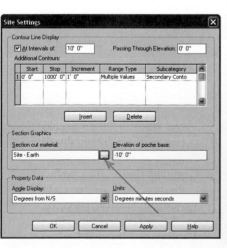

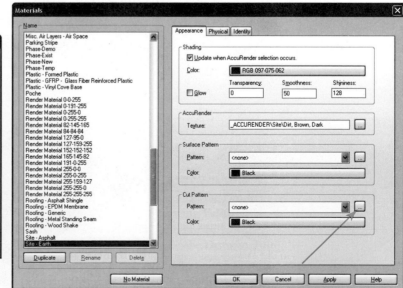

Figure 13-9

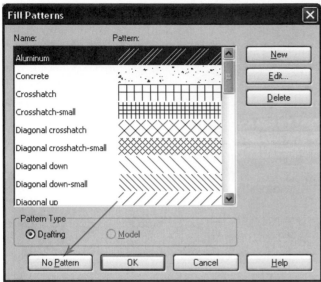

Figure 13-10

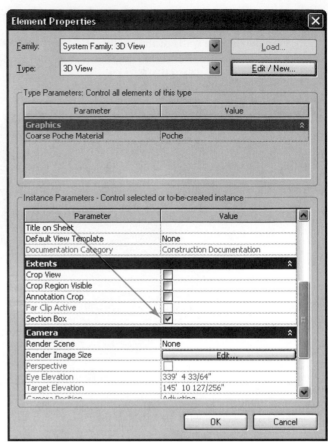

Figure 13-11

5. **RMB** in an empty spot in the **Drawing Editor** and check the **Section Box** check box (see Figure 13-11).

The **Section Box** will appear around your toposurface and building.

6. Select the **Section Box**, and drag the handles to "crop" the toposurface.
7. With the **Section Box** still selected, press the **Temporarily Hide/ isolate** button at the bottom of the **Drawing Editor** to hide the **Section Box** (see Figures 13-12 and 13-13).
8. Save this file as **TOPOSURFACE BASE**.

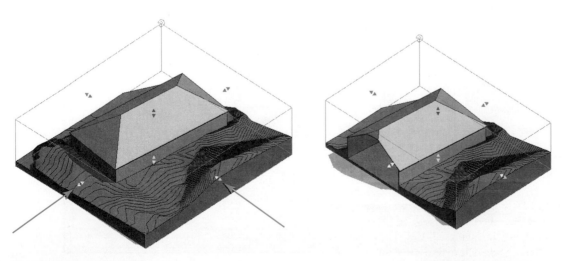

Figure 13-12

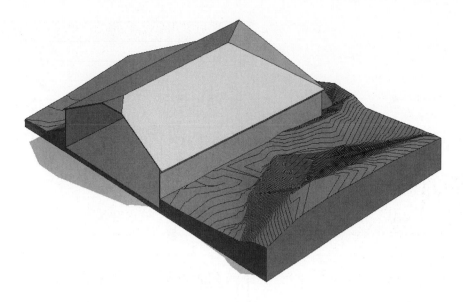

Figure 13-13

Exercise 13-4: Creating a Toposurface with Points

1. Start a new drawing using the **RAC 2009\Imperial Templates\default.rte** template.
2. In the **Project browser**, double-click on the **Site** floor plan to bring it up into the **Drawing Editor**.
3. Change the scale to **1″ = 1′-0″**.
4. Change to the **Basics** tab in the **Design Bar**.
5. Select the **Wall** and **Roof** tools and create a simple 10′ high enclosure with a roof using the dimensions shown in Figure 13-14.

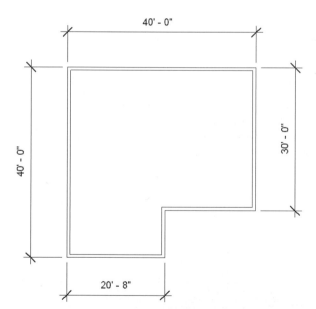

Figure 13-14

6. Change to the **Site** tab in the **Design Bar**.
7. In the **Site** tab, select the **Toposurface** tool to change to the **Toposurface** tab in the **Design Bar**.
8. In the **Toposurface** tab, select the **Point** tool.
9. In the **Options** toolbar, set the **Elevation** to **0′-0″**.
10. Place four points as shown in Figure 13-15.
11. In the **Options** toolbar, set the **Elevation** to **–4′-0″**.
12. Place more points as shown in Figure 13-16.

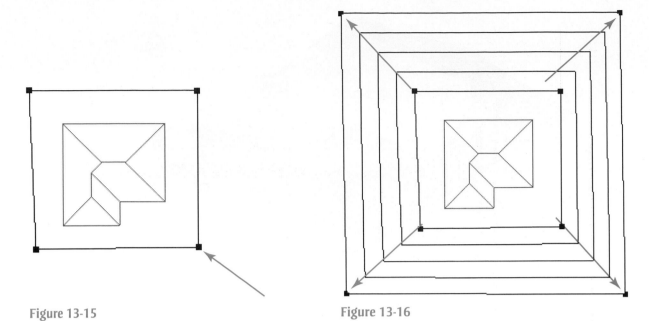

Figure 13-15

Figure 13-16

Notice that more increments appear between the levels than you created. That is because the **Site** settings are set to have **1′-0″** increments. To change these intervals, do the following:

13. Select **Settings > Site Settings** from the **Main** toolbar to bring up the **Site Settings** dialog box.
14. In the **Site Settings** dialog box, change the **Increment** setting to **0′-6″**, and press the **OK** button to return to the **Drawing Editor**.

Notice that the increments have increased (see Figure 13-17).

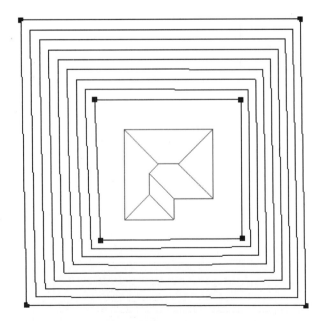

Figure 13-17

15. In the **Options** toolbar, set the **Elevation** to **–8′-0″**.
16. Place more points.
17. Press the **Finish Surface** tool in the **Site** tab and change to the **East Elevation** (see Figure 13-18).
18. Save this file as **TOPOSURFACE by POINTS**.

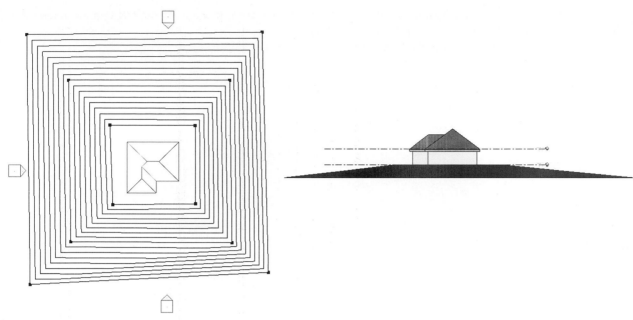

Figure 13-18

Exercise 13-5: Using the Split Surface Tool on a Toposurface

1. Using the previous exercise, change to the **Site** view.
2. Change to the **Site** tab in the **Design Bar**.
3. In the **Site** tab, select the **Split Surface** tool, and then select the toposurface you created to enter **Sketch** mode.
4. In the **Sketch** tab, select the **Lines** tool.
5. In the **Options** toolbar, select the **Pencil** tool and then the **Rectangle** tool.
6. Place a **12′** wide rectangle as shown, and press the **Finish Sketch** button to create the split surface (see Figure 13-19).

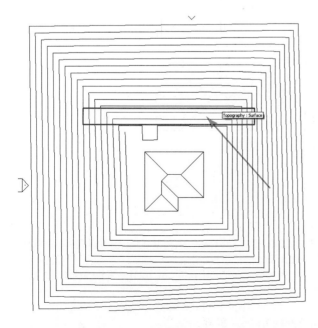

Figure 13-19

7. Select the split surface, **RMB**, and select **Element Properties** from the contextual menu to bring up the **Element Properties** dialog box.
8. In the **Element Properties** dialog box, select the button to the right of the **Materials** field to bring up the **Materials** dialog box.

9. In the **Materials** dialog box, select **Site – Asphalt** and press the **OK** buttons to return to the **Drawing Editor**.
10. Change to the **Default 3D View** (see Figure 13-20).

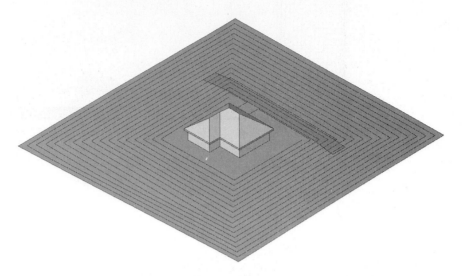

Figure 13-20

The split surface (road) is not level, but follows the contours. To fix this, do the following:

11. Select the road you just created, and select the **Edit** button in the **Options** toolbar to bring up the **Toposurface** tab in the **Design Bar**.
12. Select all the vertices in the road and enter **0** in the **Elevation** field in the **Options** toolbar.
13. Press the **Finish Surface** button in the **Toposurface** tab to make the entire road **0** elevation (see Figure 13-21).

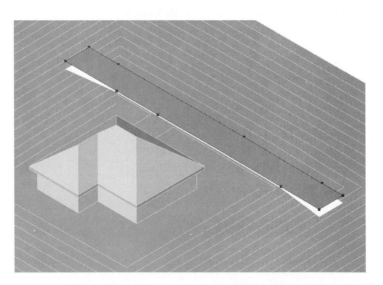

Figure 13-21

14. Select the main toposurface and select the **Edit** button in the **Options** toolbar to bring up the **Toposurface** tab in the **Design Bar**.
15. Select all the vertices adjacent to the road and enter **0** in the **Elevation** field in the **Options** toolbar.
16. Press the **Finish Surface** button in the **Toposurface** tab to make the toposurface match the elevation of the road (see Figure 13-22).
17. **RMB** in an empty spot in the **Drawing Editor** and check the **Section Box** check box.
18. Select the **Section Box** and drag the handles to "crop" the toposurface.
19. With the **Section Box** still selected, press the **Temporarily Hide/ isolate** button at the bottom of the **Drawing Editor** to hide the **Section Box** (see Figure 13-23).
20. Save this file as **SPLIT SURFACE**.

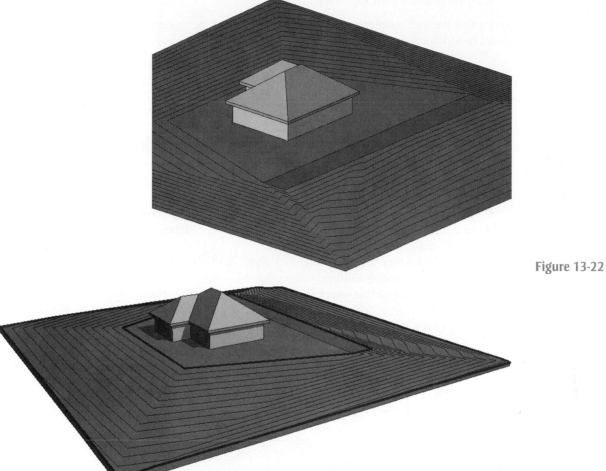

Figure 13-22

Figure 13-23

Exercise 13-6: Adding Site Components to a Toposurface

1. Using the previous exercise, change to the **Site** view.
2. Change to the **Site** tab in the **Design Bar**.
3. In the **Site** tab, select the **Site Components** tool.
4. In the **Options** toolbar, select **RPC Tree Deciduous: Red Maple –30′**.
5. Continue to place trees on the toposurface as shown in Figure 13-24.

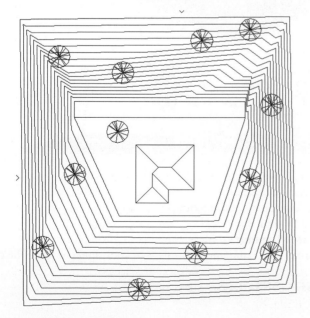

Figure 13-24

6. Change to the **East Elevation**.

Notice that the trees automatically attach to the level of the toposurface upon which they were placed in **Site** view (see Figure 13-25).

Figure 13-25

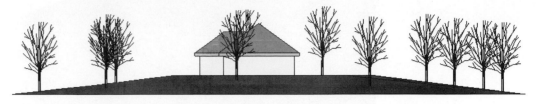

7. Change back to the **Site** view.
8. In the **Site** tab, select the **Site Components** tool.
9. In the **Options** toolbar, press the **Load** button to bring up the **Open** dialog box.
10. In the **Open** dialog box, change to the **Imperial** (or **Metric**) **Library**.
11. Select and open the **Entourage** folder.
12. In the **Entourage** folder, double-click on the **RPC Beetle** to close the dialog box and return to the **Drawing Editor**.
13. In the **Options** toolbar, check the **Rotate after placement** check box.
14. Place and then rotate the car on the road.
15. Change to the **Default 3D** and **North** views (see Figure 13-26).

Save this file as **SITE COMPONENTS**.

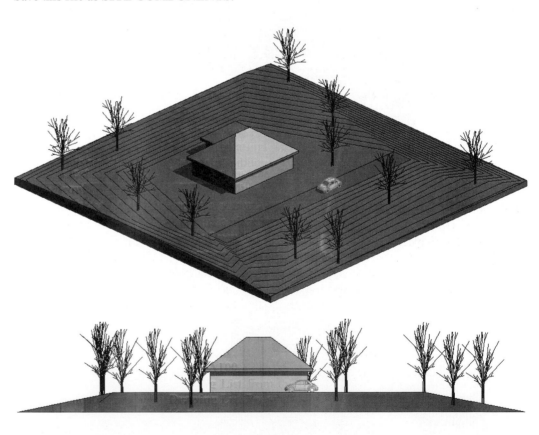

Figure 13-26

Exercise 13-7: Labeling Contours

1. Using the previous exercise, change to the **Site** view.
2. Change to the **Site** tab in the **Design Bar**.
3. In the **Site** tab, select the **Label Contours** tool.
4. Select the spot shown in Figure 13-27, drag downwards, and click again to place the contour labels.
5. Save this file as **LABELING CONTOURS**.

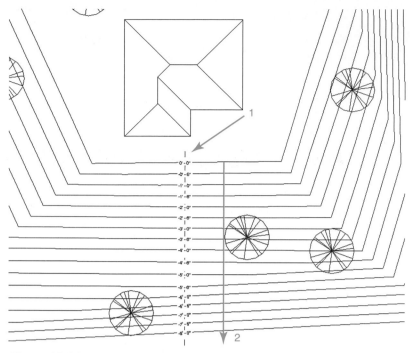

Figure 13-27

Exercise 13-8: Sloped Building Pads

In prior releases **Pads** (building pads) could not be sloped. In Revit Architecture this option has been added through the use of a new **Slope Arrow** tool.

1. Double-click on **Site** view in the **Project browser** to bring the **Site** view up in the **Drawing Editor**.
2. Change to the **West** elevation.
3. Create three **Levels** named **Level 1**, **BASEMENT**, and **GRADE**.
4. Set **Level 1** to **0′-0″**, **BASEMENT** to **10′-0″**, and **GRADE** to **20′-0″**.
5. Change to the **Site** tab in the **Design Bar**.
6. In the **Site** tab, select the **Toposurface** icon to enter the **Sketch** tab.
7. Create a **Toposurface** that is **20′-0″** high, **110′** long × **110′** wide.
8. Double-click on the **BASEMENT** floor plan in the **Project browser** to bring the **BASEMENT** view up in the **Drawing Editor**.
9. Return to the **Site** tab, and select the **Pad** tool to bring up the **Sketch** tab (see Figure 13-28).
10. In the **Sketch** tab, select the **Lines** tool, and place a rectangle as shown in Figure 13-29.
11. In the **Sketch** tab, select **Finish Sketch** to create the first pad.
12. Return to the **Site** tab, and again, select the **Pad** tool to bring up the **Sketch** tab.

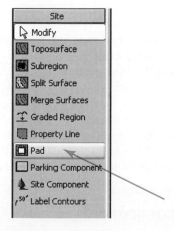

Figure 13-28

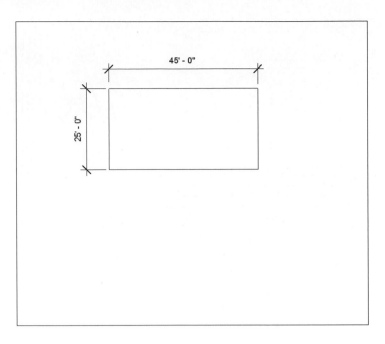

Figure 13-29

13. In the **Sketch** tab, select the **Lines** tool, and place a rectangle again, as shown in Figure 13-30.

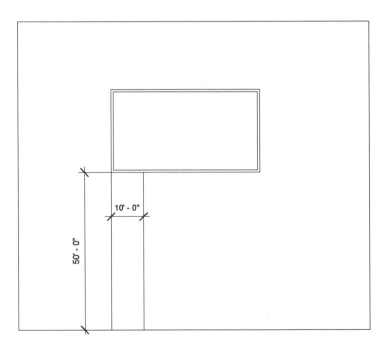

Figure 13-30

14. In the **Sketch** tab, select the **Slope Arrow** and place it as shown in Figure 13-31.
15. Select the **Slope Arrow**, and press the **Element Properties** button on the **Options** toolbar to bring up the **Element Properties** dialog box.
16. In the **Element Properties** dialog box, setting the **Level at Head** and **Level at Tail** to named levels is an easy way to control the **Slope Arrow** (see Figure 13-32).
17. In the **Sketch** tab, again select **Finish Sketch** to create the sloped **Pad**.
18. From the **Basics tab** in the **Design browser**, place a **Section callout** (see Figure 13-33).
19. Double-click on the **Section 1** that you just created in the **Project browser** to bring the **Section 1** view up in the **Drawing Editor** (see Figure 13-34).

Adding a building creates an excellent presentation (see Figures 13-35 and 13-36).

20. Save this file as **SLOPED BUILDING PADS**.

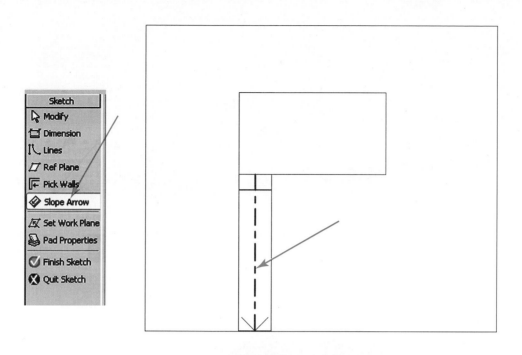

Figure 13-31

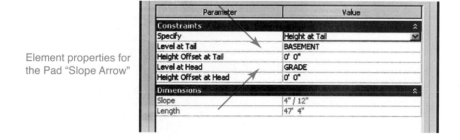

Element properties for the Pad "Slope Arrow"

Figure 13-32

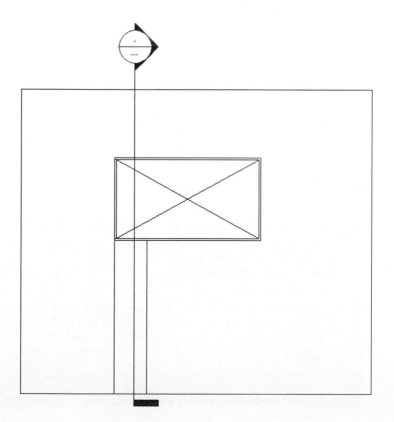

Figure 13-33

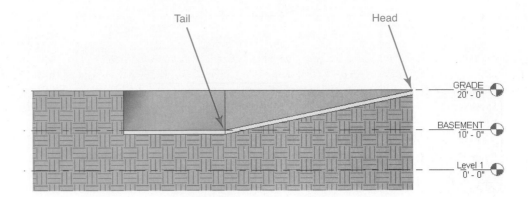

Figure 13-34

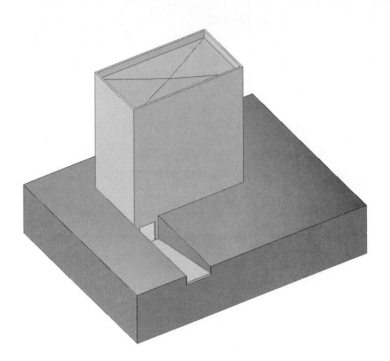

Figure 13-35

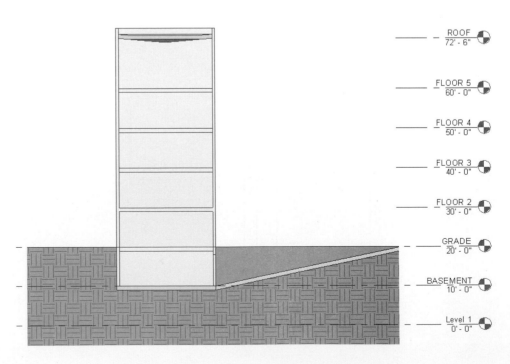

Figure 13-36

SUMMARY

This section discussed the tools and methods available to document building sites. Several methods were shown for the construction and presentation of the topography. Included were demonstrations of the **Toposurface** tool, the **Pad** tool, the **Section Box**, and the **Split Surface** tool. Finally, Revit Architecture 2009's new **Sloped Pad** enhancements were illustrated.

SECTION TEST QUESTIONS

Questions

1. What does the **Toposurface** tool do?

2. How does the **Section Box** help in 3D views of a toposurface?

3. What is the purpose of the **Pad** tool?

4. How do you use the **Label Contours** tool?

5. How do you control the edges of a split surface?

6. What does **Toposurface by Points** do?

7. Where do you set the contour increments?

8. Where are the **Site Component** families located?

Room and Area

14

Section
Objectives

- Understand **Rooms** and **Room Volumes**.
- Understand **Gross Building** and **Areas**.
- Understand **Rentable Areas**.
- Create **Area Schedules**.
- Create **Color Scheme Legends**.
- Create **Area Reports**.

Volume and area are important pieces of information for architects, engineers, contractors, and owners. In Autodesk Revit 2009, this type of information is handled by the **Room** and **Area** tools found in the **Room and Area** menu of the **Design Bar**.

The **Room** object is a 3D volumetric object. The following elements are considered to be bounding elements for room area and volume calculations:

- Walls (curtain, standard, in-place, face-based)
- Roofs (standard, in-place, face-based)
- Floors (standard, in-place, face-based)
- Ceilings (standard, in-place, face-based)
- Columns (architectural, structural with material set to concrete)
- Curtain systems
- Room separation lines

Below is the **Element Properties** dialog box for Room objects.

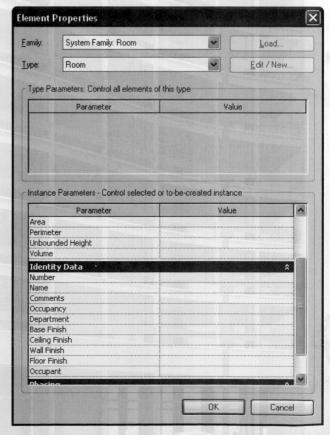

Room Properties	
Name	**Description**
Constraints	
Level	The base level the room is on. This is a read-only value.
Upper Limit	The level specified in **Upper Limit** plus the value in **Limit Offset** define the upper boundary of the room.
Limit Offset	May be negative. The **Limit Offset** plus the **Upper Limit** define the upper boundary of the room.
Dimensions	
Area	The net area calculated from the room-bounding elements. This is a read-only value.
Perimeter	The perimeter of the room. This is a read-only value.
Unbounded Height	The height of the room as defined by the distance between the room's base level and the Upper **Limit + Limit Offset**. This is a read-only value.
Volume	The volume of the room if volume computations are enabled. This is a read-only value.
Identity Data	
Number	Sets the room number, such as 1. This value must be unique for each room in a project. Revit Architecture warns you if the number is already used but allows you to continue using it. You can see the warning using the **REVIEW WARNINGS** command. Room numbers are assigned sequentially.
Name	Sets the room name, such as **Conference Room**.
Comments	Specific comments about the room.
Occupancy	Type of occupancy for structure, such as **Retail**.
Department	Department name.
Base Finish	Finish for the base.
Ceiling Finish	Finish for the ceiling, such as stucco.
Wall Finish	Finish for the wall, such as painted.
Floor Finish	Finish for the floor, such as carpeting.
Occupant	Occupant name.

Exercise 14-1: Rooms and Room Volumes

1. Start a new drawing using the **RAC 2009\Imperial Templates\default.rte** template.
2. In the **Project browser**, double-click **Floor Plans > Level 1** to bring it up into the **Drawing Editor**.
3. Using the **Wall** tool in the **Basics** tab of the **Design Bar**, create a **10'-0" × 10'-0"** enclosure **10'-0"** high. Make sure that the interior of the enclosure is **10'-0" × 10'-0"** (see Figure 14-1).

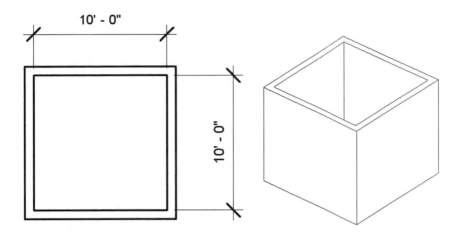

10' - 0"

10' - 0"

Figure 14-1

4. Using the **Floor** and **Roof** tools from the **Basics** tab of the **Design Bar**, place a flat roof (no slope) and floor to bound (enclose) the enclosure. Make sure the walls are attached to the **Roof** (see Figure 14-2).
5. Change to the **Room and Area** tab in the **Design Bar**.
6. In the **Room and Area** tab, select the **Settings** icon to open the **Area and Volume Computations** dialog box.
7. In the **Area and Volume Computations** dialog box, select the **Areas and Volumes** radio button and press the **OK** button to return to the **Drawing Editor** (see Figure 14-3).

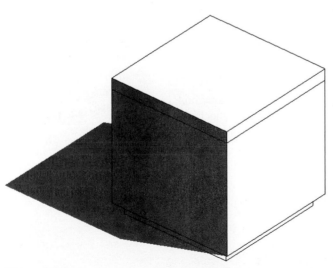

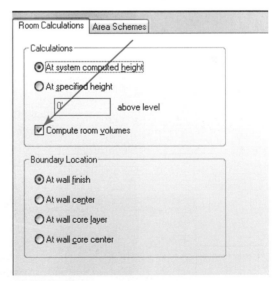

Figure 14-2   Figure 14-3

8. Select the **Room** tool from the **Room and Area** tab in the **Design Bar**.
9. Press the **Element Properties** button on the **Options** toolbar to bring up the **Element Properties** dialog box.
10. In the **Element Properties** dialog box, select **Room Tag With Volume** from the **Type** drop-down list and press the **OK** button to return to the **Drawing Editor** (see Figure 14-4).
11. In the **Level 1 Floor Plan**, move your cursor over the enclosure to place the room, and click to complete the command.

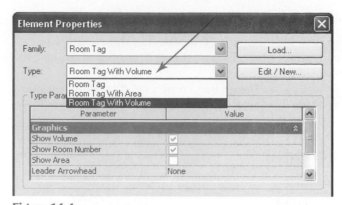

Figure 14-4

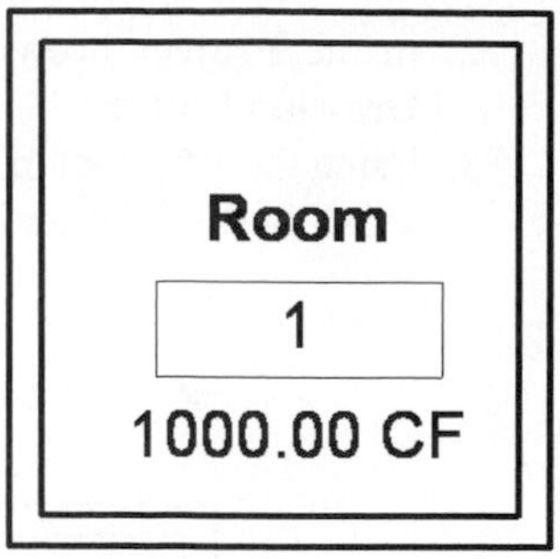

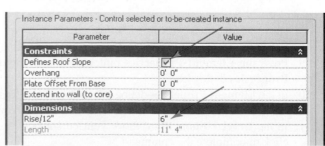

Figure 14-5

12. Notice that the room tag reads **1,000.00 CF** (see Figure 14-5).

13. To select a room, move your cursor over the room until the crosshairs graphic is displayed, and then click.

14. **RMB** on the crosshairs to bring up the contextual menu.

15. In the contextual menu, select **Element Properties** to bring up the **Element Properties** dialog box.

16. In the **Element Properties** dialog box, change the **Limit Offset** to **50′-0″**. (This now allows you to calculate the volume for a room with a pitched roof.) Press the **OK** button to return to the **Drawing Editor** (see Figure 14-6).

17. Change to **Level 2**.

18. Select the roof, and then press the **Edit** button in the **Options** toolbar to change to **Sketch** mode for the roof.

19. Select the southmost sketch line of the roof, and press the **Element Properties** button in the **Options** toolbar to bring up the **Element Properties** dialog box.

20. In the **Element Properties** dialog box, check the **Defines Roof Slope** check box, and change the **Rise/12″** to **2″** (see Figure 14-7).

Note:
From the Revit help file:
"The volume calculation uses room area multiplied by upper limit only when the default height is lower than the ceiling or floor or roof. If it is higher than those elements, then Revit Architecture calculates the room volume based on the room-bounding elements, regardless of their shape. Therefore, for rooms under roofs, such as attic spaces, specify a room height (upper limit) that is greater than the height of the roof. This will ensure that the volume will be calculated up to the roof pitch. Note that the graphical representation in section does not reflect the actual boundaries used by the calculation."

Note:
Although you have changed the **Limit Offset**, the **Room** tag still reads **1,000.00 CF**. If you change to a pitched roof, the volume will change.

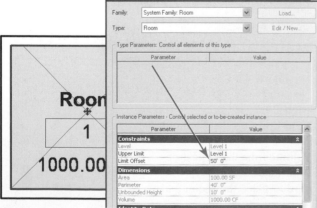

Figure 14-6

Figure 14-7

21. Press the **OK** button to return to the **Drawing Editor**.
22. Press the **Finish** roof button in the **Sketch** tab to complete the roof.
23. Return to **Level 1** where you placed the **Room** tag.

The **Room** tag now reads **1298.18 CF** (see Figure 14-8).

24. Save this file as **ROOM VOLUMES**.

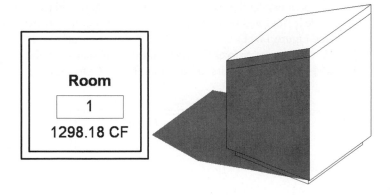

Figure 14-8

Exercise 14-2: Gross Building and Areas

1. Start a new drawing using the **RAC 2009\Imperial Templates\default.rte** template.
2. In the **Project browser**, double-click **Floor Plans > Level 1** to bring it up into the **Drawing Editor**.
3. Using the **Wall** tool in the **Basics** tab of the **Design Bar**, create the enclosure shown in Figure 14-9.
4. Change to the **Room and Area** tab in the **Design Bar**.
5. In the **Room and Area** tab, select the **Area Plan** tool to bring up the **New Area Plan** dialog box.
6. In the **New Area Plan** dialog box, select **Gross Building** from the type drop-down list, **Level** 1 from the **Area Plan Views**, and then press **OK** to create the new **Area Plan** (see Figure 14-10).
7. Press the **Yes** button on the Revit dialog box that asks **Automatically create boundary lines associated with all external walls?**

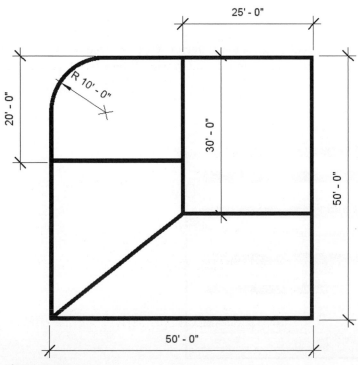

Figure 14-9

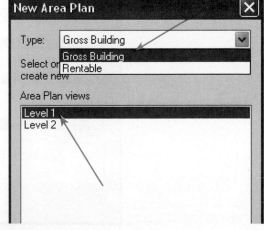

Figure 14-10

8. Double-click **Area Plans [Gross Building] > Level 1** from the **Project browser** to bring it up in the **Drawing Editor.**

Blue boundary lines will appear around the entire enclosure.

9. Select the **Area** tool from the **Room and Area** tab, and place an area tag in the middle of the enclosure.
10. The area tag will appear with the area in square feet.
11. Double-click on the word **Area** in the tag you just placed, enter **GROSS BUILDING** in the text field, and then click in an empty area in the **Drawing Editor** to complete the tag (see Figure 14-11).
12. Move your cursor over the area until the crosshairs graphic is displayed, and then click.
13. **RMB** on the crosshairs to bering up the contextual menu.

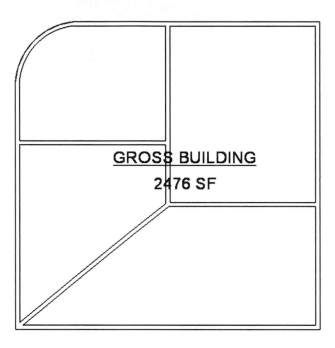

Figure 14-11

14. In the contextual menu, select **Element Properties** to bring up the **Element Properties** dialog box.
15. In the **Element Properties** dialog box, select **Exterior Area** from the **Area Type** drop-down list, and press the **OK** button to return to the **Drawing Editor** (see Figure 14-12).

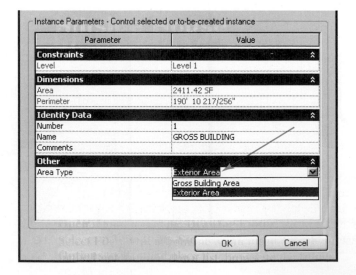

Figure 14-12

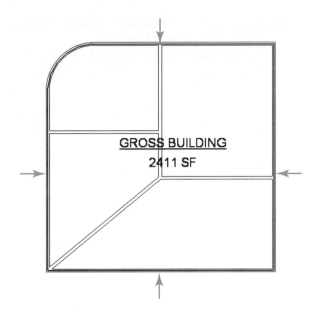

GROSS BUILDING
2411 SF

Figure 14-13

Notice that the blue boundary lines now appear around the entire enclosure, but in the center of the walls. Notice also that the **Area** in square feet has changed (see Figure 14-13).

Revit Architecture 2009 uses **Area Rules** to control the area calculation. The following are the rules for **Gross Building Area** and **Exterior Area** calculations.

Gross Building Area Scheme Types		
Area Type Selected	**Bordering Area Type**	**Measurement Rule**
Gross Building Area		
Gross Building Area	None	Area Boundary measured to the outside surface of the building.
Gross Building Area	Exterior Area	Area Boundary measured from the outside surface of the building.
Exterior Area		
Exterior Area	Exterior Area	Area Boundary measured from the wall centerline.
Exterior Area	Gross Building Area	Area Boundary measured from the outside surface of the building.

16. Save this file as **GROSS AND EXTERIOR AREAS**.

Exercise 14-3: Rentable Areas

1. Use the previous exercise.
2. In the **Room and Area** tab, select the **Area Plan** tool to bring up the **New Area Plan** dialog box.
3. In the **New Area Plan** dialog box, select **Rentable** from the type drop-down list, **Level 1** from the **Area Plan Views**, and then press **OK** to create the new **Area Plan**.
4. Press the **No** button on the Revit dialog box that asks **Automatically create boundary lines associated with all external walls?**
5. Double-click **Area Plans [Rentable] > Level 1** from the **Project browser** to bring it up in the **Drawing Editor**.

6. Select the **Area Boundary** tool from the **Room and Area** tab in the **Design Bar**.
7. In the **Options** toolbar, select the **Pick Lines** button and check the **Apply Area Rules** check button.

Checking the **Apply Area Rules** check button before applying an area boundary will allow you to calculate the area based on the type of area you boundary. The following are **Rentable Area Scheme Types** that are included in Revit Architecture 2009.

Note:

Windows in Rentable Area Scheme Types: If you place windows within the exterior walls, Revit Architecture places the area boundary lines according to the following rules based on the height of the windows: If window height is greater than 50% of wall height, area boundary lines go to the face of the glass. If window height is less than 50% of wall height, area boundary lines go to the interior face of the exterior walls.

Gross Building Area Scheme Types		
Area Type Selected	**Bordering Area Type**	**Measurement Rule**
Building Common Area		
Building Common Area	Building Common Area, Office, Store	Area Boundary measured from the wall centerline.
Building Common Area	Exterior, Major Vertical Penetration	Area Boundary measured from the wall face bordering the Building Common Area.
Office Area		
Office Area	Building Common Area, Office, Store	Area Boundary measured from the wall centerline.
Office Area	Exterior, Major Vertical Penetration	Area Boundary measured from the wall face bordering the office area.
Exterior Area		
Exterior Area	Exterior	Area Boundary measured from the wall centerline.
Exterior Area	Store	Area Boundary measured from the wall face bordering the Exterior Area.
Exterior Area	Any other areas	Area Boundary measured from the wall face bordering the other area.
Floor Area		
Floor Area	Office, Store, or Building Common Area	Area Boundary measured from the wall face bordering the other area.
Floor Area	Exterior, Major Vertical Penetration	Area Boundary measured from the wall face bordering the floor area.
Floor Area	Floor Area	Area Boundary measured from the wall centerline.

Area Type Selected	Bordering Area Type	Measurement Rule
Major Vertical Penetration		
Major Vertical Penetration	Major Vertical Penetration	Area Boundary measured from the wall centerline.
Major Vertical Penetration	Exterior	Area Boundary measured from the wall face bordering the Major Vertical Penetration area.
Major Vertical Penetration	Any other area (except Exterior)	Area Boundary measured from the wall face bordering the other area.
Store Area		
Store Area	Major Vertical Penetration, Floor	Area Boundary measured from the wall face bordering the Store area.
Store Area	Exterior	Area Boundary measured from the wall face bordering the Exterior area.
Store Area	Building Common Area, Office, Store	Area Boundary measured from the wall centerline.

8. With the **Area Boundary** tool selected, **Pick Lines** and **Apply Area Rules** applied, select the boundaries of the area you want to calculate.
9. Select the **Area** tool from the **Room and Area** tab, move it over the enclosed area you just created, and click your mouse to place the area tag (see Figure 14-15).
10. Select the area by moving your cursor over the room until the crosshairs graphic is displayed, and then click.
11. **RMB** on the crosshairs to bring up the contextual menu.

Note:
As you pick boundaries, the boundary lines will first appear in the center of the walls. After you have selected all the enclosing walls, the lines will automatically enclose the inner walls of the area (see Figure 14-14).

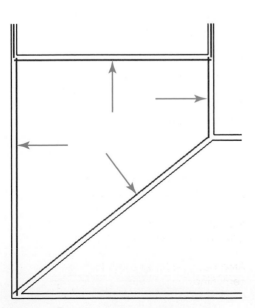

Figure 14-14

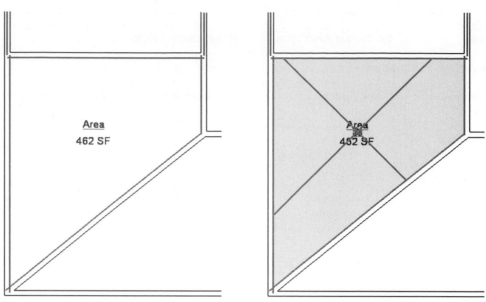

Figure 14-15

12. In the contextual menu, select **Element Properties** to bring up the **Element Properties** dialog box.
13. In the **Element Properties** dialog box, change the **Area Type** to **Store Area**, and then press the **OK** button to return to the **Drawing Editor** (see Figure 14-16).

Notice that the Area Boundary has automatically changed location, and that the area calculated has increased. This is because the rule for Store Area is automatically applied when you change the **Area Type** in the **Element Properties** dialog box to **Store Area** (see Figure 14-17).

14. Again, select the area, and change its **Area Type** to **Office**.

Notice that the Area Boundary has automatically changed location to the inside face of the walls, and the area has changed to **462 SF**.

15. Load the **Slider with Trim** window family.
16. Using the **Window** tool in the **Basics** tab, place four **Slider with Trim: 48″ × 48″** windows in the outer wall.

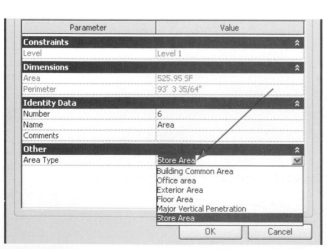

Figure 14-16

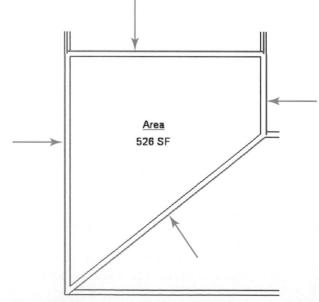

Figure 14-17

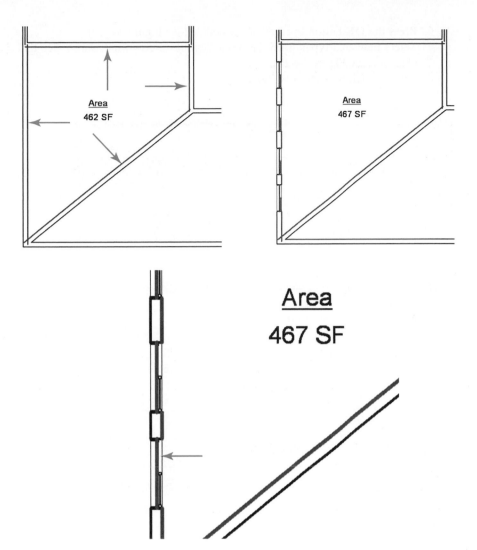

Figure 14-18

Notice that the area has changed to **467 SF**. This is because Revit calculates an **Office Area** to the face of the window glass (see Figure 14-18).

17. Change the windows to **Slider with Trim: 48″ × 48″.**

Notice that the boundary no longer calculates to the face of the glass. This is because if window height is less than 50% of wall height, Revit calculates area boundary lines to the interior face of the exterior walls.

18. Again, select the **Area Boundary** tool from the **Room and Area** tab in the **Design Bar**, and create area boundaries for the other enclosures.
19. Select the area names and change them to numbers.
20. Save this file as **RENTABLE AREAS**.

Exercise 14-4: Creating Area Schedules

1. Use the previous exercise.
2. Change to the **View** tab in the **Design Bar**.
3. In the **View** tab, select the **Schedule/Quantities** tool to bring up the **New Schedule** dialog box.
4. In the **New Schedule** dialog box, select **Areas [Rentable]** from the **Category** list, and press the **OK** button to bring up the **Schedule Properties** dialog box.
5. In the **Schedule Properties** dialog box, select **Area, Area Type, Name**, and **Perimeter** from the **Available Fields** list, and press the **Add** button.

6. Press the **OK** button to create the schedule (see Figure 14-19).
7. Select new area types from the **Area Type** drop-down list, and notice that the **Area SF** changes (see Figure 14-20).
8. Save this file as **AREA SCHEDULES**.

Area Schedule (Rentable)			
Area	Area Type	Name	Perimeter
488 SF	Office area	1	93' - 3 9/16"
445 SF	Building Common Area	2	81' - 11 15/16"
706 SF	Building Common Area	3	105' - 4"
717 SF	Building Common Area	4	123' - 1 21/32"

Figure 14-19

Area Schedule (Rentable)			
Area	Area Type	Name	Perimeter
467 SF	Office area	1	93' - 3 9/16"
473 SF	Exterior Area	2	81' - 11 15/16"
694 SF	Major Vertical Penetration	3	105' - 4"
759 SF	Exterior Area	4	123' - 1 21/32"

Building Common Area
Office area
Exterior Area
Floor Area
Major Vertical Penetration
Store Area

Figure 14-20

Exercise 14-5: Creating Color Scheme Legends

1. Use the previous exercise.
2. Double-click on **Area plans [Rentable] > Level 1** in the **Project browser** to bring it up in the **Drawing Editor**.
3. Select **Settings > Color Fill Schemes** from the **Main** menu to bring up the **Edit Color Scheme** dialog box.
4. In the edit **Color Scheme** dialog box, select **Areas [Rentable]** from the **Category** drop-down list (see Figure 14-21).

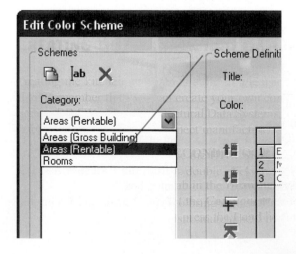

Figure 14-21

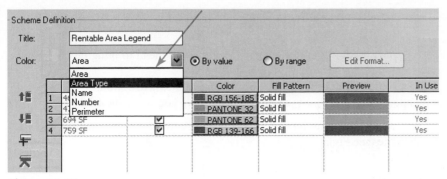

Figure 14-22

5. In the **Scheme Definition** area, select **Color** by **Area, Area Type**, **Name, Number**, or **Perimeter** (see Figure 14-22).

6. In the **Scheme Definition** area, select the **Color** and **Fill Pattern** of your choice, check the **Include Rooms/Areas from linked files** check box, and press the **OK** button to return to the **Drawing Editor**.

7. Select the **Color Scheme Legend** tool from the **Room and Area** tab in the **Design Bar**.

8. Click in the **Area plans [Rentable] > Level 1** that is in the **Drawing Editor**.

9. The **Choose Color Scheme** dialog box will now appear; press the **OK** button.

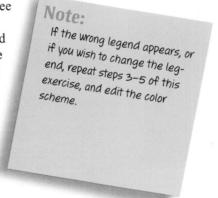

Note:
If the wrong legend appears, or if you wish to change the legend, repeat steps 3–5 of this exercise, and edit the color scheme.

The color legend will now appear, and the areas will fill with color to match the legend (see Figure 14-23).

10. Save this file as **Color Scheme Legends**.

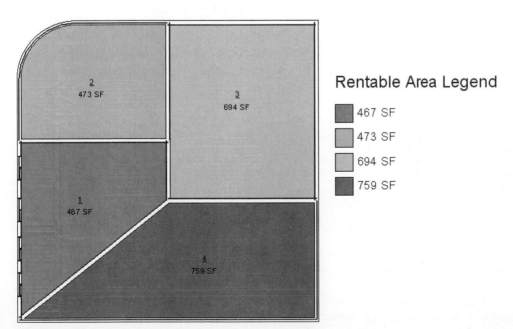

Figure 14-23

Exercise 14-6: Exporting a Room/Area Report

1. Use the previous exercise.
2. Select **File > Export > Room/Area Report** from the **Main** menu to bring up the **Export Room/Area Report** dialog box (see Figure 14-24).
3. Browse to a convenient folder to save the file, and press the **Save** button.
4. Using the Windows Explorer, browse to the folder where you saved the file.

Here you will find a new subfolder with images from the AREA REPORT you created, and an **AREA REPORT** html file (see Figure 14-25).

5. Double-click on the html file to open it in your Internet browser.
6. Save this file as **AREA REPORT**.

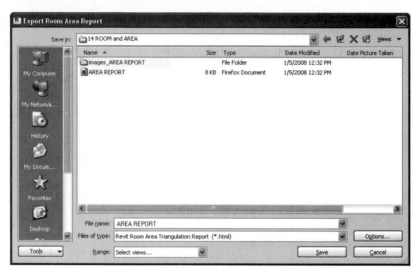

Figure 14-24

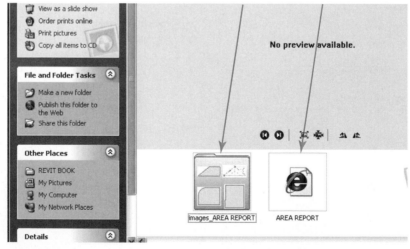

Figure 14-25

SUMMARY

This section explained and demonstrated Revit Architecture 2009's **Room** and **Area** tools. These tools are used to analyze area and volumes in buildings. Among the tools demonstrated were the **Volume** tools and the **Room** area reporting tools.

SECTION TEST QUESTIONS

Questions

1. Name three **Bounding** objects.

2. What is an **Area Boundary** used for?

3. Name three **Area Types**.

4. Where is the **Room/Area Report** located?

5. What does the **Color Scheme Legend** tool do?

6. Where is the radio button to allow volumes located?

7. In the **Store Area** type, when does Revit Architecture no longer calculate to the face of the glass?

Rendering

15

Section Objectives

- Know how to render an exterior scene.
- Know how to set up an exterior model for rendering.
- Know how to set up the **Camera** view.
- Learn how to render **Elevations**.
- Learn how to render an interior scene.
- Know how to render with 3D Studio Max.
- Create grass with 3D Studio Max.
- Know how to use RPC content.

NEW MENTAL RAY RENDERING ENGINE WITH SIMPLIFIED EASE OF USE

Visualizations have always been important in the practice of architecture. Whether visualizations "sold" the project or just made it clear to the client, they came to symbolize architecture to the public. Revit Architecture 2009 now contains the "mental ray" rendering engine. Revit Architecture's rendering system is more than acceptable for most general presentation purposes; but for the best quality visualizations and animations, nothing beats Autodesk's 3D Studio Max platform. If you wish to integrate Revit Architecture with Autodesk® 3ds Max® or Autodesk® 3ds Max® Design to produce high-end renderings and add final details, you must purchase them separately.

- *3ds Max* is a professional 3D animation package that provides additional animation, modeling, and workflow functionality for the most complex problems in design visualization and visual effects.

- *3ds Max Design* is a 3D design visualization solution for architects, engineers, designers, and visualization specialists. It is designed for interoperability with FBX® files from Revit Architecture, preserving model geometry, lights, materials, camera settings, and other metadata from a Revit project. With Revit Architecture and 3ds Max Design working together, designers can extend the building information modeling process to include design visualization.

Before we start, it is best that you understand a few terms.

Rendering

The word *render*, according to the *Dictionary.com Unabridged (v 1.1)* website (http://dictionary.reference.com accessed March 2, 2008), is "to represent; depict, as in painting: *to render a landscape*". Computer rendering is used to create realistic and photorealistic visualizations or presentations. These presentations can be made in either still or animated form. Typically, the operator will export the still presentations in JPG or TIFF file format. For animations, MOV or

AVI formats are very popular, and can easily be played back through the Internet, or placed on CD or DVD.

mental ray®

mental ray® is an Academy Award® winning, high-performance, photorealistic rendering software. It produces realistic images for digital content creation and design in the areas of entertainment, product design, and data visualization, including such applications as visual effects for motion pictures, full-length feature animations, content creation for computer games, Computer Aided Design (CAD), product design and styling, architectural design, lighting design, fluid flow simulation, seismic data studies, and medical imaging. mental ray features patented and proprietary ray tracing and rasterizer algorithms. It supports 32-bit and 64-bit CPUs and Graphics Processing Units (GPUs) and parallel computer architectures, including networks of computers, for maximum performance. mental ray combines the physically correct simulation of the behavior of light with full programmability to create any imaginable visual phenomenon.

Ray Tracing

Ray tracing is a general technique of modeling the path of light by following the light rays as they interact with optical surfaces. It is used in the design of optical systems, such as camera lenses, microscopes, telescopes, and binoculars. The term is also applied to a specific rendering algorithmic approach in 3D computer graphics, where mathematically modeled visualizations of programmed scenes are produced using a technique that follows rays from the eye outward, rather than originating at the light sources. Ray tracing produces advanced optical effects, such as accurate simulations of reflection and refraction, and is still efficient enough to frequently be of practical use when such high-quality output is sought.

Texture Maps

Texture maps are bitmap (raster) images (such as a picture of bricks) that can be placed on objects such as walls. When these objects are rendered, they will appear to be made of these materials. By using texture maps effectively, you can render visualizations quickly, and with great realism.

RPC

RPC stands for Rich Photorealistic Content, a term used to describe the software and content associated with ArchVision's award-winning Image-Based Rendering (IBR) technology. (RPC is also the file extension for this image-based content.) RPC is the first major commercial project in the evolution of image-based rendering technology. Since its introduction in 1998, the company's solutions have become the preferred method of incorporating complex objects into 3D computer graphics environments. Because RPCs rely on photo image data, their richness of detail and quality of images far surpasses those of even the best computer-generated models.

Before starting a rendering, you must set up a render scene.

RENDERING AN EXTERIOR SCENE

Exercise 15-1: Setting up the Exterior Model

1. Go to http://www.hegra.org/REVIT_BOOK_PRACTICE_FILES.html and download the **Chapter 15 RENDERING MODEL.rvt** file to a convenient folder on your computer.
2. Select **File > Open** from the **Main** menu to bring up the **Open** dialog box and open the RENDERING MODEL.rvt file you just downloaded.

Note: To see the shadows on the ground you will need a ground plane. If you don't already have a toposurface for the model, you can create a flat ground plane with the **Site > Toposurface** tool.

3. In the **Project browser**, double-click on the **Site** floor plan to bring it up into the **Drawing Editor**.
4. Change to the **Basics** tab in the **Design Bar**.
5. In the **Basics** tab, select the **Lines** tool.
6. Place a **280′ × 225′** rectangle around the building.
7. Select the **Offset** tool from the **Tools** toolbar, and offset another rectangle **5′-0″** from the first rectangle (see Figure 15-1).

Note:
When downloading, **RMB** on the file, select **Save as Target**, and download the file to a convenient folder.

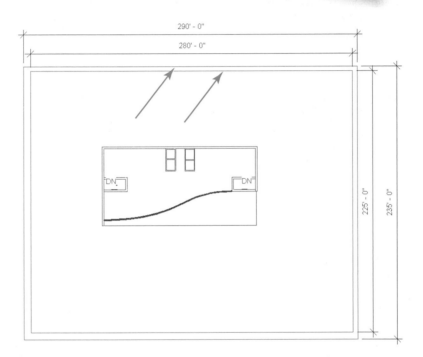

Figure 15-1

8. Change to the **Site** tab in the **Design Bar**.
9. Select the **Toposurface** tool to bring up the **Toposurface** tab.
10. In the **Toposurface** tab, select the **Point** tool.
11. In the **Options** toolbar, enter **0′-0″** in the **Elevation** field.
12. With the **Endpoint** snap on, snap to the corners of the first rectangle you placed.
13. In the **Options** toolbar, enter **-10′-0″** in the **Elevation** field.
14. With the **Endpoint** snap on, snap to the corners of the offset rectangle you created.
15. In the **Toposurface** tab, select **Finish Surface** to create the toposurface.
16. Change to the **Default 3D View.**
17. Select everything in the **Default 3D View,** and then select the **Filter Selection** button at the bottom of the interface to bring up the **Filter** dialog box.
18. In the **Filter** dialog box, select the **Check None** button to clear the check boxes, check the **Lines [Lines]** check box, and then press the **OK** button to return to the **Drawing Editor.**

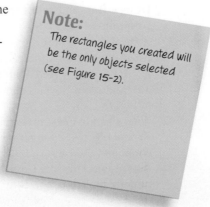

Note:
The rectangles you created will be the only objects selected (see Figure 15-2).

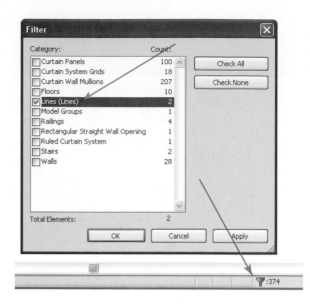

Figure 15-2

Select everything in the **Default 3D View,** and then select the **Filter Selection** button at the bottom of the interface to bring up the **Filter** dialog box.

19. Because the rectangles have been selected, press the **<Delete>** key on your keyboard to delete them.
20. Using the information on **Site** you learned in Section 13, split the toposurface, and create an asphalt road.
21. Select **File > Load from Library > Load Family** from the **Main** menu to bring up the **Load Family** dialog box.
22. In the **Load Family** dialog box, select the **Imperial Library** folder.
23. In the **Imperial Library** folder, select the **Planting** folder, and open it.
24. In the **Planting** folder, select **RPC Tree – Deciduous**, and then press the **OK** button to return to the **Drawing Editor**.
25. Press the **<Esc>** key on the keyboard twice to end the command.
26. Again, select **File > Load from Library > Load Family** from the **Main** menu to bring up the **Load Family** dialog box.
27. In the **Load Family** dialog box, select the **Imperial Library** folder.
28. In the **Imperial Library** folder, select the **Entourage** folder, and open it.
29. In the **Entourage** folder, select the **RPC Beetle** (car), the **RPC Male**, the **RPC Female**, and then press the **OK** button to return to the **Drawing Editor**.
30. Press the **<Esc>** key on the keyboard twice to end the command.
31. Change to the **Site** tab in the **Design Bar**, and select the **Site Component** tool.
32. In the **Type Selector** drop-down list in the **Options** toolbar, select **RPC Tree – Red Maple - 30'**, and place trees as shown in Figure 15-3.
33. After placing trees, press the **<Esc>** key twice to end the command.
34. Again, select the **Site Component** tool from the **Site** tab.

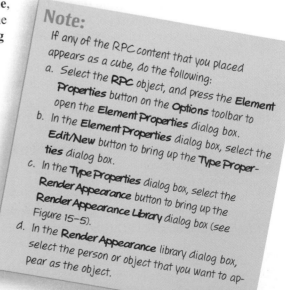

Note:
If any of the RPC content that you placed appears as a cube, do the following:
a. Select the **RPC** object, and press the **Element Properties** button on the **Options** toolbar to open the **Element Properties** dialog box.
b. In the **Element Properties** dialog box, select the **Edit/New** button to bring up the **Type Properties** dialog box.
c. In the **Type Properties** dialog box, select the **Render Appearance** button to bring up the **Render Appearance Library** dialog box (see Figure 15–5).
d. In the **Render Appearance** library dialog box, select the person or object that you want to appear as the object.

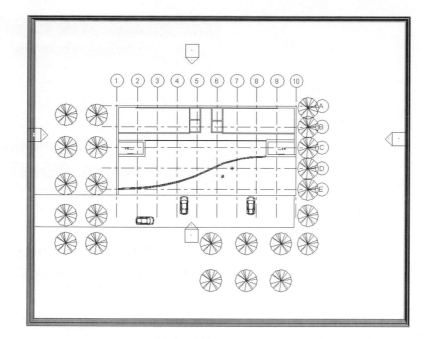

Figure 15-3

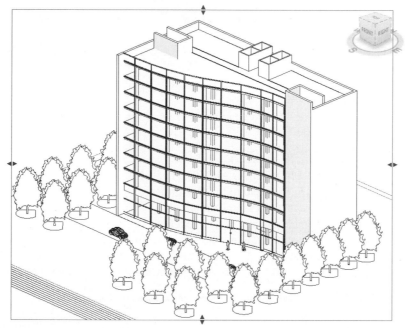

Figure 15-4

35. In the **Type Selector** drop-down list in the **Options** toolbar, select the **RPC Beetle** car, and place it on the road in your scene (see Figures 15–3 and 15–4).

36. Press the **<Esc>** key on the keyboard twice to end the command.

37. Again, select the **Site Component** tool from the **Site** tab.

38. In the **Type Selector** drop-down list in the **Options** toolbar, select the **RPC Female** and **RPC Male**, and place them in your scene (see Figures 15-3 and 15-4).

39. Select the remaining RPC objects and use the above process to change their appearance.

40. Save this file as **RENDERING MODEL**.

Note:

For a fee, you can download many more RPC libraries of people, trees, automobiles, furniture, and so on, at http://www.archvision.com. At the Archvision site there are also tutorials and a helpful staff that will guide you through all the RPC content and controls.

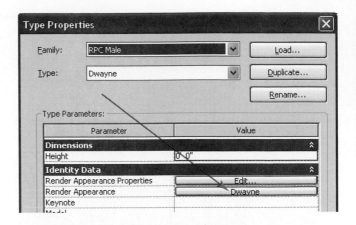

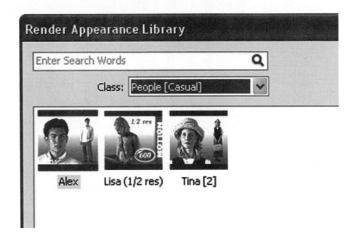

Figure 15-5

Exercise 15-2: Setting up the Camera View

1. Using the **RENDERING MODEL** file, change to the **Site** floor plan.
2. Change to the **View** tab in the **Design Bar**.
3. In the **View** tab, select the **Camera** tool.
4. Click your mouse where you expect the camera to stand.
5. Drag to the point you expect to be the target or view, and click your mouse again to create and open the new **3D View** (see Figure 15-6).
6. Select the new **3D View**, **RMB**, and rename it to **PERSPECTIVE VIEW 1**.

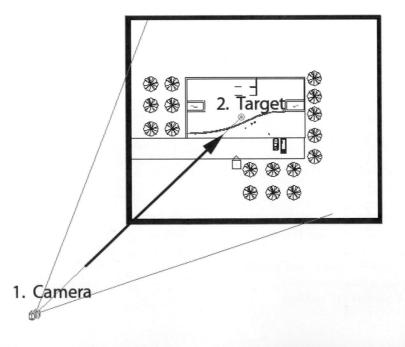

Figure 15-6

7. Hold down the **<Shift>** key on your keyboard, and the mouse wheel.
8. With the **<Shift>** key and mouse wheel held down, move your mouse to rotate the view.
9. Select the crop outline to activate its grips.
10. Move the grips to frame the **PERSPECTIVE VIEW 1** (see Figure 15-7).
11. Save this file as **PERSPECTIVE SCENE**.

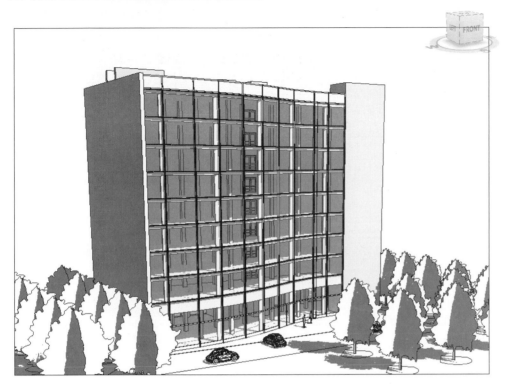

Figure 15-7

Exercise 15-3: Using the Settings Dialog Box
to Change Resolution

1. Using the **PERSPECTIVE SCENE** file, press the **Show Rendering Dialog** icon at the bottom of the **Drawing Editor** to bring up the **Rendering** dialog box (see Figure 15-8).
2. The **Rendering** dialog box will now appear (see Figure 15-9).
3. Make sure the settings are as shown in Figure 15-9, and press the **Render** button at the top of the dialog box.

Note:
The **Teapot** is the typical symbol for rendering because a teapot was the first digital object ever rendered.

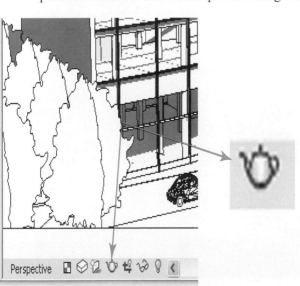

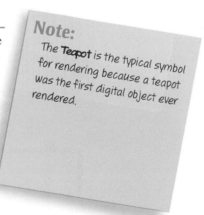

Figure 15-8

Figure 15-9

In approximately one minute, a draft (low-resolution) rendering will appear in the **Drawing Editor** (see Figure 15-10).

Figure 15-10

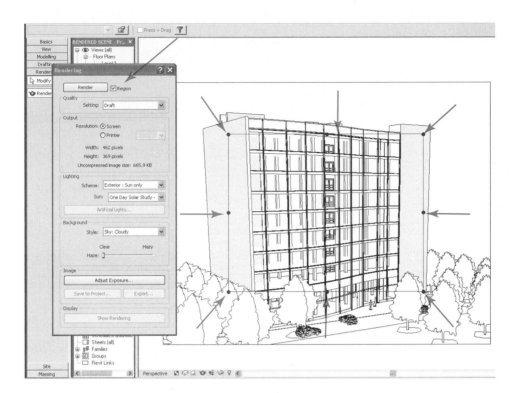

Figure 15-11

4. In the **Rendering** dialog box, check the **Region** button.

This causes a red rectangle to appear. Select it (see Figure 15-11).

5. Select the control points on the red rectangle, and adjust the rectangle to enclose the cars and people.
6. Press the **Render** button in the **Rendering** dialog box.

In about 15 seconds, the area inside the rectangle renders. This method is used to quickly check a particular part of the rendering (see Figure 15-12).

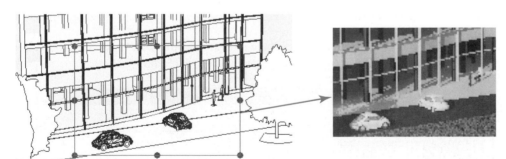

Figure 15-12

7. Press the **Show Model** button at the bottom of the **Rendering** dialog box to return the full model in the **Drawing Editor**.
8. Uncheck the **Region** check box.
9. In the **Rendering** dialog box, under **Lighting,** select **Exterior : Sun only** from the **Scheme** drop-down list (see Figure 15-13).
10. In the **Rendering** dialog box, change the **Quality** setting to **Medium**, and press the **Render** button.

In a few minutes a **Medium** (resolution) rendering will appear in the **Drawing Editor** (see Figure 15-14).

11. Select the **Export** button near the bottom of the **Rendering** dialog box to bring up the **Save Image** dialog box.

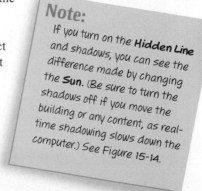

Note:
If you turn on the **Hidden Line** and shadows, you can see the difference made by changing the **Sun.** (Be sure to turn the shadows off if you move the building or any content, as real-time shadowing slows down the computer.) See Figure 15-14.

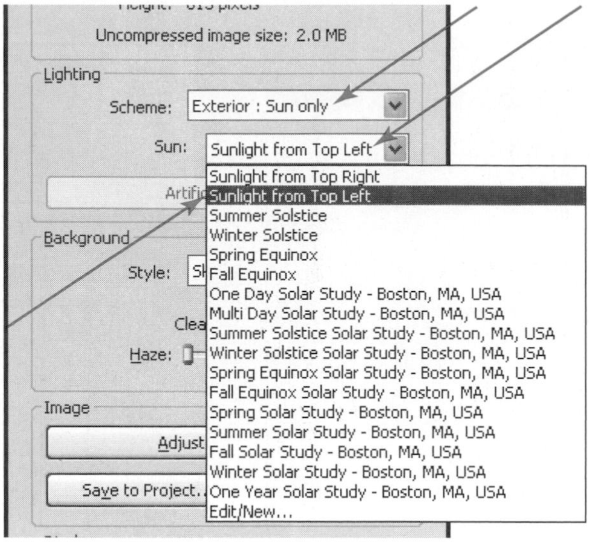

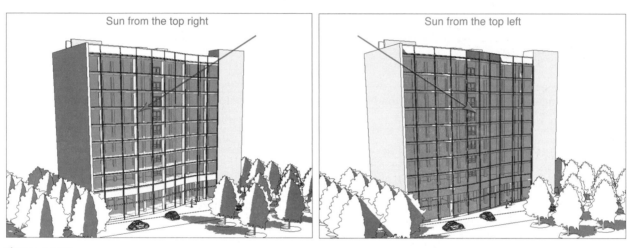

Figure 15-13

Sun from the top right

Sun from the top left

Figure 15-14

12. In the **Save Image** dialog box, save the rendering as **MEDIUM RENDERING jpg** in a convenient folder on your computer (see Figures 15-15 and 15-16).

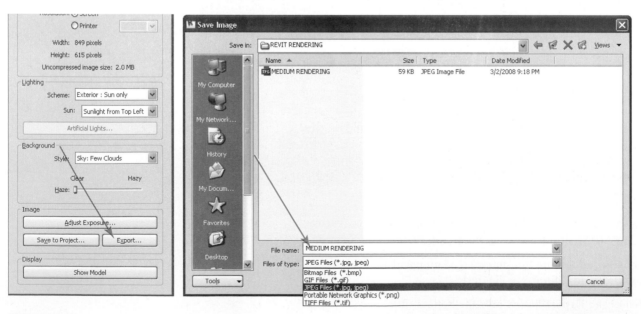

Figure 15-15

Figure 15-16

13. In the **Rendering** dialog box, select **Color** from the **Background > Style** drop-down list.
14. Again, in the **Rendering** dialog box, press the **Render** button; the background of the rendering is black (see Figure 15-17).

Figure 15-17

15. In the **Rendering** dialog box, select the **Adjust Exposure** button to bring up the **Adjust Exposure** dialog box.
16. Move the **Adjust Exposure** dialog box to the side, and slowly change the settings.
17. Press the **Apply** button, and notice the changes.
18. Continue to make adjustments until you have the presentation you like best. Then press the **OK** button and **Export** the rendering to your computer (see Figure 15-18).
19. Save this file as **RENDERED SCENE**.

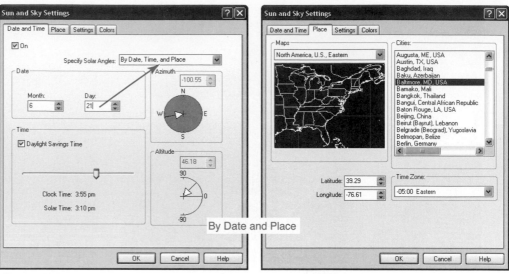

Figure 15-18

RENDERING ELEVATIONS

Save this file as **RENDERED ELEVATION.**

Note:

You cannot render elevation views. To achieve an elevation rendering, you must do the following "workaround":

a. Change to the **Default 3D View.**
b. Select **View Orient South** from the **Main** menu.
c. Repeat for the **North, East,** and **West** views.
d. Bring up the **Rendering** dialog box by pressing the "teapot" icon.
e. Render the view with a **Background Style** of the **Cobr White,** and **Quality Setting** of **Medium** (see Figures 15-19 and 15-20).

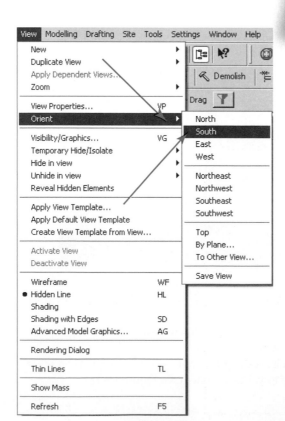

Figure 15-19

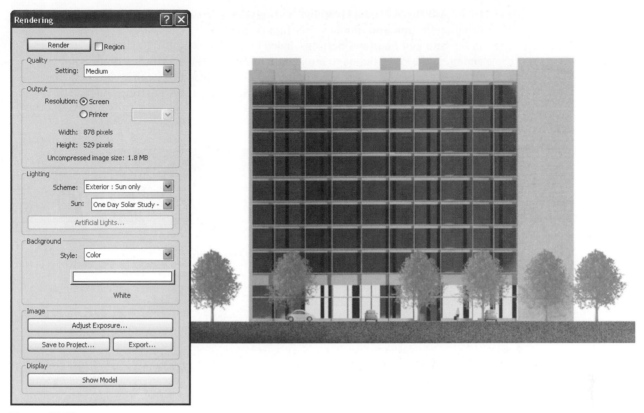

Figure 15-20

ANIMATED SOLAR STUDIES

The **Animated Solar Study** command allows you to produce shadow study movies.

1. Using the previous exercise and file, press the **Show Model** button in the **Rendering** dialog box to remove the rendering from the **Drawing Editor**.
2. Pressing the **<Shift>** key on your keyboard, hold down the right mouse button **(RMB)**, and rotate the view to a **3D View**.
3. Select **View > Advanced Model Graphics** from the **Main** menu to bring up the **Advanced Model Graphics Settings** dialog box (see Figure 15-21).

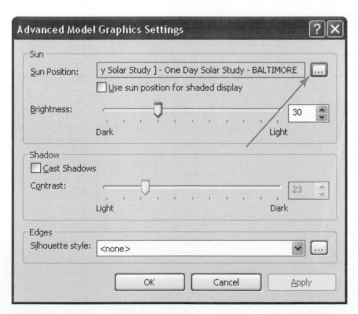

Figure 15-21

4. In the **Advanced Model Graphics Settings** dialog box, select the **Sun Position** button to bring up the **Sun and Shadows Settings** dialog box.

5. In the **Sun and Shadows Settings** dialog box, select the settings shown in Figure 15-22, and press the **Place** button to bring up the **Manage Place and Locations** dialog box.

6. In the **Manage Place and Locations** dialog box, select the city that you are in, and press the **OK** buttons to return to the **Advanced Model Graphics Settings** dialog box (Figure 15-23).

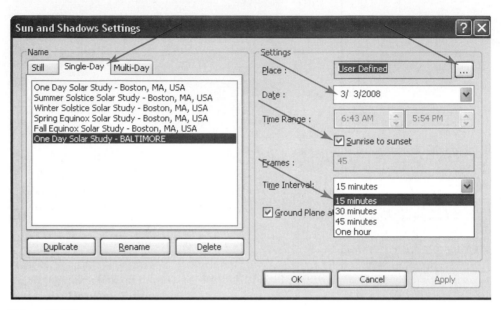

Figure 15-22

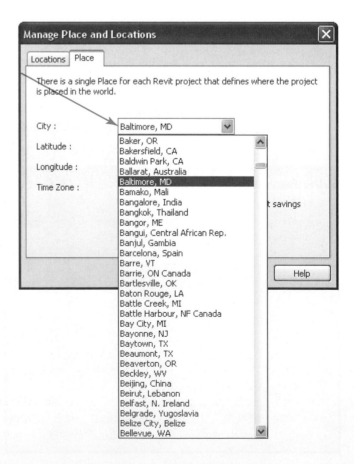

Figure 15-23

7. In the **Advanced Model Graphics Settings** dialog box, check the **Cast Shadows** check box, and then press the **OK** button (Figure 15-24).

8. Press **Preview Solar Study**, and "play" buttons will appear in the **Options** toolbar (see Figure 15-26).

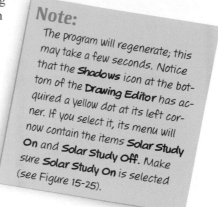

Note:
The program will regenerate; this may take a few seconds. Notice that the **Shadows** icon at the bottom of the **Drawing Editor** has acquired a yellow dot at its left corner. If you select it, its menu will now contain the items **Solar Study On** and **Solar Study Off**. Make sure **Solar Study On** is selected (see Figure 15-25).

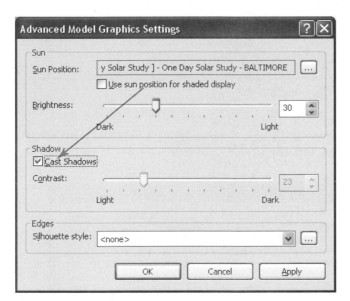

Figure 15-24

Figure 15-25

9. Press the **Play** arrow, and the program will generate the study.

10. After the study has been completed, the computer will stop generating, and the **Frame** field will show **45**.

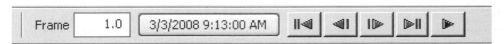

Figure 15-26

11. Select **File > Export > Animated Solar Study** from the **Main** menu (see Figure 15-27).

12. Select **File > Export > Animated Solar Study** from the **Main** menu to bring up the **Length/Format** dialog box.

13. In the **Length/Format** dialog box, select the **All frames** radio button, change the **Frames/sec** to **2,** the Model Graphics Style to <**Hidden Line**>, and press the **OK** button to bring up the **Export Animated Solar Study** dialog box (see Figure 15-28).

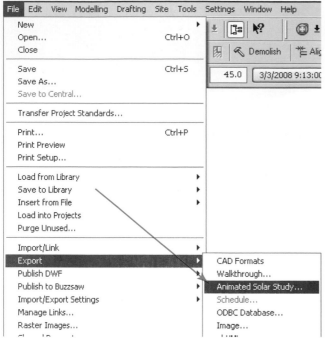

Figure 15-27

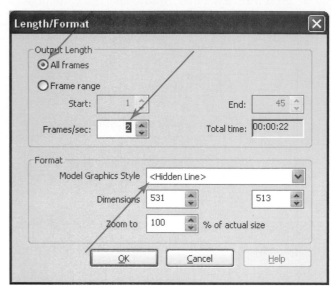

Figure 15-28

14. In the **Export Animated Solar Study** dialog box, name the file **ANIMATED SHADOW STUDY MOVIE,** and press the **Save** button (see Figure 15-29).

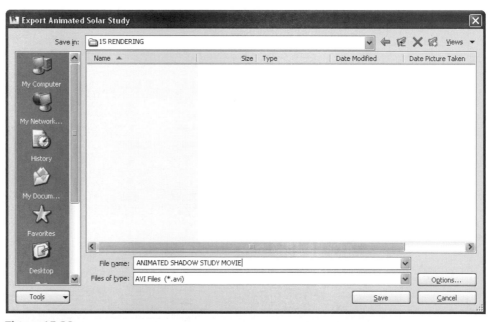

Figure 15-29

15. After a few seconds the **Video Compression** dialog box will appear.
16. In the **Video Compression** dialog box, select **Cinepak Codec by Radius** from the **Compressor** drop-down menu, and press the **OK** button (see Figure 15-30).
17. After several minutes (13 minutes on the author's 3.4 GHz AMD Athlon ™ with two GB of RAM), the program will process the AVI video movie. When it is finished, you can open the file, and view it in the Microsoft Windows Media Player on your computer.
18. Save this file as **ANIMATED SHADOW STUDY**.

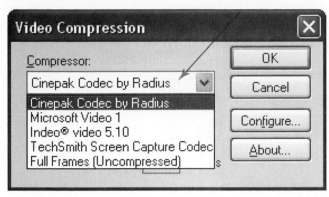

Figure 15-30

Rendering an Interior Scene

Exercise 15-4: Setting up the Interior Scene and Adding Lighting

1. Select **File > Open** from the **Main** menu to bring up the **Open** dialog box.
2. Go to http://www.hegra.org/REVIT%20BOOK%20FILES.html and download the **Chapter 15 RENDERING MODEL.rvt** file.
3. In the **Project browser**, double-click on the **Level 1 Ceiling Plan** to bring it up into the **Drawing Editor**.
4. Change to the **Modeling** tab in the **Design Bar**.
5. In the **Modeling** tab, select the **Ceiling** tool.
6. In the **Options** toolbar, select the **Compound Ceiling: 2′ × 4′ ACT System**.
7. In the **Project browser**, double-click on the **Level 1** floor plan to bring it up into the **Drawing Editor**.
8. In the **View** tab, select the **Camera** tool.
9. Click your mouse where you expect the camera to stand.
10. Drag to the point you expect to be the target or view, and click your mouse again to create and open the new **3D View**.
11. **RMB**, and **Rename** the new **3D View** to **INTERIOR SCENE** (see Figures 15-31 and 15-32).
12. Again, in the **Project browser**, double-click on the **Level 1 Ceiling Plan** to bring it up into the **Drawing Editor**.
13. Change to the **Basics** or **Modelling** tab in the **Design Bar**.
14. Select the **Component** tool.

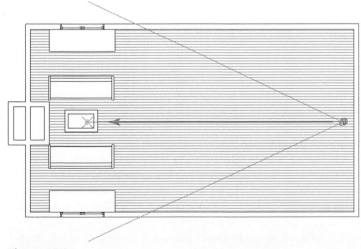

Figure 15-31

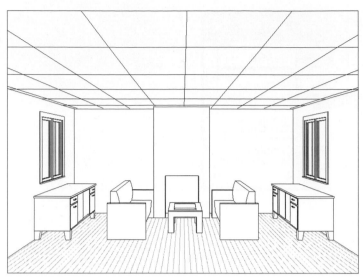

Figure 15-32

15. In the **Options** toolbar, press the **Load** button to open the **Imperial** (or **Metric**) **Library.**
16. In the **Library**, open the **Lighting Fixtures** folder.
17. In the **Lighting Fixtures** folder, locate and open the **Pendent-Hemisphere** light.
18. Place the light in the **Level 1 Ceiling Plan,** and change to the **Interior View** to check its location in the scene (see Figure 15-33).

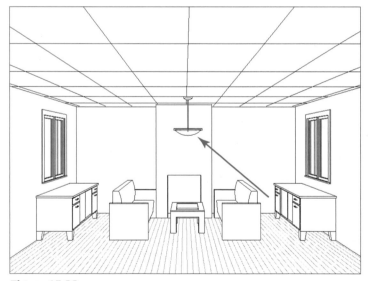

Figure 15-33

19. Change back to the **Level 1** floor plan.
20. Select the **Component** tool.
21. In the **Options** toolbar, press the **Load** button to open the **Imperial** (or **Metric**) **Library.**
22. In the **Library**, open the **Lighting Fixtures** folder.
23. In the **Lighting Fixtures** folder, locate and open the **Table Lamp-Hemispheric** light.
24. Place two **Table Lamp-Hemispheric** lights on each credenza. (You will have to select them in an elevation view and change element properties to a **2′-5″ Offset** from **Level 1.**) See Figure 15-34.
25. Double-click on **INTERIOR SCENE** in the **Project browser** to bring it up in the **Drawing Editor** (see Figure 15-35).

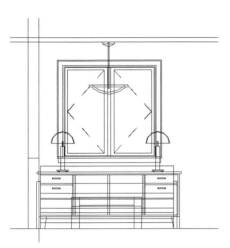

Figure 15-34

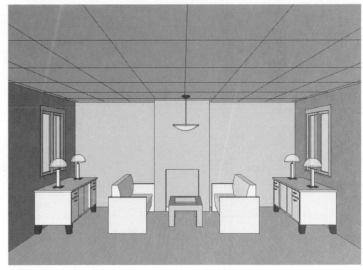

Figure 15-35

Exercise 15-5: Rendering the Interior Scene

1. Using the **INTERIOR SCENE** file, press the **Show Rendering Dialog** icon at the bottom of the **Drawing Editor** to bring up the **Rendering** dialog box.
2. In the **Rendering** dialog box, select **Interior: Sun and Artificial** from the **Scheme** drop-down list.
3. In the **Rendering** dialog box, select **Medium** from the **Quality > Setting** drop-down list, and press the **Render** button to render the file (see Figure 15-36).

Figure 15-36

4. The rendering will be dark. To fix this, select the **Adjust Exposure** button in the **Rendering** dialog box to open the **Adjust Exposure** dialog box.
5. In the **Adjust Exposure** dialog box, change the exposures to those shown in Figure 15-37, and press the **Apply** button.
6. The rendering will now adjust (Figure 15-38).
7. Select the **Table Lamps,** and then press the **Element Properties** button on the **Options** toolbar to bring up the **Element Properties** dialog box.
8. In the **Element Properties** dialog box, press the **Edit/New** button to bring up the **Type Properties** dialog box.
9. In the **Type Properties** dialog box, select **100 watt Incandescent** from the **Type** drop-down list, and press the **OK** buttons to return to the **Drawing Editor** (see Figure 15-39).

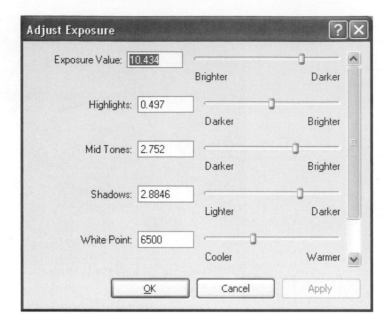

Figure 15-37

Figure 15-38

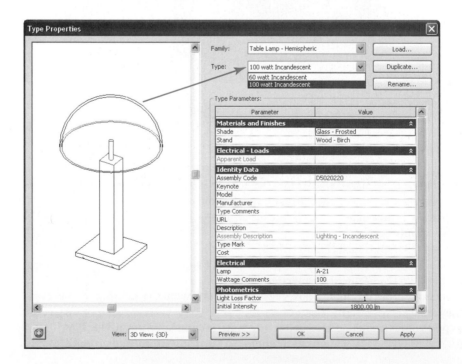

Figure 15-39

10. Repeat this process for the **Pendent – Hemisphere** light, and select **150 watt Incandescent** from the **Type** drop-down list, and press the **OK** buttons to return to the **Drawing Editor**.
11. Press the **Render** button in the **Rendering** dialog box again to re-render the scene.
12. Notice the effect of changing the wattage of the lights (see Figure 15-40).
13. Save this file as **RENDERED INTERIOR SCENE.**

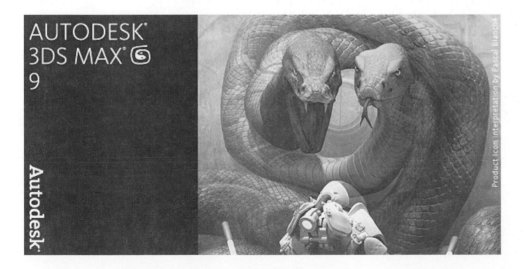

Figure 15-40

RENDERING WITH 3D STUDIO MAX

Although Revit Architecture has a good rendering system, 3D Studio MAX is much better. With its lighting capability and ability to animate, 3D Studio MAX will give you many more options for your presentations and visualizations.

1. Create a simple house in Revit Architecture.
2. Change to the **Default 3D View.** Do not use a **FLOOR PLAN VIEW.**
3. Select **File > Export > CAD Formats** from the **Main** menu to bring up the **Export** dialog box.
4. In the **Export** dialog box, save the file as an AutoCAD 2007 DWG file.

5. Name the file **REVIT CAD DRAWING**, and save it on your computer.
6. Start **3DS MAX** (this tutorial uses 3DS MAX 9).
7. Select **File > Import** from the **Main** menu to bring up the **Select File to Import** dialog box.

You will get a **Proxy Objects Detected** dialog box telling you that there are custom objects in the drawing. Press the **Yes** button to import the file anyway.

8. The **AutoCAD DWG/DXF Import Options** dialog box will appear. Accept the defaults, and press the **OK** button to import the building (see Figure 15-41).

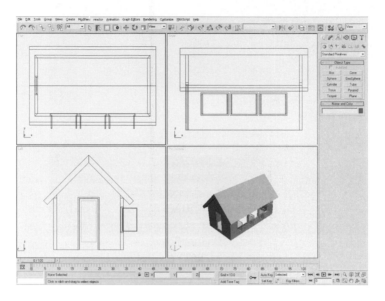

Figure 15-41

9. Select the **Zoom All** tool at the bottom right of the interface, and zoom all the viewports smaller (see Figure 15-42).

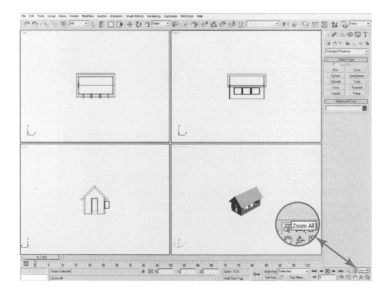

Figure 15-42

10. Using the **Create** tools, add a **Camera –Target** tool. Place a camera to the left of the building, and then drag and click its target at the center of the building.
11. After placing the camera, select the lower right viewport (Perspective), and press the <C> key on your keyboard to change it to the view through the camera (see Figure 15-43).

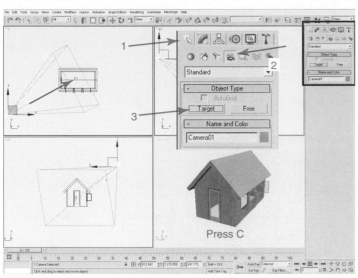

Figure 15-43

12. Select the **Camera** viewport, and using the **Navigation** tools (**Distance, Pan, and Rotate**) at the bottom right of the screen, adjust the view to the scene you wish (see Figure 15-44).
13. Using the **System** tools, add a **Sunlight** tool. Click and drag to set the **Compass**, and then drag your cursor upwards and click to set the height of the **Sunlight** (see Figure 15-45).

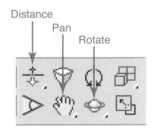

Figure 15-44

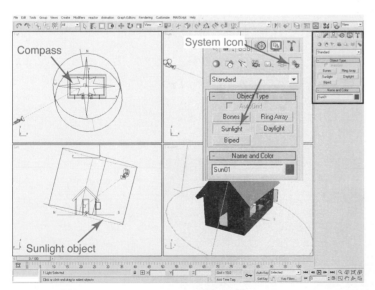

Figure 15-45

14. Click in the **Top** view to make it the active view.
15. Using the **Create** tools, add a **Plane**. Be sure to click the color box, and set it to a green color. Make the box approximately **50′ × 50′**, and set the **Length Segs** to **1** (see Figure 15-46).
16. Select the **Render** icon to bring up the **Render Scene** dialog box.

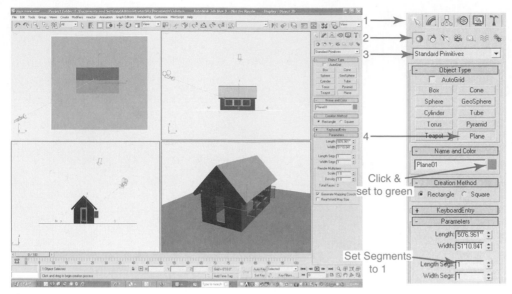

Figure 15-46

17. In the **Render Scene** dialog box, press the **Render** button to render the scene.
18. Select the **Sun** object, and then select the **Motion** icon in the upper right of the MAX 9 interface to open the **Motion** parameters.
19. Adjust the **Latitude** and **Longitude** and watch how the light changes in the scene. Here the **Latitude** is set to **75**, and the **Longitude** to **56** for the default location (see Figure 15-48).

Note:

The **Render Scene** dialog box contains all the controls for size, **Renderer**, and so on. For these tutorials, just use the defaults. Notice that the rendering is dark; that is because the sunlight is coming from the back (see Figure 15-47).

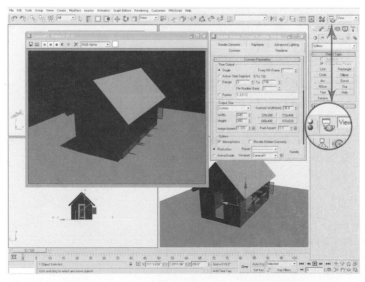

Figure 15-47

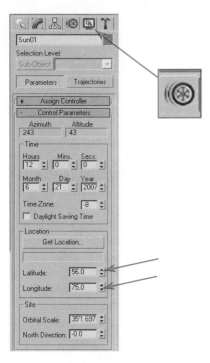

Figure 15-48

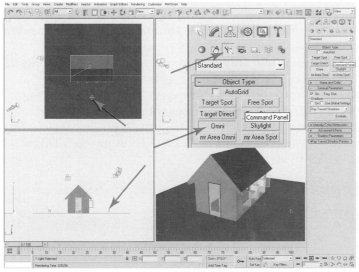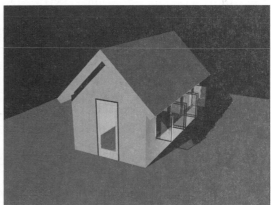

Figure 15-49

20. Re-render the scene. It is better, but the shadows are too dark on the right side.
21. To fix this, select **Lights – Omni** from the **Create** panel, and place an omni light at the right side of the building.
22. Click in the **Camera** view, re-render, and save the file (see Figure 15-49).

CREATING AND PLACING MATERIALS IN AUTODESK 3DS MAX 9

1. Select the **Material Editor** icon at the top right of the MAX interface to bring up the Material Editor.
2. In the **Material Editor,** enter **WALL MATERIAL** in the list shown in Figure 15-50.
3. Expand the **Material** display shapes, and pick the **Block** shape.

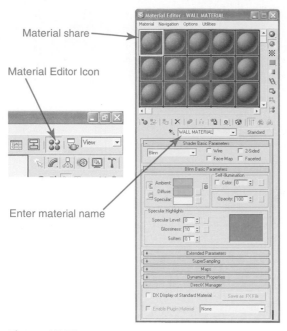

Figure 15-50

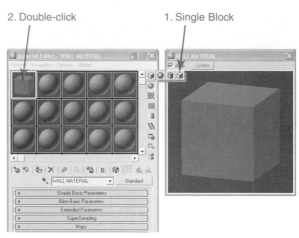

Figure 15-51

4. Double-click on the **Material** shape to expand it for better viewing (see Figure 15-51).
5. With the **WALL MATERIAL** shape selected, press the **Diffuse Color** button to open the **Material Map Browser** dialog box.
6. In the **Material Map Browser** dialog box, double-click on **Bitmap** to bring up the **Select Bitmap Image** dialog box.
7. In the **Select Bitmap Image** dialog box, browse to where your bitmap pictures are stored.
8. In the **Select Bitmap Image** dialog box, select the **Masonry.Unit Masonry.Brick.Modular.Flemish Diagonal** bitmap, and press the **Open** button to place it in the **Material Editor.** Repeat this process creating **ROOF MATERIAL** using the **Thermal-Moisture.Roof Tiles.Spanish.Red** bitmap (see Figure 15-52).

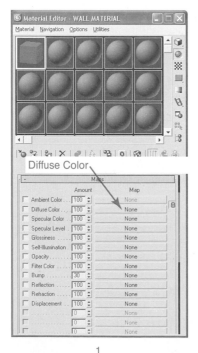

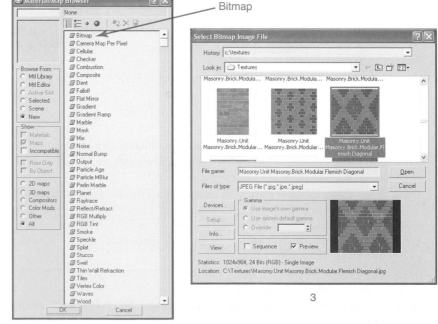

Figure 15-52

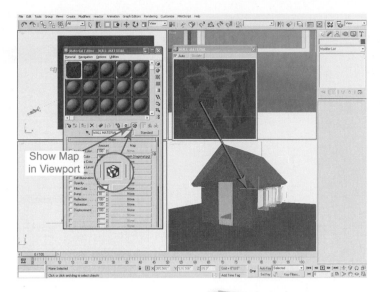

Figure 15-53

9. Select the **Show Map in Viewport** button, and drag **WALL MATERIAL** onto the walls. Repeat by dragging **ROOF MATERIAL** onto the roof (see Figure 15-53)**.**
10. Select a wall, and then select the **Modify** icon from the **Create** panel to bring up the **Modifier** list.
11. In the **Modifier** list, select the **MapScaler**.
12. Select the other walls and roof, and repeat step 11 (see Figure 15-54).

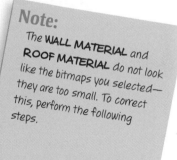

Note:
The **WALL MATERIAL** and **ROOF MATERIAL** do not look like the bitmaps you selected—they are too small. To correct this, perform the following steps.

Modify

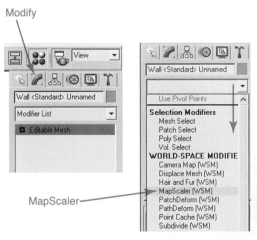

MapScaler

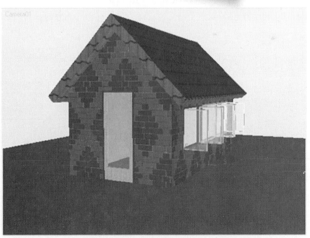

Figure 15-54

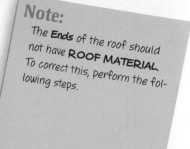

Note:
The **Ends** of the roof should not have **ROOF MATERIAL**. To correct this, perform the following steps.

13. Press the **Select by Name** icon at the top left of the MAX interface to bring up the **Select Objects** dialog box. (You can select all the objects in your scene here.)
14. In the **Select Objects** dialog box, choose **Roof Body**, and then press the **Select** button (see Figure 15-55).
15. Select the **Modify** icon from the **Create** panel to bring up the **Modifier** list.

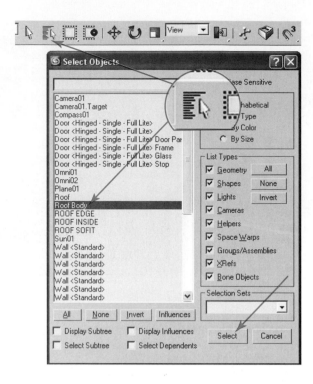

Figure 15-55

16. In the **Modifier** list, select and expand **Editable Mesh**.
17. In the expanded **Editable Mesh,** select **Polygon**.
18. Select the edge of the roof (it will turn red), and then press the **Detach** button to bring up the **Detach** dialog box.
19. In the **Detach** dialog box, enter **ROOF EDGE**, and press the **OK** button.
20. Repeat steps 13–19 to detach the other roof edges and the inside of the roof. Give each detached object a unique name such as **SOFIT** (see Figure 15-56).

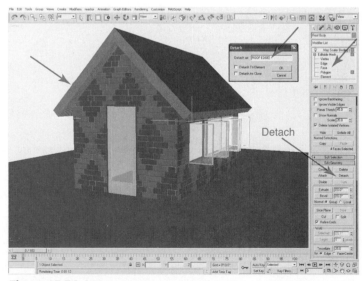

Figure 15-56

21. Open the **Material Editor**, and create a new material called **ROOF EDGE MATERIAL.**
22. Click on the **Ambient** button to open the **Ambient Color** selector, and choose a color. (The author chose white.) See Figure 15-57.

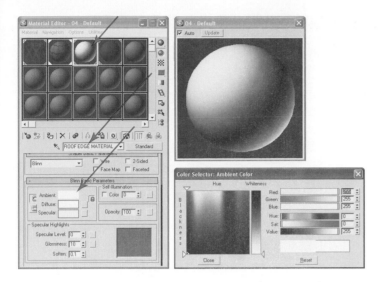

Figure 15-57

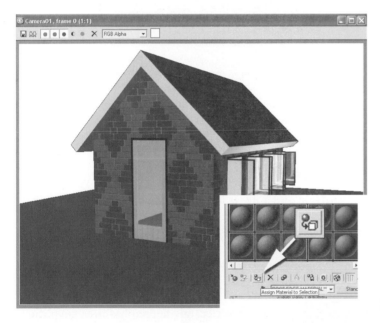

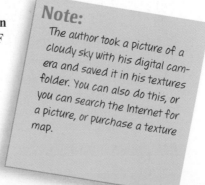

Figure 15-58

23. Again, press the **Select by Name** icon at the top left of the MAX interface to bring up the **Select Objects** dialog box.
24. In the **Select Objects** dialog box, choose the new roof objects you created to select them.
25. With the new roof objects selected, press the **Assign Material to Selection** icon to apply the **ROOF EDGE MATERIAL** to them (see Figure 15-58).

Adding the Sky in Autodesk 3DS MAX

26. In the **Select Bitmap Image** dialog box, select the **Sky** picture you have created or found, and press the **Open** button to place it in the **Material Editor.**
27. Select **Rendering > Environment** from the **Main** menu to bring up the **Environment and Effects** dialog box.

Note:
The author took a picture of a cloudy sky with his digital camera and saved it in his textures folder. You can also do this, or you can search the Internet for a picture, or purchase a texture map.

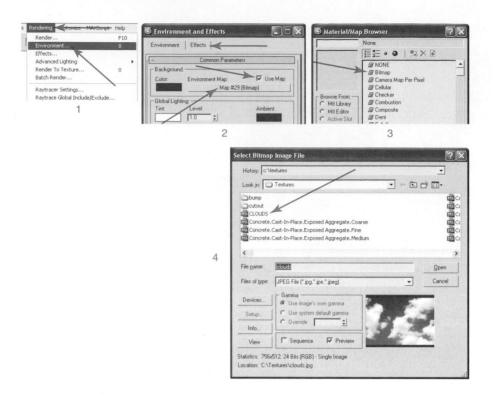

Figure 15-59

28. In the **Environment and Effects** dialog box, select the **Use Map** check box, and then press the **Environment Map** button to bring up the **Select Bitmap Image File** dialog box.
29. In the **Select Bitmap Image File** dialog box, browse to the folder where you have placed a picture of the sky, and open the picture (see Figure 15-59).

Creating Grass in Autodesk 3DS MAX 9

3DS MAX 9 has a **Modifier** called **Hair and Fur**. It has this name because MAX is often used in the gaming industry, and it is used to apply hair and fur to people and animals. This is a very sophisticated modifier, and can be easily used to create realistic grass for architectural visualizations.

Hair and Fur renders only in the **Camera** view, so you will not see its effects in any other views. For architectural visualizations, this author suggests attaching the **Hair and Fur** modifier only to a **Plane** object.

Because **Hair and Fur** is a very sophisticated modifier, this tutorial has been simplified. Please check the help file for more in-depth information.

1. Select the plane that you created in step 13 of the **Visualization with 3DS MAX** tutorial.
2. Select **Modifiers > Hair and Fur > Hair and Fur (WSM)** from the **Main** menu to apply it to the selected plane.
3. Select the **Modifier** icon in the **Create** panel to expose the **Hair and Fur** controls.
4. In the **Hair and Fur** controls, set the following:

General Parameters

Hair count = 30,000
Scale = 2 (height of grass)
Rand Scale = 40 (40% random sizes)
Root Thick = 4 (thickness of grass root)
Tip Thick = 4 (thickness of grass tip)

Material Parameters

Tip Color = light green
Root Color = dark green

Frizz Parameters

Make all the **Frizz Parameters = 0** (makes the grass vertical)

Multi Strand Parameters

Count = 3
Root Splay = 0.82
Tip Splay = 1.82 (See Figure 15-60.)

5. Render the picture. (Be patient, this render takes two passes.) Save the file (see Figure 15-61).

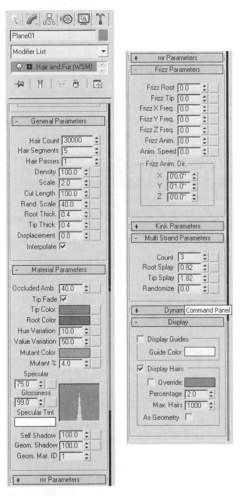

Figure 15-61

Figure 15-60

Using Archvision RPC Content in Autodesk 3DS MAX 9

1. Using your Internet browser, go to http://www.archvision.com.
2. At the first screen, select **Software Updates** from the **Support** drop-down to go to the **Software Updates** screen.

3. In the **Software Updates** screen, download and install the **RPC 3.13** plug-in.

4. Once you have installed the plug-in, select the **Geometry** icon in the **Create** panel, and then select **RPC** from the drop-down list.

5. When you have selected **RPC** from the drop-down list, the **RPC** parameters will appear.

6. From the **RPC** parameters, select the **RPC** button, select the content you want, and then place and rotate it in your scene (see Figures 15-63, 15-64, and 15-65).

Note:

All software companies are always updating software. This plug-in was the latest release as of the writing of this book (see Figure 15-62).

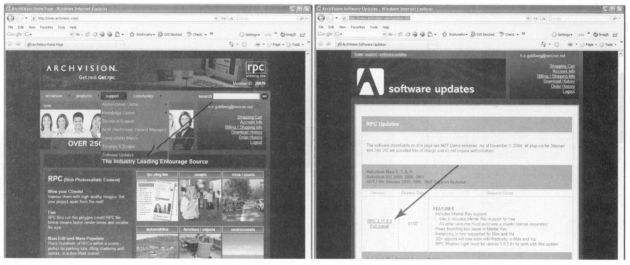

Figure 15-62

Geometry
icon

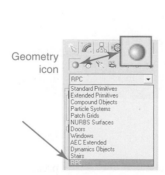

Figure 15-63

Figure 15-64

Figure 15-65

Shadowing the RPC Content

7. Select one of the **RPC** content objects you placed, and select **Mass Edit** from the **RPC** parameters to bring up the **RPC Mass Edit** dialog box.

8. In the **RPC Mass Edit** dialog box, select all the content, and then click under the **3D** column. When an **S** appears opposite the content, the object is set to shadow (see Figure 15-66).

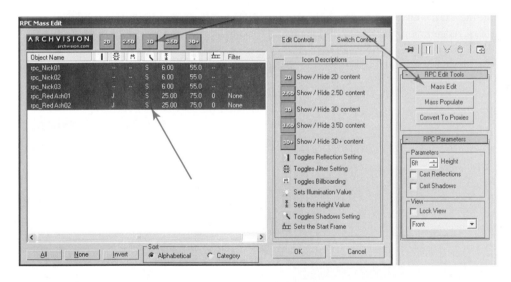

Figure 15-66

9. Press the **Select by Name** icon at the top left of the MAX interface to bring up the **Select Objects** dialog box. (You can select all the objects in your scene here.)

10. In the **Select Objects** dialog box, choose **Sun01**, and then press the **Select** button.

RPC content needs to be included in the **Sun** parameters to be seen. **Sun01** is the default name that was given when you first placed the **Sunlight** object.

11. With the **Sun01** selected, press the **Modify** icon in the **Create** panel.

12. In the **General** parameters, check the **Shadows** check box, and then press the **Include** button to bring up the **Exclude/Include** dialog box.

13. In the **Exclude/Include** dialog box, make sure that the **Include** radio button is pressed, and that all the content in the scene is together on the **Include** side (see Figure 15-67).

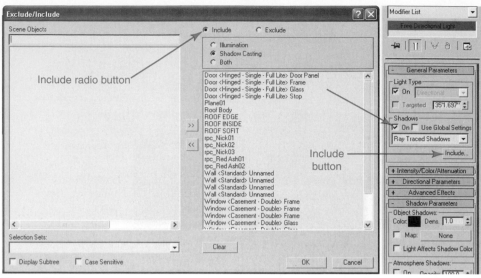

Figure 15-67

14. Finally, select **Rendering > Environment** from the **Main** menu to bring up the **Environment and Effects** dialog box.
15. In the **Environment and Effects** dialog box, select the **Effects** tab (see Figure 15-68).
16. In the **Effects** tab, select **Hair and Fur** to bring up the **Hair and Fur** effects parameters.
17. In the **Hair and Fur** effects parameters, select the **GBuffer** radio button, and then press the **Custom** radio button under **Occlusion Objects.**
18. Render the scene (see Figure 15-69).
19. Render the scene and save the file (see Figure 15-70).

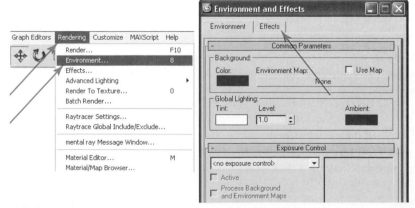

Figure 15-68

Figure 15-69

Figure 15-70

SUMMARY

This section explained and demonstrated how to render visu-alizations in Revit Architecture 2009. The concepts behind rendering were explained, as well as how to export Revit Ar-chitecture projects to 3D Studio Max for creating sophisti-cated photorealistic presentations. Also explained was how to use RPC content, and how to create grass in 3D Studio Max.

SECTION TEST QUESTIONS

Questions

1. Where did the concept of rendering come from?
2. Why does the "teapot" symbolize rendering?
3. What commands are used to prepare a 3D view for rendering as an elevation view?
4. What is mental ray?
5. What icon brings up the **Rendering** dialog box?

6. What does the **Region** tool do?
7. What does the **Adjust Exposure** tool do?
8. What are AVI files, and what program reads them?
9. When should you use **Draft** quality in Revit Architecture?
10. How do you change the wattage of a light fixture?

Part Three: Putting It All Together

Tutorial Project

16

Section
Objectives

- Place the logo in the template file.
- Create a plot sheet family from scratch.
- Set up the project.
- Know how to test the plot sheet.
- Know how to set the levels.
- Create the site.
- Create the foundation walls.
- Create the FIRST FLOOR framing and hardwood floor.
- Create the exterior walls.
- Create the HILLSIDE HOUSE exterior wall assembly.
- Place the FIRST FLOOR exterior walls.
- Create the SECOND FLOOR exterior walls.
- Create the SECOND FLOOR wing walls.
- Create the skylight side walls.
- Create the SECOND FLOOR floors.
- Create the stairway.
- Create the roof.
- Create the skylight roof.
- Create the skylight glazing.
- Create the bridge.
- Create the plot sheets.
- Create the interior walls.
- Learn how to place exterior doors and windows.
- Create the front and rear decks, and their railings.
- Create the wall detail.
- Know how to place wall tags.
- Create the door and window schedules.
- Create the kitchen and bath.
- Render the model.

The purpose of the Putting It All Together tutorial is to illustrate the Revit Architecture 2009's methodology for creating a set of construction documents while giving practical practice in using Revit Architecture 2009 tools.

For the tutorial project, the author has chosen a two-story hill side house. The project progresses through the design process to the construction documentation stage.

Before starting the project, we will create a customized plotting sheet that includes the company logo. Using Adobe Illustrator, Adobe Photoshop, Corel Draw, Paint Shop Pro, Macromedia FreeHand, Canvas, or even Windows Paint, create a JPG of your logo. Save the logo as **LOGO** in a new folder called **HILLSIDE HOUSE** on your computer. The logo the author created looks like that shown in Figure 16-1.

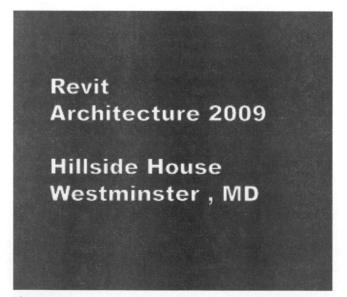

Figure 16-1

Exercise 16-1: Placing the Logo in the Template File

1. Select **File** > **Open** from the **Main** menu to bring up the **Open** dialog box.
2. In the **Look in** drop-down list, browse to the **Imperial Library** (or **Metric Library**).

3. In the **Imperial Library**, select and open the **Titleblocks** folder.

4. In the **Titleblocks** folder, select the **D 22 × 34 Horizontal** file, and press the **Open** button to bring it up in the **Drawing Editor**.

5. Select **File** > **Import/Link** > **Image** from the **Main** menu to bring up the **Open** dialog box.

6. In the **Open** dialog box, locate where you placed the **LOGO** jpg you created previously.

7. Select the **LOGO** jpg you created, and press **Open** to bring the **Image** into the **Drawing Editor**.

8. Place the logo in the drawing as shown in Figure 16-2.

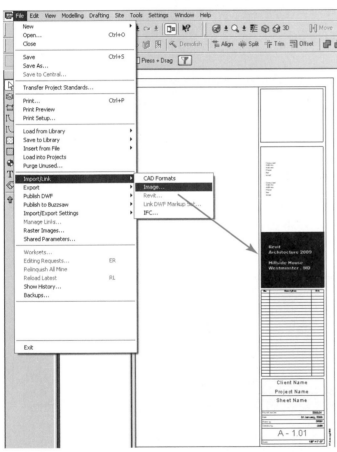

Figure 16-2

9. Delete the **Revit** logo from the top of the drawing.

10. Select **File** > **Save As** from the **Main** menu to bring up the **Save As** dialog box.

11. In the **Save As** dialog box, save the file as a **Family File [*.rfa]**, name it **HILLSIDE HOUSE SHEET FAMILY**, and place it in the folder you created named **HILLSIDE HOUSE** (see Figure 16-3).

12. Close the file.

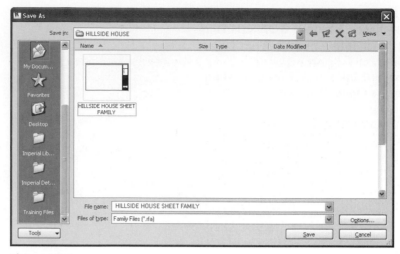

Figure 16-3

Exercise 16-2: Creating a Plot Sheet Family from Scratch

1. Select **File** > **New** > **Family** from the **Main** menu to bring up the **New** dialog box.
2. In the **New** dialog box, locate the **Imperial Templates** folder.
3. In the **Imperial Templates** folder, locate the **Titleblocks** folder.
4. In the **Titleblocks** folder, select the **D-36 × 24** template, and press the **Open** button to bring it into the **Drawing Editor**.
5. Select the **Offset** tool from the **Tools** toolbar.
6. In the **Options** toolbar, select the **Numerical** radio button, enter **1/2″** in the **Offset** field, and check the **Copy** check box.
7. Offset the top, right, and bottom margins of the **D-36 × 24** template.
8. Offset the right margin **2-1/2″** again.
9. Offset the left margin **1-1/2″**.
10. Trim the lines (see Figure 16-4).

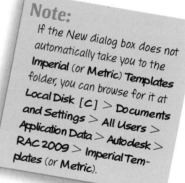

Note:
If the New dialog box does not automatically take you to the Imperial (or Metric) Templates folder, you can browse for it at Local Disk [C] > Documents and Settings > All Users > Application Data > Autodesk > RAC 2009 > Imperial Templates (or Metric).

Figure 16-4

11. Add your **LOGO** jpg as you did in the previous exercise.
12. Add a **2″** horizontal line inside the 2″ title block to separate the drawing number.
13. In the **Family** tab of the **Design Bar**, select the **Label** tool.
14. Click the **Label** tool in the **Drawing Editor** to bring up the **Select Parameter** dialog box (see Figure 16-5)

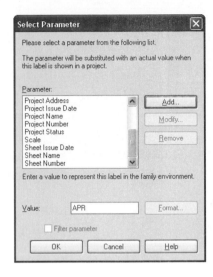

Figure 16-5

15. In the **Select Parameter** dialog box, select **Sheet Number**, and then press the **OK** button to place the **Sheet Number** tag.
16. Move the **Sheet Number** tag into position at the bottom of the title block.
17. Again, click the **Label** tool in the **Drawing Editor** to bring up the **Select Parameter** dialog box
18. In the **Select Parameter** dialog box, select **Project Name**, and then press the **OK** button to place the **Project Name** tag.
19. Rotate the **Project Name** tag, and place it in the title block.
20. **RMB** the **Project Name** tag, and select **Element Properties** from the contextual menu to bring up the **Element Properties** dialog box.
21. In the **Element Properties** dialog box, press the **Edit/New** button to bring up the **Type Properties** dialog box.
22. In the **Type Properties** dialog box, press the **Duplicate** button to bring up the **Name** dialog box.
23. In the **Name** dialog box, enter **3/8″ TAG**, and press the **OK** button to return to the **Type Properties** dialog box.
24. In the **Type Properties** dialog box, change the **Text Size** to **3/8″**, and press the **OK** buttons to return to the **Drawing Editor**.
25. Repeat the previous steps, placing tags and lines to create your own customized drawing sheet.
26. Select **File** > **Save As** from the **Main** menu to bring up the **Save As** dialog box.
27. Save the file as **CUSTOMIZED SHEET FAMILY**, and place it in your **HILLSIDE HOUSE** folder (see Figure 16-6).

Figure 16-6

Exercise 16-3: Setting up the Project

1. Select **File** > **New** > **Project** from the **Main** menu to bring up the **New Project** dialog box.
2. Accept the defaults in the **New Project** dialog box, and press the **OK** button to create the new project.
3. Select **File** > **Save As** from the **Main** menu to bring up the **Save As** dialog box.
4. In the **Save As** dialog box, name the file **HILLSIDE HOUSE PROJECT**, and save it as a **Project File** in the **HILLSIDE HOUSE** folder.

5. Select **Settings** > **Project Information** from the **Main** menu to bring up the **Element Properties** dialog box for the project (see Figure 16-7).

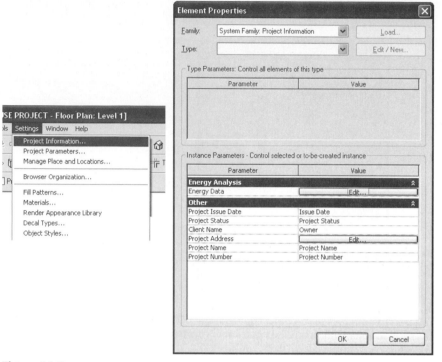

Figure 16-7

6. In the **Element Properties** dialog box, select the **Edit** button opposite the **Project Address** field to bring up the **Edit Text** dialog box.

7. In the **Edit Text** dialog box, enter **Westminster MD** as the address, and press the **OK** button to return to the **Element Properties** dialog box.

8. Fill in the rest of the information in the **Element Properties** dialog box (see Figure 16-8).

9. Press the **OK** buttons to return to the **Drawing Editor**.

10. Select **Settings** > **Manage Place and Locations** from the **Main** menu to bring up the **Manage Place and Locations** dialog box for the project.

> **Note:**
>
> Although not available for this project, which is a residence, the **Energy Data** button will set you up for export to gbXML. Using this format combined with the postal code of the project, sites such as Green Building Studio (http://www.greenbuildingstudio.com) will give you a general energy analysis of your commercial building. To set this up, do the following:
>
> - In the **Element Properties** dialog box, select the **Edit** button opposite the **Energy Data** field to bring up the **Type Properties** dialog box for **Energy Data**.
> - In the **Type Properties** dialog box for **Energy Data**, select the **Building Type** and enter the **Postal Code** of the building (see Figure 16-9).

11. In the **Manage Place and Locations** dialog box, select the **Locations** tab.

12. Here you can change the **Angle from Project North to True North** (for this project, accept the default).

13. Change to the **Place** tab.

14. Change the **City** to your project's location; the city closest to this project is **Baltimore MD**.

15. Press the **OK** button to return to the **Drawing Editor**.

16. Select **File** > **Save** from the **Main** menu to save the project.

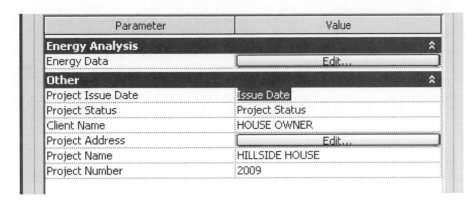

Figure 16-8

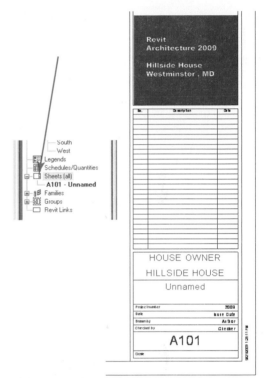

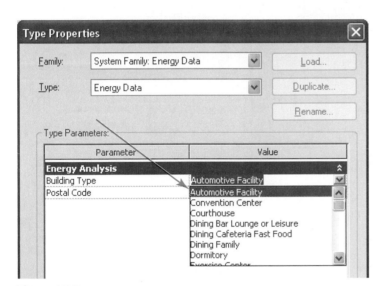

Figure 16-9

Figure 16-10

Exercise 16-4: Testing the Plot Sheet

1. Using the project you just created, **RMB** on **Sheets [all]** > **New Sheet** in the **Project browser** to bring up the **Select a Titleblock** dialog box.
2. In the **Select a Titleblock** dialog box, press the **Load** button, browse, and locate the **HILLSIDE HOUSE SHEET FAMILY** title block you previously created.
3. After the **HILLSIDE HOUSE SHEET FAMILY** title block appears in the **Select a Titleblock** dialog box, select it, and press the **OK** button to return to the **Drawing Editor**.

Notice that the plot sheet contains all the project information that you placed in the **Project Information** settings. Notice also that the plot sheet has a sheet number, and that the plot sheet appears in the **Project browser** under **Sheets [all]**.

You can now rename the sheet and sheet number, if you wish, either by clicking on those fields in the plot sheet, or renaming it in the **Project browser** (see Figure 16-10).

THE TWO-STORY CARRIAGE HOUSE PROJECT

This project is patterned after a real project that I designed, along with Rick Donally, in 1978. It is located on a hillside overlooking the Bachman Valley, and sits on 60 acres of farmland. As originally conceived, the house was to be built on an exterior exposed steel frame set on concrete piers, and the exterior walls were to be faced with plywood siding. The final building used a more conventional brick and block foundation with wood frame bearing walls and redwood siding. To take advantage of the site, Rick and I decided to place the building away from the ridge of the hillside, and enter the second level by way of a bridge. This allowed us to place the living areas at the treetop level, and access the lower bedrooms by an external stair. By doing this, the client (a bachelor at the time) could walk from his bedroom directly out to the ground level. For this project, I have simplified the building, but the main concepts still are evident. There are many methodologies for creating a virtual model in Revit Architecture 2009; this project uses one method. As you become more familiar with the program, you will discover the methods and tools that best suit the way you work. I hope you enjoy doing this project, and enjoy experiencing both the design and methodology concepts. Figures 16-11 and 16-12 show pictures of the cardboard model I created for the client.

Figure 16-11

Figure 16-12

Setting the Levels

1. Make sure that you have the **HILLSIDE HOUSE** as the current project.
2. In the **Project browser**, double-click on the **East Elevation** to bring it up in the **Drawing Editor**.
3. Select the **Levels** tool to bring up new **Levels** in the **Drawing Editor**.
4. Make or rename **Levels** to match the settings shown in Figure 16-13.

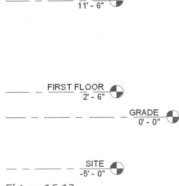

Name	Floor Elevation	Floor-to-Floor Height
PARAPET	23'-6"	0'-0"
SECOND FLOOR	11'-6"	12'-0"
FIRST FLOOR	2'-6"	9'-0"
GRADE	0'-0"	2'-6"
SITE	−5'-0"	5'-0"

Figure 16-13

Creating the Site

1. Double-click on **Site** (under **Floor Plans**) in the **Project browser** to bring the site plan (Figure 16-14) into the **Drawing Editor**.

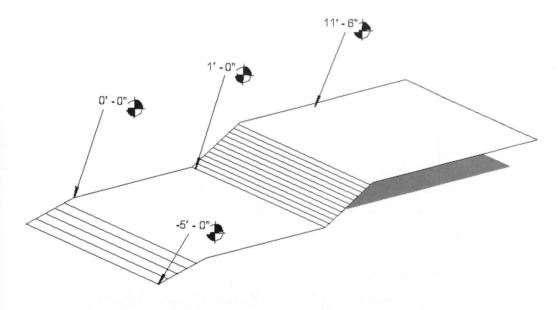

Figure 16-14

2. Set the **Scale** to **1″ = 10′**
3. Change to the **Basics** tab in the **Design Bar**.
4. In the **Basics** tab, select the **Lines** tool.
5. In the **Site** plan, place lines as shown in Figure 16-15.
6. Change to the **Site** tab in the **Design Bar**.
7. Select the **Toposurface** tool to bring up the **Toposurface** tab in the **Design Bar**.
8. In the **Toposurface** tab, select the **Points** tool.
9. In the **Options** toolbar, set the **Elevation** to **−5′-0″**.

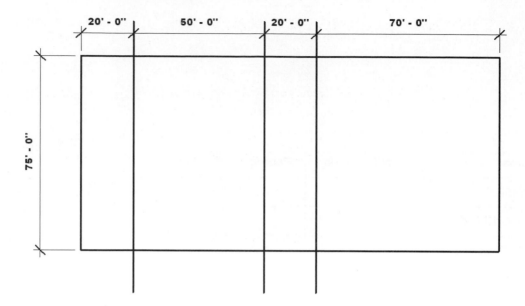

Figure 16-15

This will be the lowest point in your site.

10. Using the **Points** tool, follow the diagram shown in Figure 16-16 while changing the **Elevations** in the **Options** toolbar as you snap on the intersections of the lines you placed.

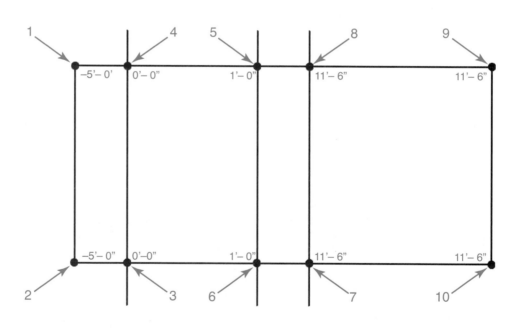

Figure 16-16

11. Press the **Finish Surface** icon in the **Toposurface** tab to complete the surface.
12. Select everything in the **Site** plan, and press the **Options** toolbar to bring up the **Filter** dialog box.
13. In the **Filter** dialog box, uncheck the **Toposurface** check box, and press the **OK** button to return to the **Drawing Editor** (see Figure 16-17).

Now, only the lines have been selected.

14. Press the **<Delete>** key on your keyboard to delete the lines you placed, leaving only the toposurface.

Save the file.

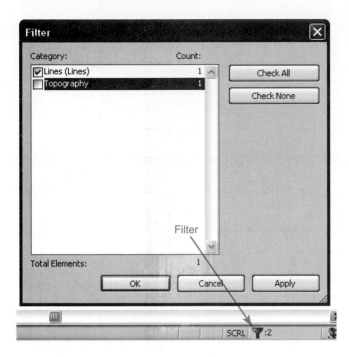

Figure 16-17

The Foundation

Creating the Foundation Wall

1. Set the **Scale** to **1/4 = 1′-0″**.
2. Make sure you are in the **Site** floor plan.
3. Change to the **Basics** tab in the **Design Bar**.
4. Select the **Wall** tool from the **Basics** tab.
5. In the **Options** toolbar, select **Basic wall: Generic –12″ Masonry**.
6. In the **Options** toolbar, select the **Element Properties** button to bring up the **Element Properties** dialog box.
7. In the **Element Properties** dialog box for the **Generic – 12″ Masonry** wall, set the **Base Constraint** to **GRADE**, the **Base Offset** to **–1′-6″**, the **Top Constraint** to **Up to Level: FIRST FLOOR**, and **Top Offset** to **–1′-0 5/8″** (the height of the trusses + plywood floor).
8. In the **Options** toolbar, select the **Pencil**, set the **Height** to **GRADE**, **Loc Line** to **Finish Face Exterior**, and select the **Rectangle** button (see Figure 16-19).
9. Place an enclosure as shown in Figure 16-20.
10. Select all the walls you just placed, and again in the **Options** toolbar, select the **Element Properties** button to bring up the **Element Properties** dialog box.
11. In the **Element Properties** dialog box, scroll down to the **Structural** area, and change the **Structural Usage** drop-down list to **Bearing**.
12. Change to the **Default 3D View**.
13. Rotate the scene so that you can see the foundation below grade.
14. Change to the **Structural** tab in the **Design Bar**.
15. In the **Structural** tab, select the **Foundation > Wall** tool.
16. In the **Options** toolbar, select the **Wall Foundation: Bearing Footing –36″ × 12″**.

Note:
This will set the bottom of the foundation wall 1–6″ below the grade (see Figure 16-18).

Note:
Setting the walls to a certain type of *Structural Usage* will automatically notify you if you are incorrectly placing a structural elements as you continue to build your model (see Figure 16-21).

Figure 16-18

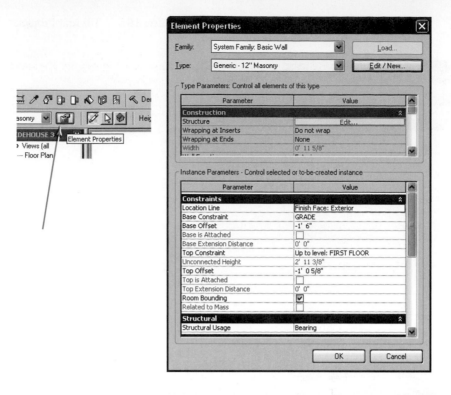

Figure 16-19

Figure 16-20

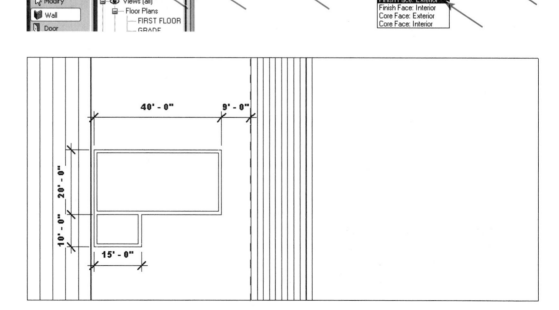

40' - 0"   9' - 0"

20' - 0"

10' - 0"

15' - 0"

Figure 16-21

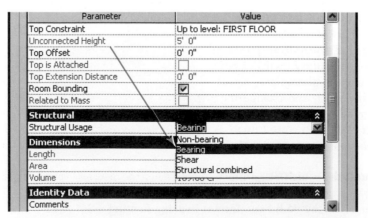

17. With the **Wall Foundation: Bearing Footing −36″ × 12″** selected, press the **Element Properties** button to bring up the **Element Properties** dialog box.
18. In the **Element Properties** dialog box, select the **Edit/New** button to bring up the **Type Properties** dialog box.
19. In the **Type Properties** dialog box, select the **Duplicate** button to bring up the **Name** dialog box.
20. In the **Name** dialog box, enter **20″ × 12″ STRIP FOOTING** and press the **OK** button to return to the **Type Properties** dialog box.
21. In the **Type Properties** dialog box, change the **Width** to **20″** and press the **OK** buttons to return to the **Drawing Editor**.
22. Touch the bottom of each wall to place the strip footing (see Figure 16-22). Note that for this picture, the toposurface has been hidden.

The foundation wall now shows its footing.
Save the file.

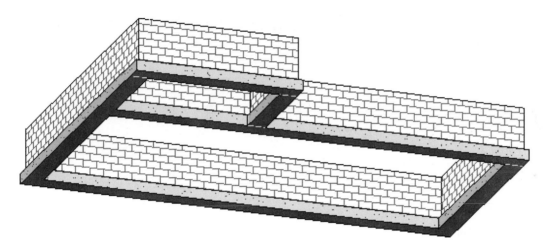

Figure 16-22

Creating the First Floor Framing and Hardwood Floor

The First Floor framing is made from **1-3/4″ × 11-7/8 Plywood Web Joists @ 2′-0″ o/c**.

1. Select **File Load from Library** > **Load Family** to bring up the **Open** dialog box.
2. Locate and open the **Structural** folder.
3. In the **Structural** folder, open the **Wood** folder.
4. In the **Wood** folder, click on the **Plywood Web Joist**, and press the **Open** button to load the joist and return to the **Drawing Editor**.
5. Double-click on the **Grade** plan to bring it up in the **Drawing Editor**.
6. Select the **Structural** tab in the **Design Bar**.
7. Select the **Beam System** tool in the **Structural** tab to bring up the **Sketch** tab (see Figure 16-23).
8. In the **Sketch** tab, select the **Structural Beam System Properties** tool to bring up the **Element Properties** dialog box.
9. Set the **Elevation** to **2′-5 1/4″**, the **Layout Rule** to **Fixed Distance**, the **Justification** to **Beginning**, and the **Beam Type** to the **Plywood Web Joist: 1 3/4 × 11 7/8** that you loaded (see Figure 16-24).
10. In the **Sketch** tab, select the **Lines** tool.
11. In the **Options** toolbar, select the **Pick Lines** button, and set the **Offset** to **1-1/4″** (the width of the siding and the sheathing).
12. Pick all the foundation walls, and then trim the lines to create a closed loop.
13. Pick the **Beam Direction** tool in the **Sketch** tab and touch the left line. This sets the beam direction (see Figure 16-25).
14. In the **Sketch** tab, press the **Finish Sketch** icon to complete the joists and return to the **Drawing Editor**.
15. Set the **Detail Level** to **Medium** to see the joists.

Figure 16-23

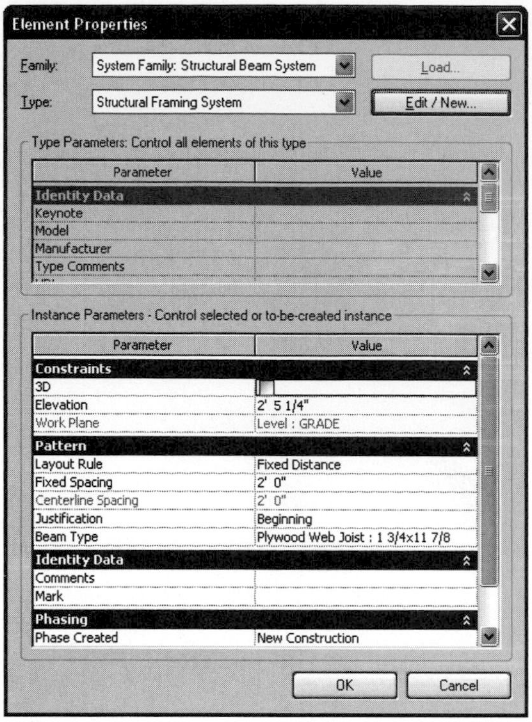

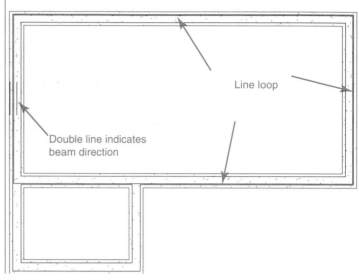

Figure 16-24

Figure 16-25

The joists will stop at the inside of the foundation. To fix this, do the following:

16. Select all the joists you placed, **RMB**, and select **Element Properties** from the contextual menu that appears to bring up the **Element Properties** dialog box.
17. In the **Element Properties** dialog box, scroll down to the **Construction** section, and set the **Start Extension** and **End Extension** to **10-3/4″**. This will extend the joists to the inside of the wall sheathing.
18. Press the **OK** button to return to the **Drawing Editor**.

You may have to add joists. To do this, select the joist, click on the pushpin to unconstrain it, and make a copy (see Figures 16-26 and 16-27).

19. Press the **OK** button to return to the **Drawing Editor** (see Figure 16-28).
20. For the hardwood floor, change to the **Basics** tab in the **Design Bar**.
21. In the **Design Bar**, select the **Floor** tool to bring up the **Sketch** tab for the floor.
22. In the **Sketch** tab, select the **Floor Properties** tool to bring up the **Element Properties** dialog box for the floor.

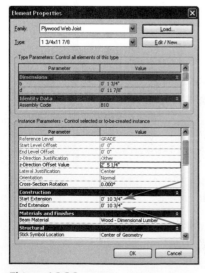

Figure 16-26

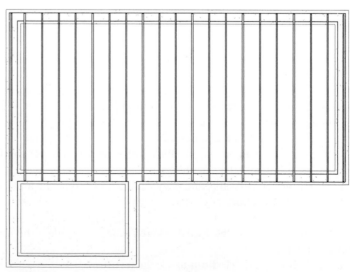

Figure 16-27

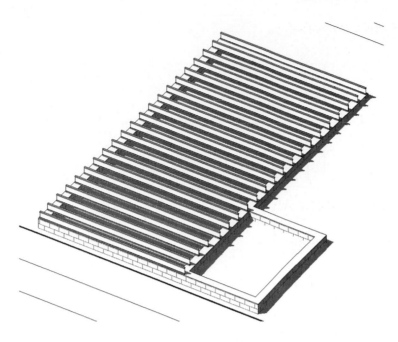

Figure 16-28

23. In the **Element Properties** dialog box, select the **Generic −12″** floor.
24. In the **Element Properties** dialog box, press the **Edit/New** button to bring up the **Type Properties** dialog box.
25. In the **Type Properties** dialog box, press the **Duplicate** button to bring up the **Name** dialog box.
26. In the **Name** dialog box, enter **3/4″ HARDWOOD FLOOR**, and press the **OK** button to return to the **Type Properties** dialog box.
27. In the **Type Properties** dialog box, press the **Edit** button in the **Structure** field to bring up the **Edit Assembly** dialog box.
28. In the **Edit Assembly** dialog box, change the **Material** for **Structure [1]** to **Wood – Flooring**, and the **Thickness** to **3/4″**.
29. Press the **OK** buttons to return to the **Element Properties** dialog box.
30. In the **Element Properties** dialog box, set the level to **Grade**, and the **Height Offset From level** to **2′-6″**.
31. Press the **OK** button to return to the **Drawing Editor** and **Sketch** tab.
32. In the **Sketch** tab, select **Lines**.
33. In the **Options** toolbar, select the **Pencil** tool and then the **Rectangle** button.
34. Place the rectangle around the joists, and then press the **Finish Sketch** icon in the **Sketch** tab to create the hardwood floor (see Figure 16-29).

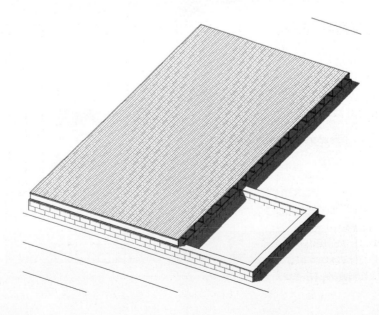

Figure 16-29

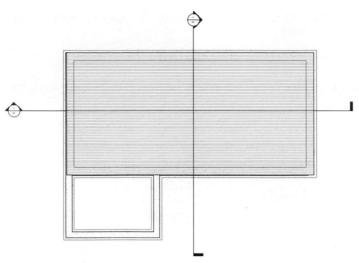

Figure 16-30

35. Change to the **FIRST FLOOR** plan view.
36. In the **Basics** tab of the **Design Bar**, select the **Section** tool.
37. Place a cross section and lateral section as shown in Figure 16-30.
38. Save the file.

CREATING THE EXTERIOR WALLS

The exterior walls for the HILLSIDE HOUSE are 2 × 6″ wood stud with a 1/2″ exterior sheathing, 3/4″ vertical wood plank, and 1/2″ gypsum wall board on the interior.

Creating the Vertical Plank Material

1. Select **Settings** > **Materials** from the **Main** menu to bring up the **Materials** dialog box.
2. In the **Materials** dialog box, in the **Graphics** tab, select **Siding - Clapboard** (see Figure 16-31).

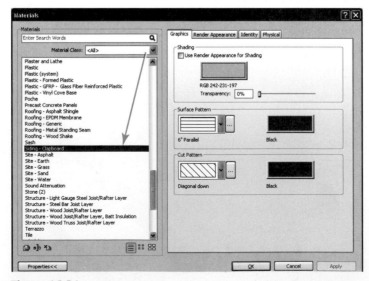

Figure 16-31

3. Click on the **Render Appearance** tab, and in the **Generic Material Properties** area, change **Rotate** to **90** degrees (see Figure 16-32a).

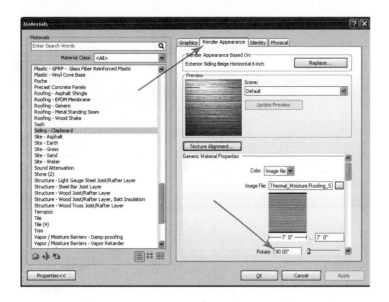

Figure 16-32a

4. Scroll down to the **Bump** area, and change **Rotate** to **90** degrees.
5. Enter **4** in the **Bump Amount** field.
6. Press the **Update Preview** button, and then press the **Apply** button (see Figure 16-32b)

The material will show when you are rendering, but you also need to set the surface texture when you are working.

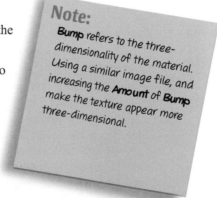

Note:

Bump refers to the three-dimensionality of the material. Using a similar image file, and increasing the **Amount** of **Bump** make the texture appear more three-dimensional.

7. Return to the **Graphics** tab in the **Materials** dialog box.
8. Click on the **Surface Pattern Pattern** button (which will be **6″ Parallel** by default) to bring up the **Fill Patterns** dialog box.
9. In the **Fill Patterns** dialog box, press the **New** button to bring up the **Add Surface Pattern** dialog box.

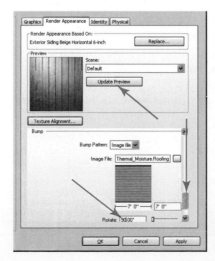
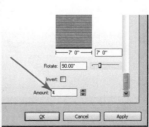

Figure 16-32b

10. In the **Add Surface Pattern** dialog box, enter **VERTICAL 6″ PARALLEL** in the **Name** field.
11. Set the **Line angle** to **90**, the **Line spacing** to **6″**, select the **Parallel** radio button, and then press the **OK** buttons to return to the **Materials** dialog box (see Figure 16-33).

You have now modified the **Siding - Clapboard** material that is to be used for your exterior walls.

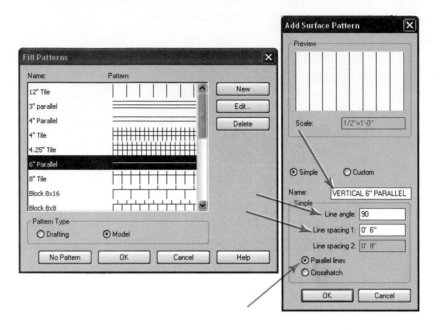

Figure 16-33

Creating the HILLSIDE HOUSE Exterior Wall Assembly

1. Double-click on **FIRST FLOOR** (under **Floor Plans**) in the **Project browser** to bring the **FIRST FLOOR** plan into the **Drawing Editor**.
2. Change the **Scale** to **1/4″ = 1′-0″**.
3. Set the **Detail Level** to **Medium**.
4. Change to the **Basics** tab in the **Design Bar**.
5. In the **Basics** tab, select the **Wall** tool.
6. In the **Options** toolbar, select the **Basic Wall: Generic −6″**.
7. With the **Basic Wall: Generic −6″** selected, press the **Element Properties** button to bring up the **Element Properties** dialog box.
8. In the **Element Properties** dialog box, select the **Edit/New** button to bring up the **Type Properties** dialog box.
9. In the **Type Properties** dialog box, select the **Duplicate** button to bring up the **Name** dialog box.
10. In the **Name** dialog box, enter **HILLSIDE HOUSE EXTERIOR WALLS** and press the **OK** button to return to the **Type Properties** dialog box.
11. In the **Type Properties** dialog box, press the **Edit** button in the **Structure** field to bring up the **Edit Assembly** dialog box.
12. In the **Edit Assembly** dialog box, press the **Preview** button at the lower left of the dialog box, and then make sure that the **View** is set to **Floor Plan: Modify type attributes** (see Figure 16-34).

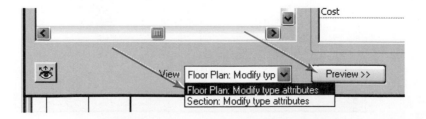

Figure 16-34

13. In the **Edit Assembly** dialog box, press the **Insert** button three times to add three layers. (They will all appear as **Structure [1]** functions and be located between the **Core Boundaries**.)
14. Click in the **Function** column of the first material to activate its drop-down list.
15. Select **Finish [1]** from the drop-down list for this material (see Figure 16-35).

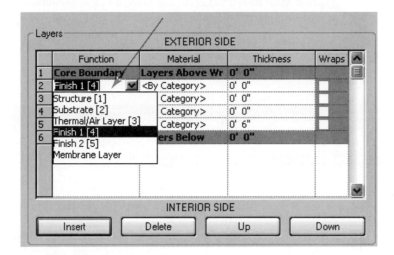

Figure 16-35

16. With **Finish [1]** selected, press the **Up** button to move it to the **Exterior Side** of the **Core Boundary**.
17. Select the **Material** next to **Finish [1]** (usually **<By Category>**) and then press the button that appears at the right side of the column to open the **Material Library**.
18. In the **Material Library**, select the **Finishes – Exterior –Siding/Clapboard** material, and press the **OK** button to return to the **Edit Assembly** dialog box.
19. Click in the **Thickness** column, and set the thickness to **3/4″**.

Note:
What does [1] ... [5] mean for the Finishes? It is the Line Width number.

Notice that the preview shows the exterior siding (see Figure 16-36).

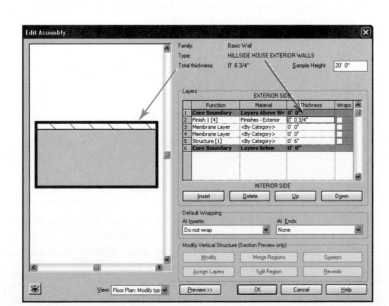

Figure 16-36

20. Repeat the process for the other layers.
21. Make **Structure [1]** the **5-1/2"** stud, with **Structure –Wood Joist/Rafter Layer** material, and place it between the **Core Boundary**.
22. Make the next layer **Substrate [2]** the **1/2"** sheathing, with **Default Wall** material, and place it above **Structure [1]** outside the **Core Boundary**.
23. Make the next layer **Finish [2]** (the inside 1/2" gypsum board) with **Finishes – Interior – gypsum Wall Board** material, and place it below **Structure [1]** outside the **Core Boundary** (see Figure 16-37).

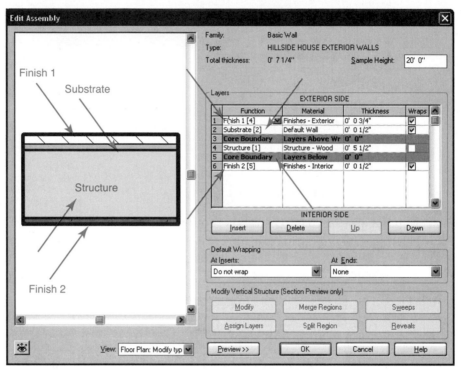

Figure 16-37

24. Press the **OK** buttons to return to the **Drawing Editor**.
25. Save the file.

Placing the FIRST FLOOR Exterior Walls

1. Select the **Wall** tool from the **Basics** tab in the **Design Bar**.
2. In the **Options** toolbar, select **HILLSIDE HOUSE EXTERIOR WALLS** from the drop-down list.
3. Select the **Element Properties** button to the right of the drop-down list to bring up the **Element Properties** dialog box.
4. In the **Element Properties** dialog box, set the **Location Line** to **Finish Face: Exterior**, **Base Constraint = FIRST FLOOR**, **Base Offset = −1'–5/8"**, **Top Constraint = Up to Level: SECOND FLOOR**, and **Top Offset = 0'-0"** (see Figure 16-38).
5. Press the **OK** button to return to the **Drawing Editor**.
6. Select the **Pick Lines** tool in the **Options** toolbar.
7. Pick the foundation walls shown in Figures 16-39 and 16-40.

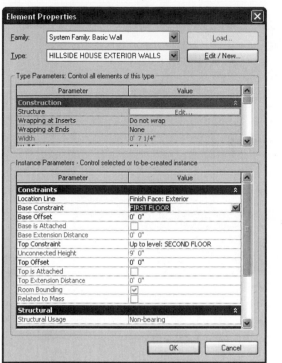

Figure 16-38

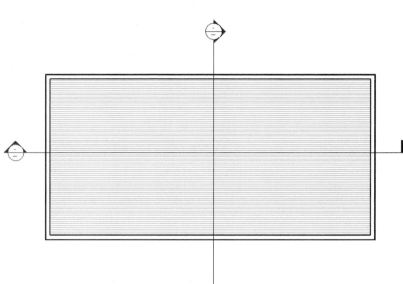

Figure 16-39

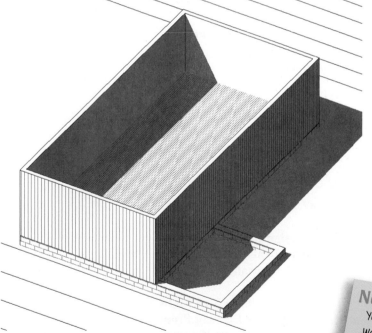

Figure 16-40

Note:
You will get a warning that the walls will overlap. Don't worry. This is because the walls you are copying have a negative base offset. You will change this next (see Figure 16-41).

Creating the SECOND FLOOR Exterior Walls

1. In the **FIRST FLOOR** plan view, select the **HILLSIDE HOUSE EXTERIOR WALLS** you just placed.
2. Select **Edit** > **Copy to Clipboard** from the **Main** menu to copy the walls.
3. Select **Edit** > **Paste Aligned** > **Select Levels by Name ...** to bring up the **Select Levels** dialog box.

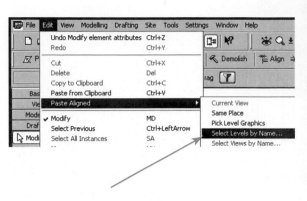 

Figure 16-41

4. In the **Select Levels** dialog box, select **SECOND FLOOR** and press the **OK** button to return to the **Drawing Editor**.
5. Select the **Default 3D View** button on the **View** toolbar to bring up the **Default 3D View** in the **Drawing Editor**.
6. Select the two walls you just placed on the **SECOND FLOOR**, **RMB**, and select **Element Properties** from the contextual menu to bring up the **Element Properties** dialog box for the walls.
7. In the **Element Properties** dialog box, change the **Base Constraint** to **SECOND FLOOR**, **Base Offset** to **0′-0″**, **Top Constraint** to **PARAPET**, **Top Offset** to **2′-0″**, **Structural Usage** to **Bearing**, and press the **OK** button to return to the **Drawing Editor**.
8. Save the file.

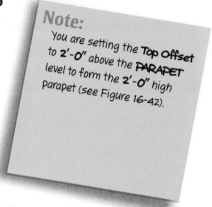

Note: You are setting the **Top Offset** to **2′-0″** above the **PARAPET** level to form the **2′-0″** high parapet (see Figure 16-42).

Note: The **SECOND FLOOR** wing walls are similar to the exterior walls except that they have sheathing and siding on both sides of the wall.

Creating the SECOND FLOOR Wing Walls

1. Double-click on **SECOND FLOOR** (under **Floor Plans**) in the **Project browser** to bring the **SECOND FLOOR** plan view into the **Drawing Editor**.
2. Change the **Scale** to **1/4 = 1′-0″**.
3. Set the **Detail Level** to **Medium**.
4. Change to the **Basics** tab in the **Design Bar**.
5. In the **Basics** tab, select the **Wall** tool.
6. In the **Options** toolbar, select the **Basic wall: HILLSIDE HOUSE EXTERIOR WALLS**.
7. With the **Basic wall: HILLSIDE HOUSE EXTERIOR WALLS** selected, press the **Element Properties** button to bring up the **Element Properties** dialog box.
8. In the **Element Properties** dialog box, select the **Edit/New** button to bring up the **Type Properties** dialog box.
9. In the **Type Properties** dialog box, select the **Duplicate** button to bring up the **Name** dialog box.
10. In the **Name** dialog box, enter **HILLSIDE HOUSE EXTERIOR WING WALLS** and press the **OK** button to return to the **Type Properties** dialog box.
11. In the **Type Properties** dialog box, press the **Edit** button in the **Structure** field to bring up the **Edit Assembly** dialog box.
12. In the **Edit Assembly** dialog box, press the **Insert** button one time in order to add one new layer above **Finish 2**.
13. Change the new layer to **Substrate [2]**, and **Finish 2** to **Finish 1 [4]**.

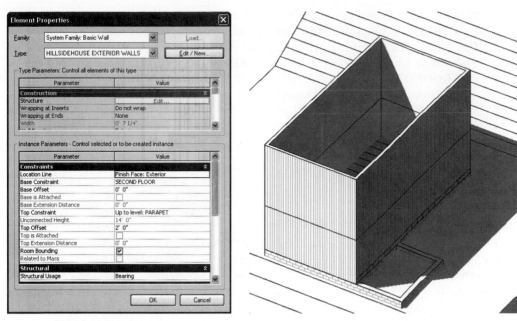

Figure 16-42

14. Set the new **Substrate [2]** material to **Wood Sheathing**, **Width** to **1/2″**, and check the **Wraps** check box.
15. Set the new **Finish 2** material to **Finishes – Exterior –Siding/Clapboard**, **Width** to **3/4″**, and check the **Wraps** check box.
16. With the **Up** and **Down** buttons, move the layers and press the **OK** button to return to the **Type Properties** dialog box.
17. In the **Type Properties** dialog box, change the **Wrapping at Ends** to **Exterior**, **Wall Function** to **Exterior**, and press the **OK** button to return to the **Element Properties** dialog box (see Figures 16-43 and 16-44).

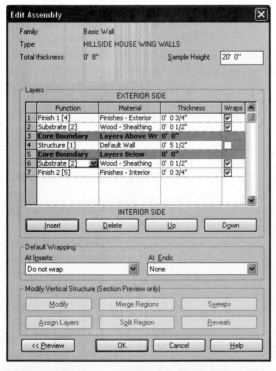

Figure 16-43

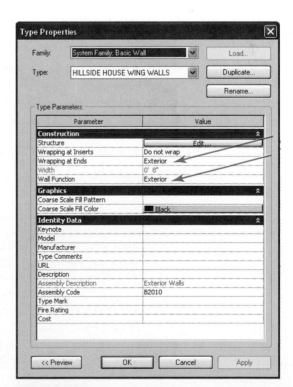

Figure 16-44

18. In the **Element Properties** dialog box, set the **Base Constraint** to **SECOND FLOOR**, **Base Offset** to **0′-0″**, **Top Constraint** to **PARAPET**, **Top Offset** to **2′-0″**, and press the **OK** button to return to the **Drawing Editor**.
19. Place **10′-0″** long **HILLSIDE HOUSE EXTERIOR WING WALLS** at the west side of the **SECOND FLOOR**, and **7′-0″ HILLSIDE HOUSE EXTERIOR WING WALLS** at the east side of the **SECOND FLOOR**.
20. Place **10′-0″** long **HILLSIDE HOUSE EXTERIOR WING WALLS** at the south side of the **SECOND FLOOR** to create the office enclosure (see Figures 16-45 and 16-46).

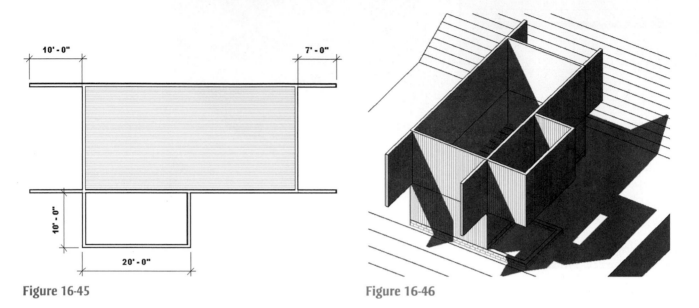

Figure 16-45

Figure 16-46

Creating the Skylight Side Walls

1. Double-click on the **South Elevation** in the **Project browser** to bring it up in the **Drawing Editor**.
2. Select the south wall, and press the **Edit Profile** button in the **Options** toolbar to bring up the **Sketch** tab in the **Design Bar**.
3. In the **Sketch** tab, select the **Lines** tool and modify the top profile of the wall as shown in Figure 16-47.
4. After you have modified the wall profile, press the **Finish Sketch** button to complete the wall, and then repeat the same operation for the other side (see Figure 16-48).
5. Save the file.

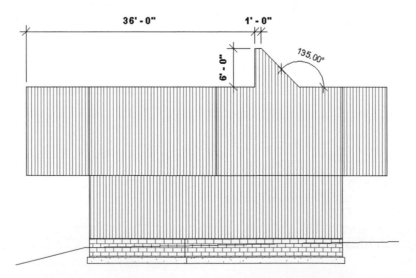

Figure 16-47

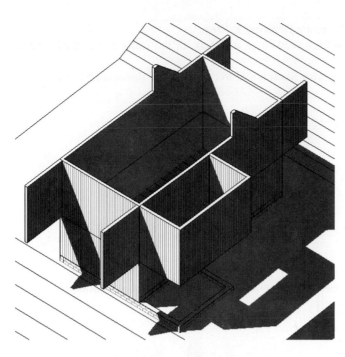

Figure 16-48

Creating the SECOND FLOOR Floors

1. Double-click on the **SECOND FLOOR** plan view in the **Project browser** to bring it up in the **Drawing Editor**.
2. Change to the **Basics** tab in the **Design Bar**.
3. In the **Basics** tab, select the **Floor** tool to bring up the **Sketch** tab in the **Design Bar**.
4. In the **Sketch** tab, select the **Floor Properties** tool to bring up the **Element Properties** dialog box.
5. In the **Element Properties** dialog box, select the **Basic wall: 3/4″ HARDWOODFLOOR**.
6. In the **Element Properties** dialog box, select the **Edit/New** button to bring up the **Type Properties** dialog box.
7. In the **Type Properties** dialog box, select the **Duplicate** button to bring up the **Name** dialog box.
8. In the **Name** dialog box, enter **SECOND FLOOR 3/4″ HARDWOODFLOOR**, and press the **OK** button to return to the **Type Properties** dialog box.
9. In the **Type Properties** dialog box, press the **Edit** button in the **Structure** field to bring up the **Edit Assembly** dialog box.
10. In the **Edit Assembly** dialog box, press the **Insert** button one time to add two new layers.
11. Move the existing **Wood Flooring** up to the top, above the **Core Boundary**, and make it **Finish 1**.
12. Make the next layer **Structure [1]** with the **Default Floor** material, **11-7/8″** thickness, and place it between the **Core Boundary**.
13. Make the third layer **Finish 1 [4]**, set its material to **Finishes – Interior – Gypsum Wall Board**, set its thickness to **1/2″**, and place it on the bottom—outside the **Core Boundary**.
14. Press the **OK** buttons to return to the **Element Properties** dialog box.
15. In the **Element Properties** dialog box, set the **Level** to **SECOND FLOOR**, and **Height Offset From Level** to **0′-0″**.

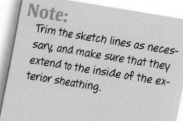

> **Note:**
> For these exercises you will use the **Floor** tool, but you will not model the structure as you did on the first floor. Either method is fine, but with this second method, you will have to use detail components later to illustrate the framing in the section views.

> **Note:**
> Trim the sketch lines as necessary, and make sure that they extend to the inside of the exterior sheathing.

16. Press the **OK** button to return to the **Drawing Editor**.
17. In the **Sketch** tab, select the **Pick Walls** tool, and pick all the walls except the east and west wing walls.
18. In the **Sketch** tab, select the **Finish Sketch** tool to complete the floor (see Figure 16-49).
19. Save the file.

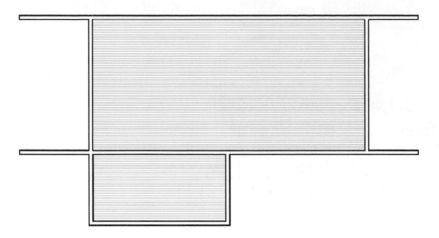

Figure 16-49

Creating the Stairway

The stairway is tied to the exterior of the building so that it doesn't subtract from the area inside the house.

1. Double-click on the **FIRST FLOOR** plan view in the **Project browser** to bring it up in the **Drawing Editor**.
2. Select one of the **HILLSIDE HOUSE EXTERIOR WALLS**, **RMB**, and select **Create Similar** from the contextual menu that appears.
3. Select the **Pencil** tool in the **Options** toolbar, and place walls as shown in Figure 16-50.

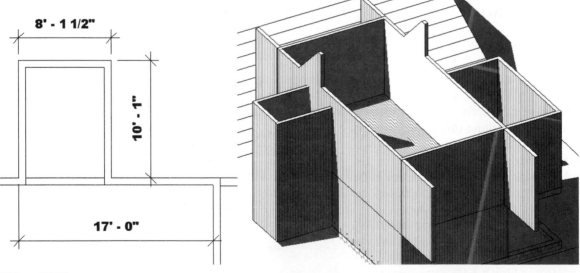

Figure 16-50

4. Select the walls you just placed, **RMB**, and select **Element Properties** from the contextual menu to bring up the **Element Properties** dialog box.
5. In the **Element Properties** dialog box set the **Top Constraint** to **PARAPET**, and the **Top Offset** to **0'-0"**.
6. Change to the **Modeling** tab in the **Design Bar**.
7. In the **Modeling** tab, select the **Stair** tool.

The **Design Bar** will change to **Sketch** mode.

8. Select **Stair Properties** in the **Sketch** tab to bring up the **Element Properties** dialog box.
9. In the **Element Properties** dialog box, use the settings and check boxes shown in Figure 16-51.
10. In the **Sketch** tab, select **Run**.
11. Click and then drag your cursor upward until the message **8 RISERS CREATED, 8 RE-MAINING** appears, and click again.
12. Drag your cursor to the **East** approximately **3′-6″**, and click again.
13. Drag your cursor to down, and click again to create the stair lines (see Figure 16-52).

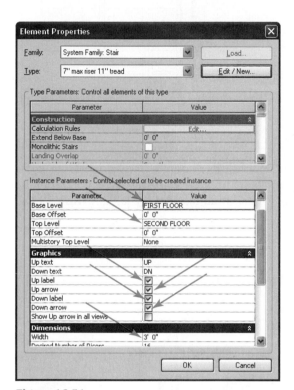

Figure 16-51

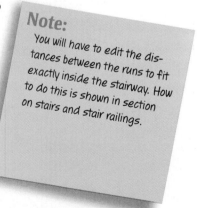

16 RISERS CREATED, 0 REMAINING

Figure 16-52

14. In the **Sketch** tab, again select the **Finish Sketch** tool to create the changed stair.
15. Delete the outside stair railing that is automatically created.
16. Select the **Align** tool from the **Tools** toolbar.
17. Select the left inside of the stairway wall, and then the left side of the stair.
18. Repeat using the **Align** tool on the top inside of the stairway, and the top of the landing. Doing this will align the stair inside the stairway (see Figures 16-53 and 16-54).
19. Double-click on the **West Elevation** in the **Project browser** to bring it up in the **Drawing Editor**.
20. Set the scale to **1/4″ = 1′-0″**, and the **Model Graphic Style** to **Wireframe**.
21. Select the stairway walls, and press the **Edit Profile** button in the **Options** toolbar to put the stairway wall in **Sketch** mode.
22. Using the **Lines** tool from the **Sketch** tab in the **Design Bar**, and the **Split** tool from the **Tools** toolbar, modify the top and bottom of the stairway wall.
23. Press the **Finish Sketch** button in the **Sketch** tab to complete the wall.

Note:
You will have to edit the distances between the runs to fit exactly inside the stairway. How to do this is shown in section on stairs and stair railings.

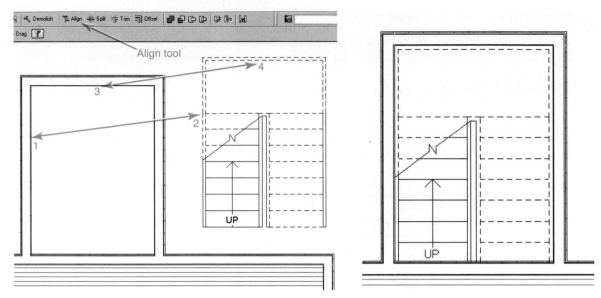

Figure 16-53

Figure 16-54

24. Repeat for the opposite wall, and then adjust the rear wall of the stairway (see Figure 16-55).
25. Using the **Opening > Wall Opening** tool from the **Modeling** tab of the **Design Bar**, create **7'-0″ × 3'-0″** wide openings leading from the stairway to the **FIRST FLOOR** and **SECOND FLOOR**.
26. Save the file.

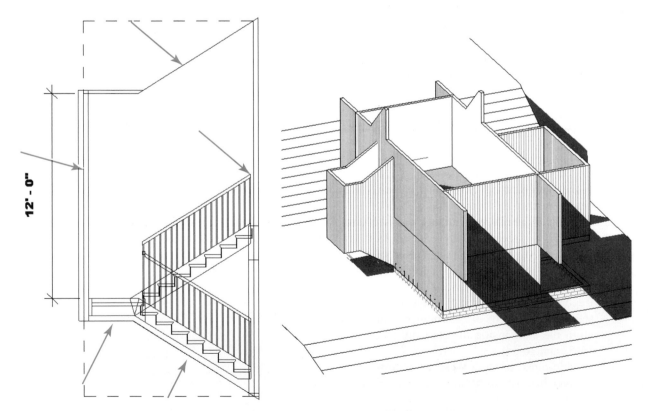

Figure 16-55

Creating the Roof

1. Double-click on the **PARAPET** level plan to bring it up in the **Drawing Editor**.
2. Change the **Scale** to **1/4″ = 1'-0″**.

3. Select **File** > **Load from Library** from the **Main** menu to bring up the **Open** menu.
4. In the **Open** menu, locate the **Imperial Library** folder.
5. In the **Imperial Library** folder, locate and open the **Structural** folder.
6. In the **Structural** folder, locate and open the **Framing** folder.
7. In the **Framing** folder, locate and open the **Steel** folder.
8. In the **Steel** folder, select the **K-Series Bar Joist-Rod Web**, then select the **18K3 Type**, and press the **Open** button to return to the **Drawing Editor**.
9. Change to the **Structural** tab in the **Design Bar**.
10. In the **Structural** tab, select the **Beam System** tool to enter the **Sketch** mode.
11. In the **Sketch** tab, select the **Structural Beam System Properties** icon to bring up the **Element Properties** dialog box (see Figure 16-56).

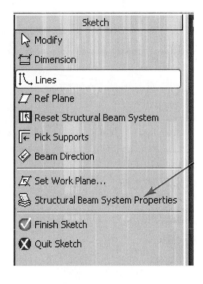

Figure 16-56

12. In the **Element Properties** dialog box, set the **Elevation** to **0'-0"**, **Layout Rule** to **Fixed Distance**, **Fixed Spacing** to **2'-0"**, **Justification** to **Beginning**, and **Beam Type** to **K-Series Bar Joist-Rod Web: 18K3**.
13. Press the **OK** button to return to the **Drawing Editor**.
14. Select the **Pencil** tool from the **Options** toolbar, and then select the **Rectangle** option.
15. Place a rectangle.
16. Select the **Beam Direction** tool from the **Sketch** tab, and select the left side of the rectangle to indicate the direction of the web joists (two small parallel lines) (see Figure 16-57).

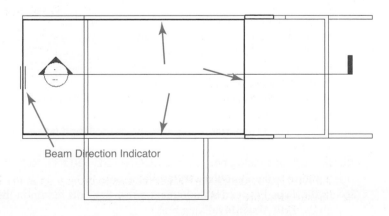

Beam Direction Indicator

Figure 16-57

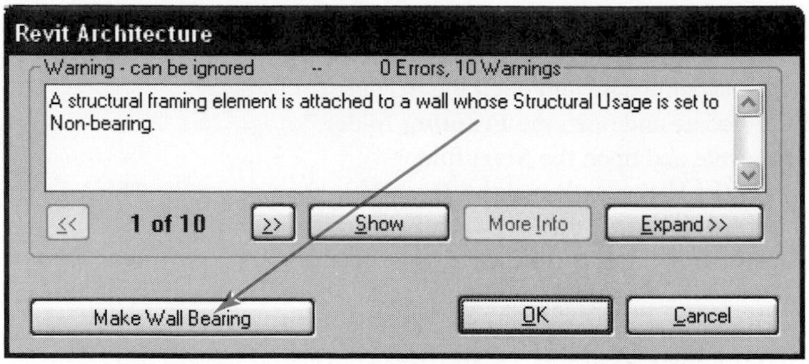

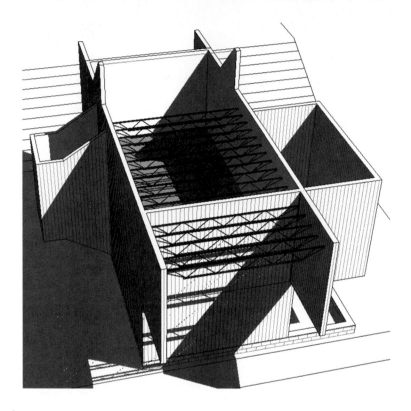

Figure 16-58

Figure 16-59

17. Press the **Finish Sketch** icon.
18. Be sure you are in the **PARAPET** plan view.
19. Select the **Basics** tab from the **Design Bar**.
20. In the **Basics** tab, select the **Roof > Roof by Footprint** tool to bring up the **Sketch** tab in the **Design Bar**.
21. In the **Sketch** tab, select the **Roof Properties** dialog box to bring up the **Element Properties** dialog box for the roof.
22. In the **Element Properties** dialog box, select **Generic-12″** from the **Type** drop-down list.
23. In the **Element Properties** dialog box, press the **Edit/New** button to bring up the **Type Properties** dialog box.
24. In the **Type Properties** dialog box, press the **Duplicate** button to bring up the **Name** dialog box.
25. In the **Name** dialog box, enter **SECOND FL FRONT ROOF**, and press the **OK** button to return to the **Type Properties** dialog box.
26. In the **Type Properties** dialog box, press the **Edit** button in the **Structure** field to bring up the **Edit Assembly** dialog box.

Note:
You may get a warning that the wall is a non-bearing wall; press the **Make Wall Bearing** button, and then press the **OK** button to create the roof joists (see Figures 16-58 and 16-59).

27. In the **Edit Assembly** dialog box, select the **Insert** button, and add a new layer.
28. Press the **Up** button to move the new layer above and outside the **Core Boundary**.
29. Change the **Function** of the layer outside the **Core Boundary** to **Finish 1 [4]**.
30. Set the **Material** for **Finish 1 [4]** to **Concrete-Cast-in-Place Lightweight Concrete**, and **Thickness** to **0′ 6″**.
31. Set the **Material** for the **Structure [1]** to **Metal-Deck**, and set its **Thickness** to **0′ 2″**.
32. Check the **Variable** check box for **Finish 1 [4]**.
33. Press the **OK** buttons to return to the **Drawing Editor** dialog box.

Note: Checking the **Variable** check box for **Finish 1 [4]** will allow that finish to have a slope.

34. In the **Sketch** tab, select the **Lines** tool.
35. In the **Options** toolbar, uncheck the **Defines slope** check box. This will cause the lines to create a flat roof.
36. Select the **Pencil** tool in the **Options** toolbar, and then select the **Rectangle** option.
37. Place a rectangle as shown in Figure 16-60, and press the **Finish Roof** button in the **Sketch** tab to create the roof.
38. Change to the **Default 3D View**.
39. Select the roof you just created.
40. Press the **Temporary Hide/Isolate** icon at the bottom of the **Drawing Editor**, and then select **Isolate Element** to isolate the roof (Figure 16-61).
41. Select the isolated roof, and then select the **Draw Split Lines** button in the **Options** toolbar.

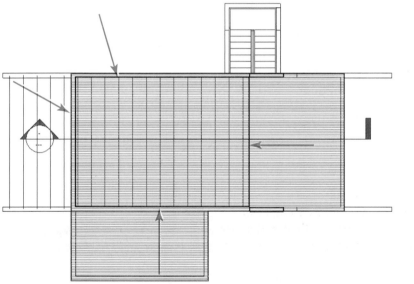

Figure 16-60   Figure 16-61

42. Draw split lines diagonally crossing the roof.
43. Select the **Modify Sub-Elements** button in the **Options** toolbar.
44. Select the grip at the intersection between the split lines, enter **−0′-3″**, c-lick outside the roof twice, and then press the **<Esc>** key on your keyboard to complete the command.
45. Select the **Temporary Hide/Isolate icon** at the bottom of the **Drawing Editor**, and then select **Reset Temporary Hide/Isolate** to unhide everything (see Figure 16-62).
46. Double-click the **Section 1** view in the **Project browser** to bring it up in the **Drawing Editor**.

In the **Section 1** view you can see the cast-in-place concrete that slopes to the center of the roof. Eventually, a roof drain will be placed in the center of this roof, and it will exit through a pipe to the drain (see Figure 16-63).

47. Save the file.

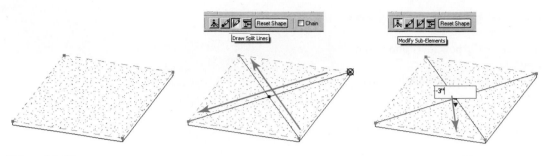

Figure 16-62

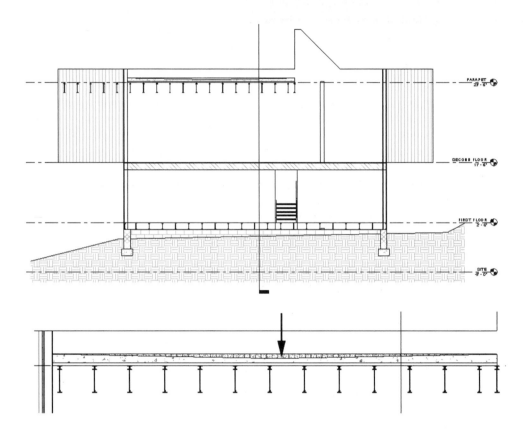

Figure 16-63

Creating the Skylight Roof

1. Double-click on the **PARAPET** level plan to bring it up in the **Drawing Editor**.
2. Change to the **Basics** tab in the **Design Bar**.
3. Select the **Ref Plane** tool from the **Basics** tab.
4. In the **Options** toolbar, select the **Pick Lines** button, and enter **0′-1″** in the **Offset** field.
5. Pick the outside of the north and south exterior walls to place reference planes.
6. **RMB** on each reference plane, and pick **Element Properties** from the contextual menu to bring up the **Element Properties** dialog box for the **Reference Plane**.
7. Enter **NORTH** in the **Name** field for the north reference plane, and **SOUTH** in the **Name** field for the south reference plane (see Figure 16-64).
8. In the **Basics** tab, select the **Roof >> Roof by Extrusion** tool.

The **Work Plane** dialog box will appear.

9. In the **Work Plane** dialog box, select the **Name** radio button, select **Reference Plane: SOUTH** from the drop-down list, and then press the **OK** button to bring up the **Go to View** dialog box.

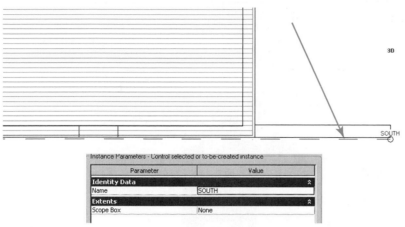

Figure 16-64

10. In the **Go to View** dialog box, select **Elevation: South**, and then press the **Open View** button to bring up the **Roof Reference Level and Offset** dialog box. Press the **OK** button to bring up the **Sketch** tab in the **Design Bar**.
11. In the **Sketch** tab, select the **Properties** icon to bring up the **Element Properties** dialog box.
12. In the **Element Properties** dialog box, select **Wood Rafter 8″ – Asphalt Shingle – Insulated** from the **Type** drop-down list, and press the **OK** button to return to the **Drawing Editor**.
13. In the **Sketch** tab, select the lines tool.
14. In the **Options** toolbar, select the **Pencil** tool, check the **Chain** check box, select the line option, and set the **Offset** to **−0′ 8 3/8″** (thickness of the roof).
15. Trace the outline of the skylight walls as shown in Figure 16-65, and press the **Finish Sketch** icon in the **Sketch** tab to create the roof.

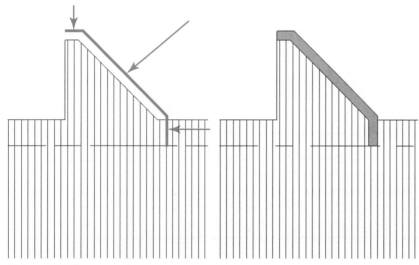

Figure 16-65

16. Double-click on the **PARAPET** plan view to bring it up in the **Drawing Editor**.
17. Select the roof you just placed to activate its grips.
18. Drag the north grip of the roof, and drag it until it snaps on the **North** reference plane.

You have now created the skylight roof (see Figure 16-66).

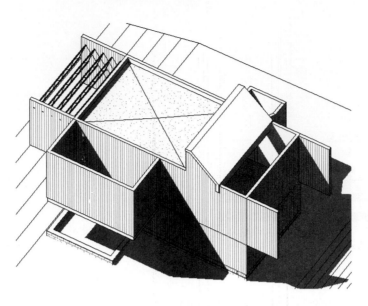

Figure 16-66

Creating the Skylight Glazing

1. Double-click on the **PARAPET** level plan to bring it up in the **Drawing Editor**.
2. Change to the **Basics** tab in the **Design Bar**.
3. Select the **Ref Plane** tool from the **Basics** toolbar, and place a reference plane at the rear of the **SECOND FLOOR FRONT ROOF**.
4. **RMB** on the reference plane, and pick **Element Properties** from the contextual menu to bring up the **Element Properties** dialog box for the **Reference Plane**.
5. Enter **SKYLITE GLAZING** in the **Name** field for the reference plane (see Figure 16-67).

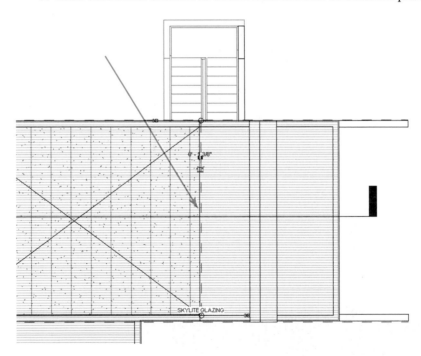

SKYLITE GLAZING

Figure 16-67

6. Double-click on the **West Elevation** in the **Project browser** to bring it up in the **Drawing Editor**.
7. In the **Basics** tab, select the **Lines** tool.
8. In the **Options** toolbar, select **Reference Plane: SKYLIGHT GLAZING** from the **Plane** drop-down list.
9. Select the **Pencil** tool, and then the **Rectangle** option (see Figure 16-68).
10. Place a rectangle where the glazing will be (see Figure 16-69).
11. Select everything with a window selection, and then press the **Filter Selection** icon in the **Options** toolbar to bring up the **Filter** dialog box.

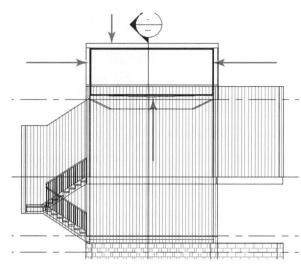

Figure 16-68   Figure 16-69

12. In the **Filter** dialog box, press the **Check None** button, press the **Lines** check box, and then press the **OK** button to return to the **Drawing Editor**. This means that only the lines will be selected.
13. With the rectangle (lines) selected, press the **Temporary Hide/Isolate** icon at the bottom of the **Drawing Editor**, and then select **Isolate Element** to isolate the rectangle.
14. Change to the **Modeling** tab in the **Design Bar**.
15. In the **Modeling** tab, select the **Curtain System** > **Curtain System by Lines** tool.
16. Select the top and bottom lines of the rectangle to create the **Curtain System** (the glazing).
17. Select the **Curtain Grid** tool from the **Modeling** tab.
18. Place grid lines to divide the curtain system into six panels.
19. Select the **Mullion** tool from the **Modeling** tab.
20. In the **Options** toolbar, select **Rectangular Mullion: 2.5″ × 5″ rectangular**, and then select the **All Empty Segments** radio button.
21. Select and click on the curtain grid you placed to create all the mullions.
22. Select the **Temporary Hide/Isolate icon** at the bottom of the **Drawing Editor**, and then select **Reset Temporary Hide/Isolate** to unhide everything.
23. Change to the **Default 3D View** (see Figure 16-70).
24. Save the file.

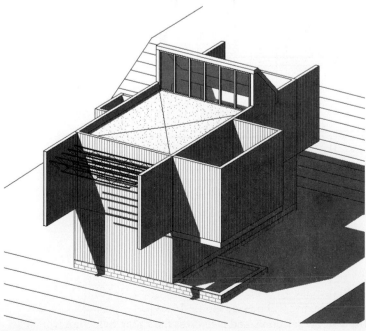

Figure 16-70

Creating the Bridge

1. Double-click on the **SECOND FLOOR** level plan to bring it up in the **Drawing Editor**.
2. Change the **Scale** to **1/4″ = 1′-0″**.
3. **RMB** in the **SECOND FLOOR** level plan, and select **View Properties** from the contextual menu to bring up the **Element Properties** dialog box for the **Floor Plan**.
4. In the **Element Properties** dialog box, select **SITE** from the **Underlay** drop-down list (see Figure 16-71).

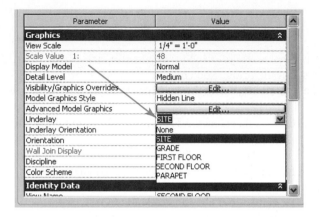

Figure 16-71

5. Change to the **Basics** tab in the **Design Bar**.
6. In the **Basics** tab, select the **Floor** tool to bring up the **Sketch** tab in the **Design Bar**.
7. In the **Sketch** tab, select the **Floor Properties** icon to bring up the **Element Properties** dialog box for the floor.
8. In the **Element Properties** dialog box, select **Generic −12″ Filled** for the **Type**.
9. In the **Element Properties** dialog box, select **SECOND FLOOR** for the **Level**, and enter **−0′-10″** for the **Height Offset From Level**.

The bridge will have a 6″ step up to the rear deck, and the rear deck will be 4″ below the **SECOND FLOOR** level.

10. Press the **OK** button to return to the **Drawing Editor**.
11. Select the **Lines** tool from the **Sketch** tab, and place a **5′-0″** wide rectangle that reaches from the upper edge of the site slope to the edge of the rear wing wall (see Figure 16-72).

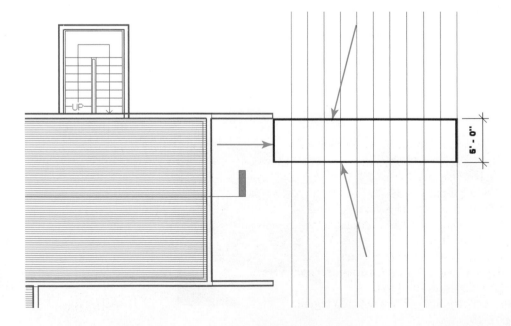

Figure 16-72

12. Press the **Finish Sketch** button in the **Sketch** tab to create the deck.
13. Change to the **Modeling** tab in the **Design Bar**.
14. In the **Modeling** tab, select the **Railing** tool to bring up the **Sketch** tab.
15. In the **Sketch** tab, select the railing properties icon to bring up the **Element Properties** dialog box for railings.
16. In the **Element Properties** dialog box, select **Handrail – Pipe** for the **Type**.
17. Press the **OK** button to return to the **Drawing Editor**.
18. In the **Sketch** tab, select the set **Host** tool, and then select the bridge you created.
19. In the **Sketch** tab, select the set **Lines** tool, and place a line where the north railing will appear.
20. In the **Sketch** tab, select the **Finish Sketch** icon to create the railing.
21. Repeat steps 18, 19, and 20 for the south railing.
22. Change to the **Default 3D View** to see the result.
23. Save the file (see Figure 16-73).

Note:
Before you create the plot sheets, open up all your views, and be sure that they are set to the correct scale and that the crop regions are correct. The crop region defines the boundaries of a view.

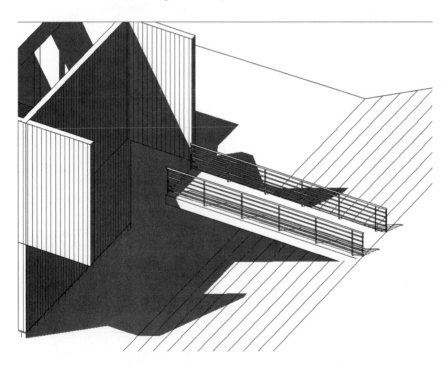

Figure 16-73

Creating the Plot Sheets

The following is an example of how to set your views correctly.

1. Bring up the **FIRST FLOOR** plan view.
2. Press the **Show Crop Region** icon at the bottom of the **Drawing Editor**.
3. Hide anything in the view (such as the toposurface) that is not important for this view.
4. Move any of your **Elevation** markers into view (if you want them to show).
5. Change any **Underlay** to **None**.
6. Set your **Detail Level**, **Model Graphic Style** (shading), and **shadows**.
7. Zoom out until you see the crop region.

Note:
If the **Crop Region** is already showing, this icon's tool tip will say **Hide Crop Region** (see Figure 16-74).

Figure 16-74

8. Select the crop region to activate its grips.
9. Drag the crop region grips until the region frames the area that you want to show on your plot sheet (see Figure 16-75).

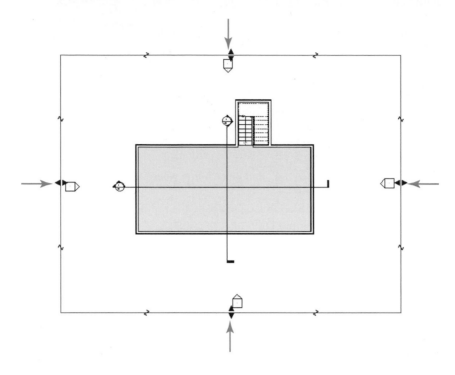

10. Press the **Hide Crop Region** icon (previously called **Show Crop Region**) at the bottom of the **Drawing Editor** to hide the region.

Once you have prepared all your views, you can proceed to place them on plot sheets.

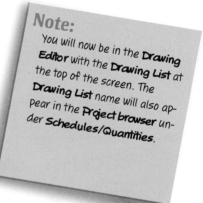

Note:
You will now be in the **Drawing Editor** with the **Drawing List** at the top of the screen. The **Drawing List** name will also appear in the **Project browser** under **Schedules/Quantities**.

11. Select the **Sheets [all]** icon in the **Project browser**, **RMB**, and select **New Sheet...** to bring up the **Select a Titleblock** dialog box.
12. In the **Select a Titleblock** dialog box, press the **Load** button to bring up the **Open** dialog box.
13. In the **Open** dialog box, browse and locate the **HILLSIDE HOUSE SHEET FAMILY** that you created in the first exercise of this section.
14. Press the **OK** button to bring the sheet into the **Drawing Editor**.
15. In the sheet's title block, select the **Unnamed** field, and change it to **TITLE SHEET**.
16. Change the sheet number to **A100**.
17. Select **View > New Drawing List** from the main menu to bring up the **Drawing List Properties** dialog box (see Figure 16-76).
18. In the **Drawing List Properties** dialog box, select the **Fields** tab.
19. In the **Fields** tab, select **Sheet Number**, **Sheet Name**, **Drawn By**, **Checked By**, and **Approved By** from the **Available fields** column, and press the **Add button** to move them to the **Scheduled fields [in order]** column.
20. Press the **OK** button to create the **Drawing List**.

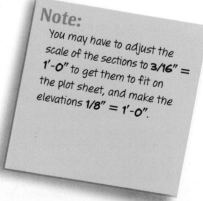

Note:
You may have to adjust the scale of the sections to **3/16" = 1'-0"** to get them to fit on the plot sheet, and make the elevations **1/8" = 1'-0"**.

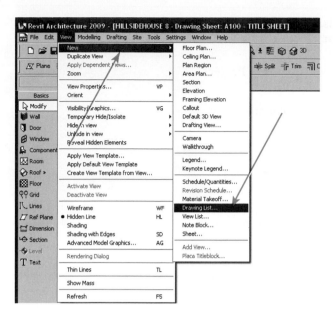

Figure 16-76

21. Double-click on **A100 – TITLE SHEET** (under **Sheets [all]**) in the **Project browser** to bring it up in the **Drawing Editor**.
22. Select the **Drawing List** name in the **Project browser** and drag it into the **TITLE SHEET** in the **Drawing Editor** (see Figure 16-77).

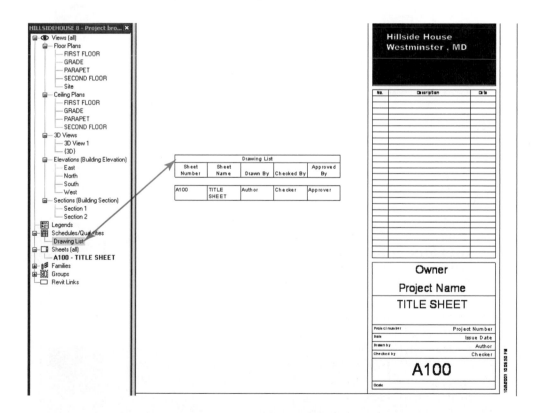

Figure 16-77

23. Again, select the **Sheets [all]** icon in the **Project browser**, **RMB**, and select **New Sheet…** to bring up the **Select a Titleblock** dialog box.
24. In the **Select a Titleblock** dialog box, the **HILLSIDE HOUSE SHEET FAMILY** will already be selected. Press the **OK** button to bring the sheet into the **Drawing Editor**. The new sheet will be automatically numbered **A101**.
25. In the sheet's title block, select the **Unnamed** field and change it to **SITE PLAN**.
26. Select **SITE** in the **Project browser**, and drag it into the sheet you just created.

27. Create four more sheets labeled **FIRST FLOOR PLAN**, **SECOND FLOOR PLAN**, **ELEVATIONS**, and **SECTIONS**.

28. Drag the appropriate views from the **Project browser** into the plot sheets.

The drawing list on the **TITLE SHEET** will now show all the drawings you created.

29. Save the file

You have now created the basic plot sheets. Now that you have created and saved the sheets, you can return to modifying the building model, and all your changes will be updated on the sheets (see Figures 16-78 through 16-83).

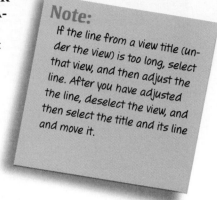

Note:
If the line from a view title (under the view) is too long, select that view, and then adjust the line. After you have adjusted the line, deselect the view, and then select the title and its line and move it.

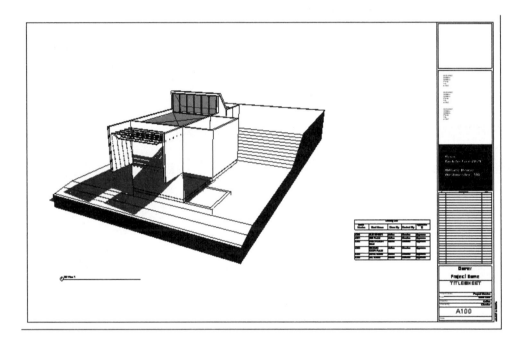

Figure 16-78

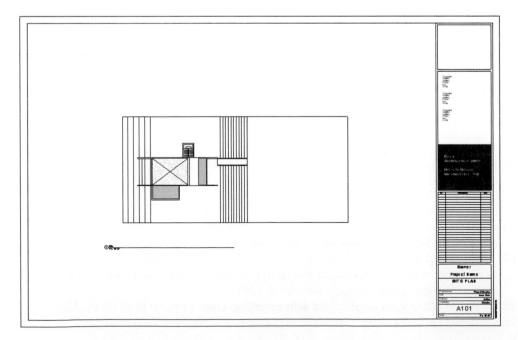

Figure 16-79

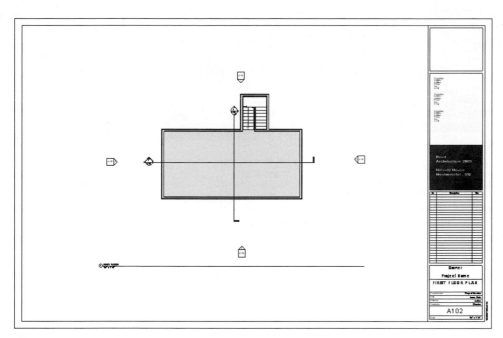

Figure 16-80

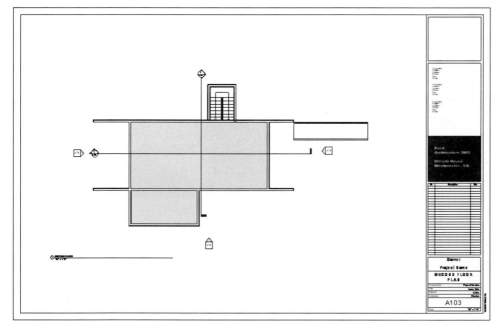

Figure 16-81

Creating the Interior Walls

1. Double-click on the **FIRST FLOOR** plan view in the **Project browser** to bring it up in the **Drawing Editor**.
2. Select the **Wall** tool from the **Basics** tab in the **Design Bar**.
3. Select the **Basic wall: Interior −4-7/8″ Partition [1-hr]** from the **Options** toolbar drop-down list.
4. Select the **Element Properties** button in the **Options** toolbar to bring up the **Element Properties** dialog box.
5. In the **Element Properties** dialog box, select the **Edit/New** button to bring up the **Type Properties** dialog box.
6. In the **Type Properties** dialog box, select the **Duplicate** button to bring up the **Name** dialog box.

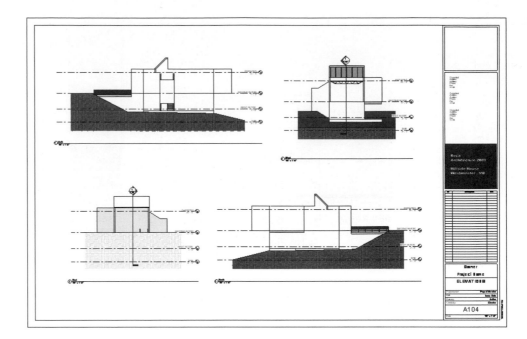

Figure 16-82

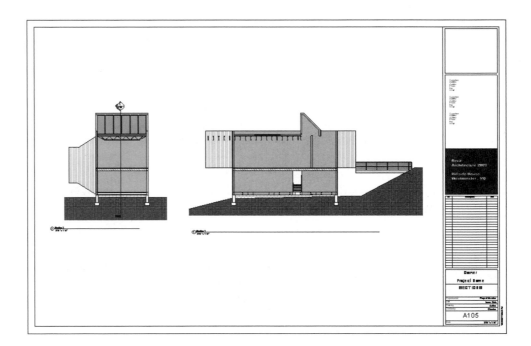

Figure 16-83

7. In the **Name** dialog box, enter **INTERIOR 4 1/2″ WALLS**, and press the **OK** button to return to the **Type Properties** dialog box.
8. In the **Type Properties** dialog box, press the **Edit** button in the **Structure** field to bring up the **Edit Assembly** dialog box.
9. In the **Edit Assembly** dialog box, change the **Structure [1] Thickness** to **3-1/2″**, and **Finish 2 Thickness** to **1/2″**.
10. Press the **OK** buttons to return to the **Drawing Editor**.
11. In the **Options** toolbar, pick the **Pencil** tool, select **Unconnected** from the **Height** drop-down list, and enter **7′-10 7/8″**.
12. In the **Options** toolbar, select **Finish Face: Exterior** from the **Loc Line** drop-down list, and the **Line** option.
13. Using the **INTERIOR 4 1/2″ WALLS** you just created, place walls and doors as shown in Figure 16-84.

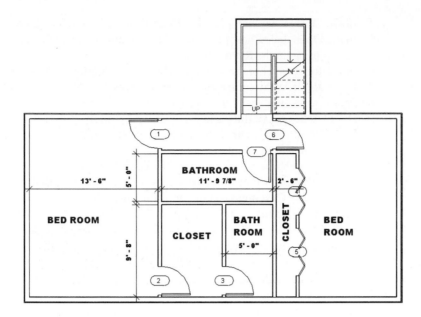

Figure 16-84

14. In the **Project browser**, double-click on the **SECOND FLOOR** plan view to bring up the **SECOND FLOOR** into the **Drawing Editor**.
15. Select the **Wall** tool again from the **Design Bar**.
16. Using the **INTERIOR 4 1/2″ WALLS** you previously created, change the height to **9′-0″**, and place walls and doors as shown in Figure 16-85.
17. Save the file.

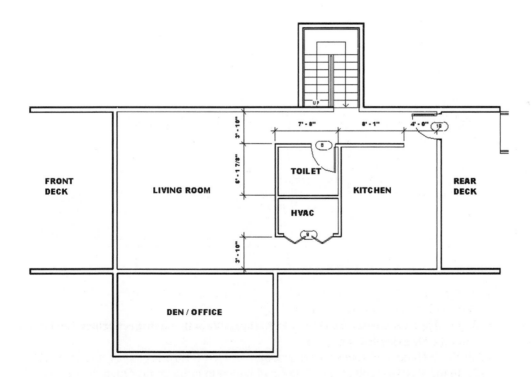

Figure 16-85

PLACING EXTERIOR DOORS AND WINDOWS

1. Double-click on the **FIRST FLOOR** plan view in the **Project browser** to bring it up in the **Drawing Editor**.
2. Change to the **Basics** tab in the **Design Bar**.
3. In the **Basics** tab, select the **Window** tool.

4. In the **Options** toolbar, press the **Load** button to bring up the **Open** dialog box.
5. In the **Open** dialog box, press the **Web Library** button at the top right side of the dialog box to bring up the Revit web library.
6. In the Revit web library, select the **Revit Architecture 2008 Library**.
7. In the **Revit Architecture 2008 Library**, press the "+" to expand the **US Library**.
8. Press the "+" to expand the **Families**.
9. Double-click on **Windows** to bring up the **Windows Library**.
10. In the **Windows Library**, select the **Casement –Triple w Trim Window**, and download and save it to your computer in the folder where you have been saving all your files.
11. Close the web library and return to the **Drawing Editor**.
12. With the **Window** tool still selected, press **Load** in the **Options** toolbar again, and locate and open the **Casement –Triple w Trim Window**.
13. Select the **Casement –Triple w Trim 72″ × 48″** from the drop-down list in the **Options** toolbar.
14. Press the **Element Properties** button in the **Options** toolbar to bring up the **Element Properties** dialog box.
15. In the **Element Properties** dialog box, press the **Edit/New** button to bring up the **Type Properties** dialog box.
16. In the **Type Properties** dialog box, press the **Duplicate** button to bring up the **Name** dialog box.
17. In the **Name** dialog box, enter **96″ × 48″**, and press the **OK** button to return to the **Type Properties** dialog box.
18. In the **Type Properties** dialog box, change the **Width** to **8′-0″**, and press the **OK** buttons to return to the **Drawing Editor**.
19. Place windows in the front of the building and back as shown in Figure 16-86.

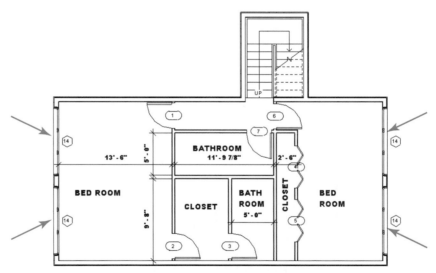

Figure 16-86

20. Double-click on the **SECOND FLOOR** plan view in the **Project browser** to bring it up in the **Drawing Editor**.
21. In the **Basics** tab, select the **Door** tool.
22. In the **Options** toolbar, press the **Load** button to bring up the **Open** dialog box.
23. In the **Open** dialog box, press the **Imperial Library** button at the left side of the dialog box to bring up the **Imperial Library**.
24. In the **Imperial Library**, select and open the **Doors** folder.
25. In the **Doors** folder, select and **Open** the **Sliding-2 panel** door.
26. Select the **Sliding-2 panel 72″ × 84″** from the drop-down list in the **Options** toolbar.
27. Press the **Element Properties** button in the **Options** toolbar to bring up the **Element Properties** dialog box.

28. In the **Element Properties** dialog box, press the **Edit/New** button to bring up the **Type Properties** dialog box.
29. In the **Type Properties** dialog box, press the **Duplicate** button to bring up the **Name** dialog box.
30. In the **Name** dialog box, enter **96″ × 108″**, and press the **OK** button to return to the **Type Properties** dialog box.
31. In the **Type Properties** dialog box, change the **Width** to **8′-0″**, the **Height** to **9′-0″**, and press the **OK** buttons to return to the **Drawing Editor**.
32. Place doors in the building as shown in Figures 16-87 and 16-88.
33. Save the file.

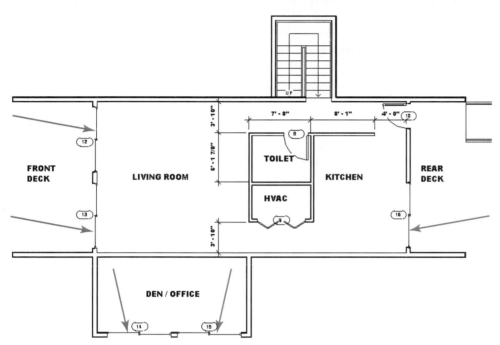

Figure 16-87

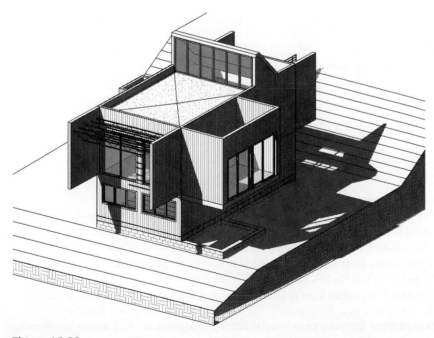

Figure 16-88

Creating the Front and Rear Decks and Their Railings

1. Double-click on the **SECOND FLOOR** plan view in the **Project browser** to bring it up in the **Drawing Editor**.
2. Select the **Floor** tool from the **Basics** tab in the **Design Bar** to bring up the **Sketch** tab.
3. In the **Sketch** tab, select the **Floor Properties** icon to bring up the **Element Properties** dialog box.
4. In the **Element Properties** dialog box, select **Wood Joist 10″ - Wood Finish** from the **Type** drop-down list.
5. In the **Element Properties** dialog box, select **SECOND FLOOR** from the **Level** drop-down list.
6. In the **Element Properties** dialog box, set the **Height Offset From Level** to **-0′ 4″** (this will set the deck 4″ lower than the SECOND FLOOR).
7. Press the **OK** button to return to the **Drawing Editor**.
8. In the **Sketch** tab, select the **Lines** tool.
9. In the **Options** toolbar, select the **Rectangle** option, and place a rectangle to form the front deck.
10. Press the **Finish Sketch** button in the **Sketch** tab to create the deck.
11. At the Revit warning **Would you like walls that go up to this floor's level to attach to its bottom**? press the **No** button.
12. Select the front deck you just created, **RMB**, and select **Create Similar** from the contextual menu to bring up the **Sketch** tab again.
13. Repeat the floor process for the rear deck.

You will now need to make the bottom of the wing walls match the bottom of the decks.

14. Double-click on the **South Elevation** in the **Project browser** to bring it up in the **Drawing Editor**.
15. Select the **Align** tool from the **Tool**s toolbar.
16. Select the bottom of the front deck, and then select the bottom of the adjacent wing wall (see Figure 16-89).

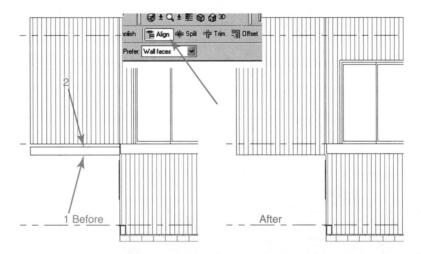

Figure 16-89

17. Repeat this process for all the wing walls in all elevations.
18. Double-click on the **SECOND FLOOR** plan view in the **Project browser** to bring it up in the **Drawing Editor**.
19. Change to the **Modeling** tab in the **Design Bar**.
20. In the **Modeling** tab, select the **Railing** tool to bring up the **Sketch** tab.
21. Select **Set Host** from the **Sketch** tab, and select the front deck.
22. Select the **Railing Properties** icon in the **Sketch** tab to bring up the **Element Properties** dialog box.
23. Select **Handrail-Pipe** from the **Type** drop-down list, and press the **OK** button to return to the **Drawing Editor**.

24. Select **Lines** from the **Sketch** tab, and place a line where the front rail will be.
25. Select **Finish Sketch** from the **Sketch** tab to create the railing.
26. Repeat steps 20–25 for the rear railing (see Figure 16-90).

Creating the Wall Detail

1. Double-click on **Section 1** in the **Project browser** to bring it up in the **Drawing Editor**.
2. Press the **Thin Lines** icon in the **View** toolbar at the top of the interface to make all the lines thin.

Notice that the stud and gypsum board of the front wall sits on the foundation and passes through the floor. This is not correct (see Figure 16-91).

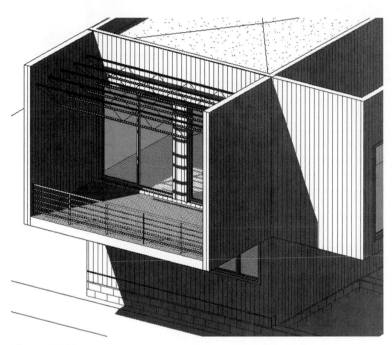

Figure 16-90

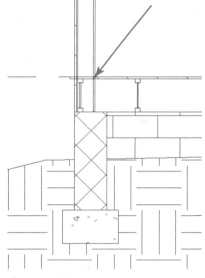

Figure 16-91

To fix this type of condition, do the following:

3. Select the wall, **RMB**, and select **Element Properties** from the contextual menu to bring up the **Element Properties** dialog box.
4. In the **Element Properties** dialog box, select the **Edit/New** button to bring up the **Type Properties** dialog box.
5. In the **Type Properties** dialog box, press the **Edit** button opposite the **Structure** field to bring up the **Edit Assembly** dialog box.
6. In the **Edit Assembly** dialog box, select **Section: Modify type attributes** from the **View** drop-down list, and scroll the image so that you can see the bottom of the wall (see Figure 16-92).
7. In the **Edit Assembly** dialog box, press the **Modify** button, and then move your cursor over the bottom line of the structure within the core boundary (the stud), and click your mouse button.
8. A "lock" symbol will appear. Click the "lock" to open it.
9. Repeat this process for the inside gypsum board adjacent to the stud (see Figure 16-93).
10. Repeat this process for the inside gypsum board adjacent to the stud.

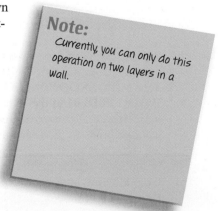

Note:
Currently, you can only do this operation on two layers in a wall.

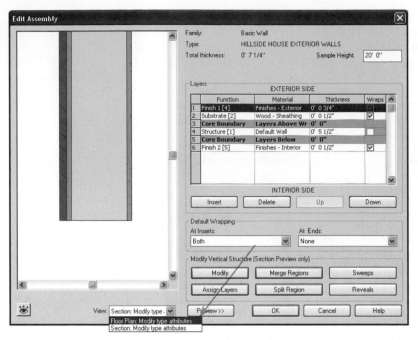

Figure 16-92

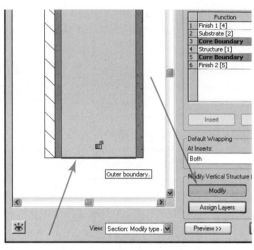

Figure 16-93

11. Select the **OK** buttons to return to **Section 1** in the **Drawing Editor**.
12. Select the wall again, and notice that small blue arrows appear at the base of the wall.
13. Drag the wall rightmost arrow upward until the stud and gypsum board are sitting on top of the floor (see Figure 16-94).

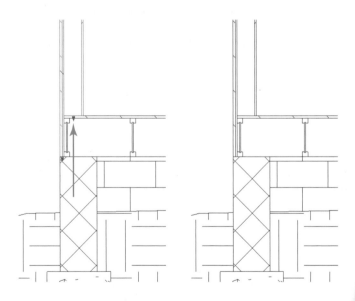

Figure 16-94

14. Repeat this process for the top of the wall, and all the other outer walls.
15. Select the **SECOND FLOOR 3/4″ HARD-WOOD FLOOR** in the section, **RMB**, and select **Element Properties** from the contextual menu to bring up the **Element Properties** dialog box.
16. In the **Element Properties** dialog box, select the **Edit/New** button to bring up the **Type Properties** dialog box.

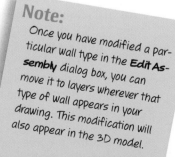

Note:
Once you have modified a particular wall type in the **Edit Assembly** dialog box, you can move it to layers wherever that type of wall appears in your drawing. This modification will also appear in the 3D model.

17. In the **Type Properties** dialog box, press the **Edit** button opposite the **Structure** field to bring up the **Edit Assembly** dialog box.
18. In the **Edit Assembly** dialog box, select the **Material** for each layer, and change its **Cut Pattern** to **None**.

This will clear the floor section, and allow you to place 2D detail components in this floor.

> **Note:**
> For learning purposes, only the first floor was modeled; the second floor was not modeled. We will now use 2D detail components to illustrate the structure in section.

19. Change to the **Drafting** tab in the **Design Bar**.
20. In the **Drafting** tab, select the **Detail Component** tool.
21. In the **Options** toolbar, press the **Load** button to bring up the **Open** dialog box.
22. In the **Open** dialog box, press the **Imperial Library** button at the left side of the dialog box to bring up the **Imperial Library**.
23. In the **Imperial Library**, select and open the **Detail Components** folder.
24. In the **Detail Components** folder, select and open the **Div 06 - Wood and Plastic** folder.
25. In the **Div 06 - Wood and Plastic** folder, select and open the **06100-Rough Carpentry** folder.
26. In the **06100-Rough Carpentry** folder, select and open the **06170-Prefabricated Structural Wood** folder.
27. In the **06170-Prefabricated Structural Wood** folder, select the **Medium Load Wood Joist-Section**, and press the **Open** button to return to **Section 1** in the **Drawing Editor**.
28. Press the **Element Properties** button in the **Options** toolbar to bring up the **Element Properties** dialog box.
29. In the **Element Properties** dialog box, press the **Edit/New** button to bring up the **Type Properties** dialog box.
30. In the **Type Properties** dialog box, press the **Duplicate** button to bring up the **Name** dialog box.
31. In the **Name** dialog box, enter **11-7/8″**, and press the **OK** button to return to the **Type Properties** dialog box.
32. In the **Type Properties** dialog box, change the **Web Diameter** to **1/2″**, the **Depth** to **0′ 11 7/8″**, and press the **OK** buttons to return to the **Drawing Editor**.
33. Place the 2D detail component of the wood joist in the drawing as shown in Figure 16-95.
34. Select the **Detail Component** you just placed, and select the **Array** tool from the **Options** toolbar.
35. On the **Options** toolbar, press the **Linear** button, check the **Group And Associate** check box, enter **20** in the **Number** field, select the **Move To: 2nd** radio button, and check the **Constrain** (horizontal or vertical) check box (see Figure 16-96).
36. Click on the center of the wood joist, drag to the right until the dimension reads **2′-0″**, and then click your mouse to array the joists.

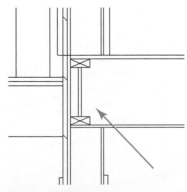

Figure 16-95

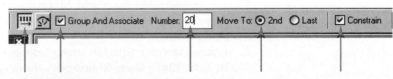

Figure 16-96

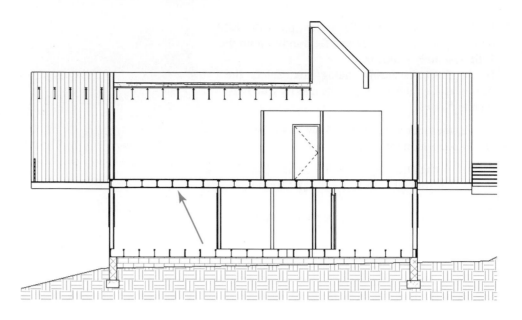

Figure 16-97

37. Click in an empty spot in the drawing to clear the command.
38. Click on the center of the wood joist, drag to the right until the dimension reads **2′-0″**, and then click your mouse to array the joists.
39. Click in an empty spot in the drawing to clear the command.
40. Again, in the **Drafting** tab, select the **Detail Component** tool.
41. In the **Options** toolbar, press the **Load** button to bring up the **Open** dialog box.
42. In the **Open** dialog box, press the **Imperial Library** button at the left side of the dialog box to bring up the **Imperial Library**.
43. In the **Imperial Library**, select and open the **Detail Components** folder.
44. In the **Detail Components** folder, select and open the **Div 06 - Wood and Plastic** folder.
45. In the **Div 06 - Wood and Plastic** folder, select and open the **06100-Rough Carpentry** folder.
46. In the **06100-Rough Carpentry** folder, select and open the **06110 - Wood Framing** folder.
47. In the **06110 - Wood Framing** folder, select **Nominal Cut Lumber-Section**, and press the **Open** button to return to the **Drawing Editor**.
48. In the **Options** toolbar, select **Nominal Cut Lumber-Section: 2 × 6**, check the **Rotate after placement** check box, place it in an empty space in the drawing, rotate it, and click your mouse.
49. Move your mouse to the lower right of the **2 × 6**, and place it as a stud plate in the first and second floor walls in section.
50. Repeat this process, selecting lumber sections from the **Options** toolbar until you have detailed the walls and the decks (see Figure 16-98).
51. Again, in the **Drafting** tab, select the **Detail Component** tool.
52. Locate and open the **05090 Metal Fastenings** folder in the **Detail Components** folder.
53. In this folder, select **A307 Bolts-Side** and **Open** it to return to the **Drawing Editor**.
54. Select **A307 Bolts-Side: 5/8″** from the **Options** toolbar and place it.

Note:
You will have to copy the last wood joist and add it at the end because the last joist is less than 2′-0″ from the previous joist (see Figure 16-97).

Note:
If you select the bolt after you place it, "arrow" grips will appear—drag on these to adjust the length of the bolt. This "arrow" grip convention for resizing is typical of many of the **Detail Components** (see Figure 16-99).

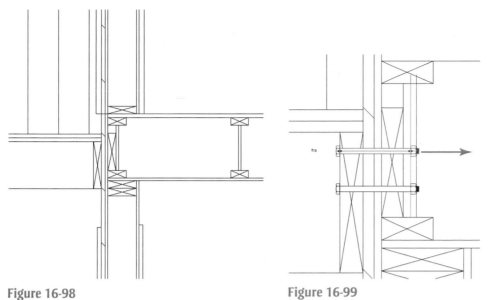

Figure 16-98   Figure 16-99

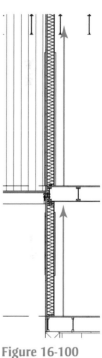

55. In the **Drafting** tab, select the **Insulation** tool.
56. In the **Options** toolbar, enter **5-1/2″** in the **Width** field.
57. Click at the top bottom middle of the first floor wall plate, and click again at the middle of the bottom of the top plate of the wall (see Figure 16-100).
58. In the **Drafting** tab, select the **Filled Region** tool to bring up the **Sketch** tab.
59. In the **Sketch** tab, select **Region Properties** to bring up the **Element Properties** dialog box for the **Filled Region**.
60. In the **Element Properties** dialog box, select the **Edit/New** button to bring up the **Type Properties** dialog box.
61. In the **Type Properties** dialog box, select the **Duplicate** button to bring up the **Name** dialog box.
62. In the **Name** dialog box, enter **STONE FILL**, and press the **OK** button to return to the **Type Properties** dialog box.
63. In the **Type Properties** dialog box, select the field **Fill Patterns** to bring up the **Fill Patterns** dialog box.
64. In the **Fill Patterns** dialog box, select the **Sand** pattern, and press the **OK** buttons to return to the **Drawing Editor**.
65. In the **Sketch** tab, select **Lines**.
66. In the **Options** toolbar, select the **Pencil** tool, and using various line options draw the drainage field at the bottom of the foundation.
67. In the **Sketch** tab, press the **Finish Sketch** tool to finish the command, and create the sand-filled drainage field.
68. Using **Detail Components**, complete the section.
69. Change to the **View** tab.
70. In the **View** tab, select the **Callout** tool.
71. In the **Options** toolbar, select **1/2″ = 1′-0″** from the **Scale** drop-down field.
72. Drag the callout around the front wall as shown in Figure 16-101.

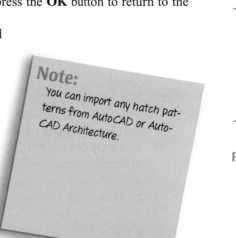

Note:
You can import any hatch patterns from AutoCAD or AutoCAD Architecture.

Figure 16-100

The callout will now appear as **Callout of Section 1** in the **Project browser** (see Figure 16-102).

73. Select **View** > **New** > **Sheet** from the **Main** menu and create a new sheet as you have done previously.
74. Name the sheet **DETAILS**.

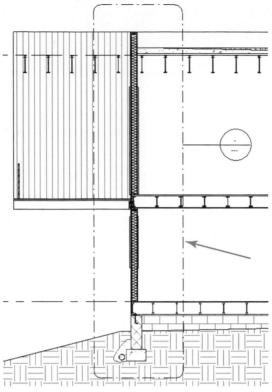

Figure 16-101

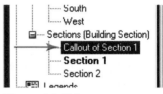

Figure 16-102

75. Drag the **Callout of Section 1** into the **DETAILS** sheet.
76. Select the **Callout** tool again, and this time make a callout of **Callout of Section 1**.
77. This callout will be labeled **Callout [2] of Section 1**.
78. Make its scale **1-1/2″ = 1′-0″**.
79. As you did previously, copy and paste the **Detail Components** into **Callout [2] of Section 1** (see Figures 16-105 and 16-106).
80. Make sure **Callout [2] of Section 1** is in the **Drawing Editor**.
81. Change to the **Drafting** tab in the **Design Bar**.
82. In the **Drafting** tab, select the **Keynote > Element** tool.
83. In the **Options** toolbar, select **Keynote Tag: Keynote Text** from the drop-down list.
84. In the **Options** toolbar, select the **Element Properties** dialog box.
85. In the **Element Properties** dialog box, select the **Edit/New** button to bring up the **Type Properties** dialog box.

Note:

The Detail Components will not show in the callout in the details sheet. There is a "work around" to fix this problem.

a. Double-click on **Section 1** in the **Project browser** to bring it up in the **Drawing Editor**.

b. Select everything in the front wall.

c. Select the **Filter** icon in the **Options** toolbar to bring up the **Filter** dialog box.

d. In the **Filter** dialog box, uncheck everything except the **Detail Groups, Detail Items,** and **Insulation Batting Lines** (see Figure 16-103).

e. Press the **OK** button to return to the **Drawing Editor**.

f. Select **Edit > Copy to Clipboard** from the **Main** menu.

g. Double-click on **Callout of Section 1** in the **Project browser** to bring it up in the **Drawing Editor**.

h. Select **Edit > Paste Aligned > Same Place** from the **Main** menu to copy all the **Detail Components** from **Section 1** into the callout (see Figure 16-104).

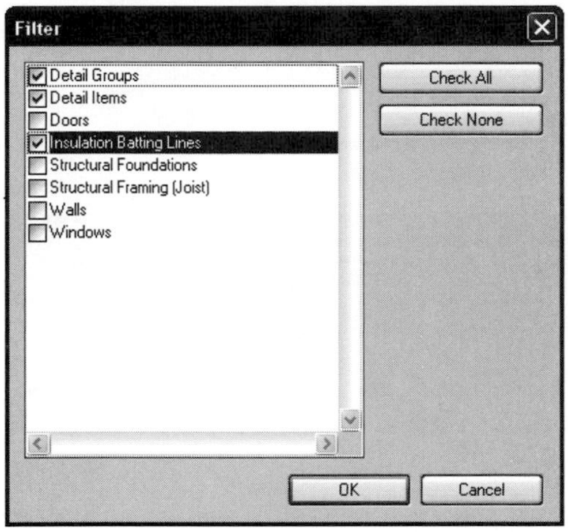

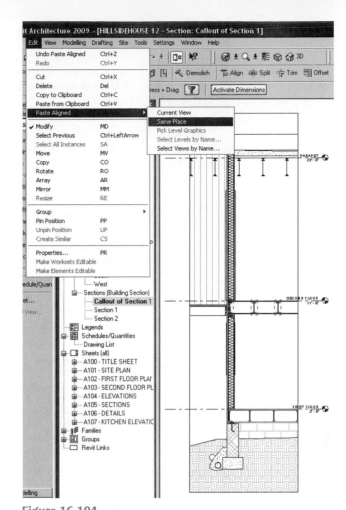

Filter

☑ Detail Groups
☑ Detail Items
☐ Doors
☑ Insulation Batting Lines
☐ Structural Foundations
☐ Structural Framing (Joist)
☐ Walls
☐ Windows

Check All
Check None

OK   Cancel

Figure 16-103

Figure 16-104

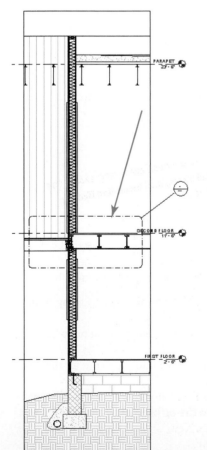

Figure 16-105

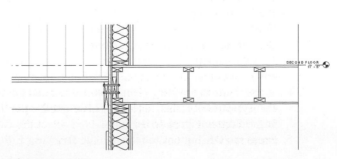

Figure 16-106

413

86. In the **Type Properties** dialog box, select **Arrow Filled 15 Degree** from the **Leader Arrowhead** drop-down list.
87. Press the **OK** buttons to return to the **Drawing Editor**.
88. Pick the batt insulation, drag to the right, and click twice to bring up the **Keynotes** dialog box.
89. In the **Keynotes** dialog box, select **07210.A3**, and press the **OK** button to return to the **Drawing Editor**.
90. Press the <**Esc**> key on your keyboard twice to complete the command and place the note.
91. Continue to add keynotes.
92. Double-click on the **DETAIL** sheet in the **Project browser** to bring it up in the **Drawing Editor**.

> **Note:**
> Once you have added a keynote for a particular material, you will not have to see its keynote thereafter; Revit will remember the material reference for that keynote. You can also add keynotes to the keynote database. Please reference the help guide for this information. You can also pre-add a keynote to a material by adding it in the **Type Properties** dialog box for a particular object (see Figure 16-107).

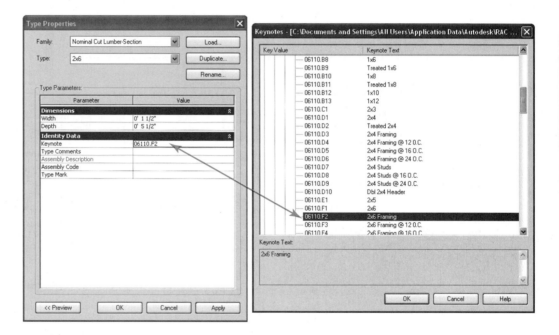

Figure 16-107

93. Drag the **Callout [2] of Section 1** into the **DETAIL** sheet (see Figure 16-108).
94. Save the file.

Placing Wall Tags

Wall tags are an excellent way to illustrate the different types of walls. You can detail the different walls in a **Legend View** (see "Creating a Legend View" in Section 11 of this book). You give the particular wall a **Fire Rating** and **Type Mark** in the wall's **Type Properties** dialog box.

1. Double-click on the **FIRST FLOOR** plan view in the **Project browser** to bring it up in the **Drawing Editor**.
2. Select a wall, **RMB**, and select **Element Properties** from the contextual menu to bring up the **Element Properties** dialog box.
3. In the **Element Properties** dialog box, select the **Edit/New** button to bring up the **Type Properties** dialog box.
4. In the **Type Properties** dialog box, enter a number or letter of your choice for the type in the **Type Mark** field. If the wall is fire rated, enter the fire rating number in the **Fire Rating** field (see Figure 16-109).
5. Press the **OK** buttons to return to the **Drawing Editor**.

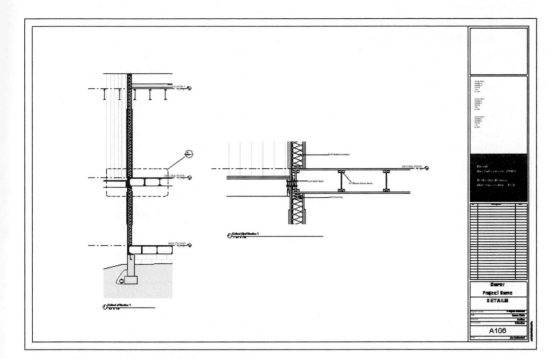

Figure 16-108

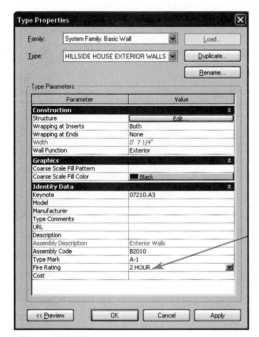

Figure 16-109

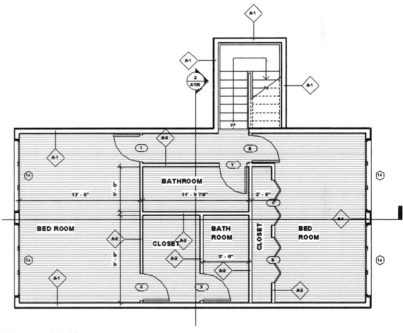

Figure 16-110

6. Change to the **Drafting** tab in the **Design Bar**.
7. In the **Drafting** tab, select the **Tag > By Category** tool.
8. Move your cursor over a wall, and a tag will appear—click to place the tag.
9. Establish **Type Marks** in the **Type Properties** dialog boxes of all the different walls, and place all the wall tags (see Figure 16-110).

Creating the Door and Window Schedules

1. Change to the **View** tab in the **Drawing Editor**.
2. In the **View** tab, select the **Schedule/Quantities** tool to bring up the **New Schedule** dialog box.
3. In the **New Schedule** dialog box, select **Doors** in the **Category** column, select the **Schedule Building Components** radio button, and press the **OK** button to bring up the **Schedule Properties** dialog box.

4. In the **Schedule Properties** dialog box, select **Width**, **Height**, and **Mark** from the **Available Fields** column on the left side of the dialog box.
5. Select **Doors** from the **Select available fields from:** drop-down list.
6. Press the **Add** button to send these fields to the **Scheduled fields [in order]** column in the right side of the dialog box.
7. Press the **Move Up** and **Move Down** buttons to arrange the fields as shown in Figure 16-111.
8. Press the **OK** button to create the **Door Schedule**. It will appear in the **Drawing Editor**, and its name will appear under **Schedules and Quantities...** in the **Project browser** (see Figure 16-112)

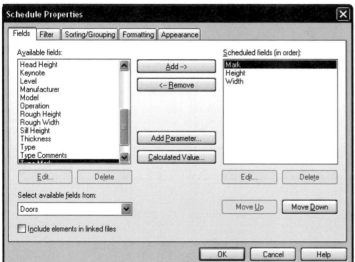

Figure 16-111

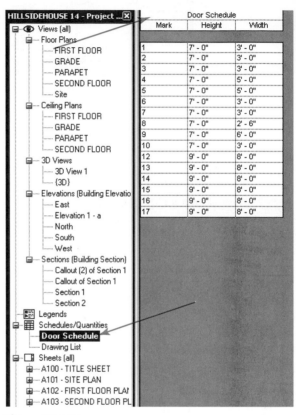

Figure 16-112

9. Repeat steps 1–8 creating a **Window Schedule** with **Type Mark**, **Height**, and **Width**.
10. Double-click on the **TITLE SHEET** in the **Project browser** to bring it up in the **Drawing Editor**.
11. Drag **Door Schedule** and **Window Schedule** from the **Project browser** into the **TITLE SHEET** (see Figure 16-113).

CREATING THE KITCHEN AND BATH

Creating the kitchen and bath is quite simple using the components and libraries that are available. Remember that you can create your own components, or buy components from companies such as BIM World or Architectural Data Systems. As Revit becomes more the standard in the architectural market, you can expect manufacturers to offer their products as digital content.

1. Double-click on the **SECOND FLOOR** plan view in the **Project browser** to bring it up in the **Drawing Editor**.
2. Change to the **Basics** tab in the **Drawing Editor**.
3. In the **Basics** tab, select the **Components** tool to bring up the **Open** dialog box.
4. In the **Options** toolbar, press the **Load** button to bring up the **Open** dialog box.

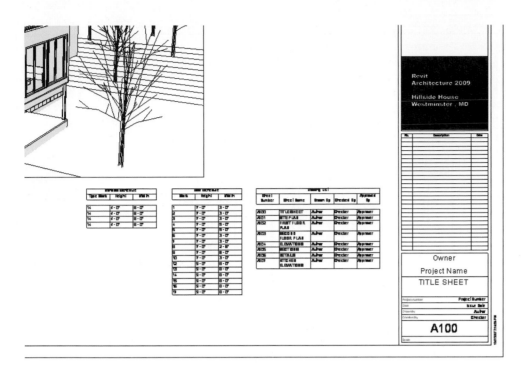

Figure 16-113

5. In the **Open** dialog box, press the **Imperial Library** button at the left side of the dialog box to bring up the **Imperial Library**.

6. In the **Imperial Library**, select and open the **Plumbing Fixtures** folder.

7. In the **Detail Components** folder, select **Toilet – Domestic -3D**, and press the **Open** button to return to the **SECOND FLOOR** plan view in the **Drawing Editor**.

8. In the **Options** toolbar, select **Toilet – Domestic -3D** from the drop-down list, and place the toilet in the **Toilet** room.

9. Repeat this process, loading and placing components from the **Casework >Domestic Bathroom** and **Domestic Kitchen** folders.

10. Change to the **View** tab in the **Design Bar**.

11. In the **Design Bar**, select the **Elevation** tool.

12. In the **Options** toolbar set the scale to $1'' = 1'\text{-}0''$.

13. Place an elevation marker in the kitchen, and check the top and left check boxes in the marker to create two elevations.

14. Dimension the new elevations.

15. Drag these two new elevations from the **Project browser** into a new plot sheet called **KITCHEN ELEVATIONS** (see Figures 16-114 and 16-115).

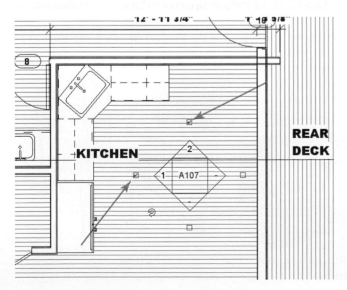

Figure 16-114

Figure 16-115

Rendering the Model

1. Double-click on the **FIRST FLOOR** plan view in the **Project browser** to bring it up in the **Drawing Editor**.
2. Change to the **View** tab in the **Design Bar**.
3. In the **View** tab, select the **Camera** tool.
4. Click your mouse where you expect the camera to stand.
5. Drag to the point you expect to be the target or view, and click your mouse again to create and open the new **3D View** (see Figure 16-116).
6. Select the new **3D View**, **RMB**, and rename it **PERSPECTIVE VIEW 1**.
7. Change the **Detail Level** at the bottom of the **Drawing Editor** to **Fine**.
8. Hold down the **<Shift>** key on your keyboard, and the mouse wheel.
9. With the **<Shift>** key and mouse wheel held down, move your mouse to rotate the view until you get a view you like.
10. Select the crop outline to activate its grips.
11. Move the grips to frame the **PERSPECTIVE VIEW 1** (see Figure 16-117).
12. Select the **Rendering** tab in the **Design Bar**.

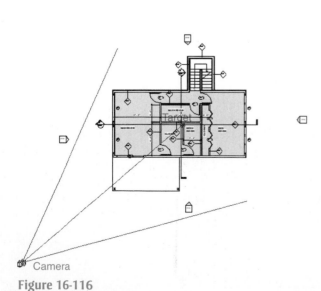

Figure 16-116

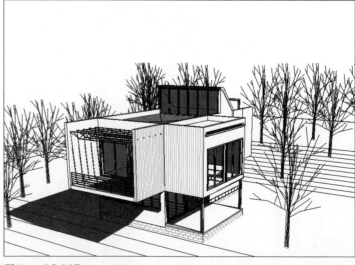

Figure 16-117

13. In the **Rendering** tab, select the **Rendering Dialog** tool to bring up the **Rendering** dialog box.

14. In the **Rendering** dialog box, set the **Quality Setting** to **Medium**, **Light Scheme** to **Exterior: Sun only**, **Sun** to **Sunlight from Top Left**, and **Background** to **Very Cloudy**.

15. Press the **Render** button to start the rendering process.

On a 3.5 GHz computer with 2 GB of RAM, you will see your rendered scene in a few minutes.

16. After the rendering process is finished, press the **Export** button in the **Rendering** dialog box, and save the image as **HILLSIDE HOUSE RENDER** in **JPEG [*.jpg,*.jpeg]** file format (see Figure 16-118).

Figure 16-118

This is as far as we go; the rest is up to you. Once you have the methodology down, the system is really quite straightforward (see Figures 16-119 through 16-127).

Save the file.

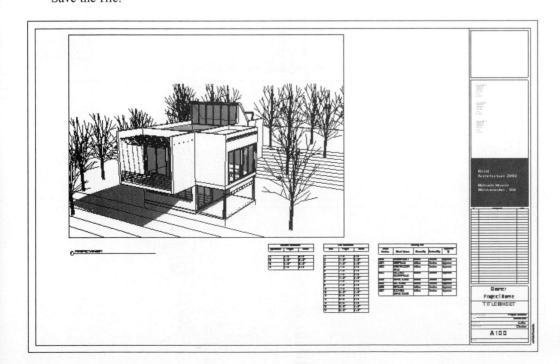

Figure 16-119

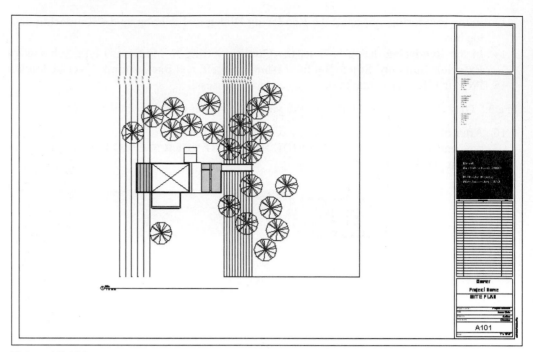

Figure 16-120

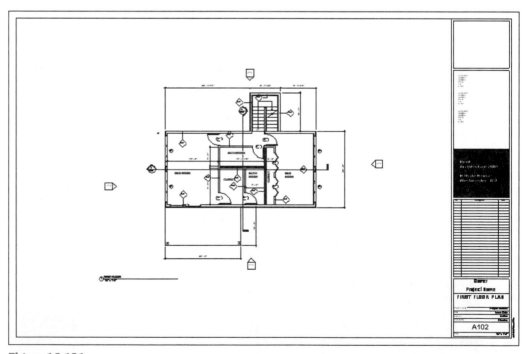

Figure 16-121

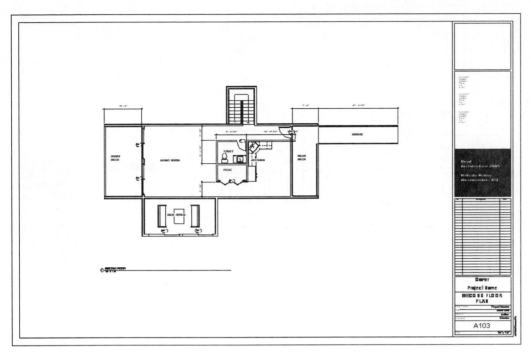

Figure 16-122

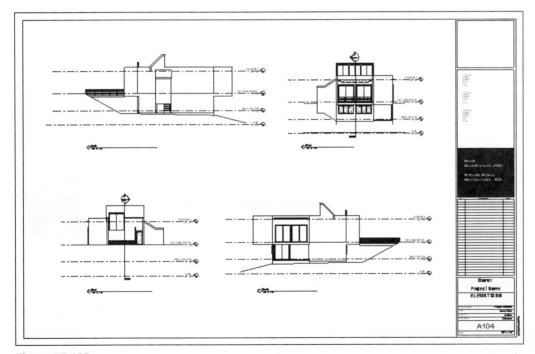

Figure 16-123

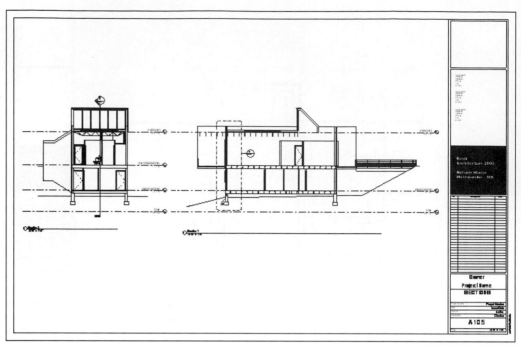

Figure 16-124

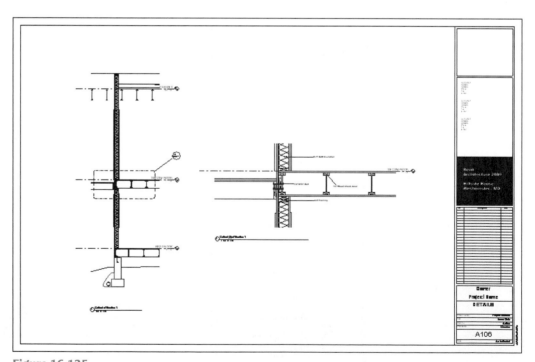

Figure 16-125

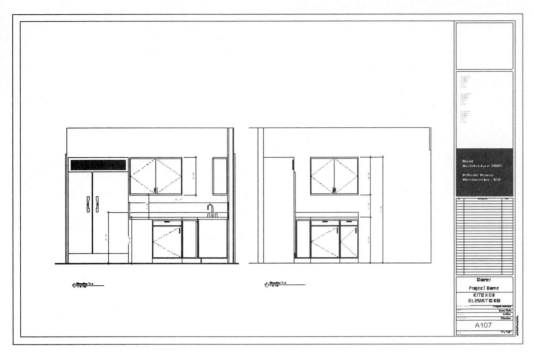

Figure 16-126

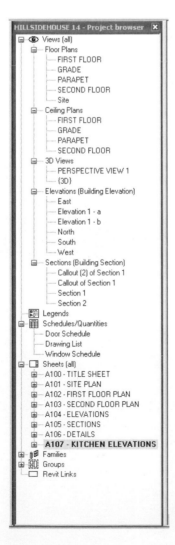

Figure 16-127

Worksharing and Worksets 17

Worksharing is Revit Architecture's technique for allowing multiple persons to work collectively on a single project. The **Worksets** toolset allows a project to be broken down into smaller parts, enabling individuals to work independently on those parts.

WORKSHARING CONCEPT

Worksharing starts with the creation of a master project file, also known as the **Central File**. This file contains a building model that requires more than one person to work on it. The model can be subdivided into functional areas, such as interior, exterior, and site. The Central File also contains a database that shows which team member is working on a designated functional area.

On many building projects, team members are assigned a specific functional area to work on. This involves simultaneously working on and saving different portions of the project. Revit Architecture projects can be subdivided into worksets to accommodate environments like this.

WORKSETS CONCEPT

Worksets function similarly to External References (Xrefs) in AutoCAD, with the additional ability to propagate and coordinate changes between designers. Team members adding elements to worksets can see the latest changes from other team members and be sure the project design is progressing in a well-coordinated manner.

LOCAL FILES CONCEPT

These are copies of the Central File that are saved on team members' computers. After a team member works on a local file, the team member then saves the changes to the Central File.

BORROWING CONCEPT

When someone has control of objects, another team member may ask for permission to work on those same objects. This is called borrowing, and the owner (controller) of the objects may grant permission.

The following tutorial is based on a tutorial written by Eric Wing in the AUGI connection newsletter. He can be reached at atpmanager@augi.com.

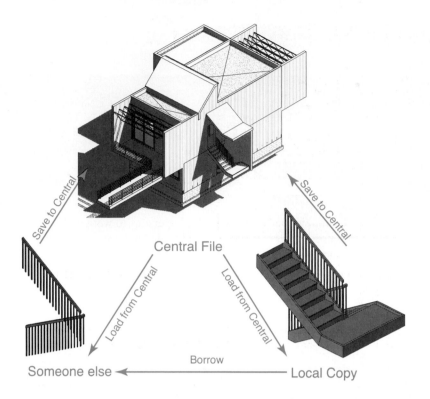

Figure 17-1 The work sharing diagram

Exercise 17-1: Creating the Central File and Worksets

1. Open the **HILL HOUSE** file that you created in the last chapter.
2. Select the walls surrounding the exterior stair, and hide them—exposing the stair and stair railing.
3. Select **Window > Toolbar** and select **Worksets** from the list that appears. This will check it and bring it into the toolbar area.
4. Select the puzzle piece button shown in Figure 17-2 to bring up the **Worksharing** dialog box.
5. In the **Worksharing** dialog box, select the **OK** button to enable **Worksharing** (see Figure 17-3).

Your computer will pause for a few seconds, and then the **Worksets** dialog box will appear. You use **Worksets** to divide your project into separate parts. In this case you will separate the stair case and railings.

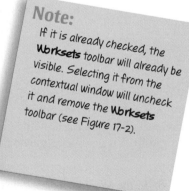

Note:
If it is already checked, the **Worksets** toolbar will already be visible. Selecting it from the contextual window will uncheck it and remove the **Worksets** toolbar (see Figure 17-2).

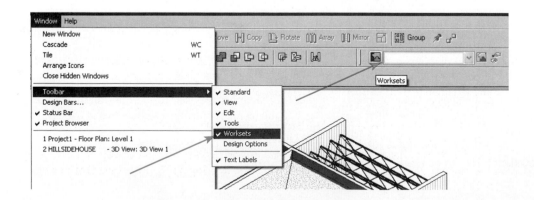

Figure 17-2

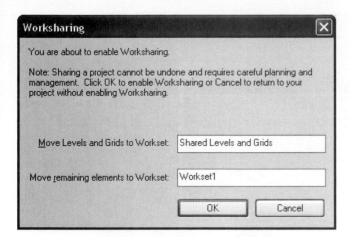

Figure 17-3

The **Worksets** dialog box always appears with **Shared Levels and Grids** and **Workset1** by default. Workset is everything other than the Shared Levels and Grids (see Figure 17-4).

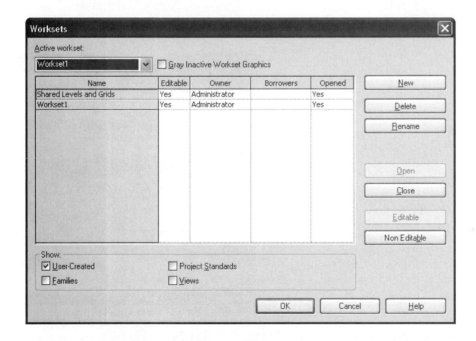

Figure 17-4

6. In the **Worksets** dialog box, press the **New** button to bring up the **New Workset** dialog box.
7. In the **New Workset** dialog box, enter **STAIR** and press the **OK** button to return to the **Worksets** dialog box.
8. Again, in the **Worksets** dialog box, press the **New** button to bring up the **New Workset** dialog box.
9. In the **New Workset** dialog box, enter **STAIR RAILING** and press the **OK** buttons to return to the **Drawing Editor** (see Figure 17-5).
10. Select the stair in the **HILLSIDE HOUSE**, **RMB**, and select **Element Properties** from the contextual menu to bring up the **Element Properties** dialog box for the stair.
11. In the **Element Properties** dialog box, scroll down to the **Identity Data** area, and select **STAIR** from the **Workset** drop-down list.
12. Press the **OK** button to return to the **Drawing Editor** (see Figure 17-6).
13. Repeat steps 9, 10, and 11 for the **STAIR RAILING**.
14. Select **File > Save As...** from the **Main** menu to bring up the **Save As** dialog box.
15. In the **Save As** dialog box, press the **Options** button to bring up the **File Save Options** dialog box.

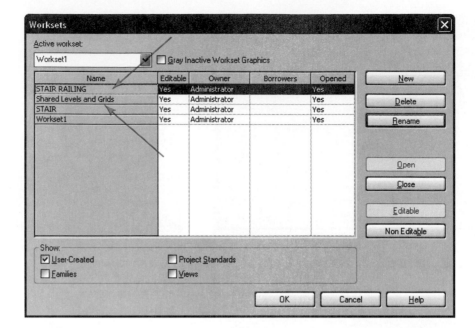

Figure 17-5

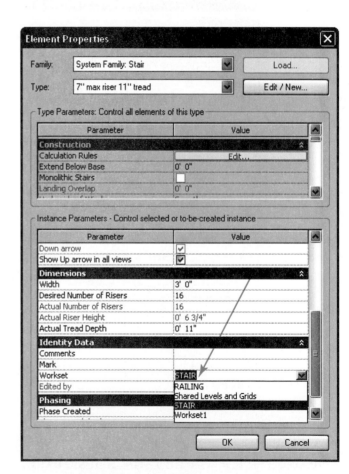

Figure 17-6

16. In the **File Save Options** dialog box, notice that the **Make this a Central File after save** check box is grayed out.

17. Change the **maximum number of backup(s)** to **1**, and press the **OK** button to return to the **Save As** dialog box (see Figure 17-7).

18. In the **Save As** dialog box, name the file **HILLSIDE HOUSE CENTRAL**, place it in your **HILLSIDE HOUSE** folder, and press the **Save** button.

The computer will work for a few seconds while it is saving the file.

Figure 17-7

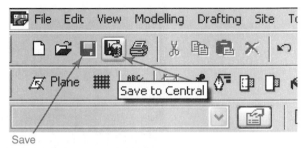

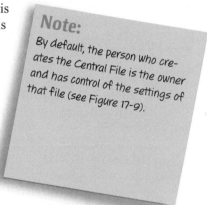

Figure 17-8

Notice that the regular **Save** icon on the **Standard** toolbar is grayed out, and that the **Save to Central** icon adjacent to it is now active (see Figure 17-8).

19. Press the puzzle icon in the **Worksets** toolbar or select **File > Worksets** from the **Main** menu to bring up the **Worksets** dialog box.
20. In the **Worksets** dialog box, select **No** from the **Editable** column for each Workset, and then press the **OK** button to return to the **Drawing Editor**.
21. Press the **Save to Central** icon in the **Standard** toolbar, and then close the file.

Note:
By default, the person who creates the Central File is the owner and has control of the settings of that file (see Figure 17-9).

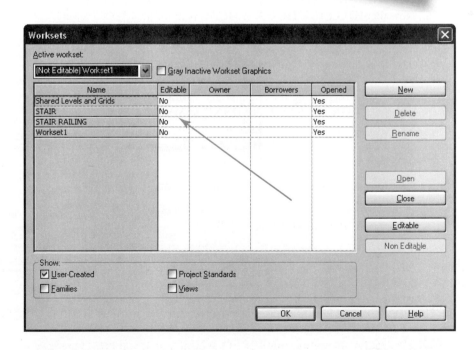

Figure 17-9

Exercise 17-2: Creating the Local File

1. Select **Settings > Options...** from the **Main** menu to bring up the **Options** dialog box.
2. In the **Options** dialog box, enter **YOUR NAME** in the **Username** field, and press the **OK** button to return to the **Drawing Editor** (see Figure 17-10).

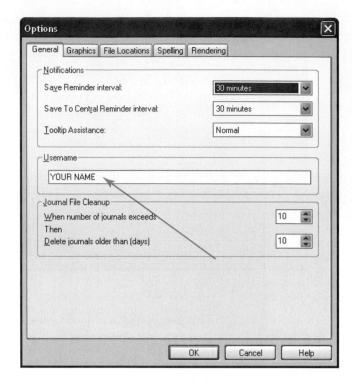

Figure 17-10

3. Open the **HILLSIDE HOUSE CENTRAL** file that you created in the last exercise.
4. Select **File > Save As** from the **Main** menu, and save the file as **HILLSIDE HOUSE LOCAL** in your **HILLSIDE HOUSE** directory.
5. Select **File > Save As** from the **Main** menu, and save the file as **HILLSIDE HOUSE LOCAL** in your **HILLSIDE HOUSE** directory.
6. Now that **HILLSIDE HOUSE LOCAL** is in the **Drawing Editor**, press the puzzle icon in the **Worksets** toolbar or select **File > Worksets** from the **Main** menu to bring up the **Worksets** dialog box.
7. In the **Worksets** dialog box, change the **Editable** column for **STAIR** and **STAIR RAILING** to **Yes**, select **STAIR** from the **Active Workset** drop-down list, and check the **Gray Inactive Workset Graphics** check box (see Figure 17-11).

Notice that your name will appear in the **Owner** column.

8. In the **Worksets** dialog box, press the **OK** button to return to the **Drawing Editor**.

Notice that everything except the stair is grayed out. This shows you what you are now editing. If everything except the stair is not grayed out, you can select **STAIR** from the **Worksets** toolbar drop-down list, and press the **Gray Inactive Workset Graphics** icon (see Figures 17-12 and 17-13).

9. Select **File > Save to Central** from the **Main** menu to bring up the **Save to Central** dialog box.
10. In the **Save to Central** dialog box, check the **Save the Local File after "Save to Central"** check box, and press the **OK** button to return to the **Drawing Editor** (see Figure 17-14).

Note: The default **Username** for the Central File is usually **Administrator**, and each team member creating a local file on his/her computer must have a unique name.

Note: Normally, **HILLSIDE HOUSE CENTRAL** will be placed on a server and team members will be making local files. Unless this exercise is done with a server, you will be maintaining both Central and local files on the same computer.

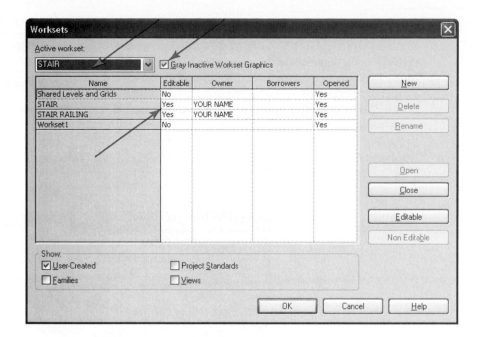

Figure 17-11

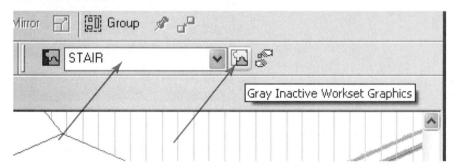

Figure 17-12

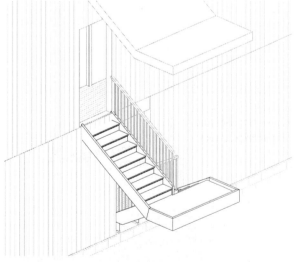

Figure 17-13   Figure 17-14

This will update the Central File, thus notifying all the team members that you are editing the
STAIR and **STAIR RAILING**.

11. Open the **HILLSIDE HOUSE CENTRAL** file.
12. In the **HILLSIDE HOUSE CENTRAL** file, open the **Worksets** dialog box and notice that
    the **STAIR** and **STAIR RAILING** have been checked out for editing by **YOUR NAME**.
13. Close the **HILLSIDE HOUSE CENTRAL** file.

Exercise 17-3: Changing Local Files, and Updating the Central File

1. In the **HILLSIDE HOUSE LOCAL** file, select the stair, **RMB**, and select **Element Properties** from the contextual menu to bring up the **Element Properties** dialog box for the stair.
2. In the **Element Properties** dialog box, press the **Edit/New** button to bring up the **Type Properties** dialog box.
3. In the **Type Properties** dialog box, under **Construction**, check the **Monolithic Stairs** check box.
4. In the **Type Properties** dialog box, under **Treads**, select **Front, Left and Right** from the **Apply Nosing Profile** drop-down list (see Figures 17-15 and 17-16).

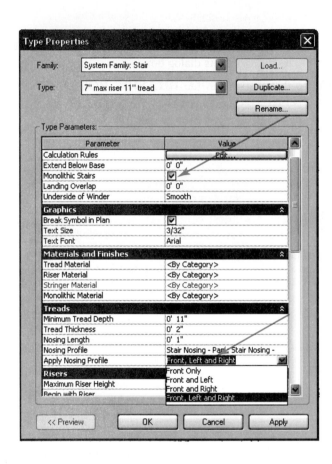

Figure 17-15

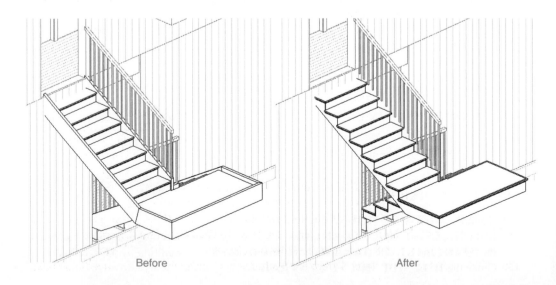

Figure 17-16   Before   After

5. Press the puzzle icon in the **Worksets** toolbar to bring up the **Worksets** dialog box.

6. In the **Worksets** dialog box, change the **Editable** column for **STAIR** to **No**, and press the **OK** button to return to the **Drawing Editor**.

7. Select **File > Save to Central** from the **Main** menu to bring up the **Save to Central** dialog box.

8. In the **Save to Central** dialog box, check the **Save the Local File after "Save to Central"** check box, and press the **OK** button to return to the **Drawing Editor**.

9. Select **File > Close** from the **Main** menu.

10. Open the **HILLSIDE HOUSE CENTRAL** file, and press the puzzle icon in the **Worksets** toolbar to bring up the **Worksets** dialog box.

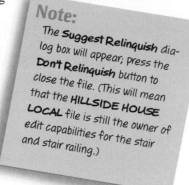

Note: The **Suggest Relinquish** dialog box will appear; press the **Don't Relinquish** button to close the file. (This will mean that the **HILLSIDE HOUSE LOCAL** file is still the owner of edit capabilities for the stair and stair railing.)

Notice that the stair in the **HILLSIDE HOUSE CENTRAL** file has changed, and that the **STAIR** in the **Worksets** dialog box says **Yes** in the **Editable** column.

11. Repeat the steps of this exercise changing the stair railing, and saving to Central.

If you can, get several people together and make more Worksets. Place the Central File on a server, and practice working as a team.

Exercise 17-4: Borrowing

When many people are working on a project, they can borrow a Workset and work on it, even if the Workset is owned by another team member. If they happen to select an object that another team member is editing, Revit will not let them work on that object. They can, though, place a request to ask that member to Relinquish the object. Borrowing a Workset gives team members access to the entire Workset with the exception of the object currently being modified by the Workset's owner.

1. Select **Settings > Options...** from the **Main** menu to bring up the **Options** dialog box.

2. In the **Options** dialog box, enter **SOME ONE ELSE** in the **Username** field, and press the **OK** button to return to the **Drawing Editor**.

3. Open the **HILLSIDE HOUSE CENTRAL** file that you created in the last exercise.

4. Select **File > Save As** from the **Main** menu, and save the file as **HILLSIDE HOUSE SOME ONE ELSE** in your **HILLSIDE HOUSE** directory.

5. Select **Settings > Options...** from the **Main** menu to bring up the **Options** dialog box.

6. In the **Options** dialog box, again, enter **YOUR NAME** in the **Username** field, and press the **OK** button to return to the **Drawing Editor**.

7. Select **File > Open** from the **Main** menu, and bring the **HILLSIDE HOUSE LOCAL** file into the **Drawing Editor**.

8. Press the puzzle icon in the **Worksets** toolbar to bring up the **Worksets** dialog box.

9. In the **Worksets** dialog box, change the **Editable** column for **Workset1** to **Yes**, and press the **OK** button.

10. When asked by the **Revit** dialog box if you want to make **Workset1 the active workset**, press the **Yes** button to return to the **Drawing Editor**.

This makes **HILLHOUSE LOCAL** the owner of **Workset1**. **Workset1** includes everything except the stair, stair railing, and **Levels and Grids**.

11. Select **File > Save to Central** from the **Main** menu to bring up the **Save to Central** dialog box.

12. In the **Save to Central** dialog box, check the **Save the Local File after "Save to Central"** check box, and press the **OK** button to return to the **Drawing Editor**.

13. Select **Settings > Options...** from the **Main** menu to bring up the **Options** dialog box.

14. In the **Options** dialog box, again, enter **SOME ONE ELSE** in the **Username** field, and press the **OK** button to return to the **Drawing Editor**.

15. Select **Settings > Options...** from the **Main** menu to bring up the **Options** dialog box.

16. In the **Options** dialog box, again, enter **YOUR NAME** in the **Username** field, and press the **OK** button to return to the **Drawing Editor**.
17. Select **File > Open** from the **Main** menu, and bring the **HILLSIDE HOUSE SOME ONE ELSE** file into the **Drawing Editor**.
18. Select the wall adjacent to the stair, **RMB**, and select **Element Properties** from the contextual menu to bring up the **Element Properties** dialog box.
19. In the **Element Properties** dialog box, change the **Top Constraint** to **Unconnected**, and enter **5′-0″** in the **Unconnected Height** field.
20. In the **Element Properties** dialog box, press the **OK** button—a Revit Architecture dialog box will appear saying **can't edit the element until "YOUR NAME" resaves the element to Central and relinquishes it, and you Reload Latest.**
21. Press the **Place Request** button to bring up the **Check Editability Grants** dialog box.
22. In the **Check Editability Grants** dialog box, press the **Continue** button to return to the **Revit Architecture** dialog box.
23. In the **Revit Architecture** dialog box, press the **Cancel** button to return to the **Drawing Editor** (see Figure 17-17).

> **Note:**
> You are continually changing the username for these exercises because they are being used as examples, and are being run on one computer. In reality, each team member will set one unique username on his/her computer.

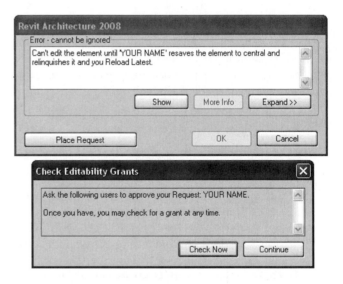

Figure 17-17

24. Select **File > Save to Central** from the **Main** menu to bring up the **Save to Central** dialog box.
25. In the **Save to Central** dialog box, check the **Save the Local File after "Save to Central"** check box, and press the **OK** button to return to the **Drawing Editor**.
26. Select **Settings > Options...** from the **Main** menu to bring up the **Options** dialog box.
27. In the **Options** dialog box, again, enter **YOUR NAME** in the **Username** field, and press the **OK** button to return to the **Drawing Editor**.
28. Press the **Editing Requests** button at the right side of the **Worksets** toolbar (see Figure 17-18).

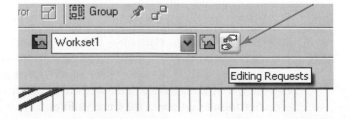

Figure 17-18

29. The **Editing Requests** dialog box will appear.
30. In the **Editing Requests** dialog box, expand **Others' pending Requests**.
31. Click on the next field shown in Figure 17-19. Notice that the **Grant** and **Deny/Retract** buttons are now available.

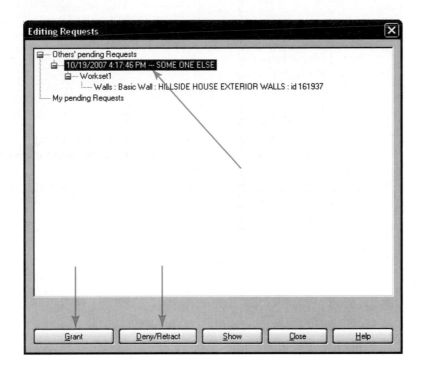

Figure 17-19

32. Press the **Grant** button, and then press the **Close** button to return to the **Drawing Editor**.
33. Select **File > Save to Central** from the **Main** menu to bring up the **Save to Central** dialog box.
34. In the **Save to Central** dialog box, check the **Save the Local File after "Save to Central"** check box, and press the **OK** button to return to the **Drawing Editor**.
35. Select **Settings > Options...** from the **Main** menu to bring up the **Options** dialog box.
36. In the **Options** dialog box, again, enter **SOME ONE ELSE** in the **Username** field, and press the **OK** button to return to the **Drawing Editor**.
37. Select **File > Open** from the **Main** menu, and bring the **HILLSIDE HOUSE SOME ONE ELSE** file into the **Drawing Editor**.
38. Select the puzzle icon at the left of the **Worksets** toolbar to bring up the **Worksets** dialog box.
39. In the **Worksets** dialog box, notice that **SOME ONE ELSE** is now in the **Borrowers** column.

This means that **SOME ONE ELSE**'s request has been granted to edit **Workset1** even though **YOUR NAME** owns it (see Figure 17-20).

40. Again, select the wall adjacent to the stair, **RMB**, and select **Element Properties** from the contextual menu to bring up the **Element Properties** dialog box.
41. In the **Element Properties** dialog box, change the **Top Constraint** to **Unconnected**, and enter **5'-0"** in the **Unconnected Height** field.

The wall changes its height to **5'-0"**, even though you are working in the **HILLSIDE HOUSE SOME ONE ELSE**, and the wall is owned by **YOUR NAME**.
    You have just borrowed! (See Figure 17-21.)

42. Select **File > Save to Central** from the **Main** menu to bring up the **Save to Central** dialog box.
43. In the **Save to Central** dialog box, check the **Save the Local File after "Save to Central"** check box, and press the **OK** button to return to the **Drawing Editor**.
44. Select **File > Open**, and open the **Central File**.

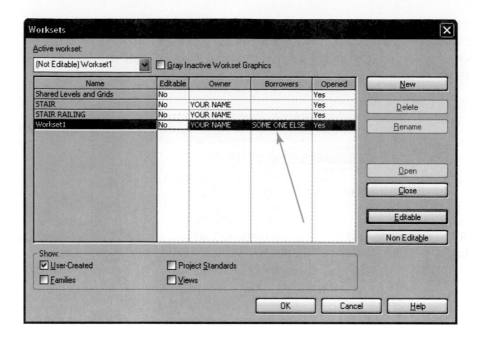

Figure 17-20

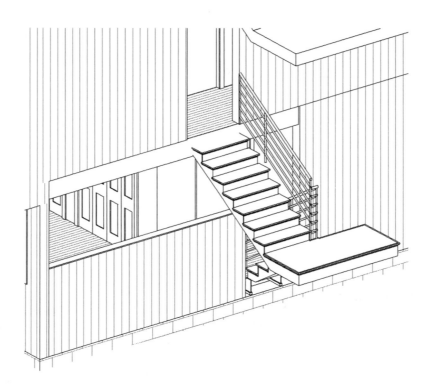

Figure 17-21

Notice that the Central File contains the changes made by both the **HILLSIDE HOUSE LOCAL** and **HILLSIDE SOME ONE ELSE** files.

As mentioned previously, it would be best to do this exercise with three separate computers, one each for the Central, and two local files.

Index